Locating Science Fiction

Liverpool Science Fiction Texts and Studies, 44

Liverpool Science Fiction Texts and Studies

Recent titles in the series

22. Inez van der Spek *Alien Plots: Female Subjectivity and the Divine*
23. S. T. Joshi *Ramsey Campbell and Modern Horror Fiction*
24. Mike Ashley *The Time Machines: The Story of the Science-Fiction Pulp Magazines from the Beginning to 1950*
25. Warren G. Rochelle *Communities of the Heart: The Rhetoric of Myth in the Fiction of Ursula K. Le Guin*
26. S. T. Joshi *A Dreamer and a Visionary: H. P. Lovecraft in his Time*
27. Christopher Palmer *Philip K. Dick: Exhilaration and Terror of the Postmodern*
28. Charles E. Gannon *Rumors of War and Infernal Machines: Technomilitary Agenda-Setting in American and British Speculative Fiction*
29. Peter Wright *Attending Daedalus: Gene Wolfe, Artifice and the Reader*
30. Mike Ashley *Transformations: The Story of the Science-Fiction Magazine from 1950–1970*
31. Joanna Russ *The Country You Have Never Seen: Essays and Reviews*
32. Robert Philmus *Visions and Revisions: (Re)constructing Science Fiction*
33. Gene Wolfe (edited and introduced by Peter Wright) *Shadows of the New Sun: Wolfe on Writing/Writers on Wolfe*
34. Mike Ashley *Gateways to Forever: The Story of the Science-Fiction Magazine from 1970–1980*
35. Patricia Kerslake *Science Fiction and Empire*
36. Keith Williams *H. G. Wells, Modernity and the Movies*
37. Wendy Gay Pearson, Veronica Hollinger and Joan Gordon (eds.) *Queer Universes: Sexualities and Science Fiction*
38. John Wyndham (eds. David Ketterer and Andy Sawyer) *Plan for Chaos*
39. Sherryl Vint *Animal Alterity: Science Fiction and the Question of the Animal*
40. Paul Williams *Race, Ethnicity and Nuclear War: Representations of Nuclear Weapons and Post-Apocalyptic Worlds*
41. Sara Wasson and Emily Alder, *Gothic Science Fiction 1980–2010*
42. David Seed (ed.), *Future Wars: The Anticipations and the Fears*
43. Andrew M. Butler, *Solar Flares: Science Fiction in the 1970s*

Locating Science Fiction

ANDREW MILNER

LIVERPOOL UNIVERSITY PRESS

First published 2012 by
Liverpool University Press
4 Cambridge Street
Liverpool
L69 7ZU

This paperback version published 2014.

British Library Cataloguing-in-Publication data
A British Library CIP record is available

ISBN 978-1-84631-842-9 (cased)
978-1-78138-116-8 (limp)

Typeset by XL Publishing Services, Tiverton
Printed and bound by CPI Group (UK) Ltd, Croydon CR0 4YY

For the five fabulous Milner boys,
Liam, Robert, Ciarán, James and David,
and in loving memory of their fabulous Aunty Joyce,
my sister, who died of cancer, aged 58, on 6 December 2011.

Contents

Acknowledgements ix
List of Figures xi

1. Memories of Dan Dare 1
Memories of Science Fiction. Literature, Genre and Popular Fiction. Memories of Dan Dare. Tales of Resonance and Wonder.

2. Science Fiction and Selective Tradition 22
Academic Definitions of Science Fiction. Modernism, Modernity and Science Fiction. Non-Academic Definitions of Science Fiction. Rethinking Genre. Rethinking Tradition.

3. Science Fiction and the Cultural Field 41
From the French Literary Field to the Global Science Fiction Field. Ideas and Effects. Science Fiction as Drama. Science Fiction as Prose. The Restricted Economy and Institutionalised Bourgeois Art.

4. Radio Science Fiction and the Theory of Genre 68
Cultural Materialism as Method. Radio Technology and Science Fiction. Radio Science Fiction Forms: Three Texts. Radio Institutions.

5. Science Fiction, Utopia and Fantasy 89
The North American Argument. The European Argument. Science Fiction and Fantasy. Utopianism in Popular Science Fiction.

6. Science Fiction and Dystopia 115
The Antipathy to Dystopia. The Strange Case of *Nineteen Eighty-Four*. Science Fiction as a Generic Context. Three Intertexts. An Ideal Typology and Some Hypotheses.

7. When Was Science Fiction? 136
Long Histories of Science Fiction. Science Fiction and the Structure of Feeling. Form and History.

8. Where Was Science Fiction? 155
Postcolonial Theory and Science Fiction. World-Systems Theory and Science Fiction: The Anglo-French Core. The European Semiperiphery. From the Semiperiphery to Core: North America and Japan.

9. The Uses of Science Fiction 178
Future Stories and Futurologies. Antipodean Utopias. *On the Beach* and *The Sea and Summer*. Anticipations of Phil Chase. Afterword.

Works Cited 199
Index 231

Acknowledgements

I am indebted to friends and colleagues in English and Comparative Literature at Monash University, English at the University of Liverpool, and English and Comparative Literary Studies at the University of Warwick; to the staffs of the Matheson Library Rare Book Collection, the Ernest Jones Library Science Fiction Foundation Collection and Special Collections Reading Room, the University of Warwick Library, the British Library at Euston and the Science Museum in South Kensington; and to Anthony Cond, Patrick Brereton and everyone at Liverpool University Press. Further individual debts of gratitude are owed to Roland Boer, Mark Bould, Ian Buchanan, Verity Burgmann, Deirdre and Jim Clarke, John Clute, Susan Cousin, Istvan Csicsery-Ronay, Jr., Rjurik Davidson, Ann Dudgeon, Nik Gladanac, Jane Montgomery Griffiths, David Jack, Darren Jorgensen, Sean Kearns, Andrew Keogh, Michal Kulbicki, Nick Lawrence, David Lockwood, the late Marie Maclean, Clare McCutcheon, Dougal McNeill, China Miéville, Richard Milner, Eugenia Mocnay, Tom Moylan, Peter Murphy, Diane Newsome, Kate Rigby, David Roberts, Stan Robinson, Matthew Ryan, Carlo Salzani, Robert Savage, Andy Sawyer, David Seed, Simon Sellars, the late Kathryn Turnier, Dimitris Vardoulakis, Walter Veit, Millicent Vladiv-Glover, Marcus Walsh, Gail Ward, Chris Williams and Chris Worth.

The Australian Research Council provided generous funding for the research on which this book is based. None of the individual chapters have been previously published in their present form, but earlier versions of different parts of the argument were rehearsed in the following journal articles: '*On the Beach*: Apocalyptic Hedonism and the Origins of Postmodernism', *Australian Studies*, 7 (1993): 190–204; 'Utopia and Science Fiction in Raymond Williams', *Science Fiction Studies*, 30.2 (2003): 199–216; 'When Worlds Collide: Comparative Literature, World-Systems Theory and Science Fiction', *Southern Review*, 37.2 (2004): 89–101; 'Framing Catastrophe: The Problem of Ending in Dystopian Fiction', *Arena Journal*, (II) 25/26 (2006): 333–54; (with Robert Savage), 'Pulped Dreams: Utopia and American "Golden Age" Science Fiction', *Science Fiction Studies*, 35.1 (2008):

31–47; 'Mis/Reading *Nineteen Eighty-Four*: A Comparatist Critique of Williams on Orwell', *Key Words*, 6 (2008): 31–45; 'Archaeologies of the Future: Jameson's Utopia or Orwell's Dystopia', *Historical Materialism*, 17.4 (2009): 101–19; 'Changing the Climate: the Politics of Dystopia', *Continuum*, 23.6 (2009): 827–38; 'Tales of Resonance and Wonder: Science Fiction and Genre Theory', *Extrapolation*, 51.1 (2010): 148–69; 'Science Fiction and the Literary Field', *Science Fiction Studies*, 38.3 (2011): 393–411.

List of Figures

Figure 1: The French literary field in the second half of the nineteenth century 42

Figure 2: The double location of early French science fiction within the late nineteenth century literary field 43

Figure 3: The global SF field in the early twenty-first century 45

Figure 4: The relation between SF, utopia and fantasy represented as a Venn diagram 104

Figure 5: Venn's diagram for four sets applied to the science fiction field 105

Figure 6: An ideal typology of possible solutions to the problem of ending in dystopian SF 134

Figure 7: Nevil Shute, George Turner and the global science fiction field 191

List of Figures

1
Memories of Dan Dare

I am by enthusiasm a science fiction fan and by profession a critical theorist, that is, an academic specialist in the theory of literary (and other) criticism. The first explains why I would choose to write about this genre, the second how I would do so, that is, by utilising the kinds of resource I canvass in my own earlier books on critical and cultural theory (Milner, 2002; Milner and Browitt, 2002). Like many other literary subfields, science fiction studies has been exposed to a wide variety of critical theories. So, for example, there are postcolonial and, more specifically, 'Afrofuturist' treatments of the genre (Rieder, 2008; Hopkinson and Mehan, 2004), feminist and post-feminist (Shaw, 2000; Melzer, 2006), Marxist and post-Marxist (Roberts, 2000; Bould and Miéville, 2009), postmodernist (Broderick, 1995; Best and Kellner, 2001), psychoanalytic (Žižek, 2001, 213–33) and ecocritical (Murphy, 2009, 89–118). No doubt, each provides very real insights, but each is also essentially the application to science fiction (henceforth SF) of a more general theory derived elsewhere. By contrast, the core critical approach specific to the genre, against which almost everything else has been obliged to define itself, remains that established by Darko Suvin in the 1970s. Mark Bould refers to Suvin's near-contemporaneous publication of the essay 'On the Poetics of the Science Fiction Genre', in 1972, and co-foundation of the journal *Science Fiction Studies*, in 1973, as 'the Suvin event', which marked the beginning of what we now know as SF studies (Bould, 2009, 18). Suvin's extraordinarily influential monograph, *Metamorphoses of Science Fiction*, followed in 1979, extending the event both spatially and temporarily. Veronica Hollinger observed some twenty years after the book's first publication that '*Metamorphoses* is *the* significant forerunner of all the major examinations of the genre' (Hollinger, 1999, 233). Over a decade later, this continues to be the case. As Bould and Vint wryly comment in the opening chapter of their *Concise History*: 'disagreeing with him [Suvin] is a considerable part of SF scholarship … he … set … the terms by which SF has subsequently been studied' (Bould and Vint, 2011, 17).

The fundamental novelty of Suvin's argument was to insist on a very close connection between SF and the much older genre of utopia, a case he has continued to prosecute in his own subsequent writings (Suvin, 1988, 42; Suvin, 2010b, 383–84). The position has been taken up and further advanced by Carl Freedman's *Critical Theory and Science Fiction* (2000) and Fredric Jameson's *Archaeologies of the Future* (2005). And it clearly informs the work of critics such as Tom Moylan, Rafaella Baccolini and Phillip Wegner (Moylan, 1986; 2000; Baccolini and Moylan, 2003; Moylan and Baccolini, 2007; Wegner, 2002). Jean Baudrillard's *Simulacres et simulation* (1981), substantial extracts from which were first published in English translation in *Science Fiction Studies* (Baudrillard, 1991), detected a similar affinity between utopia and SF, but theorised it rather differently. Each of these writers brought the resources of continental European critical theory – or 'Theory', as it has come to be known – to bear on SF, but each seems to me to have failed in significant ways, *Archaeologies of the Future* perhaps especially so. Jameson's dismissal of twentieth-century dystopian SF, in particular George Orwell's *Nineteen Eighty-Four* (Jameson, 2005, 201–2), appears not only radically over-politicised, but also directly at odds with a tradition most SF enthusiasts would regard as of central significance to the genre. I make this observation with some misgiving: *Archaeologies* had been as much anticipated by me as by Jameson's more immediate colleagues, friends and 'comrades in the party of Utopia', to whom it is dedicated.

No doubt, one could simply dismiss all this theory as irrelevant, as most fans almost certainly do. The moment of High Theory, which lasted for something like a quarter of a century in Anglophone literary and cultural studies, has now clearly passed. If even Terry Eagleton, the author of that perennial academic best-seller, *Literary Theory: An Introduction* (Eagleton, 1983, 1996), now believes us to be *After Theory* (Eagleton, 2003), then we surely are. But High Theory – theory for theory's sake – has never seemed terribly interesting to me. Quite the contrary, the point of theory is to explain the empirical, in the sense of helping to understand it rather than to explain it away, which means that literary theory really does have to be about literature, film theory about film, neither about Derrida or Foucault in and of themselves. We might, then, welcome Eagleton's licence to sidestep the increasingly interminable faction fights between post-Derridean deconstructionists and neo-Foucauldean discourse theorists. But if this licence is to mean liberty, to misquote Milton, then it must be something more than a return to simple empiricism. No matter how splendid the empirical achievement in John Clute, David Langford and Peter Nicholls's encyclopedias (Nicholls, 1979; Clute and Nicholls, 1993; Clute et al., 2011) or in Lyman Tower Sargent's bibliographies (Sargent, 1988; 1999), these are only ever means to an end, tools to understanding, not understanding itself. For the latter, what is needed isn't so much less theory as better theory.

This book will be a prolonged engagement with Suvin, Baudrillard, Freedman, Jameson and others, including Ernst Bloch, whose *The Principle of Hope* (Bloch, 1986) had very little to say about SF, but nonetheless remains an important inspiration for Suvin and Jameson. The grounds of the engagement will be what I will call the SF 'selective tradition' and the SF 'field', terms and concepts I borrow from, respectively, Raymond Williams and Pierre Bourdieu. Both notions imply more inclusive and less prescriptive understandings of the genre than in Suvin or Jameson; and both will be crucial to my own argument, especially as developed in chapters 2 and 3. The book will be an intervention into contemporary theoretical debate about SF as a literary, film, television and radio genre and its relation to the immediately cognate genres of utopia, dystopia and fantasy. It will ask and attempt to answer four very general questions: first, what positively was SF? that is, what are its relative dimensions?; second, what negatively wasn't it? that is, what are its relations to utopia, dystopia, fantasy and other genres?; third, when was it? that is, what was its time?; and fourth, where was it? that is, what was its geographical space?

The TARDIS is famously the name of Doctor Who's time machine and, although only dedicated fans remember this, it is an acronym for Time And Relative Dimension In Space, coined by the Doctor's granddaughter Susan. The question the book will pose, then, is, in short and to misappropriate the most famous invention of Gallifrey, what exactly is the time and relative dimension in space of SF itself?

1. Memories of Science Fiction

Before proceeding to these questions, however, I want to begin with a brief reconstruction of my own personal encounter with the genre, derived from a combination of memory and archive. Memory is, of course, notoriously fallible, but can be used as a kind of quasi-ethnographic resource if disciplined by access to a relevant independently collated archive, in this case the most extensive in Europe, that in the Science Fiction Collection at the University of Liverpool. Methodological apologies aside, let me proceed to record my findings. So far as I can tell, I learnt to read sometime between September 1954 and June 1955, that is, during my first year at primary school in West Yorkshire. But I remember virtually nothing of this reading before the week of 3 May 1957, when my father brought home my first ever copy of the weekly *Eagle* comic. I remember little about this, too, aside from the first two pages, which remain vividly etched in my memory: splendidly illustrated in full colour by Frank Hampson, they were an episode of *Reign of the Robots*, a story featuring Dan Dare, Pilot of the Future. Dressed in Spacefleet uniform, which was green where the Royal Air Force (RAF) uniform was blue, but with a fawn shirt and brown tie, and wearing a leather and sheepskin flying jacket, Colonel Dare had been led by the Mekon, a fearsome green-skinned tyrant, to the ominously sounding 'House of Silence' in the Venusian city of Mekonta. Now, Dare was confronted with what seemed to be the body of Sir Hubert Guest, the British Controller of Spacefleet, and immediately thereafter with those of two other Spacefleet officers, the American Captain Hank Hogan and the French Major Pierre Lafayette, along with a British scientist, Professor Jocelyn Peabody. They were not dead, however, but rather held in suspended animation, as hostages to secure Dare's future collaboration with the Mekon's megalomaniac scheme to rule the universe. There were no robots in this particular episode, but it would become clear in subsequent weeks that the Earth had already fallen to the Mekon's Treen warriors and their terrible elektrorobots.

Dan Dare provided the *Eagle* with its front-page story from the very first issue, published on 14 April 1950, the only one of the comic's original 'strip cartoons' still running when I joined the readership seven years later. Colonel Daniel McGregor Dare was the star of the British weekly comic, of the hardback *Eagle Annual*, of *Disco Volante* (*Flying Saucer*) and *Il Giorno dei Ragazzi* (*Children's Day*) in Italy, of the Adelaide Advertiser's Australian *Eagle*, and the inspiration, too, for a welter of metal and plastic toys, from ray guns to walkie-talkies. My older cousin, Colin, even listened to Dare's adventures on the 'wireless', as radio was known in those days, where Noel Johnson played the title role and Francis De Wolfe the Mekon, broadcast by Radio Luxembourg from 1951 until 1956. In Australia they were broadcast by Radio 4AK, in Spain, with Spanish actors, by Cadena SER. Dan Dare put everything else – cowboys, legionnaires, detectives – very firmly in the shade. I was instantly hooked on the *Reign of the Robots*, which ran until January 1958 (although the story that followed, *The Ship that Lived*, was a direct continuation); hooked on Dan Dare, whose adventures lasted until 1967, when he was finally promoted to Controller of Spacefleet (fortunately, the family subscription to *Eagle* had been handed down to my younger brother, Richard); and hooked on SF itself.

My father noted this enthusiasm and invited me to listen with him to the 1958 repeat of Charles Chilton's *Journey into Space* on the British Broadcasting Corporation (BBC) Light Programme. The last primetime radio serial to out-rate television in Britain, *Journey into Space* had run for three previous seasons, between 1953 and 1956. I had been too young for each of those, but avidly listened to the abbreviated, reworked and retitled repeat of the first season, broadcast as 'Operation Luna' from March to June of 1958. Here, Andrew Faulds played Jet Morgan, the Scottish Captain of the *Luna*, Guy Kingsley Poynter was Doc Matthews, the Canadian ship's doctor, David Williams played the Australian ship's engineer, Mitch, and Alfie Bass, Lemmy, the cockney radio operator. In the original, this last part had been taken by David Kossoff, whom my mother had much preferred. During the winter of 1958–59, I caught tantalisingly brief glimpses of *Quatermass and the Pit* on the screen of our new 'television set', but was hurried off to bed on the grounds that this sort of thing wasn't fit for children. The third and last of Nigel Kneale's Quatermass serials made for BBC Television between 1953 and 1959, it was a spectacular success both in this format and in a slightly disappointing movie version made by Hammer Films in 1967. I have since watched the television original on DVD and can testify that it really was astonishingly good, albeit perhaps not entirely suitable for an eight-year-old.

Warned off television, I discovered the local public library and, with it, Chilton's novelisation of *Journey into Space*. Improbably, the book's cover included a photograph of the four radio actors dressed in their space suits. I became a library stalwart and proceeded, in quick succession, through Captain W. E. Johns's SF novels, from *Kings of Space* and *Return to Mars* to *The Edge of Beyond*. But then came something much more serious, my first SF book from the senior library shelves, Nevil Shute's *On the Beach*. It provided me with an introduction to the city of Melbourne, where I have now lived for over thirty years, and to the subgenre of the doomsday dystopia. I have my own copy these days, a 1990 Mandarin Paperback, the cover of which proclaims it 'The Great Australian Novel of Our Time'. Few academic literature programmes would accept that claim, but there is an important sense in which it asserts little more than a commonplace. For this was, almost certainly, the most widely read novel ever written in Australia. Thereafter, I worked my way through Isaac Asimov's *Foundation* trilogy, which my Dad had been reading in paperback; two of J. B. Priestley's SF novels, *Saturn Over the Water* and *The Shapes of Sleep*, again borrowed from the public library; then C. S. Lewis's Ransom trilogy – *Out of the Silent Planet*, *Perelandra* and *That Hideous Strength* – and H. G. Wells's *The Time Machine*, all borrowed from the grammar school library; then John Wyndham's *Day of the Triffids* and Orwell's *Nineteen Eighty-Four*, both set as school English texts, but with the latter clearly signposted as 'Literature' rather than SF. Then on to other novels English teachers knew to be Literature, not SF: Aldous Huxley's *Brave New World,* William Golding's *Lord of the Flies,* Anthony Burgess's *A Clockwork Orange*. Interestingly, my French teachers handled this issue by insisting that Jules Verne might well be SF, but certainly wasn't Literature.

My father had never been a great reader, so he and I didn't tend to discuss the novels. But we watched BBC TV's *A for Andromeda* in 1961 and *The Andromeda Breakthrough* the following year. These were early 1960s excursions into prestige SF, with scripts co-written by the Yorkshire astronomer, Professor Fred Hoyle, who had previously written a number of SF novels. I was already old enough to note appreciatively that Andromeda, the organic life-form produced by an alien-designed computer, was played, in turn, by Julie Christie and Susan Hampshire. During the summer of 1962, Dad and I also watched ABC TV's *Out of This World,* hosted by Boris Karloff, an upmarket SF anthology spin-off from *Armchair Theatre,* which included television adaptations of short stories by Asimov and Philip K. Dick, the latter scripted by Terry Nation. It was good, intelligent stuff, which might well explain why most of its talent was promptly poached by the BBC: Sydney Newman, who had produced *Armchair Theatre,* became Head of Drama and reputedly came up with the idea for *Doctor Who,* which went to air on 23 November 1963; and Nation famously created the Daleks, who first appeared a few weeks later, on 21 December. Dad was never quite persuaded by *Doctor Who* – kid's stuff, I suppose, and in a time slot already overcommitted to the weekly Leeds United debriefing – but I certainly became so. I don't swear to have seen literally every episode, although it very much seemed that way except during my student days. But, then, I'd even been willing to join my younger brother and sister in watching Gerry and Sylvia Anderson's various adventures in Supermarionation, from *Supercar, Fireball XL5* and *Stingray* to *Thunderbirds* and *Captain Scarlet.*

Dad and I were devotees of *Out of the Unknown,* an anthology series clearly inspired by *Out of This World,* broadcast on BBC2 from 1965 to 1971. It was to the sixties what Quatermass had been to the fifties and, by the end of the first season, it had become the BBC's highest rating in-house drama. The 1965, 1966–67 and 1969 seasons were devoted to serious SF and mobilised an enormous body of talent in its service: Irene Shubik, who had worked with Newman on *Out of this World,* was appointed producer and story editor; stories came from the likes of Wyndham, Asimov, Ray Bradbury, J. G. Ballard, Frederik Pohl, C. M. Kornbluth and E. M. Forster; the adaptations for television from the likes of Nation and Priestley. In July

1969 the BBC broadcast the first episode of an American SF show named *Star Trek*. The writing didn't bear comparison with *Doctor Who*, but it had unusually sophisticated special effects by the standards of the day. I was on my way to university, however, at a time when students normally had next to no access to television, so never really got very involved with it. I missed most of the 1970–71 fourth and final season of *Out of the Unknown* for the same reason, but I gather it veered towards horror rather than SF. And I finally put away the Andersons' childish things and missed out on *Joe 90*.

And then there were the movies, mainly American, but occasionally British or French, sometimes on television but mainly at the cinema: Universal's 1930s *Flash Gordon* serial recycled for the local Saturday afternoon matinée in the mid 1950s; William Cameron Menzies' *Things to Come* and Stanley Kramer's *On the Beach*, both broadcast on television, I think by the BBC; Stanley Kubrick's *Dr Strangelove*, which I must have been too young to see legally, but nonetheless did; Gordon Flemyng's *Dr Who and the Daleks*, with Peter Cushing in the title role, a more wholesome affair we watched as a family when first released in 1965; François Truffaut's *Fahrenheit 451*, with Julie Christie from *A for Andromeda* in the double role of Clarisse and Linda; and then, in one marvellous year, my last at grammar school, Roger Vadim's *Barbarella*, Kubrick's *2001: A Space Odyssey* and Franklin J. Schaffner's *Planet of the Apes*. Then came SF-inspired rock, especially Pink Floyd between *The Piper at the Gates of Dawn* in 1967 and *The Dark Side of the Moon* in 1973, but also David Bowie during his Ziggy Stardust period. I was lucky enough to see both live.

I could go on, but won't, because we have now, finally, reached the point where my first argument can be made. The theoretical and empirical point of this exercise in autobiography as ethnography should be obvious, but rarely seems so either for literary critics, like Suvin, Freedman and Jameson, who define SF as a 'literary genre' (Suvin, 1979, 7–8; Freedman, 2000, 16–17; Jameson, 2005, 1–2), or for film critics, like Brooks Landon, Vivian Sobchak and Annette Kuhn, who insist on the distinctively 'spectacular' nature of SF cinema (Landon, 2002, 60–61; Sobchack, 1987; Kuhn, 1999, 1–11). Against each of these, I would argue that the category SF applies at its most meaningful across a whole range of forms, from the novel and short story to pulp fiction and the comic book, from radio serial and television series to drama and film, from examinable set text to rock album. The idea of the robot, for example, has its origins in the Czech high literary theatre of the 1920s, but was very rapidly exported into German popular silent cinema, thereafter into American pulp magazine fiction, and thence across the entire cultural field, from Dan Dare in 1957 to Jeanette

Winterson's *The Stone Gods* in 2007. This is certainly how I personally have understood SF and, from my experience of participant observation in SF, Star Wars and Star Trek conventions, it is also how many, probably most, fans seem to understand it. Even the much-ridiculed 'Trekkies' – a popular misnomer for Trekkers – tended to focus their enthusiasm on the *Star Trek* universe in general, as distinct from its particular manifestations in television, film, cartoon, comic book or novelisation. If this is indeed the case, then critical theory must surely aim to explain why this should be so, rather than insist that it shouldn't. What Virgil says of the farmer might thus apply equally, in our time, to the critical theorist: 'Felix qui potuit rerum cognoscere causas' [O happy he who can fathom the causes of things] (Virgil, II: 490; 2009, 68–69).[1]

There is the further point, however, that this kind of genre-defined medium-jumping isn't simply confined to 'fans', understood as a particular kind of deviant reader. For Henry Jenkins and most subsequent analysts, fans are 'consumers who also produce, readers who also write, spectators who also participate' (Jenkins, 1992a, 214). This is clearly intended as complimentary, but nonetheless describes a distinctly unusual and, at least in that sense, deviant kind of reading. I doubt my father and I were ever fans in this strong sense. Indeed, I doubt I have ever been simply a fan, although in my experience fans seldom ever are. I know that I never confined my attentions to SF, either exclusively or obsessively. The encounter I have just described occurred mainly in the (long) sixties, when there was a great deal else to command those attentions: the Beatles and the Stones; Dylan, Baez and the Grove Folk Club in Leeds; Adrian Mitchell, Adrian Henri, Roger McGough and my own feeble attempts at poetry; Don Revie's Leeds United in all their glory; *The Wednesday Play* and *That Was the Week That Was*; *US* at the Royal Shakespeare Company's Aldwych Theatre and the Campaign for Nuclear Disarmament (CND) everywhere; sex, drugs and rock and roll; the Labour Party Young Socialists and the Vietnam Solidarity Campaign; student anarchism and Trotskyism. 'Get a life', William

1 Here and throughout I have quoted from all primary texts in their original languages and included a generally acceptable English translation in square brackets immediately thereafter. In this instance, where the edition cited contains a parallel translation, both the original and the translation are taken from the same place, i.e. pp. 68–69. More commonly, however, I have cited separate editions for the original and the translation, with different page numbers for each. But wherever I have been unable to locate such a translation, the translation is mine. I have transliterated the titles of Greek, Japanese and Russian texts into Roman script, but have left direct quotations in the original script.

Shatner notoriously advised the Trekkers on *Saturday Night Live*, much as literary criticism had tended to dismiss fan readers in general. But fans already have lives. Certainly, I did. For me, the sixties was a combination of all the above, much else besides, and all of it always already in counterpoint with SF. This might have been possible without Dan Dare, but somehow I doubt it.

2. Literature, Genre and Popular Fiction

At this point, my argument will run contrary, or, at least, substantially tangential, to the widespread tendency in work on 'popular fiction' to assimilate SF to the western, the thriller and the romance, as different varieties of 'genre fiction'. So SF routinely rated a mention in the standard discussions of popular fiction of the 1980s (Pawling, 1984; Humm et al., 1986), which first defined the field, and continues to do so, for example, in Clive Bloom's *Bestsellers* (2002), John Sutherland's *Reading the Decades* (2002) and Ken Gelder's *Popular Fiction* (2004). To concentrate on what is clearly the most theoretically sophisticated of the latter, let me concede immediately that Gelder's intention to rescue popular literature from the enormous condescension of academic literary criticism is in itself thoroughly admirable, and that his theoretical framework, a loose adaptation of Bourdieu's notion of the field of cultural production, is clearly very promising. But the argument is chronically disabled, almost from its inception, by its opening assumption that 'popular fiction is best conceived as the opposite of Literature', where the latter is understood primarily as a 'kind of writing'. So Gelder defines Literature through a long list of supposedly 'Literary' writers, from Jane Austen to Tobias Wolff, conceding en route that at least two of these, William Faulkner and Martin Amis, have also written genre fiction (Gelder, 2004, 11). But almost everything Gelder attributes to popular fiction – that it is a matter of 'production and hard work' rather than 'creativity and originality'; a 'craft' rather than enmeshed in the 'art world'; 'simple' rather than 'complex'; concerned with 'fantasy' rather than 'life'; 'couldn't function' without 'a story or plot'; that it intentionally aspires to attract 'a large number of readers'; and is 'routinely produced in other entertainment fields, like cinema and theatre'; that its readers are 'leisured, fast, believing and enchanted consumers' (Gelder, 2004, 15, 17, 19, 20, 22, 28, 38) – is arguably also true of his very first example of a Literary writer, Jane Austen. More than any other writer, except perhaps the Brontë sisters, Austen established the paradigmatic form of the romance, in the Mills and Boon sense of the term, as distinct from the German or French *roman*. The few attributes that clearly don't apply to Austen, 'sensuous' rather than 'cerebral', 'excessive' rather than 'discrete' (Gelder, 2004, 19), most certainly do to others on Gelder's list, D. H. Lawrence, for example – almost as popular an inspiration for film and television adaptations as Austen – or Salman Rushdie. Gelder is right to insist that popular fiction and Literature can be defined only in relation to each other and that this relation can be analysed through Bourdieu's notion of 'field' (Gelder, 2004, 13–14). But the field in question is nonetheless not definable primarily in terms of different kinds of writing.

Nor is it primarily a matter of different kinds of reading, as Gelder also tentatively hypothesises. At one point he observes that

> Students of literary fiction at schools, colleges and universities will have been taught to read slowly and carefully, 'seriously' and 'deeply'. But readers of popular fiction may find themselves doing quite the opposite: reading fast, reading at leisure, reading to 'escape', as one might do with one of Ian Fleming's James Bond novels. (Gelder, 2004, 5)

The idea of 'slow reading' as distinctly Literary is repeated later in the argument by way of a passing nod to the academic literary criticism of J. Hillis Miller (Gelder, 2004, 37). Students of literary fiction in schools, colleges and universities are not so much Literary readers, however, as academic readers, and Hillis Miller not so much a Literary reader as a peculiarly extreme example of the academic reader. For if popular readers are those who buy and read popular genre fiction – detective fiction, romance, SF, etc. – for the purposes of pleasure rather than of employment or study, then Literary readers must similarly be those who buy and read Literary fiction for pleasure, no matter how 'serious' that pleasure, rather than for employment or study. Nearly all the writers Gelder includes in his Literary list are on sale in commercial bookshops near my home, variously marketed as 'literary fiction', 'classics', 'modern classics' or even 'Literature'. Someone buys and reads them for pleasure and that someone is the Literary reader. But Gelder has no more idea than I of exactly how or why they read. To find the answer he would need to engage in either ethnography or detailed sociological survey. And he would need to be interested in the question, rather than to assume in advance that he already has its answer. Of course, Gelder knows all about academic reading, but this is a type of reading that can be directed at any kind of text, from *Genesis* to *The X-Files* and *Buffy the Vampire Slayer*: I know because I've done precisely this (Milner, 2005, 196–203, 268–91). And it is perfectly possible to read Gelder's own example of Ian Fleming's James Bond novels slowly, carefully, seriously and deeply, which is exactly what Umberto Eco did in

The Role of the Reader (Eco, 1981, 144–72).

The Literary field, the field of popular fiction and their relations are primarily matters neither of writing nor of reading, but rather of industrial production and marketing. Gelder knows this to be true of popular fiction (Gelder, 2004, 1–2), but seems oblivious to the industrial basis of high Literature. It is crucial to Bourdieu's own approach, however, that 'all practices, including those purporting to be disinterested or gratuitous' can be treated as 'economic practices directed towards the maximizing of material or symbolic profit' (Bourdieu, 1977, 183). So he sees French publishing as comprising 'commercial' firms, which aim at short-term profit, on the one hand, and 'cultural' businesses, which aim to accumulate symbolic capital and then transform it into material capital over the much longer term, on the other (Bourdieu, 1993, 97–101). He cites a publishing house from each end of the spectrum, respectively Robert Laffont and Éditions de Minuit, and shows how their different 'temporal structures correspond to two very different economic structures'. Laffont was a large, publicly listed company, publishing about 200 titles a year, many of them best-sellers; Minuit a small private company, publishing twenty titles a year, many of which sold less than 500 copies. But both were financially profitable, the latter because of its backlist, which included, most famously, Samuel Beckett's *Waiting for Godot*. This 'sold fewer than 200 copies in 1952', but 'twenty-five years later had sold more than 500,000' (Bourdieu, 1993, 99). Bourdieu's point is that such long-term investments make financial sense, albeit only in relation to an 'economy of cultural production', where 'the intervening time ... provides a screen and disguises the profit awaiting the most disinterested investors' (Bourdieu, 1993, 101). Beckett isn't actually included in Gelder's Literary list, presumably because he wrote plays as well as novels, in French as well as in English, but the strategy Minuit adopts towards his work is exactly that pursued by Anglophone publishers of Literature, such as Faber and Faber. Bourdieu's 'restricted production' is restricted, yes, but it is production nonetheless.

What Gelder means by Literature is, as on occasion he comes close to admitting, 'the literary novel ... in its Modernist incarnations' (Gelder, 2004, 20). Remarkably little of what he attributes to Literature actually applies to pre-modernist writers like Austen, or non-modernist writers like Lawrence, or even postmodernist writers like Rushdie. For it is not so much Literature in general as modernism in particular that stands in something like binary opposition to popular fiction. And modernism was historically a very specific development, which can be located precisely in the moment between Émile Zola and Marcel Proust, George Eliot and Virginia Woolf, Mark Twain and Henry James. This leads me to conclude that literary modernism is as much a genre as SF, if not in Gelder's sense, then in Williams's, to which we turn very shortly. For Gelder, 'Popular fiction is, essentially, genre fiction' (Gelder, 2004, 10). But this sense of 'genre' as necessarily formulaic and predictable is unhelpful because, as John Frow observes, 'it obscures the extent to which even the most complex and least formulaic of texts is shaped and organised by its relation to generic structures' (Frow, 2006, 1-2).

My own sense of genre will owe less to Frow, however, than to Williams, who, in his general sociology of culture, identified three distinct levels of cultural form, termed respectively 'modes', 'genres' and 'types' (Williams, 1981, 193–97). The first refers to the deepest level of form, as in the distinction between the 'dramatic mode', where action is performed before an audience, and the 'narrative mode', where it is recounted as a tale told to an audience by a teller. The second refers to relatively persistent instances of each mode, as in the distinction between tragedy and comedy within the dramatic mode, or epic and romance within the narrative mode. Still more variable and still more dependent on particular social relations are what he terms 'types', that is, 'radical distributions, redistributions and innovations of interest, corresponding to the specific and changed social character of an epoch' (Williams, 1981, 196). The 'genres' Gelder explores are, in Williams's terms, 'types', and so too is modernist fiction. For if romance is the type that takes as its central preoccupation heterosexual courtship and marriage, and SF that which takes the social implications of scientific and technological development, then modernism takes literary form itself. In the late nineteenth and early twentieth centuries this constituted a radical redistribution and innovation of interests analogous to those in other 'types' of genre fiction.

Genre, in the sense Williams means by 'type', is thus not a matter of the quality of a text, however measured, nor of the competence of either writers or readers, however measured. It is, rather, a radical redistribution of interests (type) within a relative persistent instance (genre) of a deep form (mode). The SF 'type' was established in nineteenth-century Europe through a radical redistribution of interests towards science and technology within the novel and short story genres of the narrative mode. In the twentieth century, the same concentration of interests persists within the novel and short story, but is also redeployed into various theatrical, film, radio and television genres of the dramatic mode. Some of these SF texts have been canonised as Literature by academic criticism, albeit not normally in the cause of partisan modernism, and one self-identified SF writer, Doris Lessing, has even been awarded the Nobel Prize for Literature. The longer version of Harold Bloom's *The Western Canon* includes a plethora of SF novels and even one Hugo Award winner: Mary Shelley's *Frankenstein*, Robert Louis Stevenson's *Strange Case of Dr Jekyll and Mr Hyde*, Edgar Allan Poe's *The Narrative of Arthur Gordon Pym*, Wells's *The Science Fiction Novels*, Huxley's *Brave New World*, Orwell's *Nineteen Eighty-Four*, Anatole France's *L'île des Pingouins* (*Penguin Island*), Karel Čapek's *Válka s mloky* (*War with the Newts*) and *R.U.R.*, Stanisław Lem's *Śledztwo* (*The Investigation*) and *Solaris*, Ursula K. Le Guin's *The Left Hand of Darkness*, Russell Hoban's *Riddley Walker*, Kurt Vonnegut's *Cat's Cradle*, and so on (Bloom, 1994, 542–65). Some SF texts get much the same treatment from film critics: it is difficult to imagine a film-studies programme that doesn't, at some point, study Fritz Lang's *Metropolis* or Kubrick's *2001: A Space Odyssey*, and both were included in Paul Schrader's preliminary attempt at a film canon (Schrader, 2006). No doubt, television studies will eventually get around to canonising *Doctor Who*.

But this is nonetheless not how SF writers, readers or critics typically understand these texts. For the 'SF community', as it likes to describe itself, these are all just SF. Hence, Le Guin's prickly response to Winterson's *The Stone Gods*:

> It's odd to find characters in a science-fiction novel repeatedly announcing that they hate science fiction. I can only suppose that Jeanette Winterson is trying to keep her credits as a 'literary' writer even as she openly commits genre. Surely she's noticed that everybody is writing science fiction now? Formerly deep-dyed realists are producing novels so full of the tropes and fixtures and plotlines of science fiction that only the snarling tricephalic dogs who guard the Canon of Literature can tell the difference. I certainly can't. Why bother? I am bothered, though, by the curious ingratitude of authors who exploit a common fund of imagery while pretending to have nothing to do with the fellow-authors who created it and left it open to all who want to use it. (Le Guin, 2007, 17)

There are, of course, real differences between SF in print and SF on film, radio or television. But the generic continuity across media is nonetheless very apparent, often through the deliberate use of intertextuality. Gelder's distinction between Literature and popular fiction simply will not work for this genre in which, for example, the first issue of Hugo Gernsback's *Amazing Stories*, which is generally credited as the first American SF 'pulp' magazine, included reprints of stories by Poe and Wells, both of whom would later figure in Bloom's Western Canon. This is the same Poe who inspired Baudelaire and Verne, the same Wells who inspired Zamyatin and Čapek. Čapek's *R.U.R.* is one of only six Czech texts to be included in

Bloom's canon, but it also bequeathed the word 'robot' to SF and provided the BBC with the script for the world's first ever SF television broadcast. Orwell's *Nineteen Eighty-Four*, which also figures in Bloom's canon, almost single-handedly established the dominant paradigm for the post-war SF dystopia, as exemplified in Bradbury's *Fahrenheit 451* and Golding's *The Lord of the Flies*, so much so that Williams would describe it as virtually coextensive with 'serious "science fiction"' (Williams, 1965, 307–8). One could continue almost indefinitely with empirical example after empirical example. The theoretical point, however, is the relatively simple one, that the binary between Literature and popular fiction is almost entirely an artefact of Literary modernism, designed to valorise form over content, and cannot be applied to SF which, by contrast, is a genre of ideas and therefore privileges content over form.

3. Memories of Dan Dare

Insofar as utopia, fantasy and SF might be considered cognate forms, this is so, above all, because they are each tales of wonder. As the titles of the most famous American SF pulp magazines make clear, the genre deals in *Astounding Stories*, *Amazing Stories*, *Wonder Stories* and even *Thrilling Wonder Stories* (the first was edited by J. W. Campbell, Jr., the other three, at least initially, by Gernsback). Returning to my earlier exercise in autobiography as ethnography, I want to ask whether there is anything to learn about SF in general from my encounter with Colonel Dare, the fictional Mancunian, born seventeen years after me, who grew up to become Chief Pilot of Spacefleet. Let us note immediately that, by contrast with their less successful rivals, the Dan Dare stories were rendered unusually plausible by virtue of their consonance with what young, male readers in fifties Britain already 'knew' to be 'true'. Those marvellously realistic Spacefleet uniforms, for example, were realistic precisely insofar as they mimicked the design of existing British military and naval uniforms down to the last button and epaulette. Dan's Irish comrade, Commander Lex O'Malley, was a proper Royal Navy officer, complete with duffel coat and beard: Spacefleet, like the RAF and the British Army, were permitted only moustaches. The Mekon was precisely the kind of tyrant, an off-world Hitler – or Nasser to make the reference more exactly contemporary – British readers would have expected to find opposed to friendly relations with Earth. Sondar, the first Venusian ambassador to Earth, was precisely the kind of friendly native they would hope to encounter: as early as 10 May 1957 he was busily smuggling help to captive Earthmen, and, after the Mekon's defeat, he would become United Nations (UN) Governor of Venus.

Part of the strip's appeal lay in the depth of its backstory. By Dan Dare's time, world government has been established by the UN, the flag of which I first saw carried, not by blue berets, but by escaping Spacefleet prisoners battling Treen guards and elektrorobots on 6 December 1957. They had, of course, previously formed a Spacefleet Underground, which, as British readers would expect, had been busily digging secret escape tunnels. The all-male 'Inner Council' of the Earth Government, comprising five white faces, one black, one brown – much like the 1950s UN Security Council – heard Dare speak on 16 August 1958. Above this Inner Council, Earth had a Prime Minister, rather than a Secretary General, President or Chancellor, I learnt on 6 September 1958. In an early episode of *The Phantom Fleet*, dated 9 May 1958, Dan and his co-pilot, Digby, barely escaped collision with the Moon Mail-Rocket en route between Earth and Lunar Base. It had emblazoned on its hull 'United Nations Postal Service', but was coloured red, nonetheless, and carried the 'Royal Mail'. Even more startling, there was a cross-channel tunnel between England and France, I discovered on 18 April 1959. The new photon drive, which powered the Nimbus prototypes introduced on 9 April 1960, was a dangerous technology to be handled carefully, very much like the jet engines of the 1950s: 'NOT TO BE USED IN ATMOSPHERE' warned the control panel instructions.

The Interplanetary Spacefleet, in which Dan Dare served, was in effect a fourth, internationalised branch of the British armed forces. Again, there was for British readers in the fifties something very realistic about British command of Spacefleet. Its French, American – and presumably other – officers and spacemen are reminiscent of the Free French and Eagle Squadron volunteers of 1940. The architecture of the urban future, especially that of London, where both Spacefleet Headquarters and Earth Government were located, is a vividly plausible combination of the traditional and the futuristic. The 'Space Ministry', I learnt on 13 September 1958, was very near the City of Westminster 'Whitehall Walkway', which carried pedestrians at four miles an hour. A 1965 story, *The Big City Caper*, had the alien, Xel, make villainous use of the Post Office Tower, which opened that year, but had merely become one landmark amongst others for Dare and Digby. Interestingly, Norman Foster, Nigel Coates and Laurie Chetwood all cheerfully acknowledge their professional debt as architects to Hampson's Dan Dare stories (Glancey, 2008, 24). Lantor, the fabulous city of the five towers on Terra Nova, which Dare reached on 2 January 1960, no doubt provided an important part of their inspiration.

The Dan Dare backstory included equally credible personal biographies for the leading characters. Dan himself and his co-pilot and 'batman',

Spaceman Albert Fitzwilliam Digby, were from Manchester and Wigan respectively. It would be another half-century before Christopher Eccleston's Doctor Who would announce in similarly regional accents that 'Every planet has a North'. But this was merely a postmodern joke. The world of Dan Dare really did have a North in a way Gallifrey never could. Being English, Dan and Digby were united by region but divided by class: Dan's father had been a space pilot, his uncle a scientist and he himself had been educated at a private boarding school and, later, Cambridge and Harvard; Digby was an orphan, brought up by his Aunt Anastasia – after whom one of their spaceships was named – is married with four children and devoted to football and fish and chips. Sir Hubert is a much-decorated former RAF officer, educated at Shrewsbury and Oxford; Professor Peabody has a D.Phil. from Magdalene College, Oxford, and a B.Sc. from Bedford College, the University of London women's college in Regent's Park, sold off in 1985 unfortunately, some years before she would have been old enough to secure entry.

The virtues of Spacefleet's senior officers are clearly inherited from a long line of British heroes from Hornblower to Biggles. Hence, the wonderful exchange between Dan and Sir Hubert, on 17 May 1957, discussing a deal proposed by the Mekon:

> Dare: If we're going to beat old Melonhead, it's got to be with the *truth – not with lies!*
> Sir Hubert: Dan's right! If we defeat the Mekon by giving our word and then breaking it, how can the peoples of Earth and Venus trust us when we regain control?

Less extreme, but thereby all the more realistic, Sir Hubert's closing lines at the end of *The Ship That Lived* fictionalise very common British sensibilities from the immediate decade after 1945: 'There is a tremendous rebuilding task ahead of us, men! But, thank goodness, at last we are free to do it – *free from fear – free from tyranny!'*

The common sense of fifties Britain was monochrome, if not racist: hence, the ethnic composition of the Inner Council of Earth Government. Spacefleet, too, had a strangely uniform pallor. By contrast, the green-skinned Treens were not the only inhabitants of Venus: I met blue-skinned Atlantines on 8 November 1957 and brown-skinned Therons on 22 November. But the Earthmen were almost uniformly white: I didn't encounter a single dark skin until 12 July 1958, when a Sikh VIP – presumably, therefore, from the old Commonwealth – came to negotiate with the Cosmobes. That common sense was also, by our standards, astonishingly trusting in scientific authority. And Dan Dare mirrored that too. When the

Pescods unintentionally prompt Krakatoa to erupt and so destroy their own submarine base near Java, Dan exclaims, 'That cloud's thick with the crimson death – the fall-out will kill *millions!*' With the characteristic voice of British authority, which so reassured South Australia about nuclear testing at Maralinga,[2] Sir Hubert replies, 'No, Dan – the scientists have checked on that. It will be too diluted to do any harm by the time it falls!' Rather like Strontium 90, one supposes. My point, however, is not how misleading this all was, but rather how consonant with what its readers already believed: CND would not be launched until 1958.

However, the greater part of the serial's appeal lay altogether elsewhere, that is, in its capacity to astonish. Stories set in the future, space travel itself, life on other planets, alien cities, suspended animation, robots, all of this was utterly strange and wondrous to my six-year-old self, as it doubtless was to most *Eagle* readers. Even women scientists were pretty remarkable. When Peabody was introduced into the serial in episode 5 of Dan's first voyage to Venus, he and his colleagues expressed utter astonishment: 'Gosh!'; 'Jumpin' jets!'; '*A woman*'. Sir Hubert had even complained to the Cabinet, but, as Peabody herself commented, 'I don't see what all the fuss is about. I'm a first-class geologist, botanist, agriculturalist and the Cabinet agree I'm the best person to reconnoitre Venus as a source of food – I'm a qualified space pilot as well.' There may have been hardly any women in Spacefleet, or in Dan's world more generally, but Peabody was wonderfully proto-feminist and quite a shock to my own primary-school sensibilities.

The idea of alien life was even more remarkable: the coldly rational Treens, from Venus's northern hemisphere, whose capital city, Mekonta, was built on a network of islands floating in an artificial lake; the more pastoral, but still scientifically advanced, Therons, from the southern hemisphere, who lived quietly in their individual flying houses, in pursuit of aesthetics and virtue; and the Atlantines, descendants of Earthmen kidnapped from the Mediterranean basin for scientific experimentation by the Treens shortly before the nuclear explosion that destroyed the moun-

2 Between 1955 and 1963 the United Kingdom conducted seven major nuclear tests at the Maralinga site in South Australia. Australia thus became the first and, to date, still the only sovereign state to have invited a foreign power to explode nuclear weapons on its territory. Subsequent reports of ill health and other side effects suffered by Australian citizens of both European and Aboriginal descent called into question official assurances about the adequacy of the site's safety precautions. In 1994 the Australian Government, but not the British, agreed to a compensation settlement with the Maralinga Tjarutja people worth $A13,500,000.

tain range holding back the Atlantic Ocean. The alien geography is equally remarkable: the Flamelands, a molten belt at Venus's equator, which separates the two hemispheres; the mysterious Silicon Mass, which inhabits the lava plain and lives by consuming solid rock, into which the Mekon somehow escaped on 11 April 1958; and the mines at the North Pole.

Mars, by contrast, had long been uninhabited, its ancient quasi-human civilisation destroyed millennia ago by the space bees of asteroid 2345, the so-called 'Red Moon'; Mercury was inhabited by completely non-human rock-like crystal creatures; and beyond the solar system, the entire universe teemed with life. There were the small, highly intelligent and friendly amphibian Cosmobes, travelling through space in their water-bearing Clustaships, whom Dan encountered on 12 July 1958; and their aquatic enemies, the Pescods, who reached Earth on 18 October. There were even other Earth-like planets, including Terra Nova, discovered by Halley McHoo and introduced to Dan by Galileo McHoo, a kilt-wearing Scottish Captain Nemo, who had built his own 'Little Scotland' in the asteroid belt, on 7 March 1959. There was a complete solar system occupying less space than our moon, encountered on 30 May 1959. On Terra Nova, on 19 September 1959, Dan came up against the Nagrabs, man-eating, human-sized ants. In such pre-ecological times, the solution was simple: grab a missile, 'fly over this colony and wipe the *"Nagrabs"* out of existence for ever', as he insisted on 7 November. So much for biological diversity. The tamed giant lizards ridden by the Novads, which we met on 31 October 1959, fared much better precisely because they were tame.

4. Tales of Resonance and Wonder

The peculiar combination of the absolutely conventional and the utterly remarkable is distinctive, not only to Dan Dare, but to SF more generally. One way to theorise this compound would be as a combination between ideology and utopia, in the sense used by Jameson, not in his writings on SF, but in his general hermeneutics. In *The Political Unconscious* he developed the outline of a neo-Lukácsian 'totalising' critical method capable of subsuming other apparently incompatible critical methods, by 'at once canceling and preserving them' (Jameson, 1981, 10). Against more conventionally Marxian understandings of art as ideology, Jameson argued here for a 'double hermeneutic', which would simultaneously embrace both the negative hermeneutic of ideology critique and the positive hermeneutic of a utopian 'non-instrumental conception of culture'. For Jameson, all art, all class consciousness, can be understood as at once both ideological and utopian: 'the ideological would be grasped as somehow at one with the Utopian,' he wrote, 'and the Utopian at one with the ideological' (Jameson, 1981, 286). Spacefleet's British leadership is ideological, in these terms, but Peabody's feminism utopian. No doubt, this is so, but it nonetheless fails to explain what is specifically science-fictional about this particular amalgam of ideology and utopia.

We might find a better, or at least supplementary, answer in Stephen Greenblatt's discussion of resonance and wonder in *Learning to Curse* (1990). It has become conventional to treat the new historicists – Greenblatt himself, Catherine Gallagher, Walter Benn Michaels, Louis Montrose – either as North American Foucauldeans or, less commonly, as 'bastard offspring' of Williams's cultural materialism (Wilson, 1995, 55). I have no desire to intervene in this slightly dated controversy: suffice it to note that Greenblatt generously acknowledged his debts to Williams as well as to Foucault (Greenblatt, 1990, 2–3, 146–47). Greenblatt himself defines resonance as the object's power 'to reach out beyond its formal boundaries to a larger world' and evoke 'the complex, dynamic cultural forces from which it has emerged and for which ... it may be taken ... to stand' either as metaphor or metonym; and wonder as its power 'to convey an arresting sense of uniqueness, to evoke an exalted attention' (Greenblatt, 1990, 170). As a contextualising literary–critical method, new historicism has obvious affinities with the former. But Greenblatt is insistent that wonder can also be understood historically, citing as example its transformation 'from the spectacle of proprietorship to the mystique of the object' (Greenblatt, 1990, 179). This latter type of gaze, a 'looking whose origins lie ... in the art work's capacity to generate .. surprise, delight, admiration, and intimations of genius', is 'one of the distinctive achievements of our culture', he continues, and one of its 'most intense pleasures' (Greenblatt, 1990, 180). Hence the conclusion that, where philosophy will aim to supplant wonder with knowledge, new historicist criticism aims 'to renew the marvellous at the heart of the resonant' (Greenblatt, 1990, 181). It should be apparent that resonance has an ideological aspect, although it is not thereby reducible to ideology, and that wonder might well have a utopian aspect, although they are definitely not coextensive.

Greenblatt's main interest is in imaginative literature, as he makes clear (Greenblatt, 1990, 170), but the concepts can be applied elsewhere: the essay actually begins with a discussion of Cardinal Wolsey's hat in the library of Christ Church, Oxford, and eventually proceeds to the State Jewish Museum in Prague. If Wolsey's hat, then why not Dan Dare's cap badge? If the State Jewish Museum in Prague, then why not the Science Museum in London? The latter is one of Britain's most prestigious museums, a major tourist attraction founded in 1857 to house objects originally displayed at the Great Exhibition of 1851, located in South Kensington on a site immediately adjacent to Imperial College London, one of the 'Group of Five' leading British research universities. From 30 April 2008 to 25 October 2009 it housed an exhibition on the theme of *Dan Dare and the Birth of Hi-Tech Britain*, which aimed to chart the comic strip's influence on British science, technology and everyday life. The programme notes explain that:

> After 1945, though war-weary and broke, Britain found huge pride in wartime advances such as radar, penicillin and the jet engine. Discoveries like these were now tipped to kick-start world-beating industries, bring prosperity and bankroll the emerging welfare state.
>
> In an age before globalisation, products from rockets to radios sprang from local roots. Together they reveal a fascinating 'lost world' of British design and invention – a glimpse of a time when the TV in the corner was a Murphy, not a Sony.
>
> During the 1950s, millions of people – children and adults – followed the adventures of Dan Dare, as portrayed in Eagle magazine. Every week Dan Dare ranged across space, battling his arch foe – the power-mad Mekon. Meanwhile, back on Earth, another extraordinary future was unfolding – one which laid the foundation for today's hi-tech consumer society ...
>
> Dan Dare's adventures were created by Hampson and his team of artists using an innovative method for drawing strip cartoons, using a film-like approach where the narrative was carried in a more fluid way between frames, and employing physical models of rockets and space cities to draw from life. This evocation of the possibilities offered by future technology enthused a generation, from James Dyson to Stephen Hawking. For many people, from schoolboys to scientists and engineers, Dan Dare symbolised the bright future that technology offered to the post-war world.

In short, the adventures of Dan Dare, Pilot of the Future, were tales of resonance and of wonder. This was not simply a matter of ideological 'interpellation' in Louis Althusser's sense of the term, (Althusser, 1971, 174) on the one hand, and utopian aspiration on the other. The marvellous aspects of the tales are actually at the core of their appeal, but were only ever rendered plausible, nonetheless, by the resonant. The primary effect of

Spacefleet's Britishness, for example, was thus not the interpellation of patriotic British 'subjects', in either or both senses of the word, but rather the fictional plausibility of Peabody's feminism to an audience already constituted as British, patriotic and male. Resonance was produced textually by such 'reality effects', which were necessary in their own right, quite apart from their politico-ideological effects, for the stories to work narratologically. These reality effects are, of course, the most ideologically implicated aspects of the tales and therefore the most implausible in retrospect: a society still without a single astronaut or cosmonaut to its credit is as unlikely to command Spacefleet as it is the occupation of Iraq; female professors, by contrast, are now commonplace, even in Britain. But the resonance is nonetheless what made the wonder work. And this is true both of Dan Dare in particular and of SF in general, even literary SF, even canonical SF, so much so, indeed, as to be a constitutive feature of the genre. For SF requires this ideological resonance precisely because its narratives are, at their core, fantastic, unbelievable and unrealistic or, according to taste, marvellous and wonderful.

2

Science Fiction and Selective Tradition

To summarise the tentative conclusions of the previous chapter, I have argued that the category of SF applies meaningfully across a whole range of cultural forms, from the novel and short story to film and television, a generic continuity repeatedly signalled by way of intertextuality; that SF cannot be located exclusively on either side of any high Literature/popular culture binary, but should be seen as straddling and thereby, in effect, deconstructing them; that SF tends to be resistant to modernist aesthetics insofar as it privileges content, that is, ideas, over form; and that SF narratives are typically tales of resonance and wonder, in which quasi-ideological resonance functions primarily so as to add plausibility to the tale's wondrous core. Thus far, I have treated as SF whatever calls itself thus, but the question of definition can be postponed no further. If Le Guin is right that everybody is writing SF now, even Winterson, then it is time we attempt to describe what exactly it is they are writing. But Winterson is by no means alone in refusing the generic label 'science fiction' – here, it becomes necessary to spell the term out in full – nor with paying for that refusal at the price of Le Guin's heartfelt condemnation. Two years later, Margaret Atwood's insistence that her novels *Oryx and Crake* and *The Year of the Flood* were 'speculative fiction', but not thereby 'science fiction', prompted a very similar reaction (Le Guin, 2009). Atwood held her peace at the time, but eventually replied at length.

What she means by 'science fiction', Atwood would explain, are books descended from Wells, which deal with 'things that could not possibly happen', by 'speculative fiction' books descended from Verne, which deal with 'things that really could happen but just hadn't completely happened when the authors wrote'. Elaborating on her disagreement with Le Guin, she continued: 'what Le Guin means by "science fiction" is what I mean by "speculative fiction," and what she means by "fantasy" would include some of what I mean by "science fiction"'. 'So that clears it all up,' she concluded, 'more or less' (Atwood, 2011a, 7). Of course, it doesn't, not least because there is something very peculiar about this attempt to prise apart Verne and Wells, for if there is one thing both scholarly and fan critics tend to agree upon, it is that the two masters of the 'scientific romance' were committed to very much the same enterprise. This isn't what concerns me here, however. Rather, I want to draw attention to the underlying logic of Atwood's argument, in particular to the way she justifies a set of prospectively applicable inclusions and exclusions by reference to a set of previous texts described retrospectively, in this case, Wells's *The War of the Worlds* and Verne's 'books about submarines and balloon travel' (Atwood, 2011a, 6). In this, she is by no means unique. Quite the contrary, it seems to be exactly how the struggle for definition is normally prosecuted within SF.

1. Academic Definitions of Science Fiction

So we proceed to the first of our four main questions: what was SF? This is, at one level, essentially a question of definition. Definitions need not necessarily be academic, but academics nonetheless have a professional penchant for definition, given that it is quite fundamental to what they do, and it is difficult to imagine any more archetypically academic definitions than those proposed in Suvin's *Metamorphoses of Science Fiction*. Its foundational definition is elaborated in the first chapter:

> SF is ... a literary genre whose necessary and sufficient conditions are the presence and interaction of estrangement and cognition, and whose main formal device is an imaginative framework alternative to the author's empirical environment. (Suvin, 1979, 7–8)

Almost equally significant is the supplementary definition given on the first page of the influential fourth chapter:

> SF is distinguished by the narrative dominance or hegemony of a fictional 'novum' (novelty, innovation) validated by cognitive logic. (Suvin, 1979, 63)

In my experience, these definitions function extraordinarily well as pedagogical devices for teaching SF. The testable, even examinable, questions follow on with remarkable facility: Where is the estrangement in this novel? What exactly is its novum? Is it strangely new? Is it hegemonic? Is it validated by cognitive logic? The first definition is acceptably elitist insofar as it is confined to literature, as distinct from film or television, but also nicely contrarian, insofar as it seeks to expand the canon to include something as inherently disreputable as SF. And it is simultaneously theoretically rich and respectably radical, insofar as it derives from Russian

Formalism by way of Bertolt Brecht. The second replicates the latter achievement, insofar as it derives from Bloch out of Antonio Gramsci. Suvin's definitions were, in short, just what the Doctor of Philosophy had ordered.

Freedman's *Critical Theory and Science Fiction* accepts Suvin's stress on estrangement and cognition as 'fundamentally sound' and 'indispensable', in part, I suspect, because its author has 'struggled to obtain academic recognition for science fiction' (Freedman, 2000, 17, 15). Freedman amends Suvin's definition in only two significant respects, firstly, by substituting 'cognition effect' for cognition, so that what matters is the text's own attitude towards what it knows, as distinct from some extratextual measure of cognitive adequacy, and, secondly, by insisting that genre is better understood as a tendency than a category, so that 'a text is not filed under a generic category; instead, a generic tendency is something that happens within a text' (Freedman, 2000, 18, 20). Hence, Freedman's conclusion, simultaneously neo-Suvinian and neo-Althusserian, that a text can be described as SF only insofar as 'cognitive estrangement is the dominant generic tendency within the overdetermined textual whole' (Freedman, 2000, 20). Freedman's first amendment is necessary to save Suvin from himself. Otherwise, the science-fictionality of SF would have remained dependent on the scientificity of science and therefore subject to retrospective transformation into fantasy, since scientific knowledge is itself subject to continuous processes of development. Nonetheless, Freedman steers back toward Suvin's original position when he adds that 'the readiest means of producing a cognition effect is precisely through cognition itself' (Freedman, 2000, 19). Actually, this might very well not be the case, given that some of the most persuasive science in SF, Lem's solaristics, for example, or Asimov's psychohistory, is entirely fictional, and some of the most fundamental science in science faculties, particle physics, for example, is utterly unpersuasive to the lay reader. Which means only that both Suvin and Freedman underestimate the radical discursivity of both science and SF: science isn't cognition, it is what scientists believe to be cognition. Freedman's second amendment is more interesting insofar as it takes a first, tentative step towards a non-formalist understanding of genre, but it goes nothing like so far as I will recommend below.

Forbiddingly Hegelian in register, Jameson's *Archaeologies of the Future* is less obviously amenable to co-option into conventional pedagogy than either Suvin's *Metamorphoses* or Freedman's *Critical Theory*. Eagleton once uncharitably described Jameson's *The Political Unconscious* as part 'Californian supermarket of the mind', part 'unrepentant *bricoleur*, reaching for a Machereyan spanner here or a Greimasian screwdriver there' (Eagleton,

1986, 70–71). The same method and style informs *Archaeologies*, which exhibits the same strenuous '*mastering*' Eagleton judged 'too eirenic, easy-going and all-encompassing' for Jameson's 'own political good' (Eagleton, 1986, 71), the same commitment to *Aufhebung*, the same scholarly erudition, the same elaboration and resolution through incorporation of formalist taxonomic binaries, even the same repeated invocation of Greimas's semiotic rectangle. It is also, however, a clearly Suvinian text. So, Jameson stresses 'the role of cognition' in SF and that of magic in fantasy (Jameson, 2005, 63). SF, he writes, 'is the exploration of all the constraints thrown up by history itself – the web of counterfinalities and anti-dialectics which human production has ... produced'. Fantasy, by contrast, is 'a celebration of human creative power and freedom which becomes idealistic ... by virtue of the omission of ... material and historical constraints' (Jameson, 2005, 66). Like Suvin, Jameson also stresses the role of estrangement, arguing that SF works 'to defamiliarize and restructure our experience of our own *present* ... in specific ways distinct from all other forms of defamiliarization' (Jameson, 2005, 286). The genre's multiple mock futures, he continues, function so as to transform 'our own present into the determinate past of something yet to come' and so to make 'the present as history' available for contemplation (Jameson, 2005, 288). The function of SF, he concludes, in one of his more arresting formulations, is 'to dramatize our incapacity to imagine the future' and thereby to become 'a contemplation of our own absolute limits' (Jameson, 2005, 288–89).

These definitions each contain an implicit temporality. Although Suvin gestures towards even earlier forms, his introduction to an 'older SF history' actually begins in the fifteenth century, with Thomas More, Francis Bacon and François Rabelais (Suvin, 1979, 90–102). Freedman toys with the extremely unhelpful idea that 'all fiction is, in a sense, science fiction' (Freedman, 2000, 16), but nonetheless concentrates his attentions on post-Second World War American (and Polish) SF writers. This is so, he explains, because 'in the past forty years ... we have witnessed the production of the largest distinct body of work that strongly incarnates the generic tendency of science fiction and is explicitly and unambiguously published under the name' (Freedman, 2000, 94). Like Suvin, Jameson refers back to More, but nonetheless understands SF as a historically more recent invention, the product of a 'miraculous birth' sometime in the nineteenth century, either with Shelley's *Frankenstein* or with Wells's *The Time Machine* (Jameson, 2005, 1, 57), or, in a slightly different formulation, with Verne and Wells (Jameson, 2005, 284). All three definitions thus have a very distinctive structure, almost identical to that in Atwood's debate with Le

Guin, that is, they are at once both prospective and retrospective. So they each establish a set of inclusions and exclusions, intended to function prospectively, but only by reference to a set of previous texts, described retrospectively. The procedure is perhaps at its most transparent in Freedman, but nonetheless clearly present in Suvin and Jameson.

2. Modernism, Modernity and Science Fiction

Like Suvin, Jameson and Freedman, Wegner also attempts to apply exclusionary strategies to the SF field, but in his case through the judicious application of categories drawn from general literary theory, especially those of realism and modernism. We noted in chapter 1 how, when Gelder tropes SF as 'popular fiction' in opposition to 'Literature', he understands the latter as more or less coextensive with literary modernism. In this respect, his work unwittingly rehearses one of the most characteristic topoi in twentieth-century academic literary criticism. The binary in question sometimes manifests itself in explicit and overt hostility to popular fiction, as in the Leavisite opposition between mass civilisation and minority culture, where Eliot's modernism is a central instance of the latter, or in the Frankfurt School's opposition between the culture industries and autonomous art. At other times, it is less explicitly hostile, as in structuralist and post-structuralist distinctions between readerly and writerly texts, the text of *plaisir* and the text of *jouissance*. But mass culture invariably appears as the Other, or at least an Other, of modernist high culture. This is perhaps unsurprising: whenever we date the precise beginnings of modernism, there can be little doubt that high modernism and mass culture were roughly contemporaneous; however we characterise the cultural avant-garde, there can be little doubt that modernism and the avant-garde both stood in essentially adversarial relation, not only to bourgeois realism, but also to mass popular culture.

Yet, as we also observed in chapter 1, SF as a genre sits very uneasily on the popular side of this modernist binary. For Suvin and Jameson, as we have seen, SF is essentially a 'literary genre' and, as such, either belongs on the other side of the binary or transcends it altogether. Indeed, Jameson himself has argued that SF 'stands in complementary and dialectical relationship to high culture or modernism' (Jameson, 2005, 283). Wegner takes the argument much further, however, insisting that Jameson's *Archaeologies* 'enables us to understand science fiction ... as a *modernist* practice' (Wegner, 2007a, 7). Elsewhere, he makes similar use of Suvin: 'The formal specificity of SF as a modernist practice', Wegner writes, 'is most effectively grasped in ... Suvin's definition' of the genre (Wegner, 2009, 141). Wegner almost certainly overinterprets both Jameson and Suvin, insofar as both are drawn to much longer genealogies for SF than could ever adequately be described as either modern or modernist. He thereby incidentally almost certainly underplays the originality of his own argument.

For Wegner, as not quite for either Suvin or Jameson, SF is best understood as a peculiar variant of modernism. The genre, he writes, emerged 'as a particularly original representational technology in the late nineteenth century' and was 'always already as modernist as ... film' (Wegner, 2009, 141). Moreover, SF exhibits a form of 'realist (cognitive) modernism (estrangement)', which 'estranges through ... realistic content, whose referent is "absent"' (Wegner, 2009, 142). The result is a genre that is not only generally modernist, but also contains within itself specifically modernist moments. So Wegner rewrites the history of SF as proceeding from an initial realist moment (Wells, E. M. Forster and Alexander Bogdanov), through a first modernist moment in the 1920s (Zamyatin, Alexei Tolstoy, Huxley, Čapek, Olaf Stapledon), a second realist moment (American Golden Age SF), a second modernist moment (the New Wave), postmodernism (cyberpunk) and, finally, a post-postmodernism that actually 'repeats' the earlier modernist phases (Wegner, 2009, 142–43). This periodisation, first formulated in his review of Jameson's *Archaeologies*, is, as Wegner himself concedes, clearly 'different' from Jameson's own (Wegner, 2007a, 9–10).

What are we to make of this notion of a generally modernist form, the history of which is punctuated by particular modernist moments? Perhaps only that the term modernism is itself distinctly slippery, not only in Wegner, but also in literary theory more generally. There are at least four comparatively common, yet distinct usages currently attached to the term. First, modernism may simply denote the culture of modernity, as in Jürgen Habermas's argument that modernity is characterised by 'the separation of the substantive reason expressed in religion and metaphysics into three autonomous spheres ... science, morality and art' (Habermas, 1985, 9). So modern art becomes simply institutionally autonomous art. Ironically, a similar conception also underpins the more ambitious theorisations of postmodernism, such as Jean-François Lyotard's *The Postmodern Condition*, which seek to contrast postmodernism and postmodernity with modernism and modernity (Lyotard, 1984, 37). Setting aside the largely specious character of this version of the latter distinction, SF can no doubt plausibly be represented as a modern (and postmodern), as distinct from pre-modern, genre. But this tells us very little about what is specific to SF, as distinct from what is general to modernity. We shall return to this matter in chapter 7 below.

Second, modernism can be represented much more precisely as the kind of high art, characterised by a combination of aesthetic self-consciousness and formalist experimentalism, the origins of which are conventionally traced to late nineteenth-century Europe. So one widely used text neatly defines the high modernist period as running from 1890 to 1930 (Bradbury and McFarlane, 1976a). Jameson's *Postmodernism, or, The Cultural Logic of Late Capitalism* (1991) deploys an essentially similar conception, here linked to the periodising notion of a parallelism between three stages in the history of capitalism (competitive capitalism, monopoly capitalism and late capitalism) and three in the history of modern culture (realism, modernism and postmodernism). If we date the emergence of SF to Wells, as Wegner does, then it was indeed roughly contemporaneous with that of high modernism in this sense. But Verne's first SF novels were much earlier, nonetheless, and Wells himself was, by Wegner's own account, a literary 'realist'. The point, surely, is that a modernism of content – which is how Wegner describes SF – is not really modernism at all.

A third sense of the term, essentially a subvariant of the second, is as the type of art pursued by different kinds of cultural 'avant-garde'. Here, the role of the artist is understood as that of cultural leader, moving ahead of the wider society, much like the revolutionary vanguard in the Leninist view of politics. For the avant-gardist, art stands in opposition to the dominant 'bourgeois' culture, as an essentially 'adversarial' force, possessed of positively 'redemptive' social functions. Both Renato Poggiolo, one of the first to attempt to 'theorise' the avant-garde, and Bradbury and McFarlane see avant-gardes as integral to modernism (Poggioli, 1968, 15; Bradbury and McFarlane, 1976b, 29). By contrast, both Habermas and Peter Bürger argue for a model of the avant-garde as a movement within and against modernism, rather than coextensive with it. For Bürger, bourgeois art had consisted in a celebration in form of the liberation of art from religion, from the court, and eventually even from the bourgeoisie (Bürger, 1984, 46–49). Modernist art thus emerged as an autonomous social 'institution', the preserve and prerogative of an increasingly autonomous intellectual class, which itself, in turn, prompted the ultimately doomed rebellion of the 'historical avant-garde' of the 1920s (Bürger, 1984, 22). The avant-garde attempt to overcome the separation between art and life 'has not occurred,' Bürger concludes, 'and presumably cannot occur, in bourgeois society' (Bürger, 1984, 34). Habermas's analysis ran along similar lines, toward a similar conclusion, that the historical avant-garde's attempt to force a reconciliation between art and life, by destroying the autonomy of art, had been doomed to failure: 'A reified everyday praxis can be cured', he wrote, 'only by creating unconstrained interaction of the cognitive with the moral–practical and the aesthetic–expressive elements. Reification cannot be overcome by forcing just one of those highly stylized cultural spheres to open up and become more accessible' (Habermas, 1985, 11–12).

However we read the historical avant-garde, it is clear that SF has its own avant-gardes, but much less clear that these necessarily have anything to do with modernism. Wells, by Wegner's account a realist, was fascinated by vanguard intellectualism, whether that of the Fabian Society or of the fictional Samurai in his *A Modern Utopia*. Asimov, yet another of Wegner's realists, was actively involved in the New York Futurians, arguably yet another SF avant-garde. Zamyatin and Čapek, by contrast, were in no obvious sense avant-gardists. Some SF avant-gardes, the New Wave and cyberpunk for example, clearly post-date both modernism as defined by Bradbury and McFarlane and the historical avant-garde as defined by Habermas and Bürger. Yet the first is modernist according to Wegner, the second postmodernist and thereby, presumably, not really an avant-garde at all. Moreover, there is an important sense in which the circle around Byron and the Shelleys, which produced *Frankenstein*, might itself be considered a pre-modernist avant-garde. Interestingly, Poggioli himself traced the origins of the avant-garde to 'the various preludes to the romantic experience' (Poggioli, 1968, 15).

This is also the point of departure for David Roberts, whose fascinating account of the history of the *Gesamtkunstwerk* ('total work of art') runs interestingly parallel to Bürger's own of the avant-garde. Although the term itself was a coinage of Richard Wagner, and is usually understood as referring to the reintegration of the arts, Roberts argues both that the *Gesamtkunstwerk* is prefigured in the festivals of Revolutionary France and that it denotes, crucially, 'the idea of art … as *performance*, whose horizon is the ever-renewable present of collective participation' (Roberts, 2011, 258). This essentially avant-gardist conception reaches its self-destructive culmination, he concludes, in the totalitarian cinema of the first part of Sergei Eisenstein's *Ivan Grozniy* (*Ivan the Terrible*) and Leni Riefenstahl's *Triumph des Willens* (*Triumph of the Will*) (Roberts, 2011, 230, 249–50). SF has, of course, spawned its own *Gesamtkunstwerke*, from Lang's *Metropolis* through to James Cameron's *Avatar* and Ridley Scott's *Prometheus*, but these are neither so necessarily totalitarian as Roberts fears nor so readily defined as either modernist or realist as Wegner supposes. We shall return to this matter of the avant-garde in the chapter that follows. For the moment, however, we need only note the apparent misfit between the complexities of SF history and the available theorisations of avant-gardism.

A fourth sense of modernism is as a near-synonym for 'literary', where the latter term is used quasi-prescriptively to denote work of high literary value. This is the sense used by Gelder and also by Wegner in his account of the oscillation between realism and modernism within SF. Quite apart from the difficulty of attributing determinate objectivity to so necessarily intersubjective a category as value, the identification of modernism with modern literature per se seems distinctly fraught. Much that has been deemed of literary value – Lawrence and Orwell, for example – is in no obvious sense modernist. And there is as much bad modernism around as bad anything else (some might argue even more). What goes for literature in general also applies to SF in particular. If Wells's SF is realist and Huxley's or Stapledon's modernist, as Wegner argues, then why exactly is this so? *The Time Machine* is surely no less experimental, at the levels of both form and content, than *Brave New World*; and it is certainly held in more generally high regard than Stapledon's *Last and First Men*.

This leads me to suggest that SF cannot helpfully be defined as either realist or modernist. To describe as realist a genre that deliberately deals only with worlds that have never existed seems not only to fly in the face of all sense, but also to contradict Suvin's foundational taxonomic distinction between realistic and science-fictional literary forms (Suvin, 1979, 21–22). But to describe as modernist a genre that deliberately pastiches the conventional tropes and topoi of narrative realism seems almost equivalently perverse. The truth, surely, is that SF is neither realist nor modernist, but rather an entirely distinct third term. Here, Jameson is worth citing against Wegner: 'SF is a sub-genre with a complex and formal history of its own,' he writes, 'and with its own dynamic, which is not that of high culture...' (Jameson, 2005, 283). Wegner quotes this passage in full, but only so as to lay undue stress on the immediately following clause, which he misreads as meaning that SF is in fact a modernism (Wegner, 2007a, 8). The implied point of Wegner's intervention is clearly to valorise 'modernist' over 'realist' SF. As such, it falls short of a full attempt at redefinition, but nonetheless follows the more generally academicist logic of Suvinian and post-Suvinian definitions towards their ultimate terminus: an outright rejection of most of what most fans would recognise as SF.

3. Non-Academic Definitions of Science Fiction

Academics are by no means the only people attracted to this kind of exercise: SF history is littered with definitions and definers, be they writers, fans, editors or critics. Clute and Nicholls's version of the *Encyclopedia of Science Fiction* identified no fewer than eleven main candidates under its entry on 'Definitions of SF' (Clute and Nicols, 1993, 311–14). Less traditionally magisterial but more inclusive, *Wikipedia* currently lists twenty-nine

(Wikipedia, 2011). The most famous is probably Gernsback in 1926, describing the range and scope of his *Amazing Stories* in its first issue: 'the Jules Verne, H. G. Wells and Edgar Allan Poe type of story – a charming romance intermingled with scientific fact and prophetic vision' (Gernsback, 1926, 3). But Brian Aldiss's 1986 redefinition runs it close: 'the search for a definition of mankind' – the original 1973 definition had 'man' here rather than 'mankind' – 'and his status in the universe which will stand in our advanced but confused state of knowledge (science) ... characteristically cast in the Gothic or post-Gothic mode' (Aldiss, 1986, 25).

If Gernsback's opening editorial was essentially prospective in intent, its referents, Verne, Wells, Poe and, later on the same page, Edward Bellamy, were nonetheless very obviously retrospective. Indeed, Gernsback's editorial quite explicitly acknowledged that 'stories of this nature' had been published for 'many years', explaining that the new magazine's novelty would be in concentrating on 'the scientific fiction type of story ... exclusively', not in their publication per se (Gernsback, 1926, 3). The first issue contained stories by Verne, Wells and Poe, the promise of more by Verne and Wells in the second, the announcement of an exclusive agreement with Verne's copyright holders and with 'the best writers' of 'German, French and English stories of this kind' (Gernsback, 1926, 3). Even by his own estimate, then, Gernsback wasn't the 'Father of Science Fiction' proclaimed by Sam Moskowitz (Moskowitz, 1974a, 242), but rather its legitimate heir. Aldiss notoriously questioned even this legitimacy (Aldiss, 1986, 202–4), but his own reference to the Gothic is similarly retrospective, tracing the 'origins of the species' to Shelley's *Frankenstein* (Aldiss, 1986, 25–52). Shelley, he insisted, 'makes it plain that her central marvel shares the essential quality of scientific experiment'. By 'combining social criticism with new scientific ideas', she thus anticipated 'the methods of H. G. Wells' and those who would follow in his footsteps (Aldiss, 1986, 46). Aldiss canvassed other claims to paternity or maternity more or less respectfully, Poe and Edward Bulwer-Lytton, Samuel Butler and Charlotte Perkins Gilman, Verne and Stevenson, but Wells finally emerges as 'the Prospero of all the brave new worlds, ... the Shakespeare of science fiction' (Aldiss, 1986, 133). This is a different genealogy from Gernsback's, less impressed by Poe and Bellamy and less exclusively masculine, but it is a genealogy, nonetheless.

Behind Gernsback and Aldiss, there are yet other genealogies. Verne credited Poe as an early influence. 'Poe', he wrote in 1864, 'has created a genre of his own which owes nothing to anyone else ... he is the leader of the school of the strange' (Jules-Verne, 1976, 60; Verne, 1979). Commenting on the unresolved ending to *The Narrative of Arthur Gordon*

Pym, he asked: 'Who will ever complete it? A bolder man than I' (Jules-Verne, 1976, 62; Verne, 1979). But, as we know, Verne did himself eventually write *Le Sphinx des glaces* as the sequel, published in French in 1897 and in English translation, as *An Antarctic Mystery*, the following year. He described it thus to his publisher, Pierre-Jules Hetzel: 'I have used everything that Poe left in suspense and have developed the mystery surrounding certain of the characters ... Needless to say, I go much further than Poe' (Jules-Verne, 1976, 193). If Poe had been the leader of a genre, then Verne had, by his own account, become its chief practitioner. Similarly, Wells explicitly compared his scientific romances to Shelley. Like her, he had written 'fantasies' that aimed, not 'to project a serious possibility', but 'only at the same amount of conviction ... one gets in a good gripping dream' (Wells, 1933a, vii). Unlike her, he had substituted 'an ingenious use of scientific patter' for the kind of 'jiggery-pokery magic' she used to animate her monster. 'I simply brought the fetish stuff up to date,' he concluded, making it as 'near actual theory as possible' (Wells, 1933a, viii). This is unfair to Shelley, given that there is no magic in either *Frankenstein* or *The Last Man*. But Wells is nonetheless negotiating with a prehistory of his own texts, albeit with characteristic immodesty. Indeed, the description he gives of *The Island of Doctor Moreau*, as 'an exercise in youthful blasphemy' (Wells, 1933a, ix), might well be applied equally to *Frankenstein*. Hence, Shelley's own insistence, in the 'Introduction' to the 1831 edition, that 'supremely frightful would be the effect of any human endeavour to mock the stupendous mechanism of the Creator of the world' (Shelley, 1980, 9). Much more than Wells admitted or most subsequent critical commentary has conceded, *Moreau* was a reworking of *Frankenstein*, perhaps especially in its 1894 first draft (Wilt, 2003, 9; Philmus, 1993, 105).

Verne and Wells famously insisted on their differences from each other. For Verne, Wells's stories were quite fundamentally unscientific:

> I make use of physics. He invents. I go to the moon in a cannon-ball, discharged from a cannon. He goes to Mars in an airship, which he constructs of a metal which does away with the law of gravitation. *Ça c'est très joli* ... but show me this metal. Let him produce it. (Verne, 1997, 101–2)

For Wells, 'the great Frenchman' had settled for merely 'anticipatory inventions', whilst he had chosen to follow Shelley, holding the reader 'by art and illusion ... not by proof and argument' (Wells, 1933a, vii). Wells was careful to add, however, that

> Verne never landed on the moon because he never knew of radio and the possibility of sending back a message ... But equipped with radio ... I was able to land and even see something of the planet. (Wells, 1933a, ix)

Virtually every subsequent SF writer in the twentieth-century literary canon has insisted on their debt to and differences from Wells (cf. Zamiatin, 1970; Mánek, 2005). Huxley, for example, specifically intended *Brave New World* to expose 'the horror of the Wellsian Utopia' (Huxley, 1969, 348). Even more interesting is the case of Orwell, who was, in turn, both inspired and repelled by Wellsian futurology. So Orwell could be fulsome in retrospective praise for Wells:

> The minds of all of us, and therefore the physical world, would be perceptibly different if Wells had never existed ... Back in the nineteen-hundreds it was a wonderful experience ... to discover H.G. Wells ... here was this wonderful man who ... knew that the future was not going to be what respectable people imagined. (Orwell, 1970a, 171)

But in *The Road to Wigan Pier*, he nonetheless denounced Wells at length (Orwell, 1962, 169–72, 177–78). Wells's work had become increasingly irrelevant to the twentieth century, Orwell would eventually conclude: 'A crude book like *The Iron Heel* ... is a truer prophecy ... than ... *The Shape of Things to Come*' (Orwell, 1970a, 172; London, 1958). Moreover, he particularly disliked Wells's utopianism. As early as 1935, he had described these 'Utopiae infested by nude school-marms' as a 'kind of optimistic lie'; in 1941, he objected to the sheer uselessness of 'rigmarole about a World State'; and as late as 1946, he repeated his 'low opinion' of Wells's writing after 1920 (Orwell, 1970b, 179; Orwell, 1970a, 167; Orwell, 1970c, 293). Unsurprisingly, the great man did not take kindly to such criticism, famously dismissing Orwell as a 'Trotskyist with big feet' (Crick, 1980, 294).

Orwell had also, however, defined his work in relation to the kind of book represented by Yevgeny Zamyatin's *Mi* (We),[3] explaining to Gleb Struve that he 'heard of' this novel through the latter's *25 Years of Soviet Russian Literature* (Orwell, 1970d, 118). Unable to obtain it in English, Orwell acquired a copy of Cauvet-Duhamel's French translation, *Nous autres*, which he promptly reviewed for *Tribune*, advising its readers that

3 The title of Zamyatin's novel is written in Russian as Мы, the second letter of which, 'ы', is normally transliterated into Roman script as 'y'. But *My* looks very strange in this context, so I have therefore decided to opt for *Mi* throughout. This has the obvious advantage of not actually being an English word.

'This is a book to look out for when an English version appears' (Orwell, 1970e, 95, 99). In 1946, he wrote approvingly of the novel in his essay on James Burnham; in 1948, he offered to review a proposed English translation, which unfortunately failed to eventuate, for the *Times Literary Supplement*; and in 1949, he urged it on Fred Warburg, who had published *Animal Farm* and would shortly publish *Nineteen Eighty-Four* (Orwell, 1970f, 195; Orwell, 1970g, 473; Orwell, 1970h, 546–47).

Even the ancestors to whom more recent writers refer turn out to have ancestors of their own, even Shelley, who explained the novelty of her own fiction in similarly retrospective terms. 'The event on which the interest of the story depends', she wrote in the preface to the first edition of *Frankenstein*,

> is exempt from the disadvantages of a mere tale of spectres or enchantment. It was recommended by the novelty of the situations which it develops; and, however impossible as a physical fact, affords a point of view to the imagination for the delineating of human passions more comprehensive and commanding than any which the ordinary relations of existing events can yield. (Shelley, 1980, 13)

Her novel would thus be concerned with the possible consequences and ethical implications of a hypothetical scientific development, rather than with supernatural phenomena. In short, it would not be a conventionally Gothic romance of the kind that preceded it. Of all these definers and defined, only Aldiss would at the time have described his work as 'science fiction'. Shelley had no name for her new kind of novel, although she was careful to credit *The Last Man* to 'the author of *Frankenstein*'; Poe wrote 'tales of the grotesque and arabesque'; Verne *voyages extraordinaires* and *romans scientifique*; Wells 'scientific romances'; Gernsback's early magazines were published as 'scientifiction'; Orwell described his work as 'political writing'. But the repeated retrospective intertextual referencing suggests the presence, if not of a genre, then at least of a tradition.

The same blend of prospectus and retrospect is present in almost all definitions of SF. So, for example, Kingsley Amis described the genre as narrative dealing with a situation 'that could not arise in the world we know, but which is hypothesised on the basis of some innovation in science and technology' by reference to extracts from Wells's *The War of the Worlds* and Pohl and Kornbluth's *The Space Merchants* (Amis, 1961, 15–18). Judith Merril famously redefined the genre as 'speculative fiction', by way of a potted history of the whole of twentieth-century American and British SF, loosely centred on Campbell and Orwell (Merril, 1971, 60, 65–79). Joanna Russ described it as a literature based on 'The What If and The Serious

Explanation', by positive reference to Samuel R. Delany, Edgar Rice Burroughs and Bradbury, negative to J. R. R. Tolkien (Russ, 2007, 205). Kim Stanley Robinson argues the case for SF as a 'historical literature', by reference to Golding, Burgess, Norman Mailer, John Fowles and Guy Davenport (Robinson, 1987, 54, 61). The only important exceptions are explicitly nominalist definitions, such as Norman Spinrad's 'Science fiction is anything published as science fiction' (Clute and Nicholls, 1993, 311–14). But this necessarily begs the question of what actually does get published as SF, which in turn redirects us once again towards the SF tradition and its long history of definitions and redefinitions.

4. Rethinking Genre

The first part of Suvin's *Metamorphoses* is an account of the structure of a genre, the second, of the history of a tradition, running from More's *Utopia* to Čapek's *Válka s mloky*. If there is an obvious logical complementarity between these exercises, there is also, in this particular instance, a practically unresolved tension between the literary theorist, aiming to define the genre, and the literary historian, attempting to chart its evolution. So Suvin is simultaneously insistent that the 'concept of SF' cannot be deduced 'empirically from the work called thus', but that it is 'inherent in the literary objects'; that it can be reached only through an effort 'to educe and formulate the *differentia specifica* of the SF narration', but that 'the scholar does not invent it out of the whole cloth' (Suvin, 1979, 63). At first sight, this is bewildering, for if the concept inheres in the literary objects, then it should surely be deducible from them. The end product, but also the axiomatic premise, is the famous definition cited above, in which theory clearly triumphs over history, genre over tradition. But what follows is, nonetheless, the history of a tradition, of which 'the significant writers ... were quite aware' (Suvin, 1979, 12). Which leads me to two propositions, one on genre, the other on tradition, both deriving ultimately from Williams.

In traditional literary criticism, notions of 'form' or 'genre' are commonly used to classify literature and literary history 'not by time or place ... but by specifically literary types of organisation or structure' (Wellek and Warren, 1976, 226). They are thus deemed to possess an essential immutability, which renders their character fundamentally ahistorical. Hence, Wellek and Warren's scepticism about 'the social determination of genres' (Wellek and Warren, 1976, 109). Suvin, by contrast, is clear that form is constructed socially, at least in part. Hence, his own description of genre as 'a socioaesthetic entity with a specific inner life, yet in constant osmosis with other literary genres, science, philosophy, everyday socioeconomic life, and so on' (Suvin, 1979, 53). The phrase nicely combines a formalist sense of generic specificity with a more historicist sense of the possibilities for variation over time. But there is something strange, nonetheless, about Suvin's use of the term 'entity', suggestive as it is of a reified, perhaps even fetishistic, conception of the socioaesthetic. Socioaesthetic genre may be, but an entity it surely is not. The problem almost certainly lies with Suvin's understanding of genre as primarily a matter of classification. It is this, of course, but it is also a set of practical conventions, combining a complex mix of prohibitions, recommendations and prescriptions, which together constitute a cultural technology for the production and reception of particular kinds of text.

Williams, by contrast, had argued in *Marxism and Literature* for the theoretical superiority of notions of 'form' over 'genre-classification' (Williams, 1977, 185–86). Here, he defined the problem of form as, firstly, that of the historically variable relations between social modes and individual projects, and, secondly, that of the specifiable material practices within which those relations are enacted (Williams, 1977, 187). Form, then, is not so much a matter of classification as of social relationship: 'it is ... a social process which ... becomes a social product. Forms are ... the common property ... of writers and audiences or readers, before any communicative composition can occur' (Williams, 1977, 187–88). Form is by definition necessarily reproducible: if two texts are examples of a form, this is so only because they in some sense 'reproduce' the features of that form. But Williams distinguishes two main kinds of meaning attaching to the term 'reproduction', on the one hand, uniform copying by processes of mechanical reproduction, on the other, genetic reproduction, 'where typically forms – species – are prolonged, but in intrinsically variable individual examples' (Williams, 1981, 185). Reproduction of literary and cultural form, he observes, is analogous to reproduction only in this second sense. Moreover, culture is necessarily productive as well as reproductive: 'social orders and cultural orders must be seen as being actively made ... unless there is ... production and innovation, most orders are at risk' (Williams, 1981, 201). At their furthest reach, such innovations in form will signify what, for Williams, was the most important of all cultural possibilities, that of an emergent 'structure of feeling'.

We will return to this matter in later chapters. For the moment, however, suffice it to note that, in Williams's account, attention to the typical, the modal and the characteristic actually enables us to recognise 'innovation in process ... one of the very few elements of cultural production to which the stock adjective, "creative", is wholly appropriate'

(Williams, 1981, 200). The work of art, Roland Barthes wrote, 'is what man wrests from chance' (Barthes, 1972, 152). But it is also, as Barthes himself made clear, what form produces from chance. Formal expectations, formal conventions, whether of the sonnet or of the SF story, enter into the writing of any particular sonnet or any particular SF story as forces of production. Understood thus, that is, as a prospectively productive force within the literary mode of production, genre loses the fetishistic quality it acquires in Suvin. Understood thus, it also becomes clear why genre inheres in literary objects, but cannot be deduced from them: they bear its impress because it pre-exists them as a tool for their manufacture.

5. Rethinking Tradition

An analogous argument may be mounted with respect to tradition. For Suvin, tradition is inherited from the past, developed and modified in the present, then handed on to the future as a gift from the present-become-past. Hence, his description of Wells as 'the central writer in the SF tradition':

> He collected ... all the main influences of earlier writers – from Lucian and Swift to Kepler, Verne, and Flammarion, from Plato and Morris to Mary Shelley, Poe, Bulwer, and the subliterature of planetary and subterranean voyages, future wars, and the like – and transformed them in his own image, whence they entered into the treasury of subsequent SF. (Suvin, 1979, 220)

There are, however, other ways of theorising tradition, most importantly for my purposes Williams's notion of 'selective tradition'. In *Culture and Society*, Williams insisted that cultural tradition cannot be the objective unfolding of the consciousness of a people, as both T. S. Eliot and F. R. Leavis had argued, but must be the outcome, in part, of a set of interested selections made in the present. So Williams argues that 'a tradition is always selective, and ... there will always be a tendency for this process of selection to be related to and even governed by the interests of the class that is dominant' (Williams, 1963, 307–8). Nonetheless, he continues, tradition cannot be reduced to class. 'If we are to understand the process of a selective tradition,' he wrote,

> we shall not think of exclusive areas of culture but of degrees of shifting attachment and interaction, which a crude theory either of class or of standards is incompetent to interpret. (Williams, 1963, 310)

This argument is repeated, and significantly elaborated, in the opening theoretical chapters of *The Long Revolution*. Culture exists at three levels, Williams observes here, that of the lived culture of a particular time and place, only fully accessible to those who were part of it, the recorded culture of deposited texts, artefacts and knowledges, and the culture of the selective tradition (Williams, 1965, 66). In one sense, his point is obvious: the historical record is so large that only a 'selective process, of a quite drastic kind' can make it available to subsequent generations. This has the less obvious corollary, however, that 'Theoretically, a period is recorded; in practice, this record is absorbed into a selective tradition; and both are different from the culture as lived' (Williams, 1965, 66–67). Such selections begin within the period itself, but are continued by subsequent generations, and are always necessarily matters of evaluation, by which 'from the whole body of activities, certain things are selected for value and emphasis' (Williams, 1965, 67). The traditions thus formed are what we tend to mean by our 'culture', but they are nonetheless both more and less than that. 'The selective tradition', Williams writes,

> creates, at one level, a general human culture; at another level, the historical record of a particular society; at a third level ... a rejection of considerable areas of what was once a living culture. (Williams, 1965, 68)

Selection is a retrospective process, he continues, made and remade, not by the past, but in and for a sequence of successive 'presents', so that 'cultural tradition can be seen as a continual selection and re-selection of ancestors' (Williams, 1965, 69). It is therefore motivated above all by contemporary interests and values:

> selection will be governed by many kinds of special interest, including class interest ... The traditional culture of a society will always tend to correspond to its *contemporary* system of interests and values. (Williams, 1965, 68)

As in *Culture and Society*, the stress falls once again on selection according to class-specific criteria, but once again, also, on the reality of a truly general human culture. The theoretical novelty of the argument lies in an analytical shift from the content of the canon to the processes of canon-formation. This position is restated, in more expressly Gramscian terms, in *Marxism and Literature*. Here Williams points to the decisive importance of selective tradition in the effective operation of processes of incorporation:

> tradition is ... always more than an inert historicized segment; indeed

> it is the most powerful practical means of incorporation. What we have to see is ... a *selective tradition*: an intentionally selective version of a shaping past and a pre-shaped present, which is then powerfully operative in the process of social and cultural definition and identification. (Williams, 1977, 115)

Once again, he stresses the full extent to which such tradition is a product of contemporary culture. 'It is a version of the past', he writes, 'which is intended to connect with and ratify the present. What it offers ... is a sense of *predisposed continuity*' (Williams, 1977, 116).

Williams's argument was directed at the high literary canon and had as its immediate target cultural conservatives such as Leavis and Eliot. But what holds for Leavis's 'Great Tradition' also holds for Suvin's 'SF tradition': it too is necessarily selective. Which returns us to our starting point in that plethora of 'Definitions of SF', since each of these represents an attempt to redefine the tradition selectively by reselecting its ancestors. This is as true of Suvin and Jameson as of Gernsback or Aldiss. As Patrick Parrinder rightly observed of *Metamorphoses*: '"Cognitive estrangement" may be taken to be a fact about the 1970s, just as T. S. Eliot's "dissociation of sensibility" was a fact about the 1920s' (Parrinder, 2000, 10). This is not to suggest that all definitions are equally valid – although logically they are, since all definitions are by definition true – but only that they are all equally socioaesthetic, to borrow Suvin's term, and therefore necessarily to some extent weapons in the struggle for the power to define.

Williams's notion of selective tradition is much more persuasive than the Wittgensteinian notion of 'family resemblance', which has been applied to SF by both Kincaid and Rieder (Kincaid, 2003, 415–17; Rieder, 2008, 16–17). For the real issue is no more that of resemblance than it is of classification; what matters is the continuously changing competitive struggle to selectively define. Family resemblances of the Wittgensteinian kind might well be relevant, as Ben Ware has argued (Ware, 2011), at the level of structure of feeling, to which we turn in chapter 7 below, but they cannot explain the selectivity of the selective tradition. This selectivity is most readily apparent wherever a redefinition explicitly prescribes either inclusion or exclusion. In Suvin's case, the relevant instances are, respectively, utopia, which is included by virtue of its bearing on the novum, and fantasy, excluded by virtue of its lack of cognitive adequacy. It is to these that we will turn in the chapters that follow. In the meantime, we may conclude this preliminary discussion with a first axiom:

> *SF is a selective tradition, continuously reinvented in the present, through which the boundaries of the genre are continuously policed, challenged and*

> *disrupted, and the cultural identity of the SF community continuously established, preserved and transformed. It is thus essentially and necessarily a site of contestation.*

This sense of tradition as a process of retrospective selection is an enduring feature in Williams's work. In his later formulations, however, it is supplemented by an understanding that such selection is necessarily dependent upon 'institutions' and what he termed 'formations'. By the latter he meant the kind of intellectual movement or tendency that will have 'significant and sometimes decisive influence on the active development of a culture' (Williams, 1977, 117). So he developed an account of formations that stressed the necessary non-correspondence between selective tradition, dominant institutions and artistic formations. Within any apparent hegemony, Williams writes, 'there are not only alternative and oppositional formations ... but, within what can be recognized as the dominant, effectively varying formations which resist any simple reduction to some generalized hegemonic function' (Williams, 1977, 119). Two particular kinds of formation are distinctive to the capitalist mode of cultural production, he argues, the 'professional society', dedicated to essentially economic goals, and the artistic 'movement', 'in which artists come together in pursuit of some specific artistic aim' (Williams, 1981, 62). Both types, but especially the latter, have been of central importance to SF: obvious examples include the British New Wave and American cyberpunk. Williams himself developed a theoretical framework for the analysis of formations, which he applied to three concrete instances: the circle around William Godwin, the Pre-Raphaelite Brotherhood and the Bloomsbury Group. The details need not detain us, but we should note that what Williams calls this 'indispensable kind' of 'sociological analysis' (Williams, 1981, 86) is indeed applicable to SF, not least to Mary Shelley, whose early biography developed at the point of intersection between the Godwin circle and the circle around Percy Shelley (Milner, 2005, 219–20). Williams's gesture towards the need for sociological analysis is more instructive, however, than the details of his model. Which will lead me, in the chapter that follows, to suggest Bourdieu's notion of the 'cultural field' as a possible supplement to the concept of the selective tradition.

3

Science Fiction and the Cultural Field

In the previous chapter, we explored Williams's notion of selective tradition. Here, I want to propose Bourdieu's model of the literary field as a possible, perhaps even necessary, complement to Williams in our understanding of genre. For Bourdieu, as we noted in chapter 1, even apparently disinterested and gratuitous practices can be treated as directed towards the maximisation of material or symbolic profit. When applied directly to literature and art, this proposition produces a model of 'the field of cultural production' as structured externally in relation to the 'field of power' (Bourdieu, 1993, 37–38) and internally in relation to two 'principles of hierarchization', respectively, the 'heteronomous' and the 'autonomous' (Bourdieu, 1993, 40–41). The external relation to the field of power is Bourdieu's formulation of what Williams, after Gramsci, had referred to as hegemony and need not detain us here. But the internal relations are less obviously equivalent to ideas available in Williams. These principles of hierarchisation are alternative ways of allocating value. Bourdieu argues that the modern literary and artistic field is a site of contestation between the heteronomous principle, which subordinates art to economy, and the autonomous, which resists such subordination (Bourdieu, 1993, 40). The latter is quite specific to the cultural field: 'the theory of art for art's sake ... is to the field of cultural production what the axiom "business is business" ... is to the economic field' (Bourdieu, 1993, 62). In the short run, the two principles appear diametrically opposed: 'in the ... autonomous sector of the field of cultural production ...the economy of practises is based ... on a systematic inversion of the principles of all ordinary economies' (Bourdieu, 1993, 39). In the long run, however, he insists that '*symbolic, long-term profits*' are 'ultimately reconvertible into economic profits' (Bourdieu, 1993, 54).

1. From the French Literary Field to the Global Science Fiction Field

Bourdieu saw human sociality as the outcome of the strategic actions of individuals operating within a constraining, but not determining, context of values, which he termed 'the habitus' (Bourdieu, 1977, 72–95). The literary habitus comprises a series of 'dispositions' – 'vocations', 'aspirations' and 'expectations' – schemes of perception and appreciation which reproduce 'the fundamental divisions of the field of positions – "pure art"/"commercial art", "bohemian"/"bourgeois", "left bank"/"right bank", etc.' (Bourdieu, 1993, 64). Bourdieu's map of the French literary field in the late nineteenth century is reproduced in Figure 1. Here, the principle of autonomy governs the left of the field, that of heteronomy the right, so that the most autonomous of genres, that is, the least economically profitable – poetry – is to the left, whilst the most heteronomous, the most economically profitable – drama – is to the right, with the novel located somewhere in between. Each genre is also characterised by an internal hierarchy, which corresponds to the social hierarchy of its audiences (Bourdieu, 1993, 48). Here, the high social status audiences – the intellectuals, the old and the bourgeois – govern the upper end of the field, whilst the low status audiences – bohemia, the young, the masses – govern the lower. The entire field is also traversed diagonally by the left–right political spectrum.

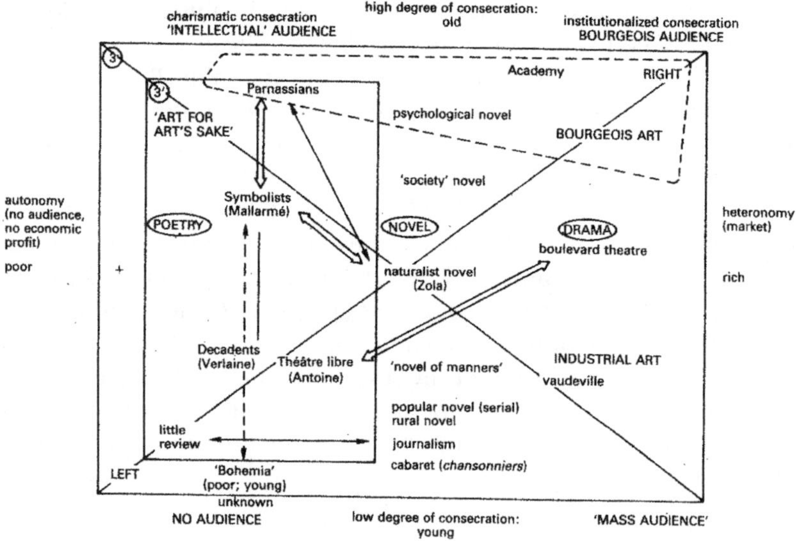

Figure 1: The French literary field in the second half of the nineteenth century. Source: Bourdieu (1993, 49).

Bourdieu's model maps the specific locations of a number of key French literary formations, the Parnassians, Symbolists and Decadents, the Théâtre libre and the Naturalist novelists. It also, however, maps the locations of vaudeville, cabaret and journalism. This is quite deliberate for, as Bourdieu himself explains, we only ever encounter 'historical definitions of the writer', which correspond to particular states of 'the struggle to impose the legitimate definition of the writer'. There is thus 'no other criterion of membership of a field than the objective fact of producing effects within it' (Bourdieu, 1993, 42). Which, incidentally, is why Gelder's view of popular fiction as a separate and distinct field from the literary is radically misconceived. I have slightly amended Bourdieu's model of the literary field so as to map on to it, in Figure 2, the location of early French SF. This was essentially double: on the one hand, the *Voyages extraordinaires* novels, first published by Hetzel, written by Verne and, on three occasions, by Jean François Paschal Grousset (under the pseudonym André Laurie); on the other, their dramatisation either for the Théâtre de la Porte Saint-Martin or the Théâtre du Châtelet by Verne and Adolphe d'Ennery. The plays are largely forgotten today, but were nonetheless hugely successful. As Margot notes of *Le Tour du monde en 80 jours*, 'After more than ten years ... barely making a living, Verne became virtually overnight a ... wealthy playwright'; between 1874 and 1900 the play had more than two thousand

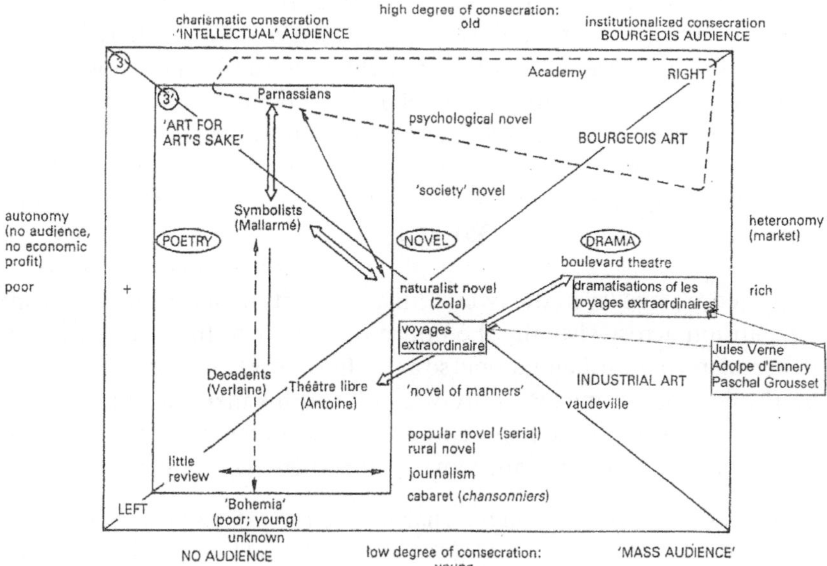

Figure 2: The double location of early French science fiction within the late nineteenth century literary field.

performances, featuring special effects that 'were the forerunners of what Hollywood ... offer audiences today (Margot, 2005, 153–54).

Here, we need to recall Bourdieu's reasons for locating drama at the heteronomous end of the literary field. 'From the economic point of view, the hierarchy is simple', he wrote: 'At the top ... is drama, which ... secures big profits' (Bourdieu, 1993, 47). Later, he added: 'The theatre, which directly experiences the immediate sanction of the bourgeois public, with its values and conformisms, can earn the institutionalized consecration of academies and official honours, as well as money' (Bourdieu, 1993, 51). The nineteenth-century theatre, in short, was 'bourgeois art' par excellence and, as such, highly profitable, both economically and symbolically. It was also ideally suited to the manufacture of SF special effects. It should come as little surprise, then, that Shelley's *Frankenstein* had occupied a very similar location within the English literary field to that of *Le Tour du monde en 80 jours* within the French. Published in novel form in 1818, its first theatrical adaptation, Richard Brinsley Peake's melodrama *Presumption, or the Fate of Frankenstein*, appeared at the English Opera House in 1823. The first French adaptation, *Le Monstre et le magicien* by Jean Touissant Merle and Antoine Nicolas Béraud, was performed in 1826 at the Théâtre de la Porte Saint-Martin – the same theatre that would later stage Verne – deploying similarly spectacular special effects. Between 1823 and 1887 there were eighteen different stage adaptations of *Frankenstein* for the British or French commercial theatre (Forry, 1990, 121–22). This, then, was SF's original location within the field of cultural production, in the overlap between the bourgeois novel and the bourgeois theatre. Wells's SF novels occupy the same space as Verne's *Voyages extraordinaires* – both were marketed in English as 'scientific romance' – but here the bourgeois theatre is finally superseded by the cinema, most obviously in his film scripts for *Things to Come* (1935) and *The Man Who Could Work Miracles* (1936).

The genre's history in the twentieth and twenty-first centuries was one of expansion across virtually the entire literary field. In Figure 3, I have further adapted Bourdieu's model so as to show how this process occurred.[4] The result is by no means entirely faithful to his method, since, where Bourdieu maps the contours of a literary field located in a particular time and place, my procedures are more science-fictional, crossing both time

4 I have made extensive use in this chapter and the next of Clute, Langford and Nicholls's various editions of *The Encyclopedia of Science Fiction*, Collins's *Encyclopedia of Australian Science Fiction and Fantasy* and the Lofficiers' *French Science Fiction, Fantasy, Horror and Pulp Fiction* (Nicholls, 1979; Clute and Nicholls, 1993; Clute, Langford and Nicholls, 2011; Collins, 1998; Lofficier and Lofficier, 2000).

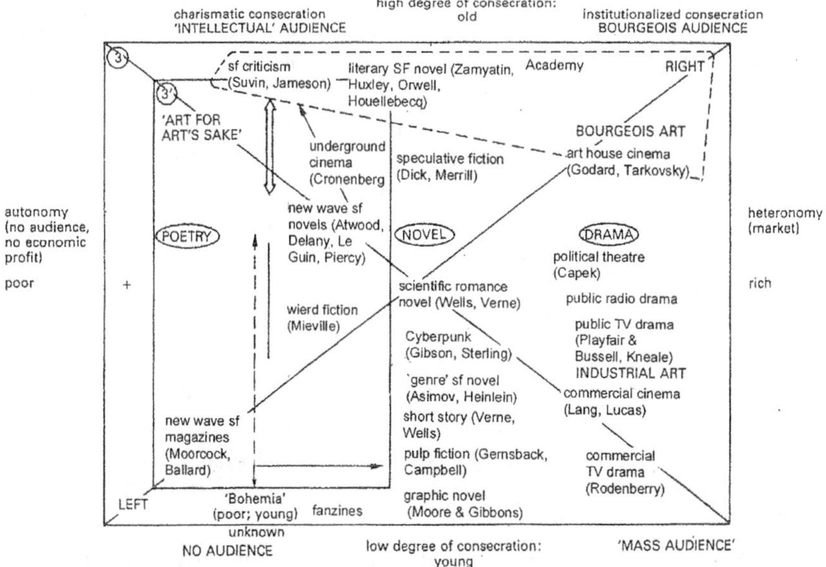

Figure 3: The global SF field in the early twenty-first century.

and space so as to render a composite account of the genesis and structure of the SF field. They do, however, come closer to producing a diagrammatic representation of contemporary SF, considered as a globalised space for the production and reproduction of the genre's distinctive selective tradition. We should stress that this SF field is located not in some different space from the globalised general literary field – or what Casanova calls the 'world literary space' (Casanova, 2005, 4) – but is rather fully included within the latter. So the SF field can be visualised as a particular two-dimensional slice of the world literary field conceived as a three-dimensional space.

2. Ideas and Effects

Unlike Bourdieu's maps, mine describes how the contemporary global field processes the legacies of its various cultural pasts. The central lines of development in the SF field, from the mid nineteenth century through to the early twenty-first, were threefold: first and foremost, the expansion of SF drama into the major new media developed through technologies of audio-visual mechanical and electronic reproduction, especially cinema, radio and television; second, the development of increasingly popular SF prose forms, especially 'pulp fiction', the comic book and the 'genre' SF novel;

third, the development of high-cultural or avant-gardist dramatic and prose forms within the area of overlap between the 'restricted economy' of symbolic profit and institutionalised bourgeois art.

The first of these immediately poses a crucial theoretical question, that of the relation between what might be termed 'ideas' and 'effects'. The subtitle to Suvin's *Metamorphoses* makes it clear that his interests – as also Jameson's – are in the poetics of a 'literary genre'. Like most fan devotees, post-Suvinian literary criticism has also tended to assume that written SF is essentially an experiment with ideas. As Suvin himself put it, 'Significant modern SF ... discusses primarily the political, psychological, and anthropological *use and effect of knowledge*' (Suvin, 1979, 15). Jameson suggests much the same when he writes that 'the scientific pretensions of SF lend the Utopian genre ... epistemological gravity' (Jameson, 2005, 57). No doubt, much written SF has indeed functioned thus, including even instances Jameson finds unpersuasive, Verne included (Jameson, 2005, 63, 93). But, equally clearly, much hasn't, for example, E. E. 'Doc' Smith's 'Skylark' and 'Lensman' series.

Doc Smith has been the butt of much academic criticism, not least Freedman's carefully understated view that 'I do not think it can be fruitfully maintained that many very complex or interesting cognitive estrangements are produced in Doc Smith' (Freedman, 2000, 19). If SF were indeed entirely a literature of ideas, then Smith's novels clearly couldn't count, since a literature of uninteresting or simple ideas is oxymoronic. But this would be an absurd judgement to make of the guest of honour at the Second World Science Fiction Convention held in Chicago in 1940. Freedman's solution is to suggest that genre is better understood as a tendency within texts rather than as a totalising description of their collective essence; that the SF tendency is indeed that identified by Suvin; and that Smith's novels, as also *Star Wars* and *Star Trek*, exhibit this tendency 'only weakly and fitfully', but also exhibit a 'spectacular hypertrophy of the specifically visual dimension associated with science-fictional tales of space travel' (Freedman, 2000, 19, 22). This is, by any count, an impressive attempt to save Suvin from himself. A more economical application of Ockham's razor would conclude, however, that Smith's novels are indeed SF, but not necessarily terribly interesting or complex examples thereof.

Freedman's reference to the specifically visual aspects of SF is nonetheless suggestive. For it is clear that, no matter how interesting the ideas in *Frankenstein* and the *Voyages extraordinaires*, sheer visuality had been a crucial element in the popular appeal of both *Le Monstre et le magicien* and Verne and d'Ennery's 1882 *Voyage à travers l'impossible* (*Journey Through the*

Impossible), which brought Captain Hatteras's son George, Doctor Ox, Otto Lidenbrock, Captain Nemo and Michel Ardan together on the stage. This tradition of SF as visual spectacle is as old as that of SF as a literature of ideas and is crucial to the development of SF drama, which, following Bourdieu, I located at the heteronomous end of the SF field. This alerts us to one of the defining features of Suvin's work, its radical indifference to drama, whether as theatre, cinema or television. But this is clearly problematic, if only because one of Suvin's own canonical SF writers – Čapek – is best-known as a dramatist. Čapek's version of SF as political theatre – *R.U.R.*, *Věc Makropulo* and *Bilá Nemoc* – moved the genre further toward the bourgeois end of the field than had Verne and d'Ennery. Suvin himself admits that Čapek was 'the most significant world SF writer between the World Wars', but nonetheless insists that the plays are 'the weakest part' of the oeuvre (Suvin, 1979, 280, 270). Suvin is entitled to his opinion, of course, but this is clearly not the judgement of the SF selective tradition nor is it reproduced in the literary field. Čapek's coinage of the word 'robot', from the Czech *robotá*, meaning hard labour, for his 1920 play *R.U.R. (Rossum's Universal Robots)* marks a truly decisive – because productive – moment in the history of the genre, that of the invention of a radically new novum. And the play's astonishing international success powerfully attests to this productivity: first performed in Czech in 1921 (Čapek, 1966, 117), a German translation was published the following year (Čapek, 1922), an American English-language version was performed in 1922, a British version in 1923, distinct British and American translations followed in book form later that year, a Japanese translation appeared in 1923, French and Russian in 1924, Rumanian and Turkish in 1927, Italian in 1929, Bulgarian in 1931, and Swedish in 1934 (Čapek, 1966, 204–5). And, as we noted in chapter 1, *R.U.R.* also provided the BBC with the text for the first SF television programme ever broadcast. This combination of new medium and new novum is immensely suggestive of the play's wider importance in the SF field.

3. Science Fiction as Drama

The expansion of SF drama into the new audio-visual media had the character of an immanent unfolding of the specular-dramatic potential present within the genre from its very inception. What Walter Benjamin says of Dada is thus also true of early SF: it 'attempted to create by ... literary ... means the effects which the public today seeks in film' (Benjamin, 1973, 239). The earliest SF film, loosely based on Verne's *De la terre à la lune* and Wells's *The First Men in the Moon*, was Georges Méliès's *La Voyage dans la lune*, produced in 1902, less than seven years after the Lumière brothers' first film projections. The earliest SF blockbuster was Lang's *Metropolis*, nearly two years in the making and finally released in January 1927, with a screenplay co-written by Lang and Thea von Harbou, the latter of whom also wrote the novelisation (von Harbou, 1926). For Méliès and Lang, as for almost all their successors, the genre's appeal was overwhelmingly located around the use of special effects to achieve the visual, as distinct from literary, rendition of a novum.

One could trace the history of SF in the cinema through a series of similar subsequent landmarks: Henrik Galeen's 1928 *Alraune*, a huge success for Ama-Film and UFA (Universum Film Aktiengesellschaft) in both Germany and the United States; James Whale's 1931 *Frankenstein*, made for Universal, the company responsible for the American release of *Metropolis*; the 'space opera' serials of the 1930s, also from Universal, featuring Buster Crabbe, by turn, as Flash Gordon and as Buck Rogers; Cameron Menzies' 1936 *Things to Come*, made for Alexander Korda's London Films, scripted by Wells and still one of very few genuine utopias in SF cinema; the Japanese post-war monster movies, beginning with Ishirō Honda's 1954 *Gojira*; Chris Marker's extraordinarily intelligent *La Jetée* (1964) and the American film it inspired, Terry Gilliam's *12 Monkeys* (1997); Kubrick's powerfully influential SF trilogy, *Dr Strangelove* in 1964, *2001: A Space Odyssey* in 1968 and *A Clockwork Orange* in 1971; Roger Vadim's single experiment with SF cinema, the internationally successful *Barbarella* (1967); the wave of Hollywood blockbusters triggered by the success of Georg Lucas's *Star Wars* and Stephen Spielberg's *Close Encounters of the Third Kind*, both released in 1977; Scott's three forays into the genre, the two early, influential proto-cyberpunk movies, *Alien* in 1979 and *Blade Runner* in 1982, and the 3D epic, *Prometheus*, in 2012, a visually stunning but ultimately intellectually unconvincing prequel to the *Alien* series; the *Star Trek* motion pictures, launched in 1979 and still continuing well into the twenty-first century; Cameron's two *Terminator* movies, produced in 1984 and 1991, the second of which, *Judgement Day*, introduced groundbreaking computer-generated special effects into SF cinema; his 2009 movie *Atavar*, at the time both the most ambitious experiment in 3D cinema and the highest grossing film in Hollywood history; Luc Besson's various excursions into SF, *Le Dernier Combat* (*The Last Battle*) in 1983, *Kamikaze* in 1986, which he wrote but did not direct, and *Le Cinquième Élément/The Fifth Element* in 1997; a string of anime feature films, most notably Mamoru Oshii's 1995 *Gōsuto In Za Sheru/Kōkaku Kidōtai* (*Ghost in the Shell*) and its 2004 sequel; Paul Verhoeven's 'American' SF films, *Robocop* in 1987, *Total Recall* in 1990 and *Starship Troopers* in 1997; Alex Proyas's experiment in

Australian gothic, *Dark City* (1998); the three wonderfully subversive SF films by New Zealand director, Andrew Niccol, *Gattaca* (1997), *S1m0ne* (2002) and *In Time* (2011); and Larry and Andy Wakowski's famously post-Baudrillardian *Matrix* trilogy (1999–2003).

Cinematic special effects do not come cheap: *La Voyage dans la lune* had a budget of 10,000 francs, 'an unbelievable amount of money at the beginning of the twentieth century' (Vallorani, 2005, 320); *Metropolis* cost DM 5 million and would have bankrupted UFA had it not acquired near-simultaneous distribution in Britain and the United States; *Terminator 2: Judgement Day* was the first American film to cost over $US 100,000,000; and, according to *Forbes* magazine in 2005, SF then accounted for eleven of the twenty-five most expensive films made in Hollywood (Rose, 2005). A recent commentator remarks that the narrative of *La Voyage dans la lune* was merely 'a frame upon which to string a demonstration of the magical possibilities of cinema' (Cornea, 2007, 250). This isn't quite true of *Metropolis*, but the architecture of the film's cityscape is, nonetheless, its central dystopian novum, a synecdoche for the city's radically inegalitarian, social structure. Much the same might be said of *Terminator 2*, where the T-1000, made of a 'mimetic polyalloy' liquid metal, able to take the shape of anything it touches, simply *is* the film's novum.

Film theorists generally take exception to Theodor Adorno and Max Horkheimer's thesis that 'the culture industry has led to the predominance of the effect ... over the work itself – which once expressed an idea, but was liquidated together with the idea' (Adorno and Horkheimer, 1979, 125). But the argument seems oddly pertinent to SF cinema, for in this particular genre, where the literary novum has, indeed, often been an 'idea', the central cinematic and dramatic device has typically been the translation of 'idea' into 'effect'. Comparing SF novels with 1950s Hollywood SF cinema, Susan Sontag astutely observed that the latter operated 'by means of images and sounds, not words that have to be translated by the imagination' (Sontag, 1966, 212). There is thus a certain necessary tension between the novum as imaginative idea and its representation as spectacle. This is only a tendency, however, towards the conceptualisation of the novum as idea in the written medium, towards its 'specularisation' – to borrow a term from Lacanian psychoanalysis (cf. Lacan, 1977; Irigaray, 1966) – as effect in the cinematic, with each understood as points on a continuum, or, more accurately, locations within a cultural field, rather than as permanent structural properties of any particular medium. Given the sheer expense of special effects, it was virtually unavoidable that commercial SF cinema should have been located further towards the heteronomous end of the field than the SF novel.

Radio and television are cheaper to produce than cinema and also more likely to be publicly owned and subsidised. The linked questions of ownership and subsidy have a direct bearing on the kinds of drama available in these media. As a general rule, to which there are necessarily a great many exceptions, public broadcasting's greater immunity from direct commercial pressure has tended to make for more adventurous scripts, its relative shortage of funding for worse special effects, especially in the case of television. Commercial television thus had a distinct advantage in the manufacture of specularity. Radio dates from the early 1920s, television from the late 1930s. In Britain, the BBC began broadcasting radio in 1920, television in 1936, with state-sanctioned monopolies lasting until 1955 in television, 1973 in radio. Thereafter it had private competitors, but nonetheless continued to dominate the market. Most European and Commonwealth countries began with state monopolies, which were eventually opened up to private competition. In the United States, by contrast, both radio and television were organised around a system of publicly licensed but privately owned commercial stations, sustained financially by advertising and sponsorship. The first licensed American radio station was Westinghouse's KDKA in Pittsburgh, which began broadcasting in 1920, the first television station W2XBS in New York, owned by RCA's subsidiary NBC, which began brodcasting in 1939. Government-funded broadcasting came much later, Public Broadcasting Service television (PBS) in 1970 and National Public Radio (NPR) in 1971, both overshadowed by their larger commercial rivals and often heavily dependent on imported BBC programming.

It is clear that commercial radio broadcast SF primarily in the United States, primarily during the 'Golden Age of Radio', from the mid 1930s until the early 1950s. Thereafter, drama was progressively displaced by music, news and talkback conversation. Since it is no longer significantly current, I have omitted commercial radio from my map of the SF field, but its previous location should be apparent: toward the mass/heteronomous corner of the field, near commercial cinema and commercial television. It is equally clear that the BBC and other public broadcasters – the Australian ABC, Radio New Zealand, the Canadian CBC, the American NPR, Radiodiffusion-Télévision Français (RTF), Société suisse de radiodiffusion, Bayerischer Rundfunk – played a crucial role in producing SF for radio, especially after the decline of American commercial SF radio. A more detailed examination of the way this institutional difference affected the forms of radio SF will be developed in the chapter that follows. For the moment, however, let us note only that the earlier differences between the American and European patterns in radio were replicated almost exactly in television.

American television SF was originally aimed overwhelmingly at children: the earliest example is *Captain Video*, which ran from 1949 until 1955, but others included *Buck Rogers* (1950–51) and *Superman* (1952–58), both of which were adapted from earlier radio serials. By contrast, the BBC's earliest efforts at television SF were distinctly 'literary': as we have noted, its first programme, and also the first in the world, was the 1938 35-minute broadcast of Čapek's *R.U.R.*, adapted from the original by Nigel Playfair and produced and directed by Jan Bussell, both of whom subsequently worked on a 90-minute version, which was broadcast in 1948. Robert Barr's production of Wells's *The Time Machine* followed in 1949 and Rudolph Cartier's of Nigel Kneale's adaptation of *Nineteen Eighty-Four* in 1954. The previous year, Cartier and Kneale had collaborated on *The Quatermass Experiment*, the first ever BBC TV serial. All of these were very definitely aimed at adults and could plausibly be represented as embodying Lord Reith's vision of a national broadcaster aiming to 'inform, educate and entertain', in that order (de Burgh, 2000, 199). Although British television experimented with children's SF and American with adult, clear national differences persisted. As Cook and Wright observe: 'British TV exported to global audiences a more sceptical, perhaps even more "realistic", view of the science fiction future ... manifested ... by way either of ironic humour ... or ... something altogether more dark and despairing' (Cook and Wright, 2006, 5). All of American television SF programming came from the private sector, most of the best-known British from the BBC: *Doctor Who* (1963–89, 1996, 2005 onwards), *Out of the Unknown* (1965–71), *Blake's Seven* (1978–81), *The Hitch Hiker's Guide to the Galaxy* (1981), *Red Dwarf* (1988–99) and *Torchwood* (2006 onwards).

In television, however, there would be no equivalent to the disappearance of drama from commercial radio. In the 1960s, American commercial television produced two important anthology series, *The Twilight Zone* (1959–64) and *The Outer Limits* (1963–65); in the decades that followed, it presided over the most successful of all SF franchises, *Star Trek* and its sequels, *Star Trek: The Next Generation*, *Star Trek: Deep Space Nine*, *Star Trek: Voyager* and *Star Trek: Enterprise*, which in combination ran from 1966 until 2005; and, in the 1990s, it produced two of the most formally innovative of late twentieth-century SF television series, J. Michael Straczynski's *Babylon 5* (1993–98) and Chris Carter's *The X-Files* (1993–2002). Moreover, Japanese commercial television also became a significant player in the global field, so much so that by the early twenty-first century it was the major source of non-Anglophone television SF. The programmes were mainly anime and mainly produced by commercial broadcasters, such as TV Tokyo Network and Fuji TV, as distinct from NHK, the national public broadcaster. They were also initially aimed overwhelmingly at children: the earliest was, of course, Osamu Tezuka's *Tetsuwan Atomu* (*Mighty Atom*), first aired in Japan in 1963 and subsequently marketed internationally as *Astro Boy*. Later examples include *Tetsujin 28-go* (*Gigantor*) (1963–66), *Mājinga Zetto* (*Tranzor Z*) (1972–74), *Chōjiku Yōsai Makurosu* (*The Super Dimension Fortress Macross*) (1982–83), *Megazōn Tsū Sun* (*Megazone 23*) (1985–89), *Doragon Bōru* (*Dragon Ball Z*) (1986–89) and *Bishōjo Senshi Sērā Mūn* (*Sailor Moon*) (1992–97).

Other public television broadcasters appear to have been less interested in the genre than the BBC. The first German public television SF series, ARD's *Raumpatrouille Orion* (*Space Patrol Orion*) didn't appear until 1966, the Australian ABC's first SF series, *Vega 4*, not until 1968. In Canada, the CBC had broadcast *Space Command* as early as 1953, but this was a children's show, on the then American model. There have been subsequent experiments with television SF in these three countries, but the rising cost of special effects resulted in an increasing reliance on imported American, British or Japanese material. By the early twenty-first century the best-known SF shows from all three were commercially produced in co-production with American or British companies: *LEXX* (1997–2002), a German–Canadian co-production partly funded by the British Channel Five; *Farscape* (1999–2003, 2004), an Australian–American co-production; and a plethora of Canadian–American co-productions filmed in Canada but to all appearances American in content, which included *The X-Files*, *Stargate SG-1* (1997–2007), *Smallville* (2001–9) and *Battlestar Galactica* (2004–9).

This pattern, by which 'quality' domestic public sector broadcasting was progressively displaced by imported commercial content, is peculiarly apparent in France, where SF had occupied an unusually central position in the national culture. French public television had produced a significant body of SF in the period between the foundation of RTF in 1949 and the partial privatisation of television in the 1980s. Government-run stations ran numerous adaptations of Verne, especially *L'île mystérieuse* (the first in 1963) and *Le Tour du monde en 80 jours* (the first in 1975). They broadcast telemovies, for example ORTF's 1974 version of *Frankenstein* and FR2's 1994 adaption of Jean-Pierre Andrevon's novel *Le Travail du furet* (*The Weasel's Work*). And they produced a wide range of series and serials: *Les Atomistes* (1968), *Le Voyageur des siècles* (*Traveller of the Centuries*) (1971), *Aux Frontières du possible* (1971–74), *L'Alpomega* (1973), *Les Classiques de l'Étrange* (1974–76), *Le Mutant* (1978), *Les Visiteurs* (1980), *La Guerre des insectes* (*War of the Insects*) (1981), *Noir sont les galaxies* (*Dark are the Galaxies*) (1981), *De Bien étranges affaires* (*Some Very Strange Affairs*) (1982), *Le*

Mystérieux Docteur Cornelius (1984), *Astrolab 22* (1985), *Le Grand secret* (1989) and *Bing* (1991–92). But the progressive commercialisation of French television – which occurred in two stages, the launch of the first private stations in 1981 and the partial privatisation of state television in 1987 – seems to have led to a decline in domestic output and an increasing reliance on imported SF programming.

As with cinema, an important part of the appeal of SF to radio and television producers and consumers lies in the opportunity for special effects. The tension between idea and effect seems to be resolved differently in radio and television, however, primarily because of the comparatively low-budget nature of the media. At one level, financial constraints clearly militate against both idea and effect, which is why so much radio and television is interesting as neither. But ideas can come more cheaply than their specularisation, which leads to the possibility that these media might sometimes reverse the cinematic prioritisation of effect over idea. Moreover, this is more likely to be true for public broadcasting on the one hand, and satellite and cable television on the other, both of which enjoy comparative freedom to explore smaller 'niche markets', than for 'free to air' commercial broadcasters compelled to maximise audiences so as to maximise advertising income. SF has only ever been a niche market. Hence, its repeated failure, children's television aside, on the three major American commercial networks, the American Broadcasting Company (ABC), the National Broadcasting Company (NBC) and the Columbia Broadcasting System (CBS), from the 1950s to the 1970s, when their programming was aimed overwhelmingly at mass audiences (Reeves, Rodgers and Epstein, 1996, 24–29). Even *Star Trek* lasted for only three seasons.

The experimental potential for radio and television SF applies at the level of form as well as content. Williams's pioneering account of broadcast drama identified three main forms, the series, the serial and the single play, often included in an anthology series (Williams, 1974, 57–61). All have been used in SF: *Star Trek* and its sequels were series; *Doctor Who*, in its initial incarnation, was a serial; *The Twilight Zone* was an anthology series. The latter form seems to have become less common, probably because different combinations of production and performance personnel for each episode make it relatively high-cost. The most interesting formal innovation in late twentieth-century television SF was the development of what Reeves, Rodgers and Epstein, referring to *The X-Files*, describe as 'episodic/serial straddle', that is, the 'mini-serial within the series' (Reeves, Rodgers and Epstein, 1996, 33–34). Here, there are discrete episodes, but also multi-part episodes and, more importantly, a range of developing storylines continued from episode to episode, which allow for cumulative character development unavailable to the conventional series. This device was applied to SF by Carter in *The X-Files*, Straczynski in *Babylon 5*, Rockne O'Bannon in *Farscape* and Russell T. Davies both in the BBC Cymru relaunch of *Doctor Who* and in *Torchwood*, its 'adult' spin-off.

This leaves us with a map of the heteronomous end of the SF field, where the new forms of SF drama are all market driven, but Čapek's theatre appeals to the most bourgeois audience, anime and the *Star Trek* franchise to the most massified, with public radio, public television and commercial cinema ranged in-between. Clearly, these locations will not be accurate for each and every programme, but they will suffice as reasonably adequate generalisations: it must be obvious that Dennis Potter's 1996 television serial *Cold Lazarus* could never have been produced solely by a 'free to air' network commercial television station. These comparisons are not intended invidiously. They are merely points on a map, organised horizontally, rather than positions in a hierarchy, organised vertically, but will nonetheless generate invidious comparisons within the SF field. As Bourdieu observes: 'The *boundary* of the field is a stake of struggles ... the social scientist's task is not to draw a dividing line between the agents involved ... but to describe ... the frontier delimiting the territory held by the competing agents' (Bourdieu, 1993, 42).

4. Science Fiction as Prose

Turning from drama to prose, the most important developments in this second region were, either directly or indirectly, effects of American 'pulp fiction'. SF short stories had been published in Europe in the nineteenth century and, indeed, both Verne and Wells experimented with the form – their best examples are collected in, respectively, *Le Docteur Ox* (1874) and *The Stolen Bacillus and Other Incidents* (1895). But European prose SF was, nonetheless, overwhelmingly a matter for the 'scientific romance', or novel. Gernsback invented neither the SF short story nor the SF 'pulp' magazine: Aldiss is right to stress that the Swedish magazine *Stella* (1886-88) and the Austrian/German/Swiss *Der Orchideengarten* (1919-21) both predated Gernsback's *Amazing Stories*, which didn't appear until 1926 (Aldiss, 1986, 202). But Gernsback's achievement remains, to have used this magazine to open up an entirely new space in the SF field, which would be occupied by a succession of subsequent American 'pulps'. These included *Wonder Stories* (1930–36) and its successor, *Thrilling Wonder Stories* (1936–55), *Startling Stories* (1939–55), the *Magazine of Fantasy and Science Fiction*, established in 1949 and still publishing, *Galaxy Science Fiction* (1950–

80) and, above all, *Astounding Stories*. Founded in 1930, *Astounding* was rebranded by Campbell as *Astounding Science-Fiction* in 1938 and as *Analog Science Fact and Fiction* in 1960. For many American SF enthusiasts the genre's so-called 'Golden Age' began in 1937, when Campbell was appointed editor, and continued until the early–mid 1950s, when the magazine's dominance over the American market was gradually undermined by the paperback novel.

The pulps mattered insofar as they were able to do for prose what film, radio and television had done for drama, that is, extend the genre toward the younger and poorer end of the heteronomous part of the literary field. Gernsback was peculiarly well placed in this respect, given his interests in broadcasting, as publisher of *Radio-Craft* and co-owner of radio station WRNY. The opening to the least consecrated end of the field was further extended in 1938 by the launch of the first SF comic book, DC's *Action Comics*, as a platform for Jerry Siegel and Joe Shuster's Superman. A plethora of similar titles followed in rapid succession: DC launched the Batman in its flagship magazine, *Detective Comics*, in 1939, and Wonder Woman in *All Star Comics* in 1940; its chief rival, Marvel, countered with the Human Torch in its own flagship, *Marvel Comics*, in 1939, and Captain America in *Captain America Comics* in 1941. The comic book continues to thrive in the United States and continues to be dominated by DC and Marvel. For a period in the 1960s, when Stan Lee pioneered the notion of the flawed superhero, in titles like *The Fantastic Four*, *The X-Men* and *Spider-Man*, Marvel clearly had the creative edge. But, in the 1980s, when Frank Miller's *Batman: The Dark Knight Returns* and Alan Moore and Dave Gibbons's celebrated 1986–87 *Watchmen* series gestured towards even darker and even more self-reflexive versions of the superhero, DC seemed to have recaptured the initiative. Some of these are arguably 'graphic novels' rather than comics, but the distinction is difficult to sustain systematically. For all his antipathy to Gernsback, Aldiss pays Campbell's *Astounding* its due: 'The pulps', he writes, 'were churned out for a lower middle class or working class ... entirely without privilege ... But only Campbell's heroes had the real equalizer ... Campbell gave you the future on your chipped plate' (Aldiss, 1986, 228–29). This is exactly right, although it is difficult to see how any of it could have been achieved without Gernsback's prior intervention.

As socially effective cultural institutions, both pulps and comics were American in origin, even if the first wasn't entirely so in initial invention. And both were exported internationally, with varying degrees of success. Early British SF magazines and comics included *Tales of Wonder* (1937–42), *Fantasy* (1938–39), *Fantasy: The Magazine of Science Fiction* (1946–47), *New*

Worlds (1946–47), *Tit-Bits Science Fiction Comics* (1953) and *Science Fantasy* (1950–66). Originally a pulp, *New Worlds* was relaunched in 'digest' format in 1949 and soon became Britain's leading SF magazine. French magazines included *Fiction* (1953–90), the two different incarnations of *Galaxie* (1953–59 and 1964–77), *Bifrost*, founded in 1996, and *Lunatique*, founded in 2005. *Fiction* was the most enduring and also arguably the most important because, as George Slusser observed, it 'was the "workshop" for the French writers ... who produced ... the SF renaissance of the 1960s–70s' (Slusser, 1989, 252). French SF comics included *Fantax* (1946–49), *L'An 2000* (1953–54), *Meteor* (1953–62) and, of course, Jean-Claude Forest's *Barbarella* (1964–82). Amongst the more successful German pulps were *Utopia Zukunftsromane* (1953–68), *Utopia Magazin* (1955–59), *Galaxis-Magazin* (1958–59), *Terra SF* (1957–86) and the weekly *Perry Rhodan*, which has been published continuously since 1961, thus making it the longest-running of all SF series, according to its publisher, Pabel-Moewig. Nonetheless, the best-known European SF comics were almost certainly the British *2000 AD* (1977–) and the French *Métal Hurlant* (1974–87, 2002–4). More significant than either, however, for the global SF field were Japanese manga, beginning in 1951 with *Tetsuwan Atomu* and including, amongst many others, *Akira* (1982–90), *Appurushīdo (Appleseed)*, (1985–89), *Gōsuto In Za Sheru/Kōkaku Kidōtai* (1989–97), *Gansuringa Garu (Gunslinger Girl)*, (2002–) and *Bishōjo Senshi Sērā Mūn* (1992–97), all of which have also been adapted for anime.

In the United States the pulps were largely superseded by the 'genre' novel, published initially by specialist SF publishers, such as Fantasy Press, Hadley Publishing and Shasta. From the mid 1950s, large general publishers increasingly acquired or constructed their own SF lists, which were often published in both paperback and hardback. Important examples included Ace Books, which dominated American SF publishing in the 1970s and 80s, Doubleday, which published Harlan Ellison's *Dangerous Visions* anthologies, and Putnam, which published Damon Knight's *Orbit* anthologies. In Britain and France, where the pulps were institutionally less significant, SF publishing was normally conducted by general publishers. The most significant included Victor Gollancz, Michael Joseph and Macmillan, Denoël's 'Présence du Futur' list, Fleuve Noir's 'Anticipation', Hachette and Gallimard's 'Le Rayon Fantastique' and Laffont's 'Ailleurs et Demain'. As in the United States, British and French SF reached a mass market primarily through paperback publishers, such as Penguin and Pan, Livre de Poche and J'ai Lu. The German pattern was different again, neither pulps nor paperbacks, but rather something straddled in between, normally published by Pabel or Moewig or, eventually, Pabel-Moewig.

Whatever the objections to pulp fiction, Gernsback had created the space for later 'genre' publishing, which, in turn created that for the various 'New Wave' interventions. The continuity between pulp and genre is at its most apparent in the United States, where many early novels were, in fact, 'fix-ups' of stories previously published in the magazines (Clute and Nicholls, 1993, 432; van Vogt, 1975, 85, 135). Well-known examples include Asimov's *Foundation Trilogy* and *I, Robot,* James Blish's *Earthman, Come Home* and *They Shall Have Stars,* Robert A. Heinlein's *Orphans of the Sky* and A. E. van Vogt's *The War Against the Rull.* But British genre writers had also published in the pulps, Wyndham in *Wonder Stories,* for example, and Ballard in *Science Fantasy.* The latter would eventually traverse virtually the entire field, moving on to the avant-garde New Wave and, thence, in turn, to the realist novel. Unlike fan criticism, academic SF studies have consistently underplayed the more general significance of pulp fiction. Moylan, for example, notes the Gernsbackian moment in passing, but only to hurry on to what really concerns him, 'the work of the 1960s that broke beyond the adventure narratives and clichéd stereotypes of the 1920s and 1930s' (Moylan, 1986, 42). Suvin deliberately ends his groundbreaking analysis 'at the threshold ... of contemporary SF history' (Suvin, 1979, 206). Freedman dismisses as 'ludicrous' the equation of SF with pulp 'unless science fiction is construed ... defamatorily' (Freedman, 2000, 14) and eventually proceeds to an admittedly embarrassed theorisation of an SF canon (Freedman, 2000, 86-93). Jameson even misspells Gernsback as 'Gernsbach' (Jameson, 2005, 93). In each case, the emphasis falls on either the European 'literary' SF of the late nineteenth and early twentieth centuries or its late twentieth-century North American counterpart.

Jameson's commentary on van Vogt's pulp short stories nonetheless suggests a line of inquiry. 'These stories ...', Jameson writes,

> emerge from the world of the pulps and of commercial culture ... They cannot be read as Literature ... above all because their strongest effects are ... specific to the genre, and ... enabled only by precisely those sub-literary conventions of the genre which are unassimilable to high culture ... their conditions of possibility are very precisely pulp conventions. (Jameson, 2005, 316)

Jameson rehearses this argument in his opening response to Atwood's *The Year of the Flood* (2009), when he writes that

> mass cultural genres ... have rules and standards as rigorous and professional as the more noble forms ... But Atwood can now be considered to be a science-fiction writer, I'm happy to say ... Perhaps

> Atwood's SF apprenticeship comes with *The Blind Assassin*. (Jameson, 2009, 7; cf. Atwood, 2000)

The problem with these formulations is not so much their insistence on the generic specificities of SF as their unexamined assumption that similar such conventions do actually exist for high 'Literature'. The second formulation also suggests that Atwood's later dystopias somehow don't count as 'Literature', an indefensible proposition in itself, but one that need not detain us here. As I argued in chapter 1, these kinds of convention do exist for literary modernism, but not for 'Literature' in general. The 'literariness' of Literature is not, in fact, a property of a certain type of writing but rather a function of how different kinds of writing are socially processed, by writers themselves and by readers, publishers, booksellers, literary critics and so on. What is defined canonically as Literature are, then, isolated examples of the actually or allegedly exceptional extracted from the wider context in which they were produced, that of what Franco Moretti terms 'normal literature' (Moretti, 1988, 15). Literature is not a genre, then, even though modernism might be; it is a selection of isolated materials taken from other genres and retrospectively homogenised by what Moretti calls the 'improper and distorting centrality that contemporary "taste" has won at the expense of historical criticism' (Moretti, 1988, 14). 'Literary SF' – by which we mean merely that fraction of the current SF field currently incorporated into contemporary versions of the literary canon – and pulp SF are different subtypes of the same genre, occupying different locations in the same literary field, distinguished from each other primarily by their respective technologies of production and attendant modes of distribution and reception.

In Figure 3, I included the genre novel, the short story, pulp fiction and the graphic novel, each with examples, toward the lower end of the prose spine of the SF field, in a descending hierarchy of legitimate consecration and an ascending hierarchy of mass popularity. Doubtless, we could readily provide alternative examples of each; we might also include a separate category for the comic book, as distinct from the graphic novel, yet further toward the lower boundary, although this would sometimes be a very fine distinction to make; we could have chosen less 'literary' examples of the short story than Verne and Wells (but also more 'literary', as in Forster's 'The Machine Stops'); and more typical examples of the graphic novel than Moore and Gibbons's *Watchmen*, which, as DC's single most critically acclaimed title, is not so much representative as paradigmatic; and we might even describe the field as Euro–American–Japanese rather than global. But the general contours of the map still seem more or less accurate.

One outstanding problem remains, that of where to locate the various 'New Wave' movements, which have arisen intermittently in antipathetic reaction to the predominant formations within the SF field. I included five of these in Figure 3: the loose and not entirely satisfactory linkage of Merril's notion of 'speculative fiction' to Dick's novels; a relatively uncontentious identification of cyberpunk with William Gibson and Bruce Sterling (although one could give non-American examples, such as Oshii in Japan or the Maurice Dantec of *Là où tombent les anges* and *Babylon Babies* in France); an equally uncontentious linkage of Michael Moorcock and Ballard through the British New Wave; a defensible, but more precarious, identification of the American New Wave with countercultural political radicalisms of one kind or another (which perhaps underestimates the role of writers like Ellison and Spinrad); and 'Weird Fiction', which could better be exemplified by H. P. Lovecraft than by China Miéville, except that the latter deliberately situates his own work in relation to the SF field. I located three of these within the restricted economy and will postpone their discussion for the moment. Speculative fiction and cyberpunk fall within the extended economy, however, even though each developed at least in part in response to the logic of the restricted economy. But both escaped that logic, the first in the direction of 'literary' SF – what else can it mean for Jameson to describe Dick as the 'Shakespeare of Science Fiction' (Jameson, 2005, 345)? – the second towards the mass market. Hence, their respective locations.

5. The Restricted Economy and Institutionalised Bourgeois Art

Turning, finally, to our third region, there are two distinct, but overlapping, parts of the SF field to be addressed, the restricted economy and institutionalised bourgeois art. We might note, in passing, that SF poetry does actually exist: Aldiss, Bradbury, Joe Haldeman, Le Guin and Gene Wolfe have all written 'speculative poetry', and there is even a Science Fiction Poetry Association, which publishes the journal *Star*Line* and administers the annual Rhysling Award for best SF poem. But it yields very little in the way of even symbolic profit when compared to the genre's prose and dramatic forms. The absence of a Hugo Award for poetry speaks louder than any poem. The more significant components of the restricted SF economy are thus those strictly non-poetic forms named in Figure 3 alongside poetry. One of these is academic SF criticism, which lies at the upper end of the restricted field, consecrated 'charismatically' by intellectual rather than bourgeois audiences. This seems to command more attention than SF poetry, but only within the academic intelligentsia:

neither Suvin nor Jameson has been shortlisted for a Hugo, not even in the non-fiction categories.

More importantly, the restricted field poses the question of the avant-garde, often deemed anachronistic in much commentary on postmodernism, which tends to insist, with Bürger, that 'art has passed beyond the historical avant-garde movements' (Bürger, 1984, 94). So Jameson writes that 'we are beyond the avant-gardes ... the collaborative ... eschews the organization of a movement or a school, ignores the vocation of style, and omits the trappings of the manifesto or program' (Jameson, 1991, 167). There is some truth in this argument, but it seems oddly inapplicable to SF, a field Jameson himself knows so well. If avant-gardism is closely identified with high modernism, either as integral or internally opposed to it, then by definition there can be no avant-gardes in so unmodernist a field as SF. But SF history is nonetheless littered with intellectual formations the organisation, vocation and trappings of which bear close resemblance to those of the historical avant-garde. An obvious example, especially interesting given its close proximity to the pulp milieu, is provided by the New York 'Futurians'.

Organisationally, the Futurians were as much a 'school' or 'movement' as Futurism itself. Asimov recalls their core membership, himself, Kornbluth, Robert Lowndes, Merril, Johnny Michel, Pohl and Donald Wollheim, as a coterie of 'brilliant teenagers ... from broken homes and ... insecure childhoods' (Asimov, 1994, 61) united by violent opposition to fascism (Asimov, 1979, 211) and also, one might add, by equally violent opposition to Moskowitz's rival 'New Fandom'. Moskowitz remembered their 'Futurian Embassy' as a 'bizarre menagerie of bohemianized science fiction fans' (Moskowitz, 1974b, 246). The Embassy's name is instructive, insofar as it suggests an avant-gardist self-conception as delegates for the very future they sought to sketch in their stories. The Futurians were also actively involved in organising publication of their own alternative pulp magazines: Lowndes edited *Future Fiction* (1939–43); Pohl edited *Astonishing Stories* (1940–43) and *Super Science Stories* (1940–43) during 1940 and 1941; and Wollheim edited both *Stirring Science Stories* (1941–42) and *Cosmic Stories* (1941). These were barely viable commercially, typically avant-gardist products of a restricted rather than an extended economy: Wollheim produced only four issues of *Stirring Science Stories* and only three of *Cosmic Stories* (Ashley, 2000, 149, 159–62).

As is well known, Asimov himself published extensively in Campbell's *Astounding*, but this was not the case for the other leading Futurians. Essentially, Futurianism's vocation was to provide a socially critical alternative to the technophile utopianism Campbell had inherited from Gernsback.

So the world-city of Trantor, in Asimov's original 'Foundation' stories (1942–50), is the heart of a decadent, essentially byzantine, civilisation; and the overpopulated Earth, ruled by an oligarchy of advertising agencies, in Pohl and Kornbluth's 'Gravy Planet' (1952), the product of centuries of unrestrained commercial development. As Andrew Ross observes, this Futurian 'injection of social consciousness ... had an enduring effect at a time when the pulp stories were beginning to address the future of authoritarian social orders' (Ross, 1991, 116). The Futurians also had programmatic trappings aplenty. Michel coined them the slogan: 'Awake! The future is upon us!' (Moskowitz, 1974b, 168). Wollheim delivered a speech to the 1937 Eastern Science Fiction Convention, largely written by Michel, which denounced 'the Gernsback Delusion' and moved (unsuccessfully as it turned out) that the Convention

> shall place itself on record as opposing all forces leading to barbarism, the advancement of pseudo-sciences and militaristic ideologies, and shall further resolve that science-fiction should by nature stand for all forces working for a more unified world, a more Utopian existence, the application of science to human happiness, and a saner outlook on life. (Moskowitz, 1974b, 119)

In 1938, the Futurians formed a Committee for the Political Advancement of Science Fiction, composed a 'Science Fiction Internationale' (Moskowitz, 1974b, 149) and drafted a manifesto Pohl remembered as having 'a lot of V. I. Lenin in it, and a lot of H. G. Wells' (Pohl, 1978, 68). In 1939, Pohl even proposed a Futurian Federation of the World (Knight, 1977, 15–16). Famously, Mozkowitz excluded six of the more vociferous Futurians, amongst them Pohl, Wollheim and Michel, from the 1939 First World Science Fiction Convention. They retaliated by convening a counter-convention at the Brooklyn headquarters of the Young Communist League, much to the dismay of one of its executive members, who suspected them of Trotskyism (Del Rey, 1980, 146; Pohl, 1978, 96, 99).

Robert Savage and I have explored the vexed relationship between Campbell and Futurianism elsewhere (Milner and Savage, 2008). Suffice it to note here simply that avant-gardist styles of organisation, vocation and trapping were clearly present in American SF, even at this most apparently mass-commercial of moments. The Futurian magazines Pohl and Wollheim edited were little more than fanzines, located well within the restricted economy, but nonetheless at positions proximate to Gernsback's and Campbell's commercially more successful pulps. Many of their individual authors would later achieve success within the extended economy, but Futurianism itself remained irreparably a product of the restricted economy. It should be obvious that much the same can also be said of the British and American New Waves of the 1960s and 70s, cyberpunk in the 1980s and the 'New Weird' in the early twenty-first century.

The British New Wave cohered around *New Worlds* during Moorcock's term as editor (1964–71) and found quintessential expression in Ballard's *The Atrocity Exhibition*, published in 1970. Moorcock's opening editorial, programmatically entitled 'A New Literature for the Space Age', approvingly cited William Burroughs's argument that, if 'writers are to describe the advanced techniques of the Space Age, they must invent writing techniques equally as advanced' (Moorcock, 1964, 2). Twenty-five issues later, Moorcock would insist, equally programmatically, that Ballard had become 'the first clear voice of a movement destined to consolidate the literary ideas ... of the 20th century, forming them into ... a new instrument for dealing with the world of the future contained ... in the world of the present' (Moorcock, 1966, 2). For Moorcock, what he would describe retrospectively as the '*New Worlds* group' was clearly a 'Movement' (Greenland, 1983, 205) with its own style and programme. It was also very obviously autonomous rather than heteronomous. Partly funded by the British Arts Council, but blacklisted by W. H. Smith, then the leading British bookseller, for its serialisation of Spinrad's *Bug Jack Barron*, the magazine's financial arrangements were typical of a restricted economy. As Luckhurst observes: 'The finances remained precarious throughout the 1960s, but this helped direct it in adventurous directions' (Luckhurst, 2005, 145).

The American New Wave was in part a spin-off from the British, as Merril's interestingly conceived but embarrassingly titled *England Swings SF* suggests. Many American New Wave writers had been published in *New Worlds*, Spinrad most obviously, but also Thomas M. Disch, Ellison, Philip José Farmer and Pamela Zoline. But Ellison's 1967 *Dangerous Visions* anthology finally announced the repatriation of the American New Wave. Here, too, we find the same breathlessly avant-gardist tone as in *New Worlds*. 'What you hold in your hands is more than a book ...', Ellison wrote, 'it is a revolution ... It was intended to shake things up. It was conceived out of a need for new horizons, new forms, new styles, new challenges in the literature of our times' (Ellison, 2002, xxxiii). In the United States, however, where there was no direct counterpart to *New Worlds*, New Wave writing would be published either in mainstream SF magazines, or in anthologies like *Dangerous Visions* or as novels. Historically a few years later, and geographically closer to the epicentre of 'new social movement' radicalism, the American New Wave was also directly exposed to the impact of both feminist and Afro-American identity politics. It would thus become simultaneously more commercially successful, more politicised and less avant-gardist than the British: Le Guin's two Hugos, for *The Left Hand of Darkness* in 1970 and *The Dispossessed* in 1975, are nicely symptomatic. Both feminist SF (here represented by Le Guin and Marge Piercy, although one could easily add Russ, Carol Ermshwiller and Octavia Butler) and Afrofuturist SF (here Delany, but also Butler once again, Walter Mosley and others) are thus best understood as direct products of the New Wave, rather than as distinct successor formations akin to cyberpunk. Delany and Ermshwiller were published in *Dangerous Visions*, Le Guin and Russ in *Again, Dangerous Visions* and Butler was to have been included in the unpublished *Last Dangerous Visions*. I located this formation within the restricted economy since it is clear that some writers – Russ and Delany – vigorously resisted the claims of the extended economy; but also towards its outer edge since others – Atwood and Le Guin – achieved a kind of commercial success which pointed toward institutionalised consecration by the intelligentsia, if not by the bourgeoisie.

Like both Futurianism and *New Worlds*, early cyberpunk also espoused, rather than eschewed, the organisation of a movement: Lewis Shiner even described it as 'the Movement' (Shiner, 1992, 25); it actively embraced the vocation of style – 'they are in love with style', Sterling wrote, favouring a 'crammed' prose, with 'rapid, dizzying bursts of novel information, sensory overload that submerges the reader' (Sterling, 1986, viii, xii–xiii); and it too had its manifestos and programmes – what else is the 'Preface' to *Mirrorshades*? Cyberpunk quickly became a commercial success, which is why I located it close to scientific romance at the centre of the SF field, but its origins were in the restricted economy nonetheless. To quote Sterling again: 'Before … the labels, cyberpunk was simply … a loose generational nexus of ambitious young writers, who swapped letters, manuscripts, ideas, glowing praise, and blistering criticism' (Sterling, 1986, ix).

Weird Fiction is less obviously an SF avant-garde than either of the New Waves, if only because it is less obviously SF. Lovecraft would never have considered his writing thus, but it is clear that his work has been an important influence on others who might, Michel Houellebecq for example (Houellebecq, 1991), Miéville (Gordon, 2003, 358) and the New Weird more generally. The latter's avant-gardist aspirations are as evident as those of earlier New Waves. Witness both the characteristically programmatic introduction and the overall programmatic structure of the VanderMeers' *New Weird* anthology (2008). And Miéville, at least, is happy to locate Weird Fiction in relation to the SF selective tradition. The first and last volumes of his Bas-Lag trilogy, *Perdido Street Station* and *Iron Council*, each won Arthur C. Clarke Awards for the 'best science fiction novel' published in the United Kingdom in, respectively, 2001 and 2005. 'Weird Fiction',

Miéville has written, is 'the bad conscience of the Gernsback/Campbell sf paradigm, ... rebuke to ... theorizing that takes that paradigm's implicit self-conception as its starting point' (Miéville, 2009a, 510). The force of the sentiment is compounded by its location in *The Routledge Companion to Science Fiction*. Both literary avant-gardist and political vanguardist, and thus doubly consigned to the restricted economy, Miéville has also determinedly prosecuted his case for the Weird in the most improbably Marxist of circumstances (Miéville and Bould, 2002; Miéville, 2009b). This is in itself reminiscent of earlier encounters between avant-garde and vanguard formations, most obviously, perhaps, Vladimir Mayakovsky's attempts to negotiate a passage between Futurism and Bolshevism. Interestingly, he too wrote SF (Mayakovsky, 1968; 1985).

The first of our SF avant-gardes, Futurianism, was originally a 'fan' formation, its core membership recruited from the Brooklyn branch of Gernsback's fan-based Science Fiction League. Many, though not all, would later become professional writers, editors and anthologists, but all entered the SF field as fans. Which serves to remind us of one of the field's most distinctive features, the unusually strong set of identifications between audiences, writers and texts. This is true of written SF, which has its 'SF Community' and World Conventions, where the Hugo and similar awards are typically made by fan vote. It is also true of film and television SF, which has developed its own parallel organisation of conventions. By comparison with other 'popular' genres, SF clearly inspires unusually strong loyalties amongst relatively clearly defined and demarcated audiences. This is by no means an exclusively American phenomenon: in Britain, both *Doctor Who* and *Torchwood* have excited intensely 'fannish' enthusiasm; interestingly, *Doctor Who* episodes won Hugo Awards in 2006, 2007, 2008, 2010 and 2011. The *Star Trek* fan base nonetheless provides the paradigmatic instance of the phenomenon. When NBC threatened to cancel the series in 1967, a 'Save *Star Trek*' campaign produced over 114,500 letters of protest, which finally secured its renewal (Tulloch and Jenkins, 1995, 9). This mass movement of Trekkers subsequently became a semi-permanent accompaniment to the franchise.

Much commentary has interpreted the Trekker phenomenon in quasi-Adornian terms as manipulation by the culture industry. But Jenkins and others have cast the Trekkers and other SF fans in more positive light:

> Fans produce meanings and interpretations; fans produce art-works; fans produce communities; fans produce alternative identities. In each case, fans are drawing on materials from the dominant media and employing them in ways that serve their own interests and facilitate their own pleasures. (Jenkins, 1992a, 214)

The essay on filking, from which this quotation is taken, formed part of a larger investigation into fandom, which included both Jenkins's own *Textual Poachers* and *Science Fiction Audiences*, which he co-authored with John Tulloch. The term 'textual poaching', which appears both in the essay and in the books, was borrowed from Michel de Certeau, who had used it to describe how subordinate subcultures reappropriate materials from the dominant culture (Jenkins, 1992b, 24–27; Tulloch and Jenkins, 1995, 38-41; de Certeau, 1984, 174). The analogy is with poaching game (*braconner*) rather than eggs (*pocher*). So the 'filker', who borrows melodies from established musicians and ideas for lyrics from *Star Trek* scripts, or the 'slash fiction' writer, who explores the 'erotic aspects of the texts', including paradigmatically the 'homoerotic romance between Kirk and Spock' (Jenkins 1992a, 215), is understood as what de Certeau had meant by a *braconnier*.

If we adopt an Adornian reading of fandom, then the phenomenon belongs in the mass-audience region of the heteronomous end of the SF field. But if we were to follow Jenkins and place the emphasis on fan creativity, as much of the evidence suggests we should, then it would belong in the restricted field as art for art's sake or, to be precise, SF for SF's sake. For there is no commercial gain to be had for these filkers, slash fiction writers and fanzine editors. Theirs is a labour of love as utopian as that of any avant-garde, aimed only at symbolic profit and only before a limited audience of peers, or like-minded 'experts'. As Constance Penley observed of *The 25th Year*, a collaborative K/S (Kirk/Spock) slash fiction published in 1991, which included the work of over thirty fan writers, poets and artists: 'Nothing better exemplifies the way slash writers have developed ... a model of equality and individuality' (Penley, 1997, 143). These 'amateur women writers', she concluded, were writing their own 'sexual and social utopias' (Penley, 1997, 145) using the materials to hand from *Star Trek*. They were textual poachers, in short. I remain open to persuasion to the contrary, but for the moment it seems that the most strictly fannish of SF fan behaviour belongs where I located the fanzines in Figure 3, that is, close to the Bohemian border of the restricted economy, but also to the graphic novel in the extended economy.

One further avant-garde position remains within the SF field, that of underground cinema, represented in Figure 2 by David Cronenberg, the Canadian *auteur* film-maker. No matter how we define underground, whether as subversive, oppositional, independent, experimental, countercultural or merely 'cult', his substantial body of SF cinema, especially *Scanners* (1981), *The Dead Zone* (1983), *Videodrome* (1983), *The Fly* (1986), *Crash* (1996) and *eXistenZ* (1999), seems paradigmatic. But in the mid 1960s Jean-Luc Godard's *Alphaville* (1965) and Truffaut's *Fahrenheit 451* (1966) would have seemed equally so. The first 'New Wave' was, after all, the French *nouvelle vague* and Godard and Truffaut, both protégés of André Bazin, both writers for *Cahiers du cinéma*, were its leading *auteurs*. Andrei Tarkovsky's two SF films, *Solyaris* (*Solaris*) and *Ctankep* (*Stalker*), might also be considered 'underground' or avant-garde, although these and similar notions are not readily transferable to late-Soviet Russia. In retrospect, however, for Tarkovsky as for Godard, the claim to underground status is belied by the sheer scale of their eventual success with institutionalised (western) bourgeois audiences: Tarkovsky won the Grand Prix Spécial du Jury at the Cannes Film Festival for *Solyaris* and the Prix du Jury Œcuménique for *Ctankep*; Godard the Goldener Bär at the Berlin International Film Festival for *Alphaville*. Hence, my decision to identify both as 'art house' rather than 'underground'. But this is a fine distinction, which probably works better synchronically than diachronically. The reader determined to insist on Godard's continuing underground status should feel free to substitute Truffaut for Godard at this location.

This takes us to the single most important component of institutionalised bourgeois art, 'literary' SF. The category barely exists for 'high Literature', which treats such texts as '"not really SF" or as somehow "transcending the genre"' (Bould, 2009, 1). But it does exist for SF: witness the meticulous fashion in which both Clute and Nicholls (Clute and Nicholls, 1993, 483–84, 768–70) and Lofficier and Lofficier (Lofficer and Lofficier, 2000, 349) distinguish between, but also incorporate, both 'genre' and 'mainstream' writers. 'Literary' SF is best understood as that fraction of the SF field currently incorporated into contemporary versions of the literary canon. It includes France's *L'île des pingouins*, Zamyatin's *Mi*, Čapek's *R.U.R.*, read as literature rather than theatre, and also his *Válka s mloky*, Huxley's *Brave New World*, Orwell's *Nineteen Eighty-Four*, Lem's *Solaris*, Arkady and Boris Strugatsky's *Piknik na obochine* (*Roadside Picnic*), Houellebecq's *Les Particules élémentaires*, which won the Prix Décembre and, in English translation as *Atomised*, the International IMPAC Dublin Literary Award, and arguably his *La carte et le territoire*, which won the Prix Goncourt. Indeed, all the many SF texts included in the longer version of Bloom's *The Western Canon* clearly belong here. They do so, however, not necessarily because of any distinctively literary 'merit', as Bloom himself would argue, but because they have been canonised as 'literary' by educational and publishing institutions and, as a result, relocated away from the bookshop shelves marked 'Science Fiction and Fantasy' to those marked 'Literary Fiction', 'Modern Classics' and 'Literature'.

But this removal has little effect within the SF field, where intertextual and other references to canonical writing proceed essentially uninterrupted. Which is why nearly all the SF texts included in Bloom's canon also rate entries in Clute and Nicholls. This is not to suggest that individual SF writers are indifferent to 'literary' recognition: some clearly attempt to gain entry into the canonical field by way of either the SF restricted field or institutionalised bourgeois SF. Ballard and Dick both clearly aspired to this, though only the first with real success in his own lifetime. The Library of America's 3-volume *Philip K. Dick Collection*, edited by Jonathan Lethem, might eventually have provided the latter with posthumous recognition, but not until 2009, well over a quarter of a century after his death. Interestingly, Houellebecq, perverse as ever, seems to have moved in the opposite direction from avant-garde poet to SF novelist (Houellebecq, 1992; 1994; 2005; 2010). The critical success of *La carte et le territoire* notwithstanding, the eventual price could be exclusion from the canonical field, given that literary gatekeepers seem far more reluctant to countenance relatively free movement between canonical and SF fields than their counterparts in SF.

These reflections lead me to postulate, by way of conclusion, two further axioms:

> *SF is a subfield of the general literary field, with a structure homologous to that of the wider field, which simultaneously constructs and is constructed by, produces and reproduces, the SF selective tradition.*

and

> *The boundary between the SF field and the (modernist) canonical 'literary' field takes a form loosely analogous to that of a membrane – that is, a selective barrier, impermeable to many but by no means all elements – located in the overlap between the SF restricted field and institutionalised bourgeois SF. From the canonical side, this impermeability tends to allow SF to enter the canon, but not to return to SF; from the SF side, movement is normally permitted in both directions.*

4

Radio Science Fiction and the Theory of Genre

Perhaps the most striking feature of the previous chapter's mapping of the SF field is that, to date, only one of these many and various SF forms, commercial radio SF drama, has actually become extinct. Its absence from the contemporary cultural field is arguably 'symptomatic', in the Althusserian sense of the term, that is, it signifies something much more generally significant about the structure and function of the whole field (Althusser and Balibar, 1970, 316). What exactly that might be, will be the subject of this chapter.

In the mid 1960s, Professor A.J.P. Taylor, the distinguished Oxford historian, opined, with all the authority of the Clarendon Press behind him, that 'Radio offered words without pictures, ... the silent film ... pictures without words. Both were ... doomed to disappear when technical advance brought words and pictures together' (Taylor, 1965, 233–34). He was more or less right about silent film, but absolutely wrong about radio, which still thrives well into the twenty-first century, not only in England but also globally. Taylor's dismissive reaction to radio was, nonetheless, neither eccentric nor idiosyncratic. Quite the contrary, perhaps the strangest thing about radio drama is not that it continues to flourish, but that it continues to be an object of near indifference, not only for literary studies, but also for media and cultural studies more generally. We should not be too surprised by the former, given that academic literary criticism has tended to treat all post-print media with a certain disdain. But one might have expected media and cultural studies to have some interest in so significant a mass medium. That they have not, tells us something rather interesting about contemporary forms of the academic division of labour. In short, it suggests that the progressive institutional differentiation of drama studies, film studies, television studies, media studies and cultural studies from each other and from literary studies has had at least two negative side effects:

the first, a growing inattention to the generic continuities across different media, the second, a failure to attend adequately to media that do not fit neatly into this institutional pattern, one example of which is radio. All of this has a special relevance to SF, insofar as it is a genre that has tended to circumvent conventional academic disciplinary and subdisciplinary boundaries. What is more, my own memories, recounted in chapter 1, do seem to suggest that radio SF has at times occupied a peculiarly salient position within the genre.

Nearly a decade after Taylor published his volume in *The Oxford History of England*, Williams published *Television: Technology and Cultural Form*, a work that quickly became a key foundational text for television studies. Like Taylor, he too chose to treat television as radio with pictures, stressing the commonality as drama between theatre and cinema, and that as broadcasting between radio and television. The cinema, he argued, 'was and remains a special kind of theatre, offering specific and discrete works of one general kind' (Williams, 1974, 29). Radio and television, by contrast, 'were *systems primarily designed for transmission and reception as abstract process, with little or no definition of preceding content*' (Williams, 1974, 25). Both eventually moved beyond this 'parasitism on existing events' to produce 'kinds of original work', he concluded, radio in the mid 1930s, television in the mid 1950s (Williams, 1974, 29–30). But in both there remained a 'deep contradiction' between 'centralised transmission and privatised reception' (Williams, 1974, 30), which tended to impose severe economic constraints on the possibilities for original creative work.

This coupling of radio and television in opposition to theatre and cinema occurs virtually nowhere else in Williams's work, where, much more characteristically, he chooses to treat film and television as contemporary forms of theatre and to elide radio more or less completely. So *The Long Revolution* concludes that 'there is a direct line from … the eighteenth-century theatre through the music-halls to the mass of material now on television and in the cinemas' (Williams, 1965, 291); and *Drama from Ibsen to Brecht* that the 'largest audience for drama, in our … world, is in the cinema and on television' (Williams, 1973, 399). In so doing, Williams ignored what was, in his time as ours, an extremely important vehicle for popular drama. The majority of radio dramatic productions are, of course, adaptations, whether from theatre, novel, short story, comic book, film or television (both *Doctor Who* and *Torchwood* have been adapted for radio). But original drama has also been written for radio, some by highly respected playwrights, for example, Brecht's *Die heilige Johanna der Schlachthöfe* (*Saint Joan of the Stockyards*), Louis MacNeice's *The Dark Tower*, Dylan Thomas's *Under Milk Wood* and Friedrich Dürrenmatt's *Herkules und der Stall des Augias*

(*Hercules in the Augean Stables*) (Brecht, 1932; MacNeice, 1947; Thomas, 1954; Dürrenmatt, 1960). Beckett wrote six radio plays, Tom Stoppard eight (Beckett, 1990; Stoppard, 1994). Which makes it all the more surprising that Williams, whose specialist field was precisely drama studies, should have been so uninterested in radio.

1. Cultural Materialism as Method

In chapter 2, we made extensive use of Williams's conceptions of form and of tradition. Here, I turn to Williams yet again, not for a substantive account of radio, which he singularly failed to develop, but rather for the method deployed in *Television*, especially its focus on the interconnections between technology, cultural form and social institution. For it was this methodology that had led him to stress the continuities between radio and television. And he was, of course, absolutely right to acknowledge the technological affinities between the two media as broadcasting systems (centralised transmission/privatised reception); the formal affinities between their respective contents (music, news, entertainment, sport); and the institutional affinities between their organisation as either public broadcasters, funded by licensing and taxation, or private broadcasters, funded by sponsorship and advertising (Williams, 1974, 30). Williams described his mature method, which clearly informs both his theory of form and the later versions of his theory of tradition, as a 'cultural materialism'. He had first used this term in a short essay published in the hundredth issue of the *New Left Review*, where he defined it as 'a theory of culture as a (social and material) productive process and of specific practices, of "arts", as social uses of material means of production' (Williams, 1980a, 243).

This theoretical position can only be understood in relation to the wider intellectual context of nineteenth- and twentieth-century Western thought, especially the distinction between what are commonly termed philosophical idealisms and materialisms. For the first, culture typically represents a superior ideal, separate from and yet superior to economics and politics, which informs the whole way of life of whole peoples, as a matter of fact in pre-modern societies, but only ideally so within modernity itself. It is a view that derives ultimately from European Romanticism, although Williams himself had encountered it primarily through Leavisite literary criticism and the journal *Scrutiny*. For the second, culture is ultimately reducible to an aggregate of individual commodities, each for sale in the market place of individual taste, their values determined solely by the revealed preferences of the aggregate of individual cultural consumers.

This view clearly derives from utilitarianism, both as a philosophical system and as applied to the disciplines of economics and political science. But Williams encountered it, in distinctly collectivised form, primarily through the kind of Marxism that sought to reduce culture to the 'superstructural' effect of the so-called economic 'base'. As he explained, 'I was trying to say something very much against the grain of two traditions, one which has totally spiritualized cultural production, the other which has relegated it to secondary status' (Williams, 1979, 352–53).

In the essay entitled 'Base and Superstructure in Marxist Cultural Theory', also written for the *New Left Review*, Williams argued for a 'revaluation' of each of the three terms in the core Marxist model, 'base', 'superstructure' and 'determination'. So the first, he wrote, should denote the primary production of society itself and of people themselves, rather than the merely 'economic'; the second, the whole range of cultural practices, rather than a merely secondary and dependent 'content'; and the third, the 'setting of limits and exertion of pressures', rather than predetermined causation (Williams, 1980b, 34–35). In *Marxism and Literature*, the argument is taken further: once again, determination is understood to mean the setting of limits and exertion of pressures (Williams, 1977, 87); and once again, production is understood as applying to a wider field than the merely economic, so that the 'productive forces' are 'all and any activities in the social process as a whole' (Williams, 1977, 93). But the notions of 'base' and 'superstructure' are here effectively consigned to theoretical oblivion: 'it is not "the base" and "the superstructure" that need to be studied,' he writes, 'but specific and indissoluble real processes' (Williams, 1977, 82). Ironically, Williams was very much concerned to invoke Marx against subsequent Marxism on this point. 'Marx's original criticism', he insisted, 'had been mainly directed against the *separation* of "areas" of thought and activity ... The common abstraction of "the base" and "the superstructure" is thus a radical persistence of the modes of thought which he attacked' (Williams, 1977, 78). It is difficult to avoid the suspicion that, at this point, Williams protests too much. And yet there is a strong sense in which his position was indeed 'Marxist'. For he in effect sought to convict Marxism of, in the telling phrase of his 1979 *New Left Review* interlocutors, 'not so much ... an excess but ... a deficit of materialism' (Williams, 1979, 350).

What the base–superstructure formula failed to acknowledge, Williams wrote, is the materiality of the superstructures themselves. Hence, his characteristically ruthless judgement that 'The concept of "superstructure" was ... not a reduction but an evasion' (Williams, 1977, 93). Superstructure, he concludes, and other related usages within Marxism, such as 'ideology' or 'the realm of art and ideas', each misrepresent what are in fact real and material activities as somehow unreal and immaterial. None of these activities can then be grasped as they are, that is, 'as real practices, elements of a whole material social process; not a realm or a world or a superstructure, but many and variable productive practices, with specific conditions and intentions'. The way forward, he insisted, is 'to look at our actual productive activities without assuming in advance that only some of them are material' (Williams, 1977, 94). If Williams retained a concept of determination, as he certainly did, then it was nonetheless a concept of multiple determination, more akin to the idealist sense of a whole way of life than to the Marxist notion of a determining base and a determined superstructure. But that whole way of life is now both thoroughly material and thoroughly marked by the impress of power and domination, in all its particular aspects. The approach linked the problem of cultural form to that of cultural technology in ways that deliberately drew attention to the materiality of what most Marxists had previously regarded as 'superstructures'.

In *Television: Technology and Cultural Form* this leads Williams to a rejection of both technological determinism and the converse view that technology is merely symptomatic of other sociocultural developments (Williams, 1974, 13). Neither is adequate, he argues, because technologies are deliberately sought out, rather than simply developing an autonomous dynamic in their own right, and because they meet known social needs, to which they are central, not marginal. Hence, his conclusion that

> When there has been such heavy investment in a particular model of social communications, there is a restraining complex of financial institutions, of cultural expectations and of specific technical developments, which though it can be seen, superficially, as the effect of a technology is in fact a social complex of a new and central kind. (Williams, 1974, 31)

For Williams, the central import of this technology and these institutions was what he termed 'mobile privatisation' (Williams, 1974, 26), that is, a simultaneously mobile and home-centred way of life, in which the home 'might appear private and "self-sufficient", but could be maintained only ... from external sources'. This distinctively twentieth-century social relationship, he concluded, created both 'the need and the form' of the new kind of communication (Williams, 1974, 27).

What follows are a few preliminary cultural materialist hypotheses developed with special reference to radio SF, a field which remains seriously under-researched even by comparison with radio drama in general.

Neither the *The Cambridge Companion to Science Fiction* (James and Mendelsohn, 2003) nor *The Routledge Companion to Science Fiction* (Bould et al., 2009) contains entries on the subject. Conversely, Tim Crook's *Radio Drama*, one of few serious studies of the medium, devotes no attention at all to the genre, aside from an extended discussion of Orson Welles's *The War of the Worlds*, which is analysed, not as SF, but rather as a skit or hoax (Crook, 1999, 105–13). If for Williams himself radio figured as little more than a prelude to television, it nonetheless isn't at all difficult to imagine how a cultural materialist approach to radio might proceed. Within the framework of an understanding of broadcasting as a novel kind of communication system and mobile privatisation as a novel way of life, it would address the material specificity of radio as, by turn, technology, cultural form and social institution. These are the lines of inquiry that will be followed here.

2. Radio Technology and Science Fiction

The most obvious difference between radio and television technologies is, of course, the absence or presence of pictures. Otherwise, however, they are remarkably similar. In its earlier stages radio had been conceived as an advanced (because 'wireless') form of electric telegraphy. The shift to imagining and constructing it as a medium of mass entertainment dates from the early to mid 1920s, with national broadcasting commencing in 1923 more or less simultaneously in Europe, America and Australasia. The crucial innovation here was to cast the signal broadly to many receivers, rather than narrowly to a single receiver in two-way transmission. The search for origins is invariably a thankless task, that for the 'first' SF radio show perhaps especially so. But we can say with some certainty that in the United States in 1931 Radio WOR-Newark, one of five stations that would soon found the Mutual Broadcasting System (MBS), broadcast a very much abridged version of Shelley's *Frankenstein*, written and directed by Alonzo Deen Cole; and that in 1932 CBS launched *Buck Rogers in the 25th Century*, produced and directed by Carlo De Angelo, a children's series based on the adventures of a newspaper comic strip character. In Australia in 1934, Radio 3DB broadcast a twenty-five-part adaptation of Erle Cox's 1919 novel *Out of the Silence*. In Britain in 1938, the BBC aired a dramatisation of Conan Doyle's *The Lost World*. In the United States in the same year, CBS broadcast Welles's adaptation of Wells's *The War of the Worlds* for *Mercury Theater on the Air*. From its very beginnings, then, radio SF could be either 'literary' or 'popular', aimed at adults or at children, serious or sensational.[5]

5 I am very grateful to John Clute for discussing radio SF with me at some length during quiet moments at the 2010 World Science Fiction Convention. The main

From the 1930s until the 1950s, the 'wireless set' was a central item of domestic furniture, around which people would gather to listen. This is how the *Mercury Theater on the Air* would have been received; and *Malheurs aux barbus*, the very popular comic SF show, written by Pierre Dac and Francis Blanche and directed by Pierre-Arnaud de Chassy-Poulay, launched by RTF in 1951; or the BBC's *Journey Into Space*, which first went to air in 1953. In the 1960s and 70s, however, the domestic wireless was progressively displaced by the portable transistor radio and transistorised car radio, both of which positioned the medium as an accompaniment to other activities. During the 1980s, the compact disc, or CD, also became commercially available as a substitute for the gramophone record. Although designed as a medium for recorded music, CDs have been used by traditional radio broadcasters to distribute other recorded material, including drama. Indeed, German 'Hörspiele' – literally hearing-plays – are now increasingly produced directly for CD rather than for radio. Good SF examples include the two *Commander Perkins* series, *Der Weganer-Sechsteiler* (*The Vega Series*, 1976–78) and *Die Arrow-Trilogie* (*The Arrow Trilogy*, 1980), produced by Europa, and *Das Sternentor* (*The Stargate*, 2002–9), a set of sequels produced by Maritim. The entire sequence and their related print novels were written by Hans Gerhard Franciscowski under the pseudonym H. G. Francis.

The 1990s witnessed the development of digital radio broadcasting, that is, the direct broadcast of digitised radio signals either to personal computers or to specially designed digital radio sets, a format which became widely available in the first decade of the twenty-first century. From the mid 2000s radio shows, including drama, were also increasingly available as podcasts, that is, as internet-delivered digital audio files, downloadable to computer. Roughly contemporaneously, independently produced specialist SF magazines began podcasting both fiction and commentary: Steve Eley and Jeremiah Tolbert's *Escape Pod* in the United States in 2005, Tony C. Smith and Ciaran O'Carrol's *StarShipSofa* in Britain in 2006 and Lucas Moreno and Marc Tiefenhauer's *Utopod* in Switzerland in 2007. At the 2010 World Science Fiction Convention, *StarShipSofa* was shortlisted, alongside five print magazines, for the Hugo Award for Best Fanzine, which it went on to win (Aussiecon4, 2010, 55). If fanzine podcasts are suggestive of the prospects for more interactive relations of communication, podcasting by traditional broadcasters tends to replicate the combination

result of those discussions was his invitation for me to rewrite the entry on radio for the third online edition of the *Encyclopedia of Science Fiction* (Clute, Langford and Nicholls, 2011). This chapter draws heavily on that work.

of few production centres with many dispersed consumption points, which had prompted both Williams's concerns about mobile privatisation and Adorno and Horkheimer's about the 'rationale of domination' (Adorno and Horkheimer, 1979, 121).

It is no doubt difficult to imagine a more literally exact instance of mobile privatisation than that provided by the car radio. But radio might nonetheless be an in principle less dominative medium than either film or television. Modernist aesthetics is replete with attempts to distinguish the seriously aesthetic from the merely entertaining, almost all of which hinge on the degree of activity or passivity demanded of the reader in the process of cultural reception: Viktor Shklovsky's notion of defamiliarisation, or estrangement (Shklovsky, 1965, 12); Roman Jakobson's conception of the poetic function of language (Jakobson, 1960, 356–57); Barthes's distinction between readerly and writerly texts, or between the text of *plaisir* and the text of *jouissance* (Barthes, 1974, 4; 1975, 14); Eco's between open and closed texts (Eco, 1981, 8–9); Hans Robert Jauss's between the 'literary' and the 'culinary' (Jauss, 1982, 25). So, when Adorno and Horkheimer complained that 'the lightning takeover by the sound film ... leaves no room for imagination or reflection on the part of the audience' (Adorno and Horkheimer, 1979, 126), they did little more than repeat a modernist commonplace. We should note, however, that they clearly regarded audience passivity as an effect of sound film in particular, rather than of film per se: the silent movie, by contrast, seemed to leave room, in its very silence, for both imagination and reflection. Much the same can be said of television without pictures, perhaps especially in the case of SF. For radio drama, like the printed novel, requires of the listener–reader much more effort to conjure up its alternative worlds than do film or television. In short, for dramatic purposes radio might be a more rather than less writerly medium.

Benjamin's famous description of the cinema-goer as a distracted or absent-minded critic might also help to explain some of the difference between radio and television SF drama. 'Reception in a state of distraction', he wrote, '... is increasing noticeably in all fields of art and is symptomatic of profound changes in apperception.' 'The film', he continued, works by 'putting the public in the position of the critic', but here, 'this position requires no attention.' 'The public is an examiner,' he famously concluded, 'but an absent-minded one' (Benjamin, 1973, 242–43). Arguably, both radio and television imply even more distracted modes of reception than film, since both are normally received domestically, that is, in an environment designed for purposes other than aesthetic enjoyment. And, clearly, much radio programming is indeed intended as background noise, a kind of wallpaper for the ears. This is less true of radio drama, however, than of music, news, weather or talkback; and less still of SF drama, which can very easily become utterly incomprehensible if attended absent-mindedly. With radio, the dramatist's script prompts the listener's imagination into providing the details of the alien beings and landscapes, space and time machines, planet-destroying wars and natural catastrophes that are so elaborately 'pictured' in film or television. Sontag's distinction between SF cinema, which operates through images and sounds, and the SF novel, which operates through words translated into imagination, might actually also suggest a deep structural affinity between SF literature and SF radio. For in radio, the listener's imagination has only words, the occasional sound effect and perhaps some incidental music with which to work. And, of these, by far the most important are the words.

3. Radio Science Fiction Forms: Three Texts

This technological given, the absence of visuality and the corresponding priority of the scripted spoken word, underlines many of the distinctive formal features of radio drama. As we noted in the previous chapter, the major televisual forms, the series, the serial and the anthology, were all originally developed for radio. Indeed, many individual television SF programmes, from *Superman* and *Buck Rogers* to *The Hitchhiker's Guide to the Galaxy*, were directly adapted from earlier radio programmes. We are often inclined to see the addition of pictures as necessarily an improvement, as Taylor and Williams both did, but it is notable that most enthusiasts seem to consider the radio version of Douglas Adams's *The Hitchhiker's Guide to the Galaxy* superior to the televisual, and the televisual superior to the cinematic. The original 1978 BBC Radio 4 series was shortlisted for the Hugo Award for Best Dramatic Presentation in 1979, but neither the television version, which first aired on BBC2 in 1981, nor the 2005 film were quite so well received. And the film was, by industry standards, only a very modest success. The subtitle of its review in the London *Observer* speaks for itself: 'The Hitchhiker Movie is clever but adds little to the Radio Original' (French, 2005). Which poses the question of what exactly might be lost, as well as gained, when film or television is substituted for radio.

Analysing two of Dick's best novels, *Do Androids Dream of Electric Sheep?* and *Ubik*, Freedman observes that SF 'manifests its generic presence', not only at the level of plot, but also in the 'molecular operations of language'. The genre's distinctive linguistic register, its use of estranged temporal and spatial locations and their linguistic counterpart, the neologism, he continued, all serve to establish 'a clear otherness vis-à-vis the … empirical world', which is nonetheless 'connected … to that world in rational, nonfantastic ways'. SF's distinctive style thus works so as to 'manage' the relation between the familiar and the unfamiliar, 'through the operations of a radically heterogeneous and polyvalent prose' (Freedman, 2000, 36–37). Freedman's general argument that SF 'enjoys a privileged affinity with critical, dialectical theory' strikes me as ultimately unsustainable. But the inference drawn from it here, that written SF's linguistic style is 'in Bakhtinian terms, ... radically novelistic', or 'dialogical', seems much more persuasive (Freedman, 2000, 41; cf. Bakhtin, 1981, 285). The same cannot be true for film or television, if only because there the visual sign necessarily takes precedence over the linguistic. But it might be true for radio, insofar as what applies to writing, can also apply to scripted, that is, written, broadcast speech. Here I intend to test this argument against three well-known examples of SF radio drama, drawn from different times and different places: Welles's adaptation of *The War of the Worlds*, Dürrenmatt's *Das Unternehmen der Wega* (*The Mission of the Vega*) and Nadia Molinari's dramatisation of Iain M. Banks's *The State of the Art*.

CBS launched the *Mercury Theater on the Air*, in which Welles produced, directed and starred, as a general radio drama anthology in July 1938 and it was under this rubric that it broadcast *The War of the Worlds* on 30 October, that is, Halloween. The play begins with two clear announcements that it is a fiction, the first introducing the programme, the second introducing Welles, which is then followed by Welles himself quoting from a slightly amended version of the opening paragraph of Wells's novel:

> We know now that in the early years of the twentieth century this world was being watched closely by intelligences greater than man's and yet as mortal as his own. We know now that as human beings busied themselves about their various concerns they were scrutinized and studied ...

Aside from the relocation from the 1890s to the 1930s, this is very close to Wells's original (Wells, 2005b, 7). Thereafter, however, the play becomes much more Wellesian than Wellsian. Its action is relocated away from Woking near London, at the heart of what was in the late nineteenth century the world's greatest Empire, to Grovers Mill, New Jersey, and New York, in what was then still a geographically isolated second-rank power possessed of virtually no colonies. The most subversive aspect of the novel is thus negated, that is, its depiction of the Empire responsible for the settler colonisation of North America, Southern Africa and Australasia – Wells refers directly to the British conquest of Tasmania (Wells, 2005b, 9) – as itself the target of an equally implacable settler colonisation.

Moreover, Welles substitutes the form of the contemporary on-the-spot newscast for the narrated memoirs of Wells's anonymous participant observer. There is a weather report, some dance band music and then a series of newsflashes, which interrupt and then displace the band as the news becomes increasingly alarming. A prominent role is played by Welles, in the part of Professor Richard Pierson of Princeton University, who moves from the confident assertion that 'the chances against' intelligent life on Mars 'are a thousand to one', to the realisation that

> these creatures have scientific knowledge far in advance of our own. It is my guess that in some way they are able to generate an intense heat in a chamber of absolute nonconductivity. This intense heat they project in a parallel beam against any object they choose, by means of a polished parabolic mirror of unknown composition ...

These lines are substantially taken from the novel (Wells, 2005b, 28), but much that occurs around them is not: the commentaries by the fictional CBS commentator, Carl Phillips; the announcement of martial law by Brigadier General Montgomery Smith of the New Jersey State Militia; the special broadcast by the United States Secretary of the Interior.

About forty minutes into the play, shortly after the last CBS reporter in New York has been killed by the aliens, there is a brief intermission, which serves to remind the audience yet again that this is a fiction. It is followed by Welles, in the part of Pierson, recounting the triumph and eventual demise of the Martians, in lines that conclude with

> Strange to watch the sightseers enter the museum where the dissembled [*sic*] parts of a Martian machine are kept on public view. Strange when I recall the time when I first saw it, bright and clean-cut, hard and silent, under the dawn of that last great day.

This too is very close to a modernised and Americanised version of Wells's own text (Wells, 2005b, 180). Finally, at the very end of the play, Welles reappears, no longer in character, to reassure listeners that 'if your doorbell rings and nobody's there, that was no Martian, it's Halloween.' What, then, are we to make of this version of *The War of the Worlds*? No matter how exaggerated the subsequent reports of panic, it is clear that the play successfully passed itself off as 'reality' to a substantial proportion of the listeners, thereby positioning them, in Barthes's terms, as readerly rather than writerly. Of the audience of about six million, 1.7 million seem to have believed it 'true', 1.2 million to have been 'frightened' (Hand, 2006, 7). The next day's newspapers apparently reported a 'tidal wave of terror that swept the nation' (Cantril, 2005, 3). Adorno was a member of Paul Lazarsfeld's Radio Project, which researched the public response to the broadcast, although he had no direct involvement with this aspect of the work, which was eventually published in 1940 under Hadley Cantril's name. Nonetheless, its findings must have confirmed many of Adorno's worst fears.

Yet, the play cannot be reduced to the hoax Crook describes, if only because it repeatedly announces its own fictionality. And, for listeners who knew it to be fiction, the first forty minutes worked surprisingly well as compellingly 'realistic' drama (the shift in register for the last fifteen minutes is perhaps less successful). Clearly, the broadcast made some attempt to estrange the listener spatio-temporally, insofar as Martian invasions are not exactly commonplace events, not even in New York. But, equally clearly, for the significant minority hoaxed by it, many of whom seem to have believed the invaders to be German rather than Martian, the locations in New York and New Jersey were all too familar. Nor is the play especially dialogical; rather, it mimics, albeit to subvert, the monologic Adorno and Horkheimer would judge characteristic of the culture industries. And yet, reality is rarely if ever entirely aural: even in the 1930s, invasions – of the Rhineland, Austria, Czechoslovakia, Poland – were both filmed and photographed. What is realistically depicted here is not so much reality, then, as the forms and conventions of radio, the role of the academic expert included. And insofar as Welles's text had an estrangement effect, it was primarily with respect to the medium over which it was broadcast. So the play positions the writerly listener, that is, the majority of the audience, those who did not panic, as responding knowingly to this subversion of dominant radio conventions. Welles's version isn't in any sense a 'bad' play, but it functions very differently from the manner Freedman describes in Dick. John Fekete unkindly observed that Freedman's attempt to construct a 'tradition of critical–theoretical works of sf' doesn't actually 'validate much science fiction' at all (Fekete, 2001, 79). And, clearly, it won't work to validate Welles's *The War of the Worlds*. But this is only to say that Freedman's generalisations are over-generalising, as most often are. Interestingly, however, his model works much better for both *Das Unternehmen der Wega* and *The State of the Art*.

Dürrenmatt's play was first broadcast in January 1955, at the height of the Cold War, by Bayerischer Rundfunk. The taken-for-granted assumptions of the passengers and crew travelling aboard his *Wega* from Earth to Venus in 2255 work very much as Freedman suggests. So we learn almost immediately that there exist the 'freien, verbündeten Staaten Europas und Amerikas' – the free, confederate States of Europe and America – with a War Minister, a Minister for Off-World Territories – a near-neologism this, 'außerirdische Gebiete', albeit in a language with a particular capacity for compound neologisms – a Secretary of State and a Foreign Minister, Sir Ernest Wood, all about to board the ship (Dürrenmatt, 1966, 77). Wood is leading a delegation to the penal colony of Venus, in the hope of recruiting the convict colonists to the Euro-American side in war against Russia. Their on-board discussions casually explain to the audience that a long, fragile peace had been established by the Treaty of New Delhi between the United States, on the one hand, and the alliance of Russia, Asia, Africa and Australia, on the other; that the Russian forts on the Moon are out of range of Western weapons; and that Mars is neutral, but Venus so weak, because barely habitable, that it might be forced into taking sides (Dürrenmatt, 1966, 81–82).

The Venusians the mission eventually meets, John Smith, Petersen and, later, Irene, make it clear that the colonists have transformed their inhospitable prison planet into a practical utopia, an acephalous society possessed of no government either to threaten or with which to treat. As Petersen explains,

> Die Venus ist groß und wir sind klein. Sie ist grausam. Wir müssen kämpfen, wenn wir leben wollen. Wir können uns Politik nicht leisten. [Venus is big and we are small. She is cruel. We must fight in order to live. We cannot afford politics.] (Dürrenmatt, 1966, 90)

Supported by Bonstetten, the resident American commissioner, the colonists refuse to take sides in Earth's war. The *Wega* is armed with nuclear weapons, however, and Wood is empowered to use them should the colonists fail to comply. The play's dramatic core consists, not in any visualisable action, but in three extended exchanges of speech over the ethics both of the war on Earth and of a possible strike against the Venusian colonists: between Wood and the Venusians; between Wood, security official Mannerheim and War Minister Costello; and between Wood and Bonstetten.

Despite his having previously promised Bonstetten there would be no attack, Wood, the diplomat, finally opts for the military solution. 'Mich ekelt dies alles [All this repels me]...', he admits, but

> Diese Venus ist fürchterlich. Sind schließlich alles Verbrecher da oben. Bin sicher, daß Bonstetten sich mit den Russen verbünden wollte. War schmutziges Theater, das sie uns vorspielten ... Nun sind die Bomben gefallen und bald werden sie auch auf der Erde fallen. Froh, daß ich einen atombobensicheren Keller habe ... Werde Klassiker lesen. Am besten Thomas Stearns Eliot. Der beruhigt mich am meisten. Es gibt nichts Ungesünderes als spannende Lektüre. [These

> Venusians are frightful. They're all villains after all. I'm sure Bonstetten wants to ally with the Russians. It was just a wretched bit of theatre they put on for us ... Now the bombs are falling and we're falling back to Earth. It's good that I have a nuclear bomb shelter ... I'll be able to read the classics. Especially T. S. Eliot. He has a most calming influence on me. There's nothing more unhealthy than sensationalist reading matter.] (Dürrenmatt, 1966, 111)

The play is thus characteristically science-fictional in virtually every respect identified by Freedman: its use of temporal and spatial estrangement effects, its use of neologism and, perhaps most fundamentally, its insistently dialogical character. For this is how SF radio drama often works at the most basic of levels: as dialogue.

Very similar observations can be made of Molinari's dramatisation of Banks's *The State of the Art*, adapted by Paul Cornell, which was first aired by BBC Radio 4 in March 2009. The introductory narration immediately estranges the listener both temporally and spatially:

> In November 1976 the General Contact Unit *Arbitrary* arrived in orbit around the planet Earth. We'd found it on what the ship claimed was a random search. Earth turned out to be home to an intelligent species, a Stage 3 civilisation. Everyone in the Contact group was delighted. Maybe this was a new world for the Culture to invite into the fold. (Molinari, 2009)

This is very near to our own space and time, of course, but the narrator, Diziet Sma, is not: she is a member of the technologically hyper-advanced, alien 'Culture', and is recalling these events 'centuries later'. Her vantage point, which remains that of the play throughout, therefore has precisely the effect of spatio-temporal estrangement. Strictly speaking, there are no neologisms here, but the exact meaning of 'General Contact Unit' and 'the Culture' is nonetheless not immediately transparent.

A 'General Contact Unit', or GCU, we soon learn, is a sentient, indeed highly intelligent and in this particular case distinctly idiosyncratic kind of spaceship. The *Arbitrary* collects snowflakes as souvenirs of the planets it visits, describes itself as 'the smartest thing for a hundred light year radius' and is, according to Sma, 'quite ... mad'. Contact itself is clearly a specialist agency responsible for first contact with lower-level civilisations and 'the Culture' is the alien civilisation's own self-description. Like Dürrenmatt's Venus, it is an acephalous society, in fact quite explicitly anarcho-communist in character; but unlike Dürrenmatt's Venus, it is also hyper-affluent. As the ship explains, the Culture's 'technological expertise and productive surplus' allow its citizens 'to live as we wish, limited only by respecting the same in others'. And one Culture citizen, Dervley Linter, a former lover of Sma, has chosen to exercise that freedom by 'going native' on Earth. The *Arbitrary*'s visit is thus not at all random; rather, the ship hopes Sma will be able to persuade Linter to return to the Culture.

Whilst Linter and Sma meet, by turn, in Paris, Oslo and New York, and the latter independently pursues her own interests in East and West Berlin, the ship debates with its human companions how to respond to this newly encountered civilisation. As in *Das Unternehmen der Wega*, the play's dramatic core consists in a series of extended acts of speech, dialogues between Sma and, respectively, Linter, the ship and a third human, Li'n-dane. Linter and the ship each find much to admire in Earth's untouched 'naturalness' and are therefore inclined to allow it to continue to develop independently. 'These people are used to good and bad mixed up …', Linter explains to Sma in Paris: 'They seize brief opportunities. They understand tragedy.' In New York, shortly after announcing his decision to convert to Catholicism, he goes on to insist: 'That's what we've lost, what *you've* lost. A sense of wonder and awe – and sin. These people know there are things they don't know and things they can do wrong.' Sma, by contrast, is appalled by Earth's capitalism, its propensity to imperialism, militarism and genocide, and its pathetically hopeless attempts at socialism and, therefore, wants to establish formal contact as soon as is practicable. 'Are they ready for us?' the ship asks. 'They're ready for World War Three, ecological catastrophe and economic collapse', she responds. Later, when the ship has already decided on non-intervention, but when Linter's fate still remains unresolved, Sma insists that 'I want to hit this place with a programme for change that will make their heads spin. I want to see the junta generals soil their pants when they realise that the future is – in their terms – bright red.'

Between non-intervention and contact there is the third position argued by Li, who is quite simply bored by Earth. He founds a 'Boredom Society' to while away the time in orbit and then launches a half-serious campaign – he dresses as Captain Kirk from *Star Trek*, armed with a *Star Wars* light saber – to have himself elected ship's captain. 'You can hardly set foot there without somebody killing somebody,' Li complains to Sma:

> or painting somebody or making music or pushing back the frontier of science or being tortured or killing themselves or dying in a car crash or hiding from the police or suffering from some absurd disease. There's nowhere for the audience to stand, it's like a badly made slasher movie, it's boring. (Molinari, 2009)

At the party he holds to launch his election drive, Li serves up 'dishes grown from the cloned sampled cells of Earth's top ten tyrants', amongst them General Pinochet chilli con carne, Ian Smith in black bean sauce and Idi Amin in a flaky pastry. Li is essentially a comic character, no doubt, but his argument, that the Earth's primitivism is neither fascinating nor horrifying, but merely uninteresting, is nonetheless absolutely serious. In the novella from which the play was adapted, although not in the radio play itself, its full seriousness is made comically apparent: 'This, I submit, is the only solution; a genocide to end all genocides. We have to destroy the planet in order to save it' (Banks, 1993, 183).

The denouement comes very quickly. Linter is casually attacked and murdered by complete strangers in a New York back alley, his body returned to the ship for burial in the traditional Culture fashion, that is, sent into the sun, and then, on 2 January 1978, the *Arbitrary* collects its snowflakes and leaves Earth orbit. But Sma has nonetheless had time to deliver her own last word on Linter's religious conversion:

> You know full well that, despite what this lot think and have done, there's nothing impossible about utopia. We've removed the bad and the pain; we kept the good and the pleasure. It's not even hard. Of course, the bad and the pain are more interesting ... But ... the Culture *is* better. (Molinari, 2009)

This is clearly Banks's own position: the Culture, he has said, is 'my personal ideal for a utopian society' (Banks, 1996); and he has explored its implications, at length and in detail, in the series of novels beginning with *Consider Phlebas* in 1987 and, to date, ending with *The Hydrogen Sonata* in 2012. But, if the play leads us towards that conclusion, then it does so only dialogically, that is, by also allowing Linter to speak to his Catholicism and Li to his bored hedonism. Dürrenmatt and Banks each have a reputation for non-genre writing as well as SF, so it might be objected that this dialogism is a product of their individual talents rather than of SF radio per se. But what Freedman writes of Dick, that 'his greatness ... is bound up with his being radically *typical* of his genre' (Freedman, 2000, 35), does also seem true of Dürrenmatt and Molinari's Banks. Not all SF drama works like this, not Welles for example, but much does and, when it does, it seems especially well suited to radio.

4. Radio Institutions

Like television, radio is much cheaper to produce than cinema and also much more likely to be publicly owned and subsidised. As we observed in the previous chapter, the comparative immunity from commercial pressure in public broadcasting tends to allow for more adventurous drama. We noted how the BBC had a state-sanctioned monopoly over radio in Britain until 1973 and still continues to dominate the market, and that similar patterns exist in many other European and Commonwealth countries. We also noted how, in the United States, radio was organised around privately owned stations, advertising and sponsorship. Gernsback himself founded the private radio station WRNY in 1925, only a year before he launched *Amazing Stories*. Commercial radio SF was primarily, although not exclusively, broadcast in the United States, primarily from the 1930s until the 1950s. Amongst the most successful programmes were CBS's *Buck Rogers* (1932–46), Mutual's *Flash Gordon* (1935–36) and *Superman* (1940–52), and ABC's *Space Patrol* (1950–55) and *Space Cadet* (1952), all of which were serials or series aimed at children. Half-hour horror anthologies had begun on American radio in the 1930s and occasionally included SF: *The Witch's Tale* (1931–38) on WOR and Mutual was the vehicle for Cole's 1931 version of *Frankenstein*. NBC launched *Lights Out* in 1934, written by Wyllis Cooper until 1936, thereafter by Arch Oboler. Cooper went on to produce *Quiet Please!* (1947–49) for Mutual and ABC, yet another horror anthology which included SF. The closing years of the 'Golden Age of Radio' also produced two important SF anthology series aimed at adults, both from NBC, *Dimension X* (1950–51) and *X Minus One* (1955–58), which included versions of Bradbury's *Martian Chronicles* and Heinlein's 'Requiem'. The English-language service of the commercially-owned Radio Luxembourg broadcast *The Adventures of Dan Dare – Pilot of the Future* as a fifteen-minute serial, five days a week, between 1951 and 1956, rebroadcast in Spain by Cadena SER and in Australia by Radio 4AK. The best-known Australian-made commercial radio SF serial was *The Stratosphere Patrol*, a 1947 dramatisation by the Sydney Futurian, Vol Molesworth, of his own Lon Wynter trilogy (Blackford, Ikin and McMullen, 1999, 58; Molesworth, 1943–44). The South African commercial radio station, Springbok Radio, also broadcast SF programmes such as *No Place To Hide* (1958–70), *Strangers from Space* (1961–63), *Probe* (1969) and *The Mind Of Tracey Dark* (1974–78).

The two most important public radio SF broadcasters were almost certainly the BBC in Britain and the French RTF/ORTF/Radio France. The BBC's early, suitably Reithian, exercises in SF followed the pattern of the 1938 version of *The Lost World*, that is, readings from or radio dramatisations of existing 'literary' novels or plays. An adaptation of Selver and Playfair's translation of Čapek's *R.U.R.* was broadcast in 1941; a second version of *The Lost World*, adapted for radio by John Dickson Carr, in 1944; Wells's *The Time Machine*, adapted, produced and directed by Robert Barr, in 1949; and *The War of the Worlds*, adapted by John Manchip White and produced by David H. Godfrey, in 1950. The Corporation's most important vehicle for self-contained radio plays became the general anthology series *Saturday Night Theatre* (1943–96), which included dramatisations of SF novels by Wells, Clarke, Wyndham and Bradbury. Programmes of this kind continue to be a staple of BBC radio, which has broadcast serialised readings from SF work by writers as various as John Christopher, Aldiss and Ballard. In 2008 it aired a two-hour version of Shute's *On the Beach* as part of its *Classic Serial* anthology (Smith, 2008). The BBC also played a crucial role in adapting and developing radio forms originally devised in American commercial radio: in 1953, for example, its *Children's Hour* broadcast a serialisation of Angus MacVicar's *The Lost Planet*.

Well-known examples of the BBC's post-war work include *Journey Into Space* (1953–55), *The Day of the Triffids* (1957), *Host Planet Earth* (1965), *The Foundation Trilogy* (1973), *The Hitchhiker's Guide to the Galaxy* (1978–80 and 2004–5), *Earthsearch* (1981), *Space Force* (1984–85), *Nebulous* (2005–8) and *Planet B* (2009), all of which were serials or series. The most influential of these were almost certainly Chilton's *Journey Into Space* and Adams's *The Hitchhiker's Guide to the Galaxy*. The first was produced as three serialised stories, comprising fifty-four episodes in total, in 1953–54, 1954–55 and 1955–56, which in 1955 reached five million listeners, the largest British radio audience ever recorded. It was sold on to fifty-eight countries and was also novelised as *Journey Into Space* in 1954, *The Red Planet* in 1956 and *The World in Peril* in 1960. The first season was then abridged, reworked and rebroadcast as 'Operation Luna' in 1958. The BBC has also produced three sequels, *The Return from Mars* in 1981, *Frozen in Time* in 2008 and *The Host* in 2009. *The Hitchhiker's Guide to the Galaxy*, written by Adams and produced by Geoffrey Perkins, was first broadcast as a serial over two seasons in 1978 and 1980 (Adams, 1985). These episodes were subsequently novelised by Adams, who then also wrote three sequel novels. After his death, the sequels were adapted for radio by Dirk Maggs and co-produced by Maggs, Bruce Hyman and Helen Chattwell as the third, fourth and fifth seasons, broadcast by the BBC in 2004 and 2005. *The Guide* has been adapted for television, theatre and the cinema, rebroadcast by all the major Anglophone public radio stations and, in translation, by public broadcasters in Finland, the Netherlands, Sweden, France and Germany.

In 2009 the BBC hosted a season of SF across three of its channels, Radio 3, Radio 4 and Radio 7, which included dramatisations of Wells's *The Time Machine*, Clarke's *Rendezvous with Rama* and Ballard's *The Drowned World*. Announcing the season in September 2008, Jeremy Howe, Commissioning Editor for Drama at BBC Radio 4, explained that radio 'seems its natural home in so many ways ... some of the best creative activity is in science fiction' (Matthewman, 2008). BBC Radio 7, the digital radio station established in 2002, now broadcasts a daily SF programme, *The Seventh Dimension*, which includes readings and dramatisations, both stand-alone and serialised, both from the archive and original commissions.

BBC programmes were often sold on to other Anglophone public broadcasters, notably the Australian ABC, Radio New Zealand, the Canadian CBC and the American NPR, all of which also produced their own material. The ABC broadcast a series of children's SF programmes written by G. K. Saunders, beginning with *The Moon Flower* in 1953. It produced a serialisation of Colin Free's *Limbo City* in 1979 and a wide range of individual SF plays, often as parts of more general anthology series. The latter included original Australian work by writers such as Bill McKeown, Barry Oakley, Alfred Behrens, John Blay, Louis Nowra and Damien Broderick. Broderick's radio adaptations of his novels, *Transmitters* and *Striped Holes*, were broadcast in 1984 and 1986, his plays written for radio, *Time Zones* and *Schrödinger's Dog*, in 1992 and 1995. Original ABC radio adaptations of SF classics included Vladimir Mayakovsky's *The Bed Bug* (1981), Alfred Bester's *The Demolished Man* (1985), Cordwainer Smith's *A Planet Named Sheol* (1986) and Čapek's *The Macropoulos Secret* (1988). In 1980–81 Radio New Zealand broadcast a three-part dramatisation of *The Lost World*, produced by Peggy Wells and Barry Campbell. CBC broadcast dramatisations of Wells's *The Time Machine* in 1948, repeated in 1950, and of Huxley's *Brave New World* in 1956. It produced an SF radio anthology series *The Vanishing Point*, which ran from 1984 until 1991 and included versions of Clarke's *Childhood's End* and Le Guin's *The Dispossessed*, and also the fantasy/horror anthology *Nightfall*, which ran from 1980 until 1983 and included some SF. CBC also broadcasts comedy SF, such as *Johnny Chase, Secret Agent of Space*, which ran from 1978 to 1981, and *Canadia: 2056*, which premiered in 2007.

NPR produced highly acclaimed radio dramatisations of the first *Star Wars* trilogy, featuring some members of the original film cast, *Star Wars* itself in 1981, *The Empire Strikes Back* in 1983 and *The Return of the Jedi* in 1996 (Daley, 1994; 1995; 1996). All three were produced as serials, adapted for radio by Brian Daley, all three were given Lucas's formal approval and all three were rebroadcast in Britain by the BBC. NPR's *Radio Tales* anthology (1996–2002), created and produced by Winnie Waldron, featured a number of SF plays, including adaptations of *Frankenstein*, *The Time Machine* and *Time Warp* (based on Wells's short story 'The New Accelerator') in 1999; Stevenson's *Dr Jekyll and Mr Hyde*, Wells's *The Island of Dr Moreau*, Verne's *Journey to the Centre of the Earth* and *The Lost World* in 2000;

and Verne's *Twenty Thousand Leagues Under the Sea*, Wells's *The Invisible Man*, *Apocalypse* (based on Frank L. Pollack's story 'Finis'), *Asteroid* (based on Wells's short story 'The Star'), *Moon Voyager* (based on Wells's *The First Men in the Moon*) and *The War of the Worlds* in 2001.

In France, RTF, which became ORTF in 1964 and Radio France in 1975, was also very actively involved in SF radio. It created and broadcast the popular daily serial *Malheurs aux barbus* (*Woe to the Bearded Ones*) in 1951–52, which the private station Europe1 subsequently adopted as the sequel, *Signé Furax* (*Signed: Furax*), from 1956 to 1960. RTF's various radio stations, especially France-Inter and France-Culture, produced a string of SF radio serials and series: *Les Tyrans sont parmi nous* (*The Tyrants are Amongst Us*) in 1953, *Blake & Mortimer* from 1960 to 1963, *L'Apocalypse est pour demain* (*The Apocalypse is for Tomorrow*) in 1977, *Le Mystérieux Dr. Cornelius* and *Le Prisonnier de la planète Mars* both in 1978, *Trois hommes à la recherche d'une comète* (*Three Men in Search of a Comet*) in 1980 and *Renard, Maurice* in 1981. Like the BBC, French public radio also used the anthology series as vehicle for self-contained SF radio plays, notably *Le Théâtre de l'Étrange* (1963–74), *Les Tréteaux de la nuit* (*The Night Stage*) (1979–80) and *La Science-Fiction* (1980–81).

From 1957 on, the French-language service of Swiss public radio, Société suisse de radiodiffusion (SSR), broadcast the long-running *Passeport pour l'inconnu* (*Passport to the Unknown*) anthology, directed and produced by Roland Sassi and the French SF writer Pierre Versins. The series included original plays by Francophone writers such as Robert Pibouleau, Laurent Lourson, Martine Thomé and Sassi himself. German public radio also produced SF: as we have seen, Bayerischer Rundfunk broadcast Dürrenmatt's *Das Unternehmen der Wega*; in 1969 Westdeutscher Rundfunk broadcast Hein Bruehl's translation of Wyndham's *Day of the Triffids* as *Die Triffids*; in 1981–82 a consortium of three German public radio stations, Bayerischer Rundfunk, Südwestfunk and Westdeutscher Rundfunk, co-produced Benjamin Schwartz's German translation of *The Hitchhiker's Guide to the Galaxy* as *Per Anhalter ins All* (Hitchhiking in Space); a second series, *Per Anhalter ins All 2*, was translated and adapted for radio by Walter Andreas Schwarz and broadcast in 1990–91.

This cursory survey is obviously inadequate insofar as it omits all mention of Eastern Europe and Japan, both of which are important centres of SF writing. But certain patterns do, nonetheless, seem apparent. As we have seen, it has been a commonplace of both scholarly and fan criticism that whereas written SF has often aspired to become a literature of ideas, film and television SF are much more concerned with special effects, a view which replicates more or less exactly Adorno and Horkheimer's judgement that the development of the culture industry leads to the predominance of effect over idea. No doubt, part of the appeal of radio SF also lies in this medium's real, albeit limited, opportunities for such effects. But the tension between ideas and effects is open to very different resolution in radio, partly because of the comparatively low-budget nature of aural effects, partly because radio, like print, requires the listener/reader to make more effort to conjure up its alternative worlds. Moreover, such 'writerly' radio drama is far more likely to be attempted by public broadcasters, which enjoy a greater comparative freedom to explore smaller 'niche markets', than by commercial broadcasters compelled to maximise audiences in order to maximise advertising revenue. The result has been the absence, since the early 1960s, of commercial radio SF from even the mass/heteronomous corner of the cultural field. That this absence is an effect of specific institutional arrangements for the production of radio broadcasting, rather than of differences in national culture between the United States and the Western European liberal democracies, is strongly suggested by the American NPR's sometimes very successful engagements with the genre. These findings, limited though they may be, are nonetheless powerfully suggestive of the general structure and functioning of the globalised SF field.

5
Science Fiction, Utopia and Fantasy

We turn now to our third question, not that of what SF was, but rather of what it wasn't. It is obvious that SF isn't the romance or the Western or crime fiction, although there are hybrid instances of SF and each of these. There are even modernist–SF hybrids: one need look no further than Ballard's middle-period fictions. But the question of generic specificity really becomes acute only at the two points that will be our concern in this chapter, utopia and fantasy. If contemporary cinema and print publishing is any guide, fantasy is a far more socially influential genre than either SF or utopia. It is also clearly the oldest of the three, if we mean by fantasy, as most analysts do, fiction in which the novum is strictly incompatible with science, for example magic, the dream or the supernatural. Until comparatively recently, however, academic debates within SF studies have focused primarily on the relation between SF, utopia and dystopia, so it might be as well to begin by sorting through some of the semantic confusions that attach to these. The term 'utopia' was, of course, coined by Thomas More in 1516. The epigraphic hexastichon supposedly written by the Utopian poet laureate, Anemolius, and included in all four of the earliest editions of More's *Utopia*, reminds us that this neologism was, in the first instance, a Greek pun in Latin between 'ou topos', meaning no place, and 'eu topos', meaning good place:

> Utopia priscis dicta ob infrequentiam,
> Nunc civitatis aemula Platonicae, ...
> Eutopia merito sum vocanda nomine.
> ['No-Place' was once my name, I lay so far;
> But now with Plato's state I can compare, ...
> 'The Good Place' they should call me, with good cause.]
>
> (More, 1995, 18–19)

Dystopia, from the Greek 'dis topos', or bad place, is a more recent coinage, which has been variously ascribed to Henry Lewis Younge in 1747, Noel

Turner in 1782 and John Stuart Mill in 1868. The last is the best known and, interestingly, here the term was used to describe a political proposal rather than a literary genre (Sargent, 2006, 15; Budakov, 2010; Köster, 1983; Mill, 1868).

Academic utopian studies has subsequently formulated the now increasingly conventional set of distinctions between utopia, referring to the general form and its general conventions (the traveller, the guide, the island, etc.), eutopia, meaning its positive variant and dystopia meaning its negative (Sargent, 1994, 7–10). In Lyman Tower Sargent's famous definition, a 'utopia (eutopia, dystopia, or utopian satire)' is 'a species of prose fiction that describes in some detail a non-existent society located in time and space' (Sargent, 1976, 275). Topos means place or space, however, rather than time. And the most important historically recent transformation in the genre, clearly occasioned by European success in mapping the world, has been the relocation of plausible better and worse worlds from geographical now-space into historical future-time. This gives us the, again increasingly conventional, academic distinction between uchronia, euchronia and dyschronia, from the Greek 'u chronos', 'eu chronos' and 'dis chronos', respectively no time, good time and bad time. These analytical distinctions work well in the abstract, but are difficult to sustain consistently against the weight of established usage, where utopia is commonly used to mean both eutopia and euchronia, but not dystopia or dyschronia. In this chapter, I will be mainly concerned with utopia in the sense of common usage, deliberately postponing my discussion of dystopia until the chapter that follows.

1. The North American Argument

There is little doubt that utopia and SF are cognate literary forms, but much doubt as to precisely how cognate. For what might be described as the dominant view in North American SF studies, especially as represented by Suvin and Jameson, utopia is simply a subgenre of SF. Suvin famously defined utopia as an 'imaginary community ... in which human relations are organized more perfectly than in the author's community' (Suvin, 1979, 45). More controversially, he proceeded to argue that it 'is not a genre' in its own right, but rather 'the sociopolitical subgenre of science fiction', that is, social-science-fiction (Suvin, 1979, 61). By virtue of this move, Suvin expanded SF, at a stroke, to accommodate not only More and Bacon, Rabelais and Campanella, Saint-Simon and Fénelon, but also Aeschylus and Aristophanes. The move is controversial, insofar as it is clearly at odds with contemporary usage amongst SF writers, fans and critics (there is no entry, for example, in the *Encyclopedia of Science Fiction* for either Aeschylus or Aristophanes). But it is warmly endorsed in Jameson's *Archaeologies* on at least five occasions (Jameson, 2005, xiv, 57, 393, 410, 414–15). Wegner, a former student of Jameson, is similarly supportive of the Suvinian view that 'science fiction and utopia are inseparable' (Wegner, 2010, xviii). And Freedman argues that SF 'reinvents the older genre and energizes it with the kind of concrete utopian potentiality ... available in the age when the future has ... finally come into existence' (Freedman, 2000, 78). In effect, Freedman, Wegner, Suvin and Jameson are each attempting a redefinition of the SF selective tradition aimed at retrospectively 'englobing' (Suvin, 1979, 61) the genre of utopia. For all four, the attempt is inspired, at least in part, by Bloch's *The Principle of Hope*.

Jameson, Wegner and Freedman borrow the novum, as both term and concept, from Suvin, who in turn derived it from Bloch. The term first appears in a brief reference to 'the Front and the Novum' towards the end of Bloch's 'Introduction' (Bloch, 1986, 18), but the concepts aren't elaborated until chapter 17. There, he argues that a 'philosophy of comprehended hope' must stand on 'the Front of the world process', that is, on the historically 'foremost segment of Being of animated, utopianly open matter' (Bloch, 1986, 200). The Front, he continues, is necessarily related to newness, the New, the Novum. And, if the Novum is really new, it will be characterised by 'abstract opposition to mechanical repetition' and by a specific repetition of its own, that of 'the still unbecome total goal-content itself, which is suggested and tended, tested and processed out in the progressive newnesses of history' (Bloch, 1986, 202). Historically, the dialectical emergence of this total content, which Bloch terms the Ultimum, will end repetition, because it represents the highest newness, which will triumph by means of a total leap out of everything that has ever existed, a leap towards the newness of identity (Bloch, 1986, 202–3). Short of the Ultimum, however, there remains only the advancing Front and the series of Nova it encounters. These are not necessarily literary or artistic, but art is nonetheless both 'a laboratory and also a feast of implemented possibilities' (Bloch, 1986, 216).

Bloch's primary intentions in *The Principle of Hope* were political and philosophical, but its range is quasi-encyclopaedic, quite literally from dreams to theology. The book includes an extensive discussion of utopian literature, from Solon to Morris by way of Plato, the Stoics, St Augustine, Joachim de Fiore, Tommaso Campanella, Robert Owen, Pierre-Joseph Proudhon and Michael Bakunin, culminating in a dismissive account of Wells as 'dilettantism and chaff' (Bloch, 1986, 617). Despite Bloch's enthusiasm for older popular forms, such as the circus and the fairy-tale, post-Wellsian SF rates no mention whatsoever. Indeed, Bloch ignores both the German tradition of the *Staatsroman*, literally, the (ideal) state novel, which has been analysed as a direct precursor to SF (Schwonke, 1957), and the German SF writers published in English translation by Gernsback (Jordan, 1986). These omissions are no mere oversight. As late as 1974, Bloch would remain deeply dismissive of the 'purely technological utopias' of 'science fiction' – the American term is used in the German original (Münster, 1977, 71). The novelty of Suvin's argument was thus precisely to reverse this judgement and to insist, both with and against Bloch, that 'the novum is the necessary condition of SF' (Suvin, 1979, 65).

Like Suvin's *Metamorphoses*, Jameson's *Archaeologies* is Blochian in theoretical inspiration and in its disciplinary orientation primarily towards comparative literature; like Suvin's *Metamorphoses*, it treats utopia as SF; like Suvin's *Metamorphoses*, it is a defence of the continuing political relevance of both. Indeed, Jameson's derivation of 'anti-anti-Utopianism' from Sartre's 'anti-anti-communism' is probably as good a slogan as 'the party of utopia' will get. The terms of this derivation are interesting. Sartre, Jameson recalls, had invented this 'ingenious political slogan' in order to 'find his way between a flawed communism and an even more unacceptable anti-communism' (Jameson, 2005, xvi). The inference is clearly that utopia may be flawed, but anti-utopianism is even more unacceptable. Moreover, the reference is to communism and anti-communism, utopianism and anti-utopianism, that is, to movements rather than texts. Where Suvin's *Metamorphoses* was essentially a post-Formalist analysis of the poetics of a literary genre, Jameson's *Archaeologies* attempts to situate this level of analysis in relation to what he terms, after Bloch, the wider 'Utopian impulse' (Jameson, 2005, 2–3). Like Peter Fitting (Fitting, 2006, 42), Jameson attributes a more formal status to the distinction between 'Program' and 'Impulse' than had Bloch. Nonetheless, it is clear from the overall structure of the argument that Bloch was at least as interested in utopian impulses as utopian texts.

Jameson's argument for the continuing political importance of SF and utopia is broached in his 'Introduction'. 'What is crippling', he insists, 'is ... the universal belief ... that no other socio-economic system is conceivable, let alone practically available.' The value of the utopian form thus consists in its capacity as 'a representational meditation on radical difference, radical otherness, and ... the systematic nature of the social totality' (Jameson, 2005, xii). This very precise thesis tells us most of what we need know about the politics of utopia as a genre, if not necessarily those of SF. The argument is resumed in the last chapter of the book's first part, where Jameson writes that utopia provides 'the answer to the universal ideological conviction that no alternative is possible'. It does so, he insists, 'by forcing us to think the break itself ... not by offering a more traditional picture of what things would be like after the break.' Hence, the conclusion that utopia is 'a meditation on the impossible, on the unrealizable in its own right' (Jameson, 2005, 232).

Here, however, the argument is also linked to a distinctive case for the peculiar contemporary relevance of utopia. Ever since Marx and Engels, supposedly 'scientific' socialisms have asserted their superiority over utopian socialism on the grounds that they know, scientifically and theoretically, how to achieve what utopians can only imagine in fantasy. As *The Communist Manifesto* famously proclaimed, utopias are merely 'fantastic pictures of future society, painted at a time when the proletariat is still in a very undeveloped state and has but a fantastic conception of its own position' (Marx and Engels, 1967, 116). But Jameson picks up on an observation of the ageing Georg Lukács that, by the 1960s, this had clearly ceased to be true (Lukács et al., 1974, 115–16). The erstwhile weaknesses of utopianism, its inability to provide an adequate account of either agency or transition, therefore 'becomes a strength', Jameson concludes, 'in a situation in which neither ... seems currently to offer candidates for solution'. In the early twenty-first century, then, for much the same reasons as before 1848, utopia 'better expresses our relationship to a genuinely political future than any current program of action' (Jameson, 2005, 232). Surveying the scattered rubble of the international socialist movement, it is difficult to disagree. But this also explains why 'anti-utopianism' becomes the other of Jameson's text and 'anti-anti-utopianism' its slogan.

At the pretextual level Jameson is no doubt right to define himself against anti-utopianism. Confronted by a capitalism as hubristic as any in history, we probably do 'need to develop an anxiety about losing the future ... analogous to Orwell's anxiety about the loss of the past' (Jameson, 2005, 233). It isn't at all obvious, however, that any of this has any necessary relation to SF in general, as distinct from Jameson's own preferred examples of the genre. The first part of *Archaeologies* closes with a moving invocation of the Mattapoisett utopians, in Piercy's *Woman on the Edge of Time*, travelling back in time 'to enlist the present in their struggle to exist' (Jameson, 2005, 233; see Piercy, 1976, 197–98). Elsewhere, Jameson has used Piercy's time travellers to even greater rhetorical effect, when he writes that 'utopias are non-fictional, even though they are non-existent. Utopias in fact come to us as barely audible messages from a future that may never come into being' (Jameson, 2004, 54). This is as good a line as any in *Archaeologies* and almost seems to belong there. But the juxtaposition of Orwell and Piercy serves to remind us that Jameson's anti-anti-utopianism is textual as well as pretextual and that it is informed by and in turn informs a clear preference for the utopian SF of his own time and place, the American New Wave, as against other versions of SF, such as the American hard SF of the 1940s and 50s, or early–mid twentieth-century European dystopian SF. The vantage point from which Jameson writes is that of an American sixties radical adrift in postmodern late capitalism. This inner sympathy with novelists like Piercy and Le Guin, Robinson and Dick, provides his writing with its real strengths. But, to reverse Jameson's own reversal of Benjamin, the effectively utopian is also, at the same time, necessarily ideological (Jameson, 1981, 286). And this is as true of anti-anti-utopianism as of utopianism itself.

Both Wegner's claim that 'there has always been a deep link between the figure of utopia, the concept of totality, and the project of revolution'[6] (Wegner, 2007b, 127) and Freedman's that SF is 'a privileged and paradigmatic genre ... not only for Marxism but for critical theory' (Freedman, 2000, xv) are each presupposed in Suvin and Jameson. But they, nonetheless, tell us more about the sad fate of the North American New Left than about SF as a genre. In an early review of *Critical Theory and Science Fiction*, John Fekete concluded that what would be 'desirable for sf' is 'less ... didactic sorting' of the kind Freedman recommends and 'more attention to what sf actually does and to what readers do to and with sf' (Fekete, 2001, 94). Fekete had been previously embroiled in a largely political controversy with Freedman, Angenot, Suvin and others, during which he was accused of everything from 'cognitive relativism' to 'deconstructionist ideology' (Freedman, 1989; Angenot and Suvin, 1988). He had, perhaps, overstepped the Baudrillardian mark, as he himself would later admit (Fekete, 2001, 94–95n). But Fekete's underlying objection to post-Suvinian prescriptive criticism is nonetheless essentially right. It was Williams, after all, whose judgements Freedman and Wegner, Jameson and Suvin, would each surely respect, who had argued that 'we need not criticism but analysis ... the complex seeing of analysis rather than ... the abstractions of critical classification' (Williams, 1989, 239).

The primary methodological implication of Williams's move away from criticism had been an interest in setting literary texts, SF included, in their social contexts, which must surely mean paying attention to what SF actually does, precisely as Fekete recommends. SF may indeed be occasionally utopian (as in Bellamy's *Looking Backward*, but more recently, and perhaps more importantly, in Banks); it has more often been dystopian (Čapek, Huxley, Orwell, Zamyatin); but is even more often neither. Not one of the

6 Athough Wegner refers to utopia here, all but one of his examples are drawn from SF (Wegner, 2007b, 126–27).

fifty-four novels Verne published in his lifetime is a utopia and the sole dystopia, *Paris au XXe siècle*, remained unpublished until 1994. Of the eight novels in Gollancz's 1933 collection of *The Scientific Romances of H.G. Wells*, only *In the Days of the Comet* and *Men Like Gods* were utopias and the first, simultaneously both utopia and dystopia, was dropped from the *Seven Science Fiction Novels* collection published in the US the following year. Wells's most successful experiment with utopia as a genre, *A Modern Utopia*, is hardly science-fictional at all. This is obvious stuff, which Freedman, Wegner, Suvin and Jameson clearly know, but they tend to ignore its wider implications, nonetheless.

Jameson observes that the citizens of what he terms 'political' utopias are normally 'grasped as a statistical population', that is, that 'there are no individuals any longer, let alone any existential "lived experience"'. Hence, the 'boredom or dryness' often attributed to the form. This is not a weakness, he continues, but rather a 'central strength', insofar as it reinforces 'plebeianisation', that is, our 'desubjection in the utopian political process' (Jameson, 2004, 39–40). There is a certain perversity to this observation, which makes sense only given his subsequent insistence that utopias are non-fictional, albeit non-existent. But the instance he cites, Piercy's Mattapoisett, runs contrary to the gist of his argument. For it is precisely insofar as some utopian texts really do work as novels, that is, as fictions, as Piercy's clearly does, that those texts attempt the kind of existential plausibility Jameson discounts. This is true, not only of Morris, as distinct from Bellamy, as Jameson half concedes (Jameson, 2004, 39–40), but also of Piercy, Le Guin and many other utopian SF novelists, though not of More, who provides the template both for the form itself and for Jameson's reading of it. The sheer persistence of utopian strategies for discounting such boredom and dryness suggests how mistaken Jameson might be. Obviously relevant topoi include: the sexual romance within utopia (Morris successfully, Bellamy unsuccessfully, and almost everyone else to some extent), the distant view of utopia from its extremities (a recurring motif in both Le Guin's Hainish and Banks's Culture novels, but also, for example, in *Star Trek*), the external threat to utopia (Banks again, but also Piercy and Robinson), and so on.

If utopias are communities imagined as more perfect, then their political purposes will tend to range from negative critique of the real through to positive inspiration to the better-than-real. The nearer any particular utopian fiction – novel or film, radio or television programme – approximates to the latter, the greater will be its attempt at existential plausibility, since such plausibility tends to render the fiction, and hence the utopia itself, more credible. This is not to discount Suvin's insight that utopia is an estranged rather than naturalistic form (Suvin, 1979, 18), but merely to insist that fiction works in very different registers from the truly non-fictional utopias of political philosophy; that it must work as art or entertainment, and is therefore much more directly implicated in the conventions of literary and cinematic naturalism than Suvin or Jameson allow.

2. The European Argument

For the most influential European SF theorists, such as Williams and Baudrillard, utopia and SF are distinct, but nonetheless cognate, genres. The difference between utopia and SF is registered very forcefully in the latter's *Simulacra and Simulation*, where the two genres are used as functionally equivalent, but mutually exclusive, periodising devices. As is well known, Baudrillard uses the term 'simulacrum' to mean a sign without a referent, 'never exchanged for the real, but exchanged for itself', and 'simulation' to mean the processual aspects of simulacra, the non-referential equivalent of representation (Baudrillard, 1994, 6). He argues that there have been a succession of three orders of simulacra since the Renaissance, which he terms, respectively, the natural, the productive, and 'the simulacra of simulation', founded on information. Each of these is accompanied by a corresponding 'imaginary', so that utopia belongs to the first order, SF to the second, and a new kind of 'implosive' fiction, 'something else ... in the process of emerging', to the third (Baudrillard, 1994, 121). In this third order of simulacra, simulation becomes 'the generation by models of a real without origin or reality', which Baudrillard terms the 'hyperreal' (Baudrillard, 1994, 1). The resulting implosion of meaning obliges SF to 'evolve implosively, ... attempting to revitalize, reactualize, requotidianize ... fragments of this universal simulation that have become ... the so-called real world' (Baudrillard, 1994, 124). He cites Dick in the United States and Ballard in England, especially *The Simulacra* and *Crash* respectively, as striking instances of this 'science fiction that is no longer one' (Baudrillard, 1994, 124–25), and we might perhaps now add Houellebecq as their more recent French counterpart.

In retrospect, the assumed equivalence in Baudrillard between the shifts from first to second and second to third imaginaries seems suspect. Neither the New Wave nor cyberpunk represented anything like so decisive a break with tradition as had the shift from Saint-Simon and Fourier to Shelley and Verne. This misreading is almost certainly an effect of Baudrillard's more general tendency to exaggerate the distinction between modernity and postmodernity. There is a difference between industrial and late capitalism, no doubt, and one that has clearly impressed itself on both SF and

SF studies (Bukatman, 1993; Broderick, 1995). But this difference is by no means commensurate with the shift from pre-modernity to modernity, or from feudalism to capitalism, to be more precise, which underpinned that from utopia to what Baudrillard calls 'classical SF'. Rather, the New Wave and cyberpunk are best understood as late moments within SF, just as Jameson's 'late capitalism' is a late moment within capitalism, his 'late Marxism' a late moment within Marxism (Jameson, 1991, 35–36; 1990). I am tempted to make the observation that where Baudrillard, against Jameson, rightly stresses the discontinuity between utopia and SF, Jameson, against Baudrillard, rightly stresses the continuity between modern and postmodern SF.

But this is still to concede too much to Baudrillard's periodisation, since utopias clearly persist into his second productive order of simulacra. Confining oneself to the best-known examples from England, France and the United States, one can easily generate a quick shortlist of utopias written in response to or reaction against industrial society: Ernest Renan's *La Réforme intellectuelle et morale* (1871), Bellamy's *Looking Backward* (1888), Morris's *News from Nowhere* (1890), William Dean Howells's *A Traveler from Altruria* (1894), France's *Sur la pierre blanche* (1905), Wells's *A Modern Utopia* (1905) and *Men Like Gods* (1923), Gilman's *Herland* (1915), B. F. Skinner's *Walden Two* (1948), Teilhard de Chardin's *L'Avenir de l'Homme* (1959), Huxley's *Island* (1962). The next stop for most readers would probably be Germany. For me, however, it would have to be Australia, where the relevant examples include Catherine Helen Spence's *A Week in the Future* (1889), David Andrade's *The Melbourne Riots* (1892), William Lane's *The Workingman's Paradise* (1892), Charles Carter's *The Island of Justice* (1901), Mary Ann Moore-Bentley's *A Woman of Mars* (1901), Ralph Gibson's *Socialist Melbourne* (1938), Eleanor Dark's *Prelude to Christopher* (1934) and Morris West's *The Navigator* (1976). There is no need to labour the point. Here, as so often, Baudrillard is simply mistaken as to matters of obvious empirical fact.

Williams dispensed with periodisations of this kind, but nonetheless insisted on the close kinship, but conceptual separateness, of utopia and SF. There are four characteristic types of alternative reality, he argues: the paradise or hell, the positively or negatively externally-altered world, the positive or negative willed transformation and the positive or negative technological transformation. SF, utopia and dystopia are each centrally concerned with the 'presentation of *otherness*', he continues, and thus depend on an element of discontinuity from 'realism'. But the discontinuity is more radical in non-utopian/non-dystopian SF, since the utopian and dystopian modes require for their political efficacy an 'implied connection' with the real: the whole point of utopia or dystopia is to acquire some positive or negative leverage on the present. By contrast, other kinds of SF and fantasy are free to enjoy greater latitude in their relations to the real. The willed transformation and the technological transformation are therefore the more characteristically utopian or dystopian modes, because transformation – how the world might be changed, whether for better or worse – will normally be more important to utopia than otherness per se. SF can and does deploy all four modes, but in each case drawing on '"science", in its variable definitions' (Williams, 1980c, 196–99). SF may be utopian or dystopian, and utopias and dystopias may be science-fictional, but the genres are analytically distinguishable, nonetheless, by virtue of the presence or absence of science (and technology). This issue is carefully avoided by Suvin's treatment of science as equivalent to cognition (Suvin, 1979, 13), but remains central for Williams. And rightly so, for this is what most clearly distinguishes the SF selective tradition, not only from the 'older and now residual modes' such as the Earthly Paradise, the Blessed Islands and the Land of Cockayne, but also from non-SF utopias (Williams, 1980c, 198).

For Williams, the question of periodisation pertains less to the relation between utopia and SF than to that between utopia and dystopia. He traces the utopian tradition from More and Bacon through to Bulwer-Lytton, Bellamy, Morris and Wells, but sees it as running aground in the early twentieth century, effectively superseded by dystopia. In these chronologically subsequent dystopias, paradigmatically, Zamyatin, Huxley and Orwell, utopia 'lies at the far end of dystopia, but only a few will enter it; the few who get out from under'. Hence, Williams's conclusion that utopia and SF tend eventually to travel the path followed by 'bourgeois cultural theory' more generally, from 'universal liberation', through a phase when the 'minority' educates and regenerates the 'majority', to the 'last sour period', when 'minority culture' searches out and finds a hiding-place 'beyond both the system and the fight against the system' (Williams, 1980c, 207). This pessimism is offset, however, by his more general insistence that SF 'is always potentially a mode of authentic shift: a crisis of exposure which produces a crisis of possibility; a reworking, in imagination, of *all* forms and conditions' (Williams, 1980c, 209); and by a rereading of Bellamy and Morris which leads him, in turn, to a distinctly positive appreciation of Le Guin.

Borrowing Miguel Abensour's distinction between 'systematic' and 'heuristic' utopias, that is, those focused respectively on alternative organisational models and on alternative values (Abensour, 1973), Williams attempts to cast new light on the old controversy between Bellamy and

Morris. If Bellamy's *Looking Backward* had been an essentially systematic utopia, Williams observes, *News from Nowhere* was a 'generous but sentimental heuristic transformation'. What is properly 'emergent' in Morris, however, and what makes it the better novel, he continues, is 'the crucial insertion of the transition to utopia' as something 'fought for' (Williams, 1980c, 202–4). At this point, Morris's heuristic becomes distinctly unsentimental. Much the same occurs in Wells, moreover, so that the mid-century dystopias need to be situated in relation to these earlier willed transformations to utopia. Orwell's 1984 is neither more nor less plausible than Morris's 2003, Williams argues, but the fictional revolution of 1952 in *News from Nowhere* is more plausible than either 'because its energy flows both ways, forward and back'. This kind of openness, when the 'subjunctive is a true subjunctive, rather than a displaced indicative', calls into question 'the now dominant mode of dystopia', he concludes (Williams, 1980c, 208). Moreover, Williams detects a parallel openness in Le Guin's *The Dispossessed*. Her anarcho-feminist Anarres is a getaway, rather than a transformation, he observes, but 'an open utopia', nonetheless, 'shifted, deliberately, from its achieved harmonious condition', thereby 'depriving utopia of its classical end of struggle, its image of perpetual harmony and rest'. In its very realism, this openness represents a strengthening of the utopian impulse, he continues, which 'now warily, self-questioningly, and setting its own limits, renews itself' (Williams, 1980c, 211–12).

No doubt, Williams was right to detect a comparative shift from utopia to dystopia in the SF of the early decades of the twentieth century; a temporary renaissance of utopian writing in the aftermath of the sixties; and a certain reflexivity in the latter's utopian aspirations. But all this needs to be carefully qualified. As Matthew Beaumont reminds us, late nineteenth-century England produced its own substantial stock of dystopian fictions, or 'cacotopias', as he terms them, borrowing from Bentham (Beaumont, 2005, 129–68; Bentham, 1843, 493). And there are, in fact, mid twentieth-century utopias, not only Skinner, Teilhard de Chardin and the Huxley of *Island*, but also, to Orwell's intense irritation, Wells's *The Shape of Things to Come*. The seventies utopias, Le Guin, of course, but also Delany, Russ and Piercy, coexisted with contemporaneous dystopias and were both preceded by and, we now know, subsequently succeeded by yet more utopias, such as Banks's *Consider Phlebas* in Scotland and Robert Sabatier's *Le Sourire aux lèvres* (*The Smile on the Lips*) in France, and yet more dystopias, for example Atwood's in Canada and Houellebecq's in France. As to the comparative realism of Le Guin's own ambiguous utopia, this we may certainly concede, but to do so leads us directly into the conceptual minefield opened up by Moylan's coinage of the analytical term 'critical utopia'.

For Moylan, the new utopias of the 1970s were critical in the double sense of Enlightenment critique and the 'critical mass' required to produce an explosion (Moylan, 1986, 10). These texts were distinctive, he argued, insofar as they rejected utopia 'as a blueprint', whilst nonetheless preserving it 'as a dream'. They therefore focused both on the conflict between utopia and their 'originary world' and on 'the continuing presence of difference and imperfection' within utopia itself. The result was a more plausible, because recognisable and dynamic, set of alternative possibilities (Moylan, 1986, 10–11). Moylan's examples include Ernest Callenbach's *Ecotopia*, Sally Gearhardt's *The Wanderground*, Suzy McKee Charnas's *Motherlines* and Dorothy Bryant's *The Kin of Ata Are Waiting for You*, but the primary focus is, nonetheless, on Russ's *The Female Man*, Le Guin's *The Dispossessed*, Piercy's *Woman on the Edge of Time* and Delany's *Triton* (Moylan, 1986, 41). These last have, of course, become something like a canon for American SF studies. All four authors were American, in the sense of citizens of the United States, as distinct from Canadians like Atwood or Latin Americans like José B. Adolph, Daína Chaviano or Hugo Correa; and all four novels caught the utopian mood of the sixties, as refracted through the memory of the seventies. 'In resisting the flattening out of utopian writing in modern society,' Moylan writes, 'the critical utopia has destroyed, preserved, and transformed that writing and marks the first important output of utopian discourse since the 1890s' (Moylan, 1986, 43).

Both Moylan's particular judgement on Le Guin and the general rationale that sustains it run interestingly parallel to Williams. It is worth noting, however, that Wells's utopias are nothing like so 'uncritical' as Moylan's coinage or Williams's argument might suggest. The opening to the first chapter of *A Modern Utopia*, written in 1905 rather than either the 1890s or the 1970s, can actually be read as an anticipation of Moylan's case. 'The Utopia of a modern dreamer must needs differ' from earlier 'Nowheres', Wells wrote: 'Those were all perfect and static States ... the modern Utopia must be ... kinetic, must shape not as a permanent state but as a a hopeful stage leading to a long ascent of stages' (Wells, 2005a, 11). The difference, he was clear, dated from Darwin's formulation of the theory of evolution, rather than from the 'new social movements' of the 1960s, as it would for Moylan, but it is couched in strikingly similar terms nonetheless. An analogous argument can also be mounted for *The Shape of Things to Come*, which registered both the sheer difficulty of achieving utopia and, once achieved, the presence of difference and imperfection therein. Indeed, Atwood goes so far as to argue that 'scratch the surface a little, and ... you see ... within each utopia, a concealed dystopia; within each dystopia, a hidden utopia' (Atwood, 2011b, 85). I doubt this is strictly true and, even if it is, utopias can nonetheless be more or less critical, just as Moylan observes. But Atwood is certainly right to resist, at least by implication, Moylan's sense of criticality as a peculiar prerogative of American New Wave SF. Rather, these options are formally available and actually deployed, albeit discontinuously, throughout the history of the genre.

3. Science Fiction and Fantasy

Suvin's and Jameson's exclusion of fantasy from SF derives loosely from Brecht's insistence on the interrelation of estrangement and cognition in the *Short Organum for the Theatre*. There, Brecht argued for the *Verfremdungseffekt*, or *V-Effekt*, 'designed to free socially-conditioned phenomena from the stamp of familiarity which protects them against our grasp today'. The purpose of his theatre is thus knowledge through estrangement akin to Galileo's 'detached eye' (Brecht, 1974, 192). For Suvin, who is himself a distinguished Brecht scholar, the necessary and sufficient conditions for SF become, similarly, 'the presence and interaction of estrangement and cognition' (Suvin, 1979, 7–8). There is clear prescriptive intent, here, to exclude myth, folktale and fantasy (Suvin, 1979, 7–9, 20). Indeed, this insistence on the cognitive functions of SF is accompanied by a profound aversion to fantasy as a 'proto-Fascist revulsion against modern civilization, materialist rationalism ... organized around an ideology unchecked by any cognition, ... its narrative logic ... simply overt ideology plus Freudian erotic patterns' (Suvin, 1979, 69). To market SF alongside fantasy, as commercial bookshops do, is thus a 'rampantly socio-pathological phenomenon' (Suvin, 1979, 9). This exclusion of fantasy is perhaps less controversial than the inclusion of utopia, insofar as it echoes a long tradition amongst SF writers, editors and readers, reaching back to Gernsback and Campbell and, before them, to Wells, Verne and Shelley. And, once again, Jameson echoes Suvin, for example when he warns that SF will add to, whilst fantasy only detracts from, utopia's epistemological gravity (Jameson, 2005, 57). Like Suvin, Jameson registers the commercial pressures toward genre-blending between SF and fantasy and, like Suvin, he sees fantasy as 'technically reactionary' (Jameson, 2005, 60). The 'invocation of magic by modern fantasy', he concludes, 'is condemned by its form to retrace the history of magic's decay and fall, its disappearance from ... the disenchanted world of prose, of capitalism and modern times' (Jameson, 2005, 71). The implication seems clear that only Tolkienesque reactionaries would dabble in such stuff.

Yet, the empirical convergence between SF and fantasy seems, nonetheless, to be a fact of contemporary cultural life. The World Science Fiction Society, which for decades made its annual Hugo Awards on near-Suvinian criteria, broke new ground when it awarded its 2001 prize for the best novel to J. K. Rowling's *Harry Potter and the Goblet of Fire*, that for the best dramatic presentation to Ang Lee's film *Wo hu cang long* (*Crouching Tiger, Hidden Dragon*). The following year the latter award went to Peter Jackson for *The Fellowship of the Ring*, the first in his *Lord of the Rings* trilogy. In 2003, it was divided into two separate classes, a long-form version, which went to Jackson once again, this time for *The Two Towers*, and a short-form version, which went to a 2002 episode of *Buffy the Vampire Slayer*, 'Conversations with Dead People'. In 2004, Jackson swept the board, taking both the long-form prize for *The Return of the King* and the short-form prize for Gollum's Acceptance Speech at the 2004 MTV Movie Awards. SF 'proper' held up better in subsequent years, apart from 2007, when Guillermo del Toro won the best dramatic presentation long-form prize for *El laberinto del fauno* ('The Faun's Labyrinth', English title *Pan's Labyrinth*); 2008, when Michael Vaughn won it for *Stardust*; and 2010, when Miéville won the prize for best novel for *The City and the City*. There was no significant sentiment, however, at any of the relevant World Science Fiction Conventions, that these fantasy awards represented some kind of category mistake.

Nor did the journal *Science Fiction Studies*, which Suvin co-founded and to which Jameson has been a longstanding contributor, baulk at including, in its 2003 special issue on the British SF Boom, extensive discussion of Miéville's work (Gordon, 2003a, 2003b). Miéville's *Perdido Street Station* had, after all, won the 2001 Arthur C. Clarke Award for the best SF novel published in the UK. He would pick up a second Clarke Award, in 2005, for *Iron Council* and would be lauded, in no less a place than *Foundation*, the journal of the British Science Fiction Foundation, and by no less a figure than Freedman himself, as 'the most talented, intelligent, and interesting writer to have emerged in Anglophone speculative fiction since the 1960s and 1970s' (Freedman, 2006, 108). Interestingly, Miéville had been short-listed for the Hugo Award for Best Novel for *Perdido Street Station* in 2002, *The Scar* in 2003 and *Iron Council* in 2005, before finally going on to win in 2010. It would, of course, be difficult to argue that either Miéville or del Toro are Tolkienesque reactionaries: the first is a key figure in contemporary critical legal theory, a recent co-editor of the neo-Marxist theoretical journal *Historical Materialism*, and an active member of the British Socialist Workers Party, his novels as redolent with Marxism as with magic; and the second directed two quite explicitly anti-fascist Spanish Civil War films – *El laberinto del fauno* is, in some respects, a sequel to *El espinazo del Diablo*

(*The Devil's Backbone*). Miéville also famously described Tolkien as 'the wen on the arse of fantasy literature'. My point is, not that Suvin and Jameson are 'objectively' mistaken in their definitions of SF, but rather that those definitions are best understood as interventions into the selective tradition, which one will accept only to the extent one shares their purpose. And, to judge by the Hugo Awards and *Science Fiction Studies*, theirs seems to have been an increasingly unsuccessful intervention.

The counter-argument, as prosecuted by both Bould and Miéville, is that SF is better considered 'a subset of a broader fantastic mode' (Miéville, 2002, 43), a neat enough near-reversal of Suvin's original attempt to englobe utopia within SF. For Miéville, the near-universalisation of commodity fetishism means that 'real' life under capitalism 'is a fantasy' and conventional 'realism' therefore merely the realistic depiction of 'an absurdity which is true' (Miéville, 2002, 41–42). Acknowledging the difference between the 'not-yet-possible' estrangement effects in SF and the 'never-possible' effects in fantasy, he nonetheless insists that

> if the predicates for a fantasy are clearly never-possible *but are treated systematically and coherently within the fantastic work*, then its cognition effect is precisely that normally associated with sf. This is why the pseudo-science of so much sf is not merely a charming affectation, but radically undermines the notion that sf deals in a fundamentally different kind of 'impossible' than fantasy. (Miéville, 2002, 45)

Hence, his eventual conclusion that 'we need fantasy to think the world, and to change it' (Miéville, 2002, 48).

At one level, Miéville does little more than recapitulate Clarke's famous third law, that 'any sufficiently advanced technology is indistinguishable from magic' and its obverse, commonly attributed to Larry Niven, that 'any sufficiently rigorously defined magic is indistinguishable from science' (Clarke, 1974, 39n). More recently, however, Miéville has restated the argument more forcefully, insisting that Suvinian and post-Suvinian valorisations of science as cognition are 'ideological' in the pejorative sense. 'To the extent that SF claims to be based on "science",' he writes, 'and … on what is deemed "rationality", it is based on capitalist modernity's ideologically projected self-justification: not some abstract/ideal "science", but capitalist science's bullshit about itself' (Miéville, 2009b, 240). The 'scientific *pretensions*' of SF, so effectively endorsed by both Suvin and Jameson, are thus critiqued by Miéville as themselves little more than ideological fantasy (Miéville, 2009b, 241). Fantasy proper, by contrast, can provide a way into thinking alterity that escapes the logics of capitalist rationality. This is still not an argument for fantasy as against SF, but it most certainly is an argument for fantasy in addition to and alongside it. Hence, his conclusion that '*Red Planets* we have. We should not neglect red dragons' (Miéville, 2009b, 245).

This inclusivity seems to me the real strength of Miéville's position. But, like Suvin's, Miéville's argument is intended as an intervention into the global SF field designed to affect the shape of the SF tradition. My own position is less concerned with shaping the selective tradition than with analysing and explaining it. And, for these purposes, I find it helpful to draw on Williams's sense of SF, utopia and fantasy (and the earthly paradise, the land of cockayne, etc.) as distinct but cognate forms. One way to represent their relationship might be through one of John Venn's 'Venn diagrams', that is as a diagram, usually in the form of a set of overlapping circles, showing all the logically possible relations between a finite collection of 'sets', where a set means merely a certain class of object. So, in Figure 4 below, each of the three circles represents a different non-realistic genre, respectively utopia, SF and fantasy. The overlap between the circles marks the four logically possible hybrid forms, utopian fantasy (A),

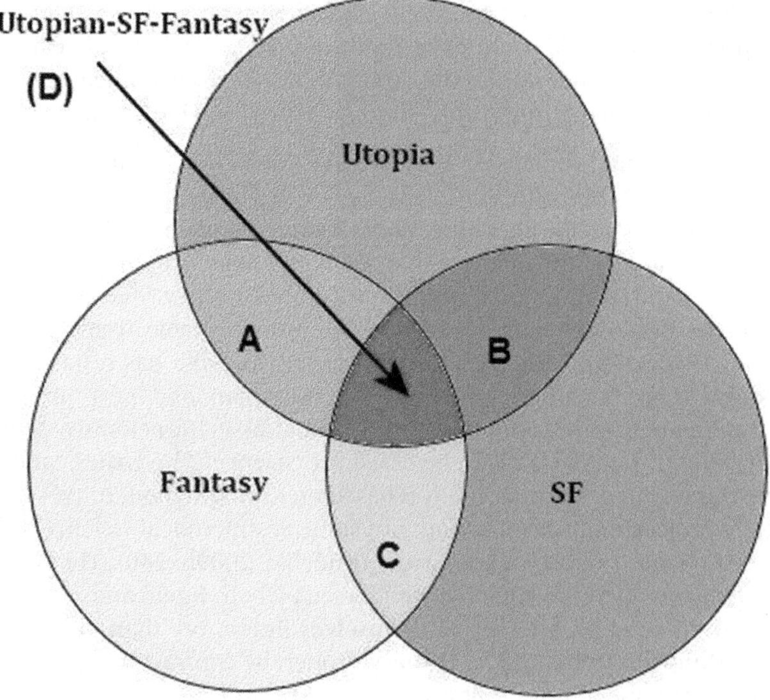

Figure 4: The relation between SF, utopia and fantasy represented as a Venn diagram.

utopian SF (B), SF-fantasy (C) and utopian SF-fantasy (D). Empirical examples of the first would include Morris's *News from Nowhere*, of the second Banks's Culture novels, the third Miéville's New Crobuzon trilogy, the fourth Piercy's *Woman on the Edge of Time*. The areas of non-overlap, by contrast, represent non-hybrid forms of utopia, SF and fantasy, examples of which could include, respectively, More's *Utopia*, Verne's *De la terre à la lune* and Tolkien's *The Lord of the Rings*. The significant point here is that More and Tolkien fall outside both the SF field and the SF selective tradition, whilst Banks, Miéville, Piercy and Verne do not.

This diagram contains only three sets and is therefore relatively simple in design. Were we to incorporate into it further non-realistic genres, such as the Gothic, then the situation would be more complex, but would still be representable by a diagram like that designed by Venn for four sets, as shown in Figure 5 below. In principle, one can design diagrams for five, six or more sets, although, beyond a certain point, their analytical value declines in direct proportion to their complexity. Because Venn was interested in logical rather than empirical relations, his diagrams are normally

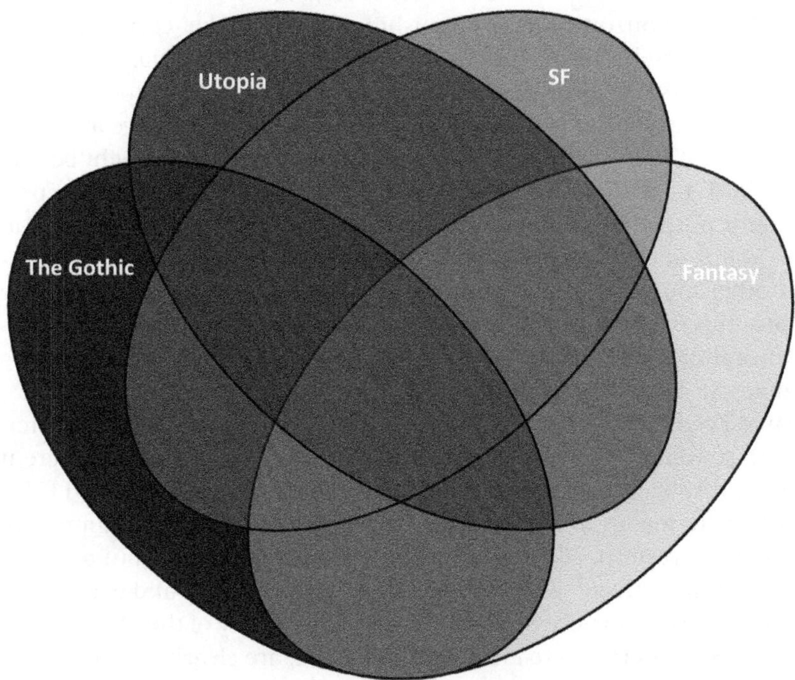

Figure 5: Venn's diagram for four sets applied to the science fiction field.

designed as symmetrical. If we were to relax this condition, however, then, for contemporary fiction at least, the fantasy circle would almost certainly be much larger than the SF circle, the utopian significantly smaller. The unmodified diagrams serve my purpose, nonetheless, as a continuing reminder of a whole range of non-realist genres, distinguishable from but cognate with each other, which exist in more or less 'pure' or 'hybrid' variants. None of this is intended to have any prescriptive value, rather its functions are wholly descriptive and analytical.

This said, we might still ask why Miéville's weird fiction – or, for that matter, Lewis's Ransom trilogy – appear more readily assimilable to SF than, say, Rowling's Harry Potter stories. The beginnings of an answer lie in Miéville's insistence that, under certain conditions, the cognition effects of fantasy can be exactly those normally associated with SF. The conditions he then specifies, as we've seen, are systematicity and coherence, but it isn't at all obvious that magic in Tolkien is any the less systematic or coherent than thaumaturgy in Miéville. The difference lies, rather, in the comparative realism with which the latter is deployed. In Miéville's Bas-Lag, thaumaturgy is used by humans and non-humans alike in a fashion very much akin to that of a scientific technology, as, for example, in its use by the New Crobuzon courts as punishment to 'Remake' criminal bodies in ways perversely 'fit' to their crimes. Moreover, the social forces that converge on its use also operate in ways recognisably akin to the structures of our own social world. Indeed, insofar as there is science at play in Miéville, then it is clearly social science. Something similar might be said of del Toro. In both cases, absolutely realistic and unsentimental representations of the dynamics of repression, oppression and exploitation, in New Crobuzon and Fascist Spain respectively, coexist with and counterpoint other more genuinely fantastic elements. At the risk of stating the obvious, this is *Magischer Realismus*, in Franz Roh's phrase. Miéville, Lewis (in Thulcandra, if not in Narnia) and del Toro each, then, provide telling examples SF-fantasy hybridity.

David Seed argues that SF in general is of a similarly hybrid character, so much so that it is better understood as a 'mode or field where different genres and subgenres intersect' than as a distinct genre (Seed, 2011, 1). This seems to me an overstatement. There are indeed many examples of SF-fantasy (-western, -detective, -thriller, etc.) hybrid texts, but as many again of comparatively 'pure' SF, whether 'hard' or 'soft'; and each of the hybrid instances also necessarily attests to the hybridity of the other genres involved. SF writers and readers, Seed included, are clearly able to recognise sets of conventions specific to their genre, even as they also enjoy the experience of subverting them. Seed himself offers no formal definition of genre, which might perhaps be forgiven in a work of only 130 very small pages, but it is clear, nonetheless, that he knows SF when he sees it. To write, as he does, that it 'has become an increasingly hybrid entity' (Seed, 2011, 123) is tacitly to concede some sense of what non-hybrid SF would be. The term 'genre' is, no doubt, problematic in SF studies, especially given its widespread use as the antonym of 'literary', where 'genre SF' means Smith and 'literary SF' Lessing. Distinctions of this kind are unhelpful, as I argued in chapter 1, and again in chapter 2, since all art, no matter how canonical, is ultimately communicable only by way of generic conventions. Genre is thus not the dirty secret of popular culture, but rather an important part of the truth of all art. And, as we concluded in chapter 2, it is not primarily a matter of retrospective academic classification, conducted with prescriptive intent, as Suvin, Jameson and Freedman believe, but rather a prospectively productive set of techniques and devices for the creative use of readers and writers.

4. Utopianism in Popular Science Fiction

If the Suvinian argument assimilates utopia and SF to each other, it does so in distinctly 'literary' a fashion, that is, by representing both genres primarily through canonical or quasi-canonical texts. It therefore tends to occlude the history, not only of popular SF and fantasy, but also of popular utopianism. The record suggests, however, the presence of a considerable body of popular utopian imaginings, fantastic, science-fictional and hybrid, within the SF selective tradition. I want to conclude this chapter, then, with a brief examination of two telling examples of popular utopianism in twentieth-century American SF, respectively 'Golden Age' pulp magazines and the *Star Trek* film and television franchise. Neither of these warrants much attention in Suvinian and post-Suvinian theory, which tends to treat popular SF with much the same disdain the Frankfurt School directed at mass culture more generally. Nonetheless, both are clearly redolent with utopian and quasi-utopian thematics.

The most influential of the American pulp fiction magazines were indisputably Gernsback's *Amazing Stories* and Campbell's *Astounding Science-Fiction*. Martin Schäfer's judgement on *Astounding* that 'utopia scarcely exists' in its pages after 1945 (Schäfer, 1977, 157) is telling, but should nonetheless not be taken as definitive. Campbell did, after all, publish the original versions of Asimov's Robot and Foundation stories, both of which were informed by a kind of technological utopianism. More importantly, *Amazing Stories* and Gernsback's other related titles had previously provided an important platform for utopian writing. Gernsback himself cited two great utopians, Wells and Bellamy, as inspirations for *Amazing* in its opening editorial (Gernsback, 1926, 3) and work by Wells appeared in each of the first twenty-nine issues (Bleiler, 1998, 546). Indeed, Davin goes so far as to argue that a distinct 'tradition of socialist and feminist utopias ... appeared in the pulps – and nowhere else – between 1920 and 1950' (Davin, 2006, 235). Some of Gernsback's key personnel were certainly involved in quasi-utopian radical politics: both David Lasser and Charles D. Hornig, who in turn managed the *Wonder* magazines, were Socialist Party activists (Bleiler, 1998, 242; Davin, 2006, 136).

In retrospect, it is clear that pulp utopianism was significantly stronger in the 1920s than in the 1930s, but there are nonetheless interesting examples from the latter decade. In 1931, Otfrid von Hanstein, writing in *Wonder Stories*, set a group of scientists to work on 'Utopia Island', secure in the conviction that it was 'destined to become the heart and brain of the entire world' (Hanstein, 1931, 1355). In 1934, *Amazing Stories Quarterly* republished a 1929 story by Harl Vincent, which told of how in 2229 Philip Barton, inventor and friend of the working man, successfully overthrows the corrupt plutocracy ruling America (Vincent, 1934, 6–27). In 1939, *Amazing* published Erwin K. Sloat's 'When Time Stood Still', the heroine of which proclaims that

> some day, all of the human race will live like this – when men finally begin to master their greed and educate their minds to use intelligently the marvelous advances science has already made, instead of thinking only to put new inventions and discoveries to use as a method of amassing money, or killing all the people you can in the next country. (Sloat, 1939, 81)

As late as 1941, *Amazing* published Eando Binder's 'Adam Link Faces a Revolt', which has its robot Adam decide to build a '*practical* Utopia' of 'science and machines', where robots and humans can live together harmoniously, even if its Eve predicts the project will end in disaster (Binder, 1941, 70–71). She is proven right, but Adam nonetheless insists that 'Utopia is a dream toward which men must work – but never achieve. Perhaps it is best so – as a shining, glorious goal that guides like a light and never goes out' (Binder, 1941, 93).

Bleiler's exhaustive analysis of early pulp SF led him to conclude that pulp utopianism took two main forms, which he termed 'technological perfectibilism' and 'social messianism', the first being generally very much more in evidence (Bleiler, 1998, xiii). But he is also clear that the genre encouraged writing critical of 'purely technological' means, so much so that the single most common categories of story motif were, in fact, 'things-go-wrong' and 'conflict' (Bleiler, 1998, xvii). Ross has also demonstrated that pulp technophilia was persistently tempered by an advocacy of 'critical technocracy', which often echoed the wider preoccupations of the progressive social movements of the 1920s and 30s (Ross, 1991, 131). Bloch's dismissive attitude towards the technological bias of American SF is thus not entirely borne out by the evidence. Indeed, there are interesting internal tensions between these two poles within Futurianism, which was, of course, by far the most utopian formation within the broader context of American pulp SF. Non-technocratic utopian consciousness is very clearly enunciated in Michel's slogan, 'Awake! The future is upon us!', which almost reads as an invocation of Bloch's own notion of 'nonsynchronous synchronicity', of the not-yet in the now (Bloch, 1977, 22–38); Asimov's utopianism, by contrast, was technocratic in exactly the sense decried by Bloch.

This is true of each of Asimov's two most famous nova, the positronic robot and psychohistory. The *I, Robot* stories depict a wholly benevolent version of the robot, constrained and motivated only by the famous three laws designed to guarantee human well-being. In the guise of a human, the positronic robot, Stephen Byerley, is eventually elected World Co-ordinator, in what is presumably a passing nod to Wells's World State. Thus entrusted to a hidden robot administration, conventionally human political questions, such as the 'ownership of the means of production', become simply 'obsolescent' (Asimov, 1950, 51). The *Foundation Trilogy* also eliminates contingency and choice from humanity's future, by subordinating it to psychohistory, that is, the 'branch of mathematics which deals with the reactions of human conglomerates to fixed social and economic stimuli' (Asimov, 1982, 14). Psychohistory is both the creation of a scientist–protagonist, Hari Seldon, Professor of Mathematics at the University of Trantor, and the collective property of a community of scientists, the First and Second Foundations. Asimov's is thus a thoroughly Baconian utopia, equating *scientia* and *potestas* in exactly the fashion of *New Atlantis*. And the goal of Seldon's Foundation is much the same as Salomon's: 'the knowledge of Causes, and secret motions of things; and the enlarging of the bounds of Human Empire, to the effecting of all things possible' (Bacon, 2002, 480).

Schäfer is right, nonetheless, to suggest that, in general, Campbell's writers tended to shy away from explicit utopianism. As Huntington observes, the 'technician manager', celebrated in *Astounding*, was a 'superior everyman whose virtues derive from his harmonious adjustment to the needs of science and technology' (Huntington, 1989, 69), rather than a visionary seeking to adjust science and technology to human needs.

Moreover, there is also a clear dystopian turn in American pulp SF after Hiroshima, nicely summarised in A. Bertram Chandler's story 'New Wings', when one of his Martian descendents of refugees from nuclear war on Earth declares: 'We've got a great future behind us!' (Chandler, 1948, 73). Ross refuses to take this apparent anti-utopianism at its face value, however, and argues that there is a subterranean strand of utopianism even here. The 'standard imperialistic components of pulp SF', he writes, 'might also be seen as utopian versions of the desire to escape the new Taylorist tyranny of organized and quantified time and space that had come to preside over the contemporary workplace' (Ross, 1991, 127). Ross has a point, no doubt, but this utopian anti-utopianism falls far short of the more explicit utopianisms in both Gernsback's *Amazing* and New York Futurianism.

The dystopian turn in 1950s pulp SF runs interestingly parallel to that in literary SF, which Williams unkindly dubbed 'Putropia' (Williams, 2010, 15–16). And, just as the 1970s produced the kind of literary 'critical utopias' celebrated by Moylan, Suvin and Jameson, so too they witnessed the popular utopianism of *Star Trek.* Gene Roddenberry's original television series ran from 1966 to 1969, *Star Trek: The Next Generation* from 1987 to 1994, *Star Trek: Deep Space Nine* from 1993 to 1999, *Star Trek: Voyager* from 1995 to 2001 and *Star Trek: Enterprise* from 2001 to 2005. The programme won Hugo Awards for Best Dramatic Presentation in 1967, 1968, 1993 and 1995 and is, after the BBC's *Doctor Who,* the second longest running SF show in the history of television. There have also been a series of eleven film spin-offs, the most recent directed by J. J. Abrams in 2009. In short, *Star Trek* has occupied a central location in late twentieth and early twenty-first-century popular culture. Jan Johnson-Smith concludes that American television SF is 'neither utopian nor dystopian', but rather 'enforces a critique of the Western mythos whilst renegotiating its finer aspects' (Johnson-Smith, 2005, 253). There is some truth in this, especially if we take Western as referring to the Western as a genre, as she intends, rather than to the culture of 'the West'. But it nevertheless seems a radically misconceived judgement on *Star Trek.* For the world of *Star Trek* – the United Federation of Planets, Starfleet, even the *USS Enterprise* itself – is precisely a utopia and, moreover, one of a very specifically American kind. The programme is set mainly in the twenty-third and twenty-fourth centuries, in a time when technological innovation has effectively solved the practical problems that confound humanity. People travel the galaxy in starships, their food and drink supplied by replicators, their fantasies enacted out and fulfilled in holodecks. Their collective social life appears similarly unproblematic: on Earth, poverty, inequality and social conflict have been eliminated, so that both genders, all races and (in the later versions) various sexualities are equal; and, in the wider universe, humanity lives at peace with neighbouring alien species in the Federation.

Commentary on the show's foundational ideology tends to situate *Star Trek* in relation to the legacy of 1960s American liberalism. So its quasi-utopian optimism about both technological and social progress can be seen as reminiscent of the official enthusiasm for both the space race and social reform under the Democratic administrations of Presidents Kennedy and Johnson. Early accounts tended to stress the positive significance of both the optimism and the liberalism. The original series featured the first 'interracial' kiss, between Kirk and Uhuru, to appear on American television. Its non-American officers included the half-alien Spock, the Russian Chekov and the Asian Sulu, as well as the African Uhuru. But the limitations were also apparent: there were more humans than aliens on the bridge of the *Enterprise*, more Americans than non-Americans, more whites than blacks, more men than women; and, although Uhuru might have been a black woman officer, she actually did very little except answer the interplanetary phone. Later versions included more non-Americans (a French captain, Picard, in *The Next Generation*), more non-whites (a black station commander, Sisko, in *Deep Space Nine*) and more women (a female captain, Janeway, in *Voyager*). But Starfleet and the United Federation of Planets remained almost as subordinate to white American men as the real-world international organisations of the late twentieth and early twenty-first centuries.

Such limitations prompted critics to question the precise extent of *Star Trek*'s liberalism: Worland stressed its cold war militarism, Blair and Cranny-Francis its sexism, Bernardi its racism (Worland, 1988; Blair, 1983; Cranny-Francis, 1985; Bernardi, 1997). But these criticisms could easily be levelled at Kennedy liberalism itself. Indeed, it might well be argued that the programme replicated the strengths and weaknesses of its home culture with some precision. Moreover, it responded, more or less creatively, to such criticism and to the increasingly postmodern character of American culture. So later commentators would see *The Next Generation* as seriously questioning existing gender stereotypes (Roberts, 1999) or even as placing 'the project of humanity ... centre-stage' (Barrett and Barrett, 2001, 204). *Star Trek*'s initial success and those of the National Aeronautics and Space Administration (NASA) space programme were roughly contemporaneous. NASA's funding had been dramatically increased in 1961, when Kennedy approved the Apollo mission to send astronauts to the moon within ten years. As the decade proceeded, the Agency's status was enhanced by the show, and the show's by the Agency.

Eventually, what began as temporal overlap evolved into institutional symbiosis, so that the first NASA space shuttle was named after the *Enterprise* and the fourth *Star Trek* movie dedicated to the astronauts killed in the shuttle *Challenger*. Penley goes so far as to argue that the Agency and the television show merged symbolically to 'form a powerful cultural icon, ... "NASA/TREK"', which 'shapes our popular and institutional imaginings about space' (Penley, 1997, 16).

The Paramount Network's decision in 2005 to cancel *Star Trek: Enterprise*, the first such cancellation since that of Roddenberry's original by NBC in 1969, might seem to threaten the link between NASA and TREK, given that there are, at present, no plans for any further television series. But the commercial and critical success of the 2009 film, the most profitable *Star Trek* movie to date, nominated for four Academy Awards, one of which it won, the first ever for the franchise, suggests the possibility that NASA/TREK might merely be relocated from small to large screen. The film's leading actors were signed for two further sequels, the first of which went into production at the beginning of 2012, with a release date scheduled for mid 2013. NASA itself suffered from declining budgets during the 1990s and, by 2011, when the space shuttle was finally retired, retained no extant manned space programmes. Nonetheless, neither Republican nor Democrat administrations seem likely to withdraw support from this aspect of NASA's work. The second President Bush formally committed himself to a return to the Moon by 2018, President Obama to a manned Mars mission by the mid 2030s (Bush, 2004; Obama, 2010). Something similar to *Star Trek* seems a very likely accompaniment to any such missions. This is so, I suspect, in part because it represents a distinctively American kind of utopia, that is, the military utopia.

Bellamy's *Looking Backward*, the most influential of all American socialist utopias, famously envisioned the United States in 2000 as a society organised around an 'industrial army', in which all citizens serve for 24 years, 'beginning at the close of the course of education at twenty-one and terminating at forty-five' (Bellamy, 2003, 81). Dr Leete, Julian West's guide to the social structure of utopia, explains that

> The people were already accustomed to the idea that the obligation of every citizen, not physically disabled, to contribute his military services to the defense of the nation was equal and absolute. That it was equally the duty of every citizen to contribute his quota of industrial or intellectual services to the maintenance of the nation was equally evident, though it was not until the nation became the employer of labor that citizens were able to render this sort of service

> with any pretense either of universality or equity. (Bellamy, 2003, 80)

The idea of an industrial army is easily caricatured as Stalinist, but Leete's own account actually appeals to the logic of military service already applied in the United States, just as its language, the use of the word 'muster', for example, reflects the common practice of American militias. The point to note here is that, unlike most European or Australasian utopian socialists, Bellamy found nothing implausible about the existing national army as a model for his ideal future society. This is unsurprising, when we recall that he came from the staunchly Unionist state of Massachusetts, as does his Julian West, and would have only just turned fifteen when General Grant accepted Lee's surrender at Appomattox Court House. For Bellamy, as for most Massachusites of his day, the United States Army would have seemed an almost wholly admirable institution.

This kind of military utopianism persists throughout the history of American SF, up to and including Roddenberry's *Star Trek*. It forms part of a wider and distinctly American cultural configuration that valorises the national military, politically and ethically, over and against all other uses of federal government power and authority. An obviously important instance is Heinlein's *Starship Troopers*, which is clearly a utopia, no matter how little it might appeal to those of liberal or social-democratic political persuasions. So Heinlein's Major Reid, Johnnie Rico's instructor in History and Moral Philosophy (H & MP) at Officer Candidates School, explains and justifies the Terran Federation's constitution, much as Dr Leete had explained and justified that of Bellamy's United States. Like Bellamy's, Heinlein's utopia is organised around the ideal of military service. Here, however, there is a real war to fight, against the arachnoid 'Bugs'; here, however, military service is optional; and here, too, only those who have served in the military are entitled to full citizenship. As Reid explains to Rico's H & MP class, the franchise is 'limited to discharged veterans' because only they have 'demonstrated through voluntary and difficult service' that they place 'the welfare of the group ahead of personal advantage' (Heinlein, 1959, 215, 217–18).

This same cultural configuration prompts the repeated elevation of successful American military leaders to the status of national hero and thence often – Washington, Jackson, Taylor, Grant, Hayes, Harrison, Garfield, the first Roosevelt, Eisenhower – to the Presidency. There is no equivalent in any other liberal democratic polity, neither in Continental Europe nor in the Commonwealth. This is not to suggest that Americans necessarily misrecognise their military. Quite the contrary, there is evidence to suggest that, unlike Continental and Commonwealth militaries, which have habitually been prone to fascism at worst, traditionalist conservatism at best, the United States armed forces are indeed a relatively progressive force within the wider society. Their collective historical memory does, after all, include both wintering at Valley Forge and marching through Georgia from Atlanta to the sea. Starfleet is thus not only a utopia, but also a characteristically American utopia, a means to project back to the Great Republic its own ideal self-image. It seems unlikely to be out of business for very long.

6
Science Fiction and Dystopia

In the previous chapter, we explored the relations between SF, utopia and fantasy, concluding that all three occupy positions within the contemporary global SF field and therefore contribute to the SF selective tradition. Twenty years ago, both fan critics and academics alike would have found the inclusion of fantasy much more problematic than that of utopia. Today, however, the central site of contention, albeit not to the point of exclusion, is almost certainly provided by dystopia.

1. The Antipathy to Dystopia

The obverse of the enthusiasm for utopia traced in chapter 5 is, in Williams, Freedman, Suvin and Jameson, something quite close to a distaste for dystopia. All four are obliged to concede, at least in passing, the obvious formal symmetries beween utopia, in the sense of eutopia, and dystopia that prompted Sargent to insist they comprise a single utopian genre. But all four are either hostile or indifferent to the most influential examples of dystopian SF. For Williams, as we've seen, SF dystopias were 'Putropias', predicated upon an elitist structure of feeling that counterposed 'the isolated intellectual' to the 'at best brutish, at worst brutal' masses (Williams, 2010, 15–16). For Suvin, 'SF will be the more significant and truly relevant the more clearly it eschews ... the ... fashionable static dystopia of the Huxley–Orwell model' (Suvin, 1979, 83). Elsewhere, he argues that such static dystopias are necessarily unable to do justice to 'the immense possibilities of modern SF in an age polarized between the law of large numbers and ethical choice' (Suvin, 1988, 106–7). Himself the author of a monograph on Orwell (Freedman, 1988), Freedman acknowledges that 'negative utopia' was 'the most significant version' in the first half of the twentieth century, but cheerfully, albeit mistakenly, proclaims that thereafter the positive utopia 'largely regains its traditional priority' (Freedman, 2000, 82–83).

The antipathy is at its most extreme in Jameson, whose anti-anti-utopianism seems to require him to counterpose 'anti-Utopia' to 'Utopia', rather than dystopia to utopia. He argues that there are two main kinds of loosely 'dystopian' text: the 'critical dystopia', which functions by way of a warning, through Heinlein's 'if this goes on' principle (Heinlein, 1940); and the anti-Utopia proper, which springs from the quite different conviction that human nature is so inherently corrupt that it can never be salvaged by any 'heightened consciousness of the impending dangers' (Jameson, 2005, 198). Jameson borrows the term 'critical dystopia' from Moylan, who in turn borrowed it from Sargent, and, like them, argues that it is essentially utopian in intent and import and thus a kind of 'negative cousin' of utopia (Jameson, 2005, 198). We shall return to critical dystopias below. For the moment, however, note that Jameson is primarily preoccupied with the second variant, the anti-utopia, which he sees as the true antonym of utopia, the textual equivalent to anti-utopianism in politics (Jameson, 2005, 199). He cites a number of examples of 'classic Cold War dystopia', from 'horror films to respectable literary and philosophical achievements', but argues that the key instance, which established several of the form's 'symptomatic and paradoxical features', was Orwell's *Nineteen Eighty-Four* (Jameson, 2005, 200).

Jameson's analysis of *Nineteen Eighty-Four* proceeds by distinguishing three levels at work in Orwell: an 'articulation of the history of Stalinism', which the novelist had 'observed and experienced empirically'; a supposed 'historical universalization' of this experience into a vision of human nature as 'an insatiable and lucid hunger for power'; and the conversion of this 'conjuncture' into 'a life-passion'. That passion, Jameson insists, has 'become the face of anti-Utopianism in our own time' (Jameson 2005, 200). Comparing Orwell's 'Cold War public' to that for eighteenth-century 'gothic nightmares of imprisonment and ... evil monks or nuns', Jameson concludes that these two 'dystopian awakenings' can each be considered 'collective responses of the bourgeoisie', the first 'in its struggle against feudal absolutism', the second in 'reaction to the possibility of a workers' state' (Jameson, 2005, 201). Orwell's anti-Stalinism is thus essentially 'bourgeois' in character and prompted by hostility to the idea of a workers' state. It may best be understood, Jameson continues, as 'a dispirited reaction to postwar Labor Britain' or 'a depressive symptom of revolutionary discouragement' (Jameson, 2005, 202). Later still, he extrapolates from Orwell to the generalising conclusion that 'a systemic perspective for which it is obvious that whatever threatens the system as such must be excluded' is 'the basic premise of all modern anti-Utopias from Dostoyevsky to Orwell' (Jameson, 2005, 205).

The objection is immediate: surely, Jameson can't mean *all* modern anti-Utopias? Zamyatin's *Mi*? Čapek's *R.U.R.*? Huxley's *Brave New World*? He ignores Čapek altogether. He argues that in Zamyatin 'it is not the personal and the political that are confused but rather aesthetics and bureaucracy'; and that, if the novel is an anti-utopia, it is one 'in which the Utopian impulse is still at work, with whatever ambivalence'. And he argues that in Huxley we find 'an aristocratic critique of the media and mass culture, rather than of any Orwellian "totalitarianism"' (Jameson, 2005, 202). It follows, then, that neither is a thoroughgoing anti-utopia in Jameson's sense. The obvious danger is that the category of the anti-utopian text becomes virtually coextensive with *Nineteen Eighty-Four*. At one point Jameson asks: 'Can we separate anti-Utopianism in Orwell from anti-communism?' (Jameson, 2005, 201). We might equally ask whether we can separate anti-anti-utopianism in Jameson from anti-anti-communism. The answer seems to be no, which is regrettable if only because, as Jameson himself notes, 'the history of the communist adventure is not co-terminous with the history of socialism as such' (Jameson, 2005, 21). And Orwell's place in the latter history deserves far greater respect than Jameson accords it.

It might be excusable to argue so dismissively if Orwell's politics were merely personal or found no expression in the novel, but neither is true. Orwell belonged to an important and continuing tradition of anti-Stalinist leftism and those politics clearly do inform the text of *Nineteen Eighty-Four*. The problem arises essentially because Jameson treats both the politics and the novel as products of the Cold War 1950s, an oddly perverse move in a theorist renowned for the injunction to 'Always historicize!' (Jameson, 1981, 9). *Nineteen Eighty-Four* was published in June 1949 and its author was already dead by the end of January 1950, which means that both author and text were necessarily products of the two decades that preceded the Cold War, but not of the Cold War itself. Jameson's misreading of Orwell and *Nineteen Eighty-Four* is no minor matter, but rather the central point of weakness in his *Archaeologies*. Clearly, *Nineteen Eighty-Four* is not a dispirited reaction to post-war Labour Britain: the very suggestion – Clement Attlee as Big Brother – would be risible were it not seriously entertained in the United States. Hence, Orwell's own explanation to the American United Auto Workers Union, written six months before his death, that the novel was 'NOT intended as an attack on Socialism or on the British Labour Party (of which I am a supporter)', but as an exposé of 'perversions' which had been 'partly realised in Communism and Fascism' (Orwell, 1970j, 564). The reference to Fascism is important because Orwell's Ingsoc was never meant to signify British Labourism, but rather

National Socialism. To read the novel as a symptom of revolutionary discouragement might remain plausible, especially given the Spanish Fascist victory in 1939, which went unreversed in 1945. But Orwell had shown little sign of discouragement in 1943 when, already at work on *Animal Farm*, he wrote thus of his experiences in Spain: 'the common man will win his fight sooner or later, but I want it to be sooner ... That was the real issue of the Spanish war, and of the last war, and perhaps of other wars yet to come (Orwell, 1966, 245). There is no universalised pessimism here, rather the very opposite, a belief that, no matter how dire the current circumstances, the working-class cause will eventually triumph.

All of this suggests the possibility that *Mi, R.U.R.*, *Brave New World* and even *Nineteen Eighty-Four* might actually be, *pace* Jameson and Suvin, closer to examples of critical dystopia than anti-utopia. This does not mean, however, that there are no anti-utopias, only that these are much less common than Jameson and Suvin fear. Obvious examples of anti-utopian fiction include the many anti-Bellamies prompted by *Looking Backward*, such as Richard C. Michaelis's *Looking Further Forward* (1890), Arthur Dudley Vinton's *Looking Further Backward* (1890), W. W. Satterlee's *Looking Backward and What I Saw* (1890) and J. W. Roberts's *Looking Within: The Misleading Tendencies of 'Looking Backward' Made Manifest* (1893). Morris's *News from Nowhere* was also an anti-Bellamy, self-consciously designed to refute Bellamy's utopia. But it nonetheless proceeded to invest the anti-utopia with a radically utopian content and, unlike the other anti-Bellamies, it also worked as an aesthetic experience, that is, as art, as fiction. The difference is the reason Morris is still read today, while Michaelis, Vinton, Satterlee and Roberts are remembered only by bibliographers: because simple anti-utopias are generally too boringly polemical to command an audience outside the immediate occasion of their polemic. In literature, as in life, it is difficult to desire dystopia consciously, not impossible certainly, but difficult nonetheless. Which is why the most effective anti-utopias are normally not dystopian fictions at all, but straightforwardly panglossian affirmations that we already live in the best of all possible worlds.

At this point, we need to say a little more about the notion of critical dystopia. Sargent coined the term to describe the socially critical dystopian American SF of the early 1990s, especially Piercy's 1991 novel *He, She and It* (Sargent, 1994, 9). It was picked up by Baccolini in her reading of feminist dystopias and applied retrospectively to Murray Constantine's (a pseudonym of Katharine Burdekin) 1937 *Swastika Night* and Atwood's *The Handmaid's Tale* (Baccolini, 2000). Moylan then gave it extensive theoretical elaboration in his account of 'the dystopian turn' in SF (Moylan, 2000,

183–99). Critical dystopias, he explained, 'burrow within the dystopian tradition', but they do so only 'in order to bring utopian and dystopian tendencies to bear on their exposé of the present moment'. They are thus 'stubbornly' utopian, in the sense that they do not move easily toward their own better worlds: 'Rather, they linger in the terrors of the present even as they exemplify what is needed to transform it' (Moylan, 2000, 198–99). Unlike Baccolini, Moylan insisted that this was an essentially 'recent development', a 'distinctive new intervention', specific to the late 1980s and early 1990s. So neither *Swastika Night* nor *The Handmaid's Tale,* still less *Nineteen Eighty-Four,* could count as such (Moylan, 2000, 188). The supposed novelty of the critical dystopia absolves Jameson from serious examination of earlier socially critical dystopias, but Moylan was too well informed to make the same mistake. He knew that Zamyatin's *Mi* takes a '*utopian* stance', that Orwell wanted *Nineteen Eighty-Four* to be 'a utopian attack on what he saw as anti-utopian historical tendencies' and that the 'outside' of Atwood's Gilead provides the novel with 'a utopian horizon' (Moylan, 2000, 160, 162–63). So, where Jameson works with a simple binary between 'anti-Utopia' and 'critical dystopia', mistakenly consigning Orwell to the former, Moylan carefully distinguishes the 'classic dystopia' and 'critical dystopia', on the one hand, both of which are socially critical, and the 'anti-utopia', 'pseudo-dystopia' and 'anti-critical dystopia', on the other, none of which are (Moylan, 2000, 195). Suvin has recently posited the slightly different distinction between the 'simple dystopia', which need have no relation to utopia, the anti-utopia, understood in much the same fashion as Sargent, and the 'fallible dystopia', concerned to demonstrate that 'no dystopian reality is nightmarishly perfect, and that its seams may be picked apart' (Suvin, 2010b, 395). Both taxonomies make better sense than Jameson's oversimplified misappropriation of the early Moylan, even though Suvin still treats *Mi* and *Nineteen Eighty-Four* as anti-utopias (Suvin, 2010b, 385), but for both this is only achieved at the price of theoretical over-elaboration.

For Baccolini and Moylan, the crucial difference between classic and critical dystopias runs thus:

> dystopias maintain utopian hope *outside* their pages ... for it is only if we consider dystopia as a warning that ... readers can hope to escape its pessimistic future ... the new critical dystopias allow both readers and protagonists to hope by resisting closure: the ambiguous, open endings of these novels maintain the utopian impulse *within* the work. (Baccolini and Moylan, 2003, 7)

Formally, this distinction might well be worth making; substantively, it is much less helpful since, as I will seek to demonstrate below, utopian impulses are clearly present within the texts of *Mi*, *Nineteen Eighty-Four* and *The Handmaid's Tale*. Determination to contextualise critical dystopia in relation to a specific historical moment, that of the triumph of Anglo-American neo-liberalism in the 1980s and 1990s, thus leads Moylan in particular, but to some extent Baccolini also, into an unnecessarily elaborate taxonomy. Suvin's revised taxonomy is similarly dependent on the supposed specificities of an immediately contemporary, albeit more loosely defined, politico-social configuration. So he writes that the fallible dystopia, which is more or less what Moylan means by the critical dystopia, is 'a new sub-genre of the US 1960s–1970s ... arising out of ... the shock of Post-Fordism and its imaginative mastering' (Suvin, 2010b, 394–95). For Suvin, as for Moylan, the novelty is both formal and historical. But if many of the earlier dystopias had in fact contained expressly utopian content, then this distinction also fails, both formally and historically. The original typology, distinguishing between dystopia and anti-utopia, might well be sufficient, so long as not misused after Jameson's fashion.

Baccolini and Moylan are nonetheless right that utopianism resides within dystopia primarily in its function as warning. But Suvin and Jameson – and Williams too – somehow contrive to miss this fairly obvious point. In his first essay on SF, Williams acknowledged that dystopian fictions were often defended as cautionary tales. But 'they are less warnings about the future', he retorted, 'than about the adequacy of certain types of contemporary feeling'. 'I believe, for my own part,' he continues, 'that to think, feel, or even speak of people in terms of "masses" is to make the burning of the books and the destroying of the cities just that much more possible' (Williams, 2010, 17). In truth, it isn't at all clear why this should be so: whatever sins of omission or commission are normally counted against Leavis's *Mass Civilization and Minority Culture* (1930), Hiroshima and Nagasaki are rarely amongst them. More to the point, it is even less clear why the examples Williams gives from Orwell, Huxley and Bradbury should not be read as cautionary tales, nor why Wyndham's fiction can't be read as a warning against the 'presumption' of science, in Shelley's phrase, even if there is little likelihood that the Triffids will ever have their day or the Kraken ever wake.

2. The Strange Case of *Nineteen Eighty-Four*

Orwell's *Nineteen Eighty-Four* is the most famous of English-language dystopias and, as we've seen, it excites considerable antipathy in Suvin, Jameson, Freedman and, to some extent, also Williams. An important part of the problem resides in the question of how exactly the novel ends. We all think we know how it goes: 'But it was all right, everything was all right, the struggle was finished. He had won the victory over himself. He loved Big Brother.' Reminding us exactly where we have arrived at, the novel then reads, in most subsequent editions as in the first, 'THE END' (Orwell, 1989, 311; 1949, 298). Little wonder, then, that Williams should have read it as 'desperate because ... on such a construction the exile could not win, and ... there was no hope at all', and its author, therefore, as 'a man committed to decency who actualized a distinctive squalor' (Williams, 1963, 283, 277). It was a judgement he would amend, but never revise. So the last of his many readings continues to deplore 'the terrifying irrationalism of the climax of *Nineteen Eighty-Four*' (Williams, 1991, 124).

Jameson shares a similarly longstanding animus towards both novel and author, evident for example when he writes that 'the force of the text ... springs from a conviction about human nature itself, whose corruptions and lust for power are inevitable, and not to be remedied by new social measures or programs, nor by heightened consciousness of impending dangers' (Jameson, 2005, 198). Both Williams and Jameson clearly grasp the central political dilemma of dystopian fiction, that, if its serious purpose is in its warning, then the more grimly inexorable the fictive world becomes, so the less effective will it be as a call to resistance. As Adams's Vogons were inclined to repeat: 'Resistance is useless!' (Adams, 1979, 57). Or as Engels had it: 'Freedom is the recognition of necessity'.[7] In short, there is no point in resisting the inevitable. Hence, Williams's judgement that 'in the very absoluteness of the fiction', it becomes 'an imaginative submission to ... inevitability' (Williams, 1991, 125–26) and Jameson's that *Nineteen Eighty-Four* is not so much a critical dystopia as an 'anti-Utopia ... informed by a central passion to denounce and to warn against Utopian programs in the political realm' (Jameson, 2005, 198–99).

There is no doubting that Orwell's later writings had express political purposes, but these are nonetheless not as Jameson has them. 'Every line of serious work that I have written since 1936', Orwell insisted in 1946, 'has been written, directly or indirectly, *against* totalitarianism and *for* democratic Socialism' (Orwell, 1970i, 28). Jameson sidesteps the question of Orwell's peculiar politics, a combination of anti-fascism, neo-Trotskyism and libertarian socialism, by dismissing all reference to the '"if this goes

7 In truth, Engels wrote 'die Einsicht in die Notwendigkeit' (Engels, 1962, 106), which is more accurately translated by Burns as 'the insight into necessity' (Engels, 1987, 105). But 'recognition' remains the best-known English translation and better suits my (apparently illegitimate) purposes here.

on" principle' in *Nineteen Eighty-Four* as 'mere biographical affirmation' (Jameson, 2005, 198). But when Orwell invited his American trade-union readers to read the novel in precisely these terms, he surely provided a gloss, not simply to his own beliefs, but also to the text's intended political effects. 'I do not believe that the kind of society I describe necessarily *will* arrive,' he explained to the United Auto Workers, 'but ... that ... it *could* arrive ... totalitarianism, *if not fought against,* could triumph' (Orwell, 1970j, 564). *Nineteen Eighty-Four* was written, at least in part, as exactly that inspiration to political resistance Williams and Jameson insist it cannot be. Their judgement is sustained, moreover, by a surprising lack of interest in the novel's more formally literary properties. Williams writes as if it were written wholly within the conventions of literary realism, which it most definitely is not: witness the lengthy extracts from Goldstein's *Theory and Practice of Oligarchical Collectivism* (Orwell, 1989, 191–208, 209, 210–26). Worse still, Jameson virtually reduces it to its American reception as the paradigmatic Cold War dystopia, uncritically repeating the dominant American reading of both author and text as 'at one with contemporary ... anti-socialisms' (Jameson, 2005, 200, 199). More importantly for my purposes, however, neither seems to register the simple fact that the novel doesn't end at 'THE END', but continues, in my edition for over fourteen more pages, in the first for over thirteen (Orwell, 1989, 312–26; 1949, 299–312).

Nineteen Eighty-Four actually ends at the conclusion to the 'Appendix' on Newspeak, with 'It was chiefly in order to allow time for the preliminary work of translation that the final adoption of Newspeak had been fixed for so late a date as 2050' (Orwell, 1989, 326; 1949, 312). In content, these lines add little, but their form is redolent with meaning. For as Atwood observes of the whole 'Appendix', it

> is written in standard English, in the third person, and in the past tense, which can only mean that the regime has fallen, and that language and individuality have survived. For whoever has written the essay on Newspeak, the world of *1984* is over. (Atwood, 2005, 337)

Thomas Pynchon makes much the same point in his 'Foreword' to the Centennial Edition of the novel (Pynchon, 2003, xxiv). They are surely right: the 'Appendix' is internal to the novel, neither an author's nor a scholarly editor's account of how the fiction works, but rather a part of the fiction, a fictional commentary on fictional events. And, although Atwood fails to notice this, it is anticipated within the main body of the text, by a footnote in the first chapter, which assures us, again in standard English, in the third person, in the past tense, that 'Newspeak was the official language of Oceania' (Orwell, 1989, 5n; 1949, 7n). Atwood uses a similar device in *The Handmaid's Tale*, the first of her three dystopian SF novels, which concludes with an extract from the proceedings of a 'Symposium on Gileadean Studies', written in some utopian future set long after the collapse of the Republic of Gilead (Atwood, 1987, 311–24). Moreover, she readily admits that *Nineteen Eighty-Four* provided her with a 'direct model' for this (Atwood, 2005, 337). If she is to be believed, then both Orwell's 'Appendix' and her 'Historical Notes' work as framing devices, by which to blunt the force of dystopian inevitability.

3. Science Fiction as a Generic Context

There are good reasons to take Atwood and Pynchon seriously, not least their own SF. But it might be more productive to pursue not so much the matter of their critical credentials as that of Orwell's own intellectual context. Let us begin by noting how SF, or at least something very close to it, provided him with a generic context and related set of intertexts. Orthodox literary criticism tends to resist such identification between Orwell and SF, on the grounds that he is a 'great writer', not some second-rate Trekkie. In 1943, however, when he began work on what was still entitled *The Last Man in Europe*, he hadn't known he was a great writer: none of his books had sold particularly well nor received much in the way of critical acclaim. But he had known about SF, not the term perhaps, still rarely used outside the United States, but certainly 'that kind of book', as he had written to Struve of Zamyatin's *Mi* (Orwell, 1970d, 118). The authors of that kind of book included, for Orwell, not only Zamyatin, but also Wells, Huxley and Čapek. Add in Shelley and Verne and one would have something close to a canon of European, as distinct from American, SF writing. Canons aside, however, we might still ask what exactly Orwell's interests were in this European tradition of utopian and dystopian future fictions.

Zamyatin is by common consent one of the most important figures in early twentieth-century Russian SF. Suvin describes him as, alongside Čapek, 'the most significant world SF writer between the World Wars' (Suvin, 1979, 280), but he was certainly not appreciated as such in Orwell's England. *Mi* had been written in Russia and in Russian during 1920–21, but wasn't published in the original language until 1952, and then only in the United States: first publication in Russia came as late as 1988. It had become available in English, however, in an American, but not British, translation, as *We*, in 1924, and in French translation, as *Nous autres*, in 1929 (Zamiatin, 1952; Zamiatine, 1929). Unable to obtain the American translation, then still unavailable in England, Orwell had, as we've seen, acquired a copy of *Nous autres*, which he then strongly recommended to *Tribune*'s readers. If Zamyatin was effectively unknown in England, Wells, by contrast, was clearly the leading English SF writer of the day, although, like Orwell, he remained unfamiliar with the term: as with Verne in English translation, Wells's novels were marketed as 'scientific romance' (James, 1994, 9). His utopian fictions included *A Modern Utopia*, *The Dream*, *Men Like Gods* and *The Shape of Things to Come* (Wells, 2005a; Wells, 1923; Wells, 1924; Wells, 1993). This last, which predicted and argued for the creation of a technocratic 'World State', became the best-known English literary utopia of the 1930s. The 1936 film version, *Things to Come*, directed by Cameron Menzies with a screenplay co-authored by Wells, occupied an equally prominent position in British SF cinema. As we noted in chapter 2, in his youth Orwell had admired Wells, but would later come to see the latter's work as increasingly irrelevant to the twentieth century, less adequate as prophecy than even London's *The Iron Heel* (Orwell, 1970a, 172). And, as we also noted, Orwell was especially antipathetic to Wells's utopianism.

For Orwell, Huxley clearly represented a more formidable figure than the later Wells. Orwell made a point of insisting that *Brave New World* had been 'plagiarized' from Zamyatin's *Mi*, a calumny later redirected at *Nineteen Eighty-Four* itself (Orwell, 1970e, 96; 1970h, 547). Unlike Orwell, always essentially a literary outsider, Huxley came from one of the leading intellectual families in England, descended on his father's side from T. H. Huxley and on his mother's from Matthew Arnold. When *Brave New World* was published in 1932, its author was already a well-established writer, with *Crome Yellow*, *Point Counter Point* and *Do What You Will* to his credit (Huxley, 1921; 1928; 1929). He had been a friend of D. H. Lawrence, whose letters he was then editing for publication, and of writers like Virginia Woolf and Forster (Huxley, 1932). Orwell, by contrast, was out of work, impoverished and staying with his elder sister in Leeds, where he borrowed Huxley's novel from the local public library (Crick, 1980, 137). Orwell would in retrospect treat Huxley, along with Joyce, Eliot and Lawrence, as part of 'the movement' of the 'middle and late twenties' (Orwell, 1970k, 554). And, despite mixed initial responses – the book was much more successful in Britain, where it sold 13,000 copies in 1932 and 10,000 in 1933, than in the United States (Bedford, 1973, 251) – *Brave New World* had indeed become one of the intellectual landmarks in what we might now think of as the long twenties.

Orwell is at his most enthusiastic about Huxley in *The Road to Wigan Pier*, where he denounces Wells (Orwell, 1962, 169–72, 177–78), citing *Brave*

New World with approval for its caricature of Wellsian utopianism as a 'paradise of little fat men' (Orwell, 1962, 169). Huxley had indeed intended the novel to expose the horrors of Wellsian utopia, but in writing *Brave New World*, he acquired a series of other targets – American capitalism and Soviet Communism; state planning and eugenics; sexual, pharmacological and mass-media-induced hedonism; Keynesian economics and Lawrentian primitivism – many of which he would elsewhere explore more positively. Part of the novel's peculiar character, at once both strength and weakness, is its capacity to represent sympathetically many different sides of many different questions, but this was hardly an Orwellian virtue. By 1940, Orwell would dismiss Huxley's dystopia as having no bearing on the actual future; the following year, he judged its failure reminiscent of Wells (Orwell, 1970l, 33; 1970m, 46; 1970a, 172).

Orwell's primary objection to *Brave New World* was directed at its anti-political pessimism. So he found Huxley guilty of a 'refusal to believe that human society can be fundamentally improved. Man is non-perfectible, merely political changes can effect nothing, progress is an illusion.' 'The connection between this belief and political reaction', he continued, 'is ... obvious. Other worldliness is the best alibi a rich man can have' (Orwell, 1970c, 82). Here, the argument is specifically directed at Huxley's pacifism, rather than at his dystopian novel, but in the review of *Nous autres* for *Tribune*, where the charge of plagiarism was first aired, Orwell was explicit that what distinguished Huxley from Zamyatin was precisely the latter's 'political point'. The irony should be obvious: these were exactly the charges – that he plagiarised Zamyatin; that he was pessimistic about the possibilities for political change; that there was no practicable political point to his argument – which would be directed at *Nineteen Eighty-Four* by later leftist critics.

But Orwell continues:

> In Huxley's book ... no clear reason is given why society should be stratified in the elaborate way ... described. The aim is not economic exploitation, but the desire to bully and dominate does not seem to be a motive either. There is no power hunger, no sadism, no hardness of any kind. (Orwell, 1970e, 97)

By contrast:

> It is [the] ... intuitive grasp of the irrational side of totalitarianism – human sacrifice, cruelty as an end in itself, the worship of a Leader ... – that makes Zamyatin's book superior to Huxley's. (Orwell, 1970e, 98)

The political point of Orwell's own dystopia was already becoming apparent. It would need to be so unremittingly horrible as to expose the sheer ghastliness of totalitarianism, but would therefore need something external to itself to inspire belief in the possibility of resistance. Which is why 'THE END' could not actually be the end.

Čapek interested Orwell less than Wells, Zamyatin or Huxley. Presumably this is so, in part, because *R.U.R.* is unconcerned with the issue of totalitarianism. Orwell seems to have been unfamiliar with Čapek's 1937 SF play, *Bílá nemoc* (*The White Plague*), which addressed the question very directly and was very promptly translated into English under the title *Power and Glory* (Čapek, 1937b, 1938). The Čapek brothers, Karel and Josef, were nonetheless amongst the best-known figures in inter-war Czech literary life. Moreover, *R.U.R. Rossum's Universal Robots*, the title of which is given in English even in the Czech original, had proven an extraordinary international success. Orwell could not have attended the 1923 London production, since he was serving in Burma at the time, but might well have noticed the reviews. He seems not to have owned a television set, so nor is he likely to have seen the BBC's 1938 adaptation, although, at the time, he was living in Wallington, Hertfordshire, and might conceivably have known someone with access to a set. He could certainly not have seen the BBC's 1948 version, since, by then, he was already in a sanatorium near Glasgow, where the facilities would not have extended to television. And, in any case, the first draft of *Nineteen Eighty-Four* was already completed.

Nonetheless, Orwell certainly knew of the play and seemed familiar with its themes. In *The Road to Wigan Pier*, he cites Čapek approvingly as a critic of mechanical progress for its own sake. '[T]he unfortunate thing', Orwell writes,

> is that Socialism, as usually presented, is bound up with the idea of mechanical progress … as an end in itself, almost as a kind of religion … Karel Capek hits it off well enough in the horrible ending of *R.U.R.*, when the Robots, having slaughtered the last human being, announce their intention to 'build many houses' (just for the sake of building houses, you see). (Orwell, 1962, 165–66)

This is interesting for two reasons, because it directly addresses our own question of horrible endings, and because the (slight mis-) quotation suggests direct familiarity with the play, at least in book form. For this is indeed what their leader, Radius, demands of the robots, production for production's sake:

> Roboti budou mnoho stavět. Budou stavět nové domy pro nové Roboty.

> [The Robots will build much. They will build new houses for new Robots.]
> (Čapek, 1966, 85; 1961, 89)

The sentiment is repeated in the Epilogue:

> 2. ROBOT/ Pane, měj slitování. Padá na nás hrůza. Všechno napravíme, co jsme učinili.
> 3. ROBOT/ Znásobili jsme práci. Není už kam dát, co jsme vyrobili.
> (Čapek, 1966, 89)

In Paul Selver's British English translation these two different speeches are compounded and elaborated into a single speech by Radius expressing the same sentiment:

> Sir, have pity. Terror is coming upon us. We have intensified our labour. We have obtained a million million tons of coal from the earth. Nine million spindles are running by day and night. There is no more room to store what we have made. Houses are being built throughout the world. (Čapek, 1961, 93)

But, as we shall see, Orwell was mistaken to describe the play as ending thus.

4. Three Intertexts

We have traced Orwell's responses to Wellsian utopia and to the dystopias of Zamyatin, Huxley and Čapek. The problem of ending remains to be examined, however, at least for the dystopias, since here the formal issues confronting utopian and dystopian writers become very different. Let us elaborate a little. We noted in the previous chapter that utopian novels and films necessarily work in different registers from utopian political philosophy proper, insofar as they must work as art or entertainment and are therefore implicated in the conventions of literary and cinematic naturalism. The worse worlds of dystopian fiction are similarly implicated, but here the relevant political purpose is the warning, rather than the inspiration. As Huxley observed of *Brave New World*: 'This ... was the message of the book – *This is possible: for heaven's sake be careful*' (Bedford, 1973, 245). Unlike utopias, dystopias are rarely charged with either boredom or dryness, since their stock in trade of human beastliness remains captivating to our conventional postlapsarian sensibilities. The problem remains, however, of how to represent a naturalistically plausible danger sufficiently terrible to be threatening, but insufficiently so as to be demoralising. Hence, what we might term the problem of ending in dystopia. How, then, is it resolved in Orwell's three dystopian intertexts?

Zamyatin's *Mi/Nous autres* has much in common with *Nineteen Eighty-Four*, but is far more directly a critique of scientific positivism than of totalitarianism per se. So its 'Единое Государство'/'l'Etat Unique'[8] (the Sole State or the One State) is ruled by mathematics and science as much as by the dictatorial 'Благодетель'/'Bienfaiteur' (Benefactor). Like all its members, the novel's central protagonist, 'Д-503'/'D-503', the builder of the 'ИНТЕГРАЛА'/'*Intégral*' space probe, is merely one of many 'нумера'/'numéros'; like all these numbers, his daily routine is ordered with arithmetical precision by the 'Часовая Скрижаль'/'Tables des Heures' (Table of Hours); and each of the novel's chapters is famously represented as a laboratory 'Запись'/'Note' (Record or Entry) (Zamyatin, 1967, 5–6, 12; Zamiatine, 1929, 7–8, 16). D-503 is seduced into the cause of rebellion, both sexually and politically, by I-330. At one level, she provides the model for Orwell's Julia, a sexually proactive woman whose affections serve to promote the male protagonist's resistance to the state, but whom he will therefore eventually be forced to betray. D-503's final Record, reporting his subjection to the Benefactor's lobotomy-like 'Великая Операция'/'Grande Opération' to eliminate the imagination, and his subsequent impassive witness to I-330's torture under 'Колокол'/'la Cloche' (the Bell), is thus a moment of simultaneous defeat and betrayal, a model for the moment in *Nineteen Eighty-Four* when 'I sold you and you sold me' (Zamyatin, 1967, 199–200; Zamiatine, 1929, 233–34; Orwell, 1989, 307).

There are obvious differences, however. Where Orwell's tripartite structure of rival totalitarianisms, Oceania, Eurasia and Eastasia, is a self-sealing, fully enclosed system of domination, Zamyatin's Sole State remains encircled by the wild country outside 'Зеленая Стена'/'le Mur Vert' (the Green Wall) and threatened from within and without by the 'МЕФИ'/'Méphi' underground. Moreover, I-330 is a much stronger character than Julia, not only a leader in the Mephi, but also the novel's chief intellectual antagonist to official positivism. Her insistence that there can be no final number, and therefore no final revolution, radically undermines D-503's faith in the mathematical foundations of the social order (Zamyatin, 1967, 149; Zamiatine, 1929, 179). If there is some homology between the destruction of Julia and Winston in *Nineteen Eighty-Four* and that of I-330 and D-503 in *Mi/Nous autres*, there is, nonetheless, no equivalent to the latter's illicit

8 I have cited both the original Russian text and the French translation, the first because it is indeed the original, the second because it was the first published version in Europe and, hence, the only version that Orwell and (arguably) Huxley could have read.

child by O-90, who will be born and brought up beyond the Green Wall. If the Benefactor still rules the Sole State at Zamyatin's conclusion, his rule has been challenged more effectively in the course of the narrative by the unsuccessful Mephi revolution, than is Big Brother's by either the illusory promise of the Brotherhood or Winston's vague hope in the proles.

The contrast between the two novels is perhaps at its keenest in their respective accounts of the mathematics of totalitarianism. For where Orwell's O'Brien can make Winston see five fingers, I-330's insistence that there is no final number will haunt D-503 through to this novel's 'КОНЕЦ'/ 'La Fin' (The End) in Record 39:

> Слушайте, – дергал я соседа. – Да слушайте же, говорю вам! Вы должны – вы должны мне ответить: а там, где кончается ваша конечная Вселенная? Что там – дальше?
> Ecoutez, je vous dis! Répondez-moi: de l'autre côte de la limite de votre univers fini, qu'y a-t-il?
> [Listen ... Just listen to me! ... you must give me an answer: out there, where your finite universe ends! What is out there, beyond it?] (Zamyatin, 1967, 198; Zamiatine, 1927, 232; Zamyatin, 1972, 202)

This isn't quite the end, of course, since Record 40 is still to come. But even there, in the novel's closing paragraphs, Zamyatin reminds us that the Green Wall has been successfully breached from the outside, that the Sole State is actually already in retreat:

> Откладывать нельзя – потому что в западных кварталах – все еще хаос, рев, трупы, звери и – к сожалению – значительное количество нумеров, изменивших разуму. Но на поперечном, 40-м проспекте удалось сконструировать временную Стену из высоковольтных волн.
> On ne peut différer l'exécution car il y a encore, à l'ouest, des régions où règnent le chaos et les bêtes sauvages et qui, malheureusement, renferment une grande quantité de numéros ayant trahi la raison. Nous avons cependant réussi à établir, dans la 40° avenue, un mur provisoire d'ondes à haute tension.
> [This cannot be postponed, because in the western parts ... there is still chaos, roaring, corpses, beasts, and – unfortunately – a considerable group of numbers who have betrayed Reason. However, on the Fortieth cross-town avenue, we have succeeded in erecting a temporary barrier of high-voltage waves.] (Zamyatin, 1967, 200; Zamiatine, 1927, 234; Zamyatin, 1972, 204)

The particular defeats of D-503 and I-330 are thus contextualised and mitigated against by the overarching promise of infinite revolution. As Suvin comments. 'the protagonist's defeat is of the day but not necessarily of the epoch. The defeat in the novel ... is not the defeat of the novel itself, but an exasperated shocking of the reader into thought and action' (Suvin, 1979, 259).

Like *Nous autres, Brave New World* is set in the twenty-sixth century and, like *Nous autres,* its target is an affluent, technologically sophisticated dystopia. But where Zamyatin's Sole State anticipated Oceanian sexual puritanism, Huxley explored the dystopian potential of the mass commodification of sexual, pharmacological and mass-media pleasures. As Orwell observed, it was directed at 'the hedonistic principle', at a world 'turned into a Riviera hotel' and was thus a 'brilliant caricature' of the 'present of 1930', that is, the 1920s. From a twenty-first century vantage point, we might want to add the present of 1960, 1970, 1980, 1990, 2000 and perhaps even 2010, but for Orwell, writing in 1940, it seemed to cast 'no light on the future' (Orwell, 1970m, 46). Like *Nous autres, Brave New World* famously ends with a death, but a media-saturated suicide rather than a political execution:

> 'Mr Savage!'
>
> Slowly, very slowly, like two unhurried compass needles, the feet turned towards the right; north, north-east, east, south-east, south, south-south-west; then paused, and after a few seconds, turned as unhurriedly back towards the left. South-south-west, south, south-east, east, ... (Huxley, 1955a, 237)

If John, the Savage, were the novel's hero and his resistance to the pseudo-Wellsian World State heroic, then this ending would be tragic. But it is closer to bathetic comedy, for he is clearly neither hero nor protagonist: he doesn't actually appear until chapter 7, his rebellion is comically excessive, his public self-flagellation in the closing chapter is near-ludicrous, and the Savage Reservation that nurtured him is as drug-obsessed and socially conformist as the civilisation he pits it against. If the novel had a central protagonist, it would probably be the intelligent but self-important and self-pitying Bernard Marx, but he is too obviously yet another butt for the novel's humour to be its hero.[9] And this, surely, is the point. *Brave New*

9 Donald Watt's careful examination of the novel's manuscript revisions shows that 'Huxley at first thought of Bernard as the novel's hero, then switched to John as more fitting for the hero's role, and finally decided that Helmholtz, if anyone, should be the book's only authentically uplifting character' (Watt, 1966, 80).

World is above all a comic novel, a scattershot satire of Huxley's contemporary intellectual landscape, from Hollywood hedonism to Pavlovian psychology, Freudianism to Fordism, both in the sense used in the novel and that of more recent sociology and economics. As Huxley explained in a letter to his father, it is 'a comic, or at least satirical, novel about the Future' (Huxley, 1969, 351). In this respect, it remains very different from our other three dystopias. The first act of *R.U.R.* is comic and, indeed, vaguely reminiscent of Shaw, but thereafter the dominant register becomes closer to Chekhov or Ibsen; there are comic moments in *Mi/Nous autres*, as for example when D-503 imagines I-330 as one of the Valkyries (Zamyatin, 1967, 171; Zamiatine, 1929, 204), but these are comparatively few; and there is virtually no comedy to speak of in *Nineteen Eighty-Four*.

The one character exempt from such satire in *Brave New World* is Mustapha Mond, the World Controller for Western Europe. Significantly, it is only in the debate with him, in chapters 16 and 17, that the Savage becomes a truly serious figure. This is the philosophical core of the novel, where Mond speaks for Enlightenment *civilisation* and the utilitarian felicific calculus, the Savage for Romantic *Kultur*, but also for primitivist barbarism. The first of these chapters ends with Bernard and Helmholtz's banishment to an island reserved for those 'too self-consciously individual to fit into community-life' (Huxley, 1955a, 178). This is handled with explicit comic effect for Bernard, less so for Helmholtz, but in neither case is there much suggestion that the outcome is especially intolerable. The World State inspires satirical amusement rather than terrified dread. The second ends with the interestingly ambivalent philosophical conclusion to the entire novel. 'What you need', the Savage argues, 'is something *with* tears for a change. Nothing costs enough here.' 'We prefer to do things comfortably', Mond retorts a little later. 'But I don't want comfort', the Savage replies,

> 'I want God, I want poetry, I want real danger, I want freedom, I want goodness. I want sin.'
>
> 'In fact,' said Mustapha Mond, 'you're claiming the right to be unhappy.'
>
> 'Not to mention the right to grow old and ugly and impotent; the right to have syphilis and cancer; the right to have too little to eat; the right to be lousy; the right to live in constant apprehension of what may happen tomorrow; the right to catch typhoid; the right to be tortured by unspeakable pains of every kind.'
>
> There was a long silence.
>
> 'I claim them all,' said the Savage at last.

> Mustapha Mond shrugged his shoulders. 'You're welcome,' he said. (Huxley, 1955a, 186–87)

Chapter 18, narrating the Savage's self-exile, self-mutilation and self-destruction, is still to come, but the philosophical argument ends here, with an unresolved choice between what Huxley would later describe as 'an insane life in Utopia, or the life of a primitive in an Indian village, ... in some respects ... hardly less queer and abnormal' (Huxley, 1955b, 7). In short, Huxley's ending surrounds a philosophical impasse with a set of highly elaborate comic and satiric trappings.

We noted Orwell's description of Čapek's *R.U.R.* as ending with the Robots producing for production's sake, after their slaughter of the human race. But this isn't how the play ends in either the Czech original or its British translation. The original was organised into a comic prologue and three acts, with the speech to which Orwell refers coming at the end of the second act. Selver's translation, as adapted for the London stage by Playfair, had three acts and an epilogue, with the speech coming at the end of the third act. But in both one human remains alive, R.U.R.'s head of construction, Stavitel Alquist, and in both his function is to provide the play with a less horrible ending than Orwell recalled. Alquist has been retained by the Robots in an apparently futile effort to find ways to reproduce themselves in the absence of humans, who alone knew the secret of their creation. In *R.U.R.* humankind is led to extinction, through a combination of technological excess and unbridled capitalism; the Robots to a parallel near-extinction, through their cruelty in disposing of their one-time human masters. The play's logic thus tends remorselessly toward the self-destruction of both, just as Orwell remembered. Indeed, the play might plausibly have ended there, with the theatrical equivalent of what Marx and Engels had called 'the common ruin of the contending classes' (Marx and Engels, 1967, 79).

Its actual conclusion, however, is that life will continue even though humanity might not, which is more optimistic, but nonetheless distinctly improbable because belied by almost everything that precedes it. Where no politics will work, the alternative turns out to be unconditional romantic love. In ways both unexplained and inexplicable, the play insists that self-sacrificial heterosexual love between the Robot, Primus, and the Robotess, Helena, will yield the promise of new life. Alquist is thus given the play's last speech, in which to pronounce them the new Adam and Eve. Opening the Bible, he quotes directly from *Genesis* and then concludes by citing the song of Simeon from the Gospel according to St Luke:

> Nyní propustíš, Pane, služebníka svého v pokoji; nebot uzřely oči mé

> – uzřely – spasení tvé skrze lásku, a život nezahyne! ... Nezahyne! ... Nezahyne! (Čapek, 1966, 102)

This is rendered slightly misleadingly in Selver's British translation, but with much more dramatic effect for an inter-war English audience, as a near direct quotation from both the King James Bible and the Church of England's daily 'Order for Evening Prayer':

> Now, Lord, lettest Thou Thy servant depart in peace, according to Thy will, for mine eyes have seen Thy salvation (Čapek, 1961, 104; cf. St Luke, 2: 29–30).

Čapek's conclusion is clear: that no matter what the sterilities of human (capitalist) robotics and inhuman (communist) Robots, love and life will finally survive. Christian rhetoric thus serves to underwrite the essentially pantheist solution that life will out, no matter what the actions of humans and their robotic creations. In some ways, this anticipates more recent deep-ecological speculation about the planet's capacity to survive the depredations of our species. But for Čapek it was, rather, the way to square a circle, to produce an optimistic resolution where none was available. Certainly, it seems to have been insufficiently persuasive for Orwell to remember its details.

5. An Ideal Typology and Some Hypotheses

To summarise: Zamyatin's *Nous autres* resolves the problem of dystopian ending by framing the particular catastrophes that overcome D-503 and I-330 in relation to a surrounding context of infinite, or at least continuing, revolution; Huxley's *Brave New World* by framing its philosophical impasse comically and satirically; and Čapek's *R.U.R.* by the contrivance of an optimistic outcome, in many respects at odds with the main narrative. The first seems to me the most persuasive, the last the least. But, however effective, they together provide three out of the four instances of a possible ideal typology, arranged around measures of internality and externality applied, respectively, to the formal question of narrative structure and to the dystopian content of the imaginary worlds represented in the fiction. So the solution in *Nous autres* is internal both to the text's main narrative and to the fictional history of the world it describes. That in *Brave New World* is also internal to the main narrative, but external to the fictional history of AF 632, insofar as satire necessarily implies a position outside the reality it satirises. That in *R.U.R.* is external to the main narrative in form – the English translation is right to represent the fourth act as an epilogue – and also in content, insofar as the closing transcendental religiosity occupies a quite different conceptual space from that postulated in the first three acts. This ideal typology is represented in diagramatic form in Figure 6 below.

	FORM (continuity with the main narrative)		
		Internal	**External**
CONTENT (continuity with the imaginary world represented in the fiction)	**Internal**	*Nous autres*	*Nineteen Eighty-Four*
	External	*Brave New World*	*R.U.R.*

Figure 6: An ideal typology of possible solutions to the problem of ending in dystopian SF.

The fourth possibility, that of narrative externality in form, but historical internality in fictional content, is what we find in Orwell's 'Appendix'. Given that we know he was familiar with each of the other texts, we may plausibly infer that this device was in fact a deliberate invention, an experiment in relation to 'that kind of book', that is, in relation to the genre of SF. Interestingly, there is no trace of the 'Appendix' on Newspeak in what remains of Orwell's own manuscript (Orwell, 1984). Given its dilapidated state – there is much missing – this in itself proves very little. But it is suggestive of the possibility that the 'Appendix' really was written last, as the real 'END' to the novel, the solution to a problem that had only become apparent once the main text was more or less complete. These inferences are strongly supportive of Atwood's and Pynchon's readings of the novel itself and of its more general significance. We may reasonably conclude, then, that readings of *Nineteen Eighty-Four*, which remain premised on the assumption that the novel ends at 'THE END', are radically misconceived.

As we noted in chapter 5, Williams compares *Nineteen Eighty-Four* unfavourably with *News from Nowhere*, arguing that the latter's fictional revolution provides an instance of the kind of 'true subjunctive' that is entirely absent from Orwell. Williams was right to draw our attention to what he elsewhere termed 'the tenses of the imagination' (Williams, 1984), but he was mistaken, nonetheless, in his understanding of *Nineteen Eighty-Four*. For this true subjunctive is precisely what occupies the space between 'THE END' of the novel and the 'Appendix' on 'THE PRINCIPLES OF

NEWSPEAK'. Moreover, the subjunctive takes a particularly interesting form within the actual text of the 'Appendix', that of the subjunctive future perfect. Citing Freud's notion of 'working through' and Paul Cohen on mathematical 'forcing', Alain Badiou has observed that: 'Forcing is the point at which a truth ... authorizes anticipations of knowledge concerning not what is but *what will have been if truth attains completion*'. 'This anticipatory dimension', he continues, 'requires that truth judgements be formulated in the future perfect' (Badiou, 2004, 127). To be able to say something about a truth means, then, that at some future moment this truth will have been realised, that it will have been true. 'A forcing', Badiou writes elsewhere, 'is the powerful fiction of a *completed* truth' (Badiou, 2003, 65). Effective political and religious myths are therefore, for Roland Boer, precisely instances of such forcings, since they construct or postulate worlds the truth of which will have been upon their completion (Boer, 2006). To be more precise, however, the tense to which Badiou and Boer both refer is the indicative future perfect. And, as such, it is the informing tense of all positively utopian myth, as in Boer's own example of Exodus. This has the interesting theoretical corollary that the equivalent tense of dystopian prevention, of that we seek to avoid by negative example, will be the subjunctive future perfect.

We began with Atwood's observation that Orwell's *Appendix* had been written in the past tense. We should now add that there are other tenses at work there, notably the subjunctive future perfect. So that, in the sentences which provide its chronological frame, Orwell writes that it 'was expected that Newspeak would have finally superseded Oldspeak ... by about the year 2050' and that 'within a couple of generations even the possibility of such a lapse would have vanished ... When Oldspeak had been once and for all superseded, the last link would have been severed' (Orwell, 1989, 312, 324). Orwell's use of the subjunctive functions here almost exactly as Williams observed it in Morris, that is, to mean that these events will not necessarily have eventuated. The subjunctive future perfect is by no means always empirically present in dystopian SF – its use in Atwood's 'Historical Notes', for example, is merely trivial – but, even when this is so, even where the tense fails to appear altogether, it remains nonetheless the logically informing tense of dystopia. For this is what dystopian future fictions recount, what *would have happened* if their empirical and implied readerships had not been moved to prevent it. Orwell knew this and that might well be an important part of his lasting significance. It is also why *Nineteen Eighty-Four* cannot be considered in any real sense an anti-utopia, but must rather be judged a critical dystopia in the full sense of the term.

7
When Was Science Fiction?

Between 20 May and 25 September 2011 the British Library in London held a public exhibition devoted to SF under the rubric *Out of This World: Science Fiction but Not as You Know It*. The Library is a United Kingdom deposit library and was thus able to draw on an extensive collection of first editions by British publishers, including Shelley's *Frankenstein* and *The Last Man*, Bellamy's *Looking Backward* (the London version), Wells's *The Time Machine*, Huxley's *Brave New World* and Orwell's *Nineteen Eighty-Four*. It also houses an extensive collection of archives, for example the Ballard papers, and was able to draw on these too, so as to include, for example, a page from the annotated typescript of an early draft of *The Burning World*. A series of related 'Out of This World Events' were also organised, including, two days before the exhibition closed, a distinguished panel of speakers on 'J. G. Ballard: Further Reflections'. The overall effect of the entire four-month event, extensively advertised both in the London press and on local public transport, remains deeply impressive. Yet, its title was, in at least one significant respect, oddly inappropriate to its content. For at no point did any exhibit actually address either ABC TV's early-1960s *Out of This World* anthology series, from whence the exhibition's title was taken, or *Star Trek*, from whence came its subtitle, in an obvious reference to Commander Spock's much misquoted line from the first of the movies: 'It's life, Captain, but not life as we know it' (Wise, 1979). Both the exhibition itself and the companion book by Mike Ashley clearly assumed that their audiences already knew SF as television, but nonetheless not as literature.

As Ashley explained:

> There is often a narrow perception that science fiction is primarily for a juvenile readership and concentrates on adventures in time and space ... science fiction tends to be judged by its worst examples, whilst its best examples are redefined as 'literature'. (Ashley, 2011, 6)

However, he continues: 'It is all science fiction – but not necessarily as you know it!' (Ashley, 2011, 7). Both the exhibition and the book were insistent that the genre has 'an ancient pedigree,' in Ashley's phrase, 'dating back ... at least as far as the ancient Greeks' (Ashley, 2011, 7). Both placed particular emphasis on Lucian of Samosata's *Alēthēs Historia* (*The True History*), which dates from the second century AD. So, too, do a range of well-known academic texts, from Suvin's *Metamorphoses* through to Seed's *Very Short Introduction* (Suvin, 1979, 54, 97–98; Seed, 2011, 2–3). Yet the vast majority of SF readers have almost certainly never heard of Lucian. The conclusion seems inescapable, then, that the British Library exhibition was, at least in part, an academic or quasi-academic intervention into the SF field. As such, it serves nicely to return us to the third of our original questions: When was SF? That is, what was its time?

1. Long Histories of Science Fiction

We need to recall here that one effect of Suvin's definition of SF was to expand the genre so as to incorporate into it a substantial part of the western literary and philosophical canon. There are thus, according to Suvin, six main instances of SF in the 'Euro-Mediterranean tradition': the Hellenic (Aeschylus, Aristophanes, Plato, Theopompus, Euhemerus, Hecataeus, Iambulus); the Hellenic-cum-Roman (Virgil, Antonius Diogenes, Lucian); the Renaissance–Baroque (More, Rabelais, Bacon, Campanella, Cyrano, Swift); the democratic revolution (Mercier, Saint-Simon, Fourier, Blake, Shelley); the *fin-de-siècle* (Bellamy, Morris, Verne, Wells); and the modern (from Wells, Zamyatin and Čapek through Gernsback and Campbell to the present) (Suvin, 1979, 87, 205). More recently, Adam Roberts's *The History of Science Fiction* has taken a similarly long view, tracing the genre back, firstly, to the ancient Greek novel rather than to the drama and, secondly, to Reformation Protestantism, the two beginnings seen as separated by an 'interlude' between AD 400 and 1600, during which fantasy prevailed over SF (Roberts, 2005, ix, 32–35). Unlike Suvin, Roberts insists on the specifically religious context of the genre's seventeenth-century re-emergence, through what he terms 'a cultural dialectic between "Protestant" rationalist post-Copernican science on the one hand, and "Catholic" theology, magic and mysticism, on the other' (Roberts, 2005, 3). Elsewhere, in an engagement with Moretti, Roberts has identified twenty-three 'generational "vogues"', ranging from the lunar adventures of the first half of the seventeenth century to the cyberpunk novels and films of the late twentieth and early twenty-first (Roberts, 2011, 50–55). Here, however, I will concentrate on his *History*.

Suvin himself complained that both utopian and SF scholars have failed to consider seriously 'anything in the 120 pages between the theory and Wells' in his *Metamorphoses* (Suvin, 2010a, 220). Whether this is fair comment on the wider community of scholars remains moot, but let us, at least, attempt to take the full measure of Suvin's and Roberts's arguments here. For Suvin, as we have seen, the science in SF is essentially a matter of cognitive rationality. It follows, then, that the genre has no necessary connection with any specifically modern understandings of science and technology. Indeed, he is at pains to insist that SF embraces a whole range of subgenres 'from Greek and earlier times', including 'the Islands of the Blessed, utopias, fabulous voyages, planetary novels, *Staatsromane*, anticipations, and dystopias' (Suvin, 1979, 12). For Suvin, however, as for Jameson, the core of the genre is in its connection with utopia. Hence, his stress on More and Wells. 'More's *Utopia*', Suvin writes, 'subsumes all the SF forms of its epoch … it translates the Land of Cockayne and the Earthly Paradise into the language of the philosophical dialogue on the ideal state and of Renaissance discovery literature' (Suvin, 1979, 92). As we have seen, he makes a very similar claim for Wells, who 'collected … all the main influences of earlier writers … and transformed them in his own image, whence they entered the treasury of subsequent SF' (Suvin, 1979, 219–20).

Roberts's notion of science is similarly disconnected from contemporary understandings of the relation between science and technology. SF is not so much about science, he argues, as about *technē*, in the Heideggerian sense of the term, not as an instrument, but as a way of knowing the world by 'enframing' it (Roberts, 2005, 11–12). This is a 'fundamentally philosophical outlook', he adds, closer to soft than to hard SF. It also suggests a version of the genre, he concedes, that 'many readers of SF will not recognise' (Roberts, 2005, 18). Roberts's overall sense of the genre is thus similar to Suvin's in general outline, except that *voyages extraordinaires*, to the sky, the moon and the planets, displace utopia at its centre: 'Travels "upwards" through space, or sometimes "downwards" into hollow-earth marvels … are the trunk … from which the various other modes of SF branch off' (Roberts, 2005, vii). The two main branches, he adds, are travels through time and stories about the technologies of travel (Roberts, 2005, viii). Utopias do figure in Roberts's account, just as voyages had in Suvin's, but only insofar as they deal with 'lands that might actually be reached by a voyager, strange but *material* new forms of human life and society' (Roberts, 2005, 54).

Despite their very different theorisations, these two long histories are devoted to a similar range of pre-modern subgenres. Both also see SF as fundamentally incompatible with totalising versions of religious idealism (Suvin, 1979, 7, 26–27; Roberts, 2005, xiii) and both cite the burning at the stake of Giordano Bruno the Nolan by the Inquisition in 1600 as a crucial turning point in the development of the genre (Suvin, 1979, 98; Roberts, 2005, 36). Although there are certainly differences in emphasis – Suvin ignores Plutarch's *Peri tou empainomenou prosōpou to kuklō tēs selēnēs* (*Concerning the Face Which Appears in the Orb of the Moon*), whilst Roberts ignores Rabelais's *La vie de Gargantua et de Pantagruel* – both are directed at a similar range of pre-modern writers, notably Aristophanes, Antonius Diogenes, Lucian, More, Bacon, Campanella, Cyrano and Swift. Interestingly, both also draw attention to Lucian as, respectively, providing the 'paradigm for the whole "prehistory" of SF' (Suvin, 1979, 98) and the 'father of science fiction' (Roberts, 2005, 27). There is no doubting the connections Suvin and Roberts establish between particular classical texts and their seventeenth- or twentieth-century counterparts. Aristophanes' *Ornithes* (*The Birds*), Campanella's *La città del Sole* (*The City of the Sun*) and Le Guin's *The Dispossessed* are indeed all utopias, just as Lucian's *Alēthēs Historia*, Cyrano's *L'Autre Monde ou les États et Empires de la Lune* (*The Other World or the States and Empires of the Moon*) and 'the voyages of the starship *Enterprise*' are all *voyages extraordinaires*. It remains open to doubt, however, whether either or both lineages yield any adequate sense of the functioning of the SF selective tradition in the early twenty-first century.

I confess to some scepticism about these long histories, not for the reason Roberts imputes to his imagined opponents, 'because … critics prefer the later writing, and don't really enjoy so-called "proto-science" fiction', but rather for the one he discounts, that '*something* happened to science in the Victorian age' (Roberts, 2005, xv, 4). Something did, indeed, happen to science in the nineteenth century, not the cultural division between arts and sciences Roberts addresses, but rather the development of new kinds of relationship between science and technology. When Suvin treats science as cognition and Roberts as philosophical outlook, both overlook the fundamental historical difference between our contemporary understandings of science and those of antiquity and early modernity, that the Industrial Revolution decisively and definitively redefined science into an intensely practical activity inextricably productive of new technologies, in the everyday rather than the Heideggerian sense. And this is clearly how contemporary SF continues to understand science: Le Guin's Hainish Ekumen is made possible by the ansible eventually produced from Shevek's science, and Roddenberry's United Federation of Planets by the science that produced Starfleet's warp drive. Nothing even vaguely similar exists in Aristophanes or Lucian, Campanella or Cyrano.

When Delany describes 'genealogies, with Mary Shelley for our grandmother or Lucian of Samosata as our great-great grandfather' as 'preposterous and historically insensitive' (Delany, 1994, 26), he is quite right about the second, but nonetheless mistaken about the first. For part of the novelty of *Frankenstein* was precisely that it imagined biological science as practically applicable to medical technology. Which is why Aldiss was right to trace the 'origins of the species', and Jameson the genre's first 'miraculous birth', to Shelley's novel (Aldiss, 1986, 25–52; Jameson, 2005, 1). It is also why *Frankenstein*, like Wells's *The Time Machine* and Verne's *Vingt mille lieues sous les mers*, is still actively present in the contemporary SF field, continuously available as an intertextual reference point in SF literature, film, radio and television. To take only one recent example, Gibson's *Zero History* can have its Hollis Henry refer to her boyfriend Garreth's seriously damaged and reconstructed leg as 'Frank' (Gibson, 2011, 300) only because it knows that SF readers always-already know about Frankensteinian science, in a way they simply do not about Lucian's King Endymion. But let us take Suvin and Roberts, and, with them, the British Library, Ashley and Seed, at face value, and test their argument against a particular text, the *Alēthēs Historia*.

Lucian's novel is claimed for SF primarily as an early example of a *voyage extraordinaire* to the moon. The narrator tells of how, sailing west from the Pillars of Heracles, his ship and crew were swept into the sky by a waterspout, which carried them, after a week, to an island in the air we soon learn to be the moon:

> Περὶ μεσημβρίαν δὲ οὐκέτι τῆς νήσου φαινομένης ἄφνω τυφὼν ἐπιγενόμενος καὶ περιδινήσας τὴν ναῦν καὶ μετεωρίσας ὅσον ἐπὶ σταδίους τριακοσίους οὐκέτι καθῆκεν εἰς τὸ πέλαγος, ἀλλ᾽ ἄνω μετέωρον ἐξηρτημένην ἄνεμος ἐμπεσὼν τοῖς ἱστίοις ἔφερεν κολπώσας τὴν ὀθόνην.
> [But about midday, when we were out of sight of the island, a waterspout suddenly came upon us, which swept the ship round and up to a height of some three hundred and fifty miles above the earth. She did not fall back into the sea, but was suspended aloft, and at the same time carried along by a wind which struck and filled the sails.] (Lucian, 1972, I, 9: 6–10; 1905, 139).

They are taken prisoner by Endymion, king of the Moon, whose side they join in war against Phaethon, king of the Sun. The Sunites are victorious, however, after which articles of peace are concluded and the voyagers left free to explore the Moon: 'Ἃ δὲ ἐν τῶι μεταξὺ διατρίβων ἐν τῆι σελήνηι κατενόησα καινὰ καὶ παράδοξα, ταῦτα βούλομαι εἰπεῖν [I am now to put on record the novelties and singularities which attracted my notice during our stay on the Moon]' (Lucian, 1972, I, 22: 7–8; 1905, 145). These novelties include a universal diet of the fumes from roast flying frogs, mucus made of honey and sweat made of milk, glass clothing for the rich and brass for the poor, removable eyes and a capacity to overhear and see everything on Earth (Lucian, 1972, I, 23–26).

The voyagers take their leave of Endymion and journey on through the skies, to the Morning Star, the Zodiac and the Sun, swept along by the wind:

> ἐν δὲ τῶι παράπλωι πολλὰς μὲν καὶ ἄλλας χώρας παρημείψαμεν, προσέσχομεν δὲ καὶ τῶι Ἑωσφόρωι ἄρτι συνοικιζομένωι, καὶ ἀποβάντες ὑδρευσάμεθα. ἐμβάντες δὲ εἰς τὸν ζωιδιακὸν ἐν ἀριστερᾶι παρήιειμεν τὸν ἥλιον, ἐν χρῶι τὴν γῆν παραπλέοντες· οὐ γὰρ ἀπέβημεν καίτοι πολλὰ τῶν ἑταίρων ἐπιθυμούντων, ἀλλ' ὁ ἄνεμος οὐκ ἐφῆκεν. ἐθεώμεθα μέντοι τὴν χώραν εὐθαλῆ τε καὶ πίονα καὶ εὔυδρον καὶ πολλῶν ἀγαθῶν μεστήν.
> [We passed on our way many countries, and actually landed on Lucifer, now in process of settlement, to water. We then entered the Zodiac and passed the Sun on the left, coasting close by it. My crew were very desirous of landing, but the wind would not allow of this. We had a good view of the country, however, and found it covered with vegetation, rich, well watered, and full of all good things.] (Lucian, 1972, I, 28: 25–30; 1905, 147).

They sail on to Lampton, which is inhabited entirely by lamps, and then to Aristophanes's Cloud-cuckoo-land, where they are prevented from landing by the direction of the wind. Eventually, however, the wind drops and their vessel is returned to the ocean from which it had been plucked (Lucian, 1972, I, 29). All this occurs in the first 29 of 42 sections in Book I, with a further 47 to follow in Book II. In the remainder, there are a series of subsequent Terrestrial adventures, which include being swallowed by a 200-mile-long whale and living inside it for many months (Lucian, 1972, I, 30–42; II, 1–2), a visit to the Island of the Blest, where the dead heroes live (Lucian, 1972, II, 6–29), and to the Isle of Dreams, the inhabitants of which are, quite literally, dreams and nightmares (Lucian, 1972, II, 32–35).

All this is great fun, to be sure, and Suvin quite right to describe it as 'a string of model parodies', but less obviously so to add that each parody translates 'a whole literary form into a critical, that is, cognitive, context' (Suvin, 1979, 97). That parody is critical is indisputable; that it is cognitive seems open to question if cognition is non-identical with ethical or aesthetic judgement; that it is scientific, as the use of the term cognitive seems to connote, seems simply wrong. Roberts is similarly effusive about *Alēthēs Historia*, which he describes as 'outrageous, inventive, bizarre and very funny ... The ironic title indicates the way in which the book explores the playful exuberance of lies and lying' (Roberts, 2005, 28). This, too, seems fair comment. Nonetheless, it is not at all obvious that these particular qualities have any necessary connection with anything we today regard as SF. Lucian's adventures in the skies are essentially of a piece with those on the Earth and both are part of the wider world of classical myth. Antiquity made extraordinary scientific advances, especially in mathematics, but there is little or no trace of any of these in Lucian. Still less is there any evidence of our modern sense of science as technology: he is simply uninterested in how a ship designed to sail the seas might be adapted to sail the skies; rather, it is all left to a waterspout and the winds.

Roberts eventually has the good grace to admit that 'Lucian's sympathy is ... with the mythic, not the scientific, mode' and that the work is 'anti-SF rather than proto-SF', but spoils the effect by adding that 'anti-SF nevertheless involves an engagement in the terms of SF' (Roberts, 2005, 29). Not necessarily, one should add, especially not if the terms of SF were defined in the nineteenth and twentieth centuries, as I have argued, rather than in the second and seventeenth. Indeed, neither Lucian nor any other classical author could ever have imagined science as productive of technologies. Their societies were organised around slave economies, in which labour was both debased and cheapened, and labour-saving therefore a matter of indifference. As Perry Anderson observed of what he calls 'slave relations of production', 'no major cluster of inventions ever occurred to propel the Ancient economy forward ... Nothing is more striking ... than the overall technological stagnation of Antiquity' (Anderson, 1974, 25–26). The society for which Lucian wrote, imperial Rome, 'possessed very little objective impetus for technological advance', Anderson concludes. Hence, its inability to apply and develop the two most important inventions actually made within its boundaries during the first century AD, the watermill and the reaping machine (Anderson, 1974, 79–80). The sixteenth and seventeenth centuries are a different matter, but remained so distracted by the ideological warfare between Protestantism and Catholicism that science figured primarily as world view, rather than as potentially productive technique.

Roberts's argument serves to remind us of the general significance for the long-term development of modern European culture of the Reformation and Counter-Reformation. Let me be clear that I have no quarrel with this. Max Weber's *The Protestant Ethic and the Spirit of Capitalism* (1930), with which Roberts seems oddly unfamiliar, seems to me crucial to any adequate understanding of cultural modernity; indeed, I have made use of it as such in my own work on Milton (Milner, 1981; Milner, 1999; Milner, 2005, 203-217). When Roberts writes that the genre 'still bears the imprint of the cultural crisis that gave it birth' (Roberts, 2005, 3) he is absolutely right, but when he adds that the crisis 'happened to be a European religious one', he surely misrecognises the relevant cultural crisis. In the sense that we now understand the terms, both science and SF emerge, not from the culture wars of the sixteenth and seventeenth centuries, but from those of the eighteenth and nineteenth. The genre's foundational dialectic is therefore not that between Catholicism and Protestantism, but rather between the Enlightenment and Romanticism. Both native Londoners and tourists alike are familiar with the Latin inscription, describing the course of the Great Fire of London of 1666, mounted on the North face of Christopher Wren and Robert Hooke's Monument, erected between 1671 and 1677. Few, however, recall the line, blaming the Fire on Popish frenzy, which was added in 1681 but removed in 1830. The addition marks the dialectic between Protestantism and Catholicism, the removal that between Enlightenment and Romanticism.

The novelty of the Enlightenment's version of science was, in Adorno and Horkheimer's phrase, that it 'behaves toward things as a dictator toward men. He knows them in so far as he can manipulate them' (Adorno and Horkheimer, 1979, 9). This kind of science had, of course, been anticipated in Bacon and Newton, but was only made practicable by the key developments of the Industrial Revolution: Cartwright's invention of the power-operated loom in 1785, Watt's of the rotary steam engine in 1782, the construction of a national canal network across Britain between 1790 and 1794. All this, in turn, gave force to the Romantic counter-critique:

> For was it meant
> That we should pore, and dwindle as we pore ...
> On solitary objects, still held
> In disconnection dead and spiritless,
> And still dwindling and dwindling still,
> Break down all grandeur ... (Wordsworth, 1949, 402)

As Kate Rigby observes, Wordsworth here represents the objects of scientific study as doubly dead, literally so because killed, metaphorically so because isolated 'in disconnection' (Rigby, 2004, 18). The monster forged by Shelley's Victor Frankenstein from the disconnected parts of dead bodies would be the fictional product of exactly this kind of alienated science.

2. Science Fiction and the Structure of Feeling

The abbreviation 'SF' can stand, not only for 'science fiction' or 'speculative fiction', but also for Gernsback's 'scientifiction' and, we might add, Robert Scholes's 'structural fabulation' (Scholes, 1975), Hollywood cinema's 'scifi' and even 'science fantasy' (Attebery, 1987, 182). During my own childhood it on occasion also stood for Spacefleet: when Frank Bellamy took over from Hampson in 1959 as the chief artist of the Dan Dare stories, he redesigned the vehicles, helmets and spacecraft to include an 'SF' logo, which I am now inclined to consider a generic in-joke. For cultural materialists, however, the abbreviation might also signify 'structure of feeling'. I have had repeated recourse to Williams's cultural materialism throughout this study and will do so again here. For where Suvin and Roberts detect formal continuities, not only between Wells and More, but between both and Lucian, Williams tended to stress the historical discontinuities between the pre-modern and the modern. This is the general significance of his 'long revolution', but also the more specific significance of his use of the notion of 'structure of feeling'.

By the 'long revolution', Williams meant the history of the emergence and development of modernity, and of the interrelationships, in the first instance within British society, but later elsewhere, between the democratic revolution, the industrial revolution and the 'cultural revolution' embodied in the extension and actual or potential democratisation of communications (Williams, 1965, 10–12). This long revolution dates from the late eighteenth century and runs roughly contemporaneously with the 'tradition' Williams charted in *Culture and Society 1780–1950*. In this respect, he tended to follow Leavis, rather than Eliot, in stressing the long-term cultural consequences of the Industrial Revolution, as distinct from those of the Reformation. This lack of interest in the sixteenth and seventeenth centuries was the occasion for much criticism and even prompted Williams himself to a 'Postscript' on Milton in the 1963 edition of *Culture and Society* (Williams, 1963, 324–25). Later, he would volunteer the more general admission that 'my historical perception … made it difficult to see the real connections with the Civil War' (Williams, 1979, 131). All of which suggests something in the fashion of an oversight rather than an insight. But, in fact, it was both. What Williams had overlooked, as the reference to Milton and the Civil War alerts us, was the decisive long-term political significance of the English Revolution of 1649. But what his 'historical perception' had nonetheless understood was how, from the late eighteenth century on, the experience of industrialisation produced a progressive displacement of the dialectic between Catholicism and Protestantism by that between the Enlightenment and Romanticism.

This displacement registers in the emergence of what Williams called a new 'structure of feeling'. The latter term is an original coinage of his, but has subsequently been widely cited elsewhere. Eagleton described it as 'vital' in understanding the articulation between sign systems and practices, Jameson toyed with the idea that it might be used to analyse postmodernism, Said thought it 'seminal' to his own account of the relationship between culture and imperialism (Eagleton, 1984, 110; Jameson, 1991, xiv; Said, 1993, 61). More interestingly for our purposes, the concept has even been taken into SF itself: it is used – accurately and precisely – both by the time-travelling human settlers from the Jovian moons of 3020 in Robinson's *Galileo's Dream*, and by the anonymous twenty-fourth-century historian-narrators of the 'Extracts' in his *2312*. Williams's first attempt at a theorisation of the concept was in his early work on cinema, *Preface to Film*, where he observed that it is a common experience to realise that, when one measures the whole work of art against its separable parts, 'there yet remains some element for which there is no external counterpart'. This element, he continued, 'is what I have named the *structure of feeling* of a period' (Williams, 2001, 33). Exactly the same concept appears in his earliest discussion of SF, to which we referred briefly in the previous chapter. There, he argued that stories of 'a secular paradise of the future' had 'reached their peak' with Morris and thereafter were 'almost entirely converted into their opposites: the stories of a future secular hell'. Here, too, he distinguished the three main types of contemporary literary SF, 'Putropia, Doomsday, and Space Anthropology' (Williams, 2010, 15).

By the first of these, he meant dystopian SF of the kind exemplified by Huxley, Orwell, Bradbury and Zamyatin; by the second, the kind of fictional catastrophe in which human life itself is extinguished, as in van Vogt's 'Dormant', Philip Latham's 'The Xi Effect', Christopher's 'The New Wine' and almost, but not quite, Wyndham's *The Day of the Triffids*; by the third, 'stories ... which consciously use the SF formula to find what are essentially new tribes, and new patterns of living' (Williams, 2010, 18). The last is exemplified by James Blish's *A Case of Conscience*, a later version of which would win the 1959 Hugo Award, and its 'beautifully imagined tribe' of eight-foot tall, reptilian Lithians, which Williams deems 'a work of genuine imagination, and real intelligence' (Williams, 2010, 19). Williams confessed to an intense dislike of 'most of the examples' of the other two types, but added that even these were interesting 'because they belong, directly, to a contemporary structure of feeling' (Williams, 2010, 15). As we noted in chapter 6, he considered this to be that of the isolated intellectual versus the masses, as enjoined by English conservative intellectuals from Eliot to Leavis.

Whatever we make of the merits of this particular reading, and I have my doubts, especially as it applies to Zamyatin and Orwell, the theoretical purchase of the concept of structure of feeling should be clear. It is one of a series of related concepts – discourse, ideology and world vision are obvious alternatives – available for use in literary and cultural studies to denote the patterned 'articulation' of different texts and sign systems. As Williams later glossed the term:

> The point of the deliberately contradictory phrase ... is that it was a structure in the sense that you could perceive it operating in one work after another which weren't otherwise connected ... yet it was one of feeling much more than of thought ... for which the best evidence was often the actual conventions of literary or dramatic writing. (Williams, 1979, 159)

Some such concept seems essential to cultural analysis; the only relevant question is which. The term itself is used only sparingly, and in relatively untheorised fashion, in *Culture and Society* (Williams, 1963, 56, 100), but it seems clear that Williams intended it to refer to a much more generally common possession than the specifically intellectual content of the cultural tradition (Williams, 1963, 119).

Moreover, there is also an important sense in which that particular study performatively illustrates the practical workings of the concept. The novelty of the general argument in *Culture and Society* is foreshadowed in its initial unlikely pairing of Edmund Burke and William Cobbett, the one a reactionary opponent of the French Revolution, the other a radical critic of the new industrial class system. Williams's point, however, was that 'we can only understand this tradition of criticism of the new industrial society if we recognize that it is compounded of very different and at times even directly contradictory elements' (Williams, 1963, 38). At issue, then, are not only a series of individual opinions, although these certainly matter, but also, and more centrally, the 'historical formation' of a 'structure of meanings, ... a wide and general movement in thought and feeling' (Williams, 1963, 17). In *The Long Revolution*, Williams developed a more theoretical elaboration of the concept. Using an analogy with solution and precipitate, where the former is the whole lived experience and the latter an aspect of the whole subsequently recovered only abstractly, he writes that 'The most difficult thing to get hold of is this felt sense of the quality of life at a particular place and time: a sense of the ways in which the particular activities combined into a way of thinking and living' (Williams, 1965, 63). He cites Erich Fromm's notion of 'social character' and Ruth Benedict's 'pattern of culture', but concludes that both are too 'abstract' for his purposes.

To get the sense of the lived 'experience', he continues, we need the sense of 'a further common element', 'a particular community of experience hardly needing expression, through which the characteristics of our way of life ... are in some way passed, giving them a particular and characteristic colour' (Williams, 1965, 63–64). This further common element is the structure of feeling, 'as firm and definite as "structure" suggests, yet it operates in the most delicate and least tangible parts of our activity' (Williams, 1965, 64). 'In one sense', Williams writes,

> this structure of feeling is the culture of a period: it is the particular living result of all the elements in the general organization. And it is in this respect that the arts of a period ... are of major importance. For here, if anywhere, this characteristic is likely to be expressed; often not consciously, but by the fact that here ... the actual living sense, the deep community that makes the communication possible, is naturally drawn upon. (Williams, 1965, 64–65)

A structure of feeling, he makes clear, is neither universal nor class specific, although it is 'a very deep and wide possession'. Nor is it formally learned, whence follows its often peculiarly generational character: 'the new generation will have its own structure of feeling, which will not appear to have come "from" anywhere' (Williams, 1965, 65).

Structure of feeling clearly designates something different from ideology, if by ideology we mean, as most Marxists did, a relatively formalised belief system. In *The Long Revolution,* Willliams had used the term 'social character' in preference to ideology, but he was clear nonetheless as to the distinction he intended to make: 'structure of feeling ... is different from any of the distinguishable social characters, for it has to deal not only with public ideals but with their omissions and consequences, as lived' (Williams, 1965, 80). In *Marxism and Literature,* he would repeat this argument, more or less exactly, but in opposition to more explicitly Marxist concepts, such as 'world-view' and 'ideology' (Williams, 1977, 132). In both cases, he intended 'structure of feeling' to include a strong sense of the experiential, which he saw as excluded from most conceptions of ideology. And what applies to ideology, applies almost equally to other parallel, non-Marxist concepts, such as discourse or episteme. The crucial difference between structure of feeling and other alternative theoretical conceptions lies in Williams's debt to Leavis and to the Romantic tradition more generally. As he would later explain: '"experience" was a term I took over from *Scrutiny* ... Leavis's strength was in reproducing and interpreting what he called "the living content of a work"' (Williams, 1979, 163–64).

In *Marxism and Literature*, the emphasis on both the immediately experiential and the generationally specific aspects of artistic process are retained, but here they are conjoined to a stress on cultural pre-emergence. In this reformulation, the experiential remains at odds with official, 'formal' culture precisely insofar as it is indeed genuinely new: 'practical consciousness is what is actually being lived, ... not only what it is thought is being lived' (Williams, 1977, 130–31). Similarly, the generationally specific remains different from the experience of previous generations insofar as it too is indeed genuinely new. Structures of feeling, Williams writes,

> can be defined as social experiences *in solution*, as distinct from other social semantic formations which have been *precipitated* and are more evidently and more immediately available ... The effective formations of most actual art relate to already manifest social formations, dominant or residual, and it is primarily to emergent formations ... that the structure of feeling, *as solution*, relates. (Williams, 1977, 133–34)

Structures of feeling are thus no longer in any sense 'the culture' of a period; they are, rather, precisely those particular elements within the culture that most actively anticipate subsequent mutations in the general culture itself; that is, they are quite specifically counter-hegemonic. A structure of feeling is therefore the element within the general culture that most actively anticipates subsequent mutations in the general culture itself. In Bloch's terms, it is the Novum encountered by the advancing Front.

In *The Long Revolution*, Williams tested his method against the England of the 1840s. If we are to understand the culture of this period, he argued, we should begin with the Sunday newspapers, which were by far the most widely read, rather than with the daily *Times*, as most histories tended to do. To understand the literature, we need to consider the 'most widely read writers', Lytton, Maryatt, James and Grant, as well as Dickens, Thackeray and the Brontës; and the pornographic, the philosophical, historical, religious and poetic writing as well as the prose fictions (Williams, 1965, 70–72). This will lead us, in turn, into a 'social history' of the period's institutions (Williams, 1965, 72). 'This is the reality', Williams concludes, 'that various strands of the selective tradition tend to reduce, seeking always a single line of development' (Williams, 1965, 74). Moreover, a crucial element in the emergent structure of feeling of the mid nineteenth century was the new industrial science and its technologies. 'Again and again,' Williams wrote, 'even by critics of the society, the excitement of this extraordinary release of man's powers was acknowledged and shared ... "These are our poems", Carlyle said in 1842, looking at one of the new locomotives, and this element ... is central to the whole culture' (Williams, 1965, 88). This is precisely the element that would most clearly distinguish the new worlds of SF from the alternative islands of older utopian fictions.

3. Form and History

Williams's distinction between dominant, residual and emergent cultures is well known. What particularly interested him were the latter, that is, those genuinely new meanings and values, practices, relationships and kinds of relationship, which are substantially alternative or oppositional to the dominant culture (Williams, 1977, 123). An emergent culture, Williams observed, requires not only distinct kinds of immediate cultural practice, but also and crucially 'new forms or adaptations of forms' (Williams, 1977, 126). The nineteenth-century SF novel was exactly this, a new form radically different from those that preceded it. Moreover, insofar as it had been an adaptation of any pre-existing form, this wasn't so much the utopia, or, indeed, the fantasy, as the historical novel. Both Suvin and Jameson have registered the affinities between the latter and SF. So, when Suvin introduces pluridimensional temporality into his basic taxonomy of literary forms, he treats SF as the estranged counterpart of historical realism (Suvin, 1979, 21). More interestingly, because historical rather than formalist in its implications, Jameson notes how the historical novel ceased to be 'functional' roughly contemporaneously with the beginnings of SF, in the simultaneous historical moment of Flaubert's *Salammbô*, first published in 1862, and Verne's *Cinq Semaines en ballon* (*Five Weeks in a Balloon*), first published in 1863 (Jameson, 2005, 285). The latter observation is empirically very astute, for just as French publishing in the early decades of the nineteenth century was dominated, in terms of both sales and translations, by the historical novels of Alexandre Dumas, so in the later decades it would be dominated by Verne's *voyages extraordinaires*. We might add that Verne was a protégé of Dumas and that Verne's second SF novel, written in the same year as *Cinq Semaines en ballon*, but rejected by Hetzel as too pessimistic and therefore left unpublished until 1994, was in fact the future history *Paris au XXe siècle*.

How, then, does Jameson theorise this shift from the historical novel to SF? His understanding of the older genre is heavily dependent on Lukács's

The Historical Novel, which had argued that the achievement of the early nineteenth-century historical novel – his exemplar is Sir Walter Scott – lay in its capacity to represent the difference between the pre-capitalist past and the capitalist present through historically different typical characters in historically different typical situations. 'What is lacking in the so-called historical novel before ... Scott,' Lukács wrote, is 'the specifically historical ... derivation of the individuality of characters from the historical peculiarity of their age' (Lukács, 1969, 15). Whilst earlier 'historical' novels had imagined characters from the past as essentially identical to people in the present, Scott was able to portray 'the struggles and antagonisms of history by means of characters who, in their psychology and destiny, always represent social trends and historical forces' (Lukács, 1969, 33). This difference is not merely a matter of individual talent, but of collective historical experience, insofar as 'the French Revolution, the revolutionary wars and the rise of Napoleon ... for the first time made history a *mass experience* ... on a European scale' (Lukács, 1969, 20). Just as Scott's Waverley novels marked the emergence of this new historical sensibility, so Flaubert's *Salammbô*, according to Lukács, marks its decline into 'decorative monumentalization, the devitalizing, dehumanizing and at the same time making private of history' (Lukács, 1969, 237). This, too, is a matter of collective experience rather than individual talent, a direct product of the successful bourgeois revolutions of 1848 and the consequent changes in dominant conceptions of history and progress, which led increasingly to the elimination of notions of contradiction (Lukács, 1969, 202–7).

Lukács's editorialising against post-1848 bourgeois dominance is the political corollary of the anti-modernist aesthetics he developed elsewhere, here prefigured in the polemic against 'naturalism' in the historical novel. Neither seems especially pertinent to a world that has become both post-bourgeois (although not thereby post-capitalist) and postmodernist. And his predictions of the genre's decline are clearly falsified by the evidence of its continuing vitality in what Agnes Heller calls the 'contemporary historical novel' (Heller, 2011). Lukács's argument might, then, seem hopelessly anachronistic to the twenty-first century reader. Indeed, it is interesting that, when presented with the opportunity to become 'the Lukács of postmodernism', Jameson chose, rather, to insist on the latter's 'moment of truth' (Jameson, 1991, 49; cf. Fehér, 1990, 92; Huyssen, 1988, 200). Stripped of its more aggressively prescriptive aspects, however, that is, rendered more properly sociological, Lukács's account provides Jameson with the raw materials for his reading of SF. The 'new genre', Jameson writes, is 'a form which ... registers some nascent sense of the future ... in the space on which a sense of the past had once been inscribed', that is, the space of the historical novel (Jameson, 2005, 286). The connection between the genres arises, he argues, because each is 'the symptom of a mutation in our relationship to historical time' (Jameson, 2005, 284).

Jameson sees both the emergence of SF and the decline of the historical novel into 'archaeology' as functions of an increased collective inability to understand the present as history. The new genre's sense of the future cannot therefore entail the imaginary representation of any real future, but must rather work primarily 'to defamiliarize and restructure our experience of our own *present*' (Jameson, 2005, 286). And it does so, furthermore, primarily by 'transforming our own present into the determinate past of something yet to come' (Jameson, 2005, 288). His conclusion is worth quoting:

> SF ... enacts and enables a structurally unique 'method' for apprehending the present as history ... irrespective of the 'pessimism' or 'optimism' of the imaginary future world which is the pretext for that defamiliarization. The present is ... no less a past if its destination prove to be the technological marvels of Verne or ... the shabby and maimed automata of P. K. Dick's near future. (Jameson, 2005, 288)

Jameson is, however, much more interested in late twentieth-century American SF than in nineteenth-century French, so the argument slips very quickly from Verne to Dick, thence to the critical utopian writers of the American 1970s, and finally to the proposition, repeated throughout *Archaeologies*, that the 'deepest vocation' of both SF and utopia is to bring home 'our constitutional inability to imagine Utopia' (Jameson, 2005, 289).

As I argued in chapter 5, utopia and SF are nothing like so implicated in each other as Jameson believes. Nor, however, is it at all obvious that, when SF writers do attempt to imagine utopia, they find themselves constitutionally incapable of doing so. Robinson is a distinguished SF writer, winner of two Hugo Awards for Best Novel, a would-be ecotopian and, interestingly, a former student of Jameson, who has explicitly argued to the contrary. 'All portrayed societies are stylised and hypothetical', he writes:

> Seen in that way, a utopian novel is only a tiny bit less realistic than the most naturalistic realist novel ... this notion that we cannot imagine utopia is mistaken. We can imagine utopia ... The constraints are very slack and our imaginations strong. We are quite capable of taking the present situation, and all history too, and ringing every

> possible physical and logical change in our ideas to make something new. (Robinson, 2011, 13–14)

The problem, he adds, is not that of imagining utopia but of 'getting from here to there' (Robinson, 2011, 14). Hence, his diagnosis of the central weakness of his own utopian novel, *Pacific Edge*, that it cannot deal with the fact that 'there are guns under the table' (Robinson, 2011, 9).

This said, Jameson's notion that SF and the historical novel are closely cognate genres, insofar as, at the most fundamental of levels, both take human historicity as their central subject matter, seems a much more productive starting point than the post-Suvinian preoccupation with More which actually directs most of *Archaeologies*. For the typical subject matter of SF is, indeed, future history, uchronia and dyschronia rather than utopia and dystopia, its precursors therefore Scott and Dumas rather than More and Bacon. Hence, the ritualistic invocation of 'tomorrow' by Gernsback in *Amazing Stories*, even of 'tomorrow and tomorrow's tomorrow' by Campbell in *Astounding* (Gernsback, 1926, 3; Campbell, 1938, 37). Hence, more interestingly, Robinson's argument that SF 'is an historical literature', in which there is always 'an explicit or implicit fictional history that connects the period depicted to our present moment'. 'The two genres are not the same', he continues, but 'more alike ... than either is like the literary mainstream'. 'They share some methods and concerns,' he concludes,

> in that both must describe cultures that cannot be physically visited by the reader; thus both are concerned with alien cultures, and with estrangement. And both genres share a view of history which says that times not our own are yet vitally important to us. (Robinson, 1987, 54–55)

Robinson is, of course, a political optimist and an avowed humanist. But a similarly historical conception seems to inform the work of as pessimistic a misanthrope as Houellebecq. The posthuman narrators of his first SF novel, *Les Particules élémentaires*, explain that

> Ce livre est avant tout l'histoire d'un homme, qui vécut la plus grande partie de sa vie en Europe occidentale, durant la seconde moitié du XX siècle ... fréquemment guettés par la misère, les hommes de sa génération passèrent en outre leur vie dans la solitude et l'amertume. [This book is principally the story of a man who lived out the greater part of his life in Western Europe, in the latter half of the twentieth century ... often haunted by misery, the men of his generation lived out their lonely, bitter lives.] (Houellebecq, 2000a, 7; 2000b, 3)

The novel is, in short, a history of how post-1968 France produced a culture so dire as to prompt humanity to preside over its own abolition. Houellebecq's third and, to date, final future history novel, *La carte et le territoire,* repeats the trope:

> L'oeuvre qui occupa les dernières années de la vie de Jed Martin peut ainsi être vue – c'est l'interprétation la plus immédiate – comme une méditation nostalgique sur la fin de l'âge industriel en Europe, et plus généralement sur le caractère périssable et transitoire de toute industrie humaine.
> [The work that occupied the last years of Jed Martin's life can thus be seen – and this is the first interpretation that springs to mind – as a nostalgic meditation on the end of the industrial age in Europe, and, more generally, on the perishable and transitory nature of any human industry.] (Houellebecq, 2010, 428; 2011, 291)

It does not follow that a proposition is true merely because supported by such unlikely bedfellows as Robinson and Houellebecq. But I do think we can take the connection between SF and the historical novel to be established at least tentatively, far more so than that between SF and utopia, and sufficiently so that we might now proceed to a few concluding remarks on the history of SF as a form. We argued in chapter 1 that, of Williams's three levels of form, SF is a 'type', that is, a radical distribution, redistribution and innovation of interest within the novel and short story genres. In the twentieth century, this type was expanded to embrace other media, notably film, radio and television, but its beginnings are in the novel and short story nonetheless. We have argued in this chapter that these innovations of interest were focused above all on the practical capacity of sciences to become technologies and that they first occurred only in the early nineteenth century. At one level, this is merely to restate an older position in SF studies, with Aldiss, Williams and Jameson, but against Suvin and Roberts. This is not to deny that SF texts have rifled through the broader western cultural legacy in search of inspiration: Wilcox's *Forbidden Planet* famously rewrote *The Tempest* with Robby the Robot in the role of Ariel. But SF readers, writers and critics do not claim Shakespeare for their own in anything like the way Gernsback claimed Poe, Verne and Wells; nor in which Sterling claims Shelley's *Frankenstein* as 'a wellspring of science fiction as a genre', albeit only 'humanist' SF (Sterling, 1990, 39–41). Borrowings from Shakespeare or Lucian or More can be important and interesting, but they are borrowings from outside the selective tradition of SF, nonetheless.

I have also suggested that the genre's initial emergence was overwhelmingly conditioned by the dialectic between Enlightenment and Romanticism, a proposition that will acquire renewed relevance in my concluding chapter. The history of the genre, I hypothesise, is inextricably connected to this dialectic, which is, in turn, the most fundamental of all the dialectics of western cultural modernity. David Roberts and Peter Murphy argue that Enlightenment and Romanticism are 'the divided unity of modernism', where the latter term means not so much any particular variant of avant-gardism as cultural modernity in general. There is thus a continuing dialectic between the Enlightenment project to denaturalise the human and Romanticism's attempt to renaturalise it. 'Enlightenment autonomy is always threatened by the immanent contradiction of denaturalization: the reversal of freedom into unfreedom', they observe at the conclusion to the first part of their study (Roberts and Murphy, 2004, 75). Conversely, they proceed, 'romantic incarnation is always threatened by the immanent contradiction of renaturalization: the reversal of the spiritualization of nature into the naturalization of spirit.' 'Each bears witness', they conclude, 'to the failed internal dialogue of modernity' (Roberts and Murphy, 2004, 76).

This reading of the continuing force of the dialectic of Enlightenment and Romanticism is very persuasive, more so than Roberts and Murphy's own canvassed solutions thereto. Which is why it seems highly improbable that SF will either decline or disappear at any time in the likely near future. It is also, incidentally, why Baudrillard is mistaken to read Dick and Ballard as precursors to an entirely new kind of post-SF, the difference of which from SF would be as great as that between utopia and SF itself. No doubt, these newer SFs, which we can agree to call postmodern, have indeed been deeply preoccupied with the simulacra of simulation: this is at least as true of cyberpunk and 'posthuman' SF as of Dick and Ballard. But they all remain irretrievably bound to the quintessentially modern founding assumption that their fictional sciences can and will produce technologies sufficiently effective as to shape human being itself.

8

Where Was Science Fiction?

Although heavily weighted towards England, France and the United States, the British Library's 2011 *Out of This World* exhibition, cited in the previous chapter, clearly presented a version of the history of SF that not only reached back to classical antiquity, but also stretched across Eurasia and North America, from the Japanese Haruki Murakami's *Sekai no owari to hādo-boirudo wandārando* (*Hard-Boiled Wonderland and the End of the World*) to the Canadian Margaret Atwood's *Oryx and Crake* and *The Year of the Flood* (Ashley, 2011, 66, 114). Germany, Poland, Russia and Czechoslovakia were all comparatively well represented; on 9 September the Library even hosted an 'Out of This World Event' on Lem, in association with the Polish Cultural Institute; Enrique Gaspar y Rimbau's *El Anacronópete* was acknowledged as pre-dating Wells's 'The Chronic Argonauts' by a year (Ashley, 2011, 50); and at least one Australian SF writer rated a mention, Greg Egan, for *Permutation City* (Ashley, 2011, 71). Although fan-based World Science Fiction Conventions were first organised in the United States and remain heavily weighted towards that country, they have now also been held in Canada since 1948, in England since 1957, Germany since 1970, Australia since 1975, the Netherlands since 1990, Scotland since 1995 and Japan since 2007. From the most academically legitimated institutions through to the most fan-legitimated, the genre is, then, slowly becoming increasingly aware of itself as transcending national boundaries. Which takes us to the last of my theoretical questions, that of the cultural geography of the genre: Where was SF? What was its geographical space? What, in short, is the geographical provenance of the SF selective tradition, the temporal origins of which were sketched in the previous chapter?

At one level, the empirical answer is doubly unsurprising, firstly, because we already know that the selective tradition goes back only to Wells, Verne and Shelley and, secondly, because their particular national contexts occupied a peculiarly central location within the general nineteenth-century literary economy. SF begins, then, as a literary genre located in England and France, which is subsequently exported to other media and other regions. Its more recent geographical trajectory is less predictable, however. The genre's frontiers seem to have expanded to include the Weimar Republic, early Soviet Russia, inter-war Czechoslovakia, the United States (and Canada) at roughly the same time, Japan and Poland in the post-Second World War period and, finally, late-Communist Russia. No doubt, there are other minor centres, Latin America and Australia, for example (Bell and Molina-Cavilán, 2003; Dann and Webb, 1998; Dann, 2008), but the genre's primary boundaries are nonetheless roughly those described above. These, then, are the frontiers that require mapping and explanation. As we observed in passing in chapter 3, such explanation poses a problem for the habitually national assumptions around which academic life is conventionally organised. Hence, the need to redefine Bourdieu's notion of the national literary field into that of a globalised SF field. The implied criticism here, that the analytical frame remains determinedly national in focus and therefore increasingly inappropriate to an increasingly globalised culture, is as applicable to Williams as to Bourdieu. We will therefore need to look elsewhere for theoretical inspiration. Two obvious candidates suggest themselves, both grounded in the determinedly non-national discipline of comparative literature: the kind of postcolonial literary studies developed and inspired by writers like Said and Gayatri Chakravorty Spivak; and Moretti's application of Immanuel Wallerstein's world-systems theory to literary sociology. Insofar as both can be extended from literature per se to cultural texts in general, both also imply the possibility of a comparative cultural study.

1. Postcolonial Theory and Science Fiction

Postcolonial literary theory ultimately derives from the empirical datum of the collapse of European imperialism, the British Empire in particular. The combination of 'Third Worldist' cultural politics and post-structuralism, which it denotes, was a defining feature of the late twentieth-century occidental radical academy. Insofar as it was constituted by any particular body of work, this was above all that associated with Said and Spivak, whose careers can easily be run together as paradigmatically, but also caricaturally, 'postcolonial'. Both were preoccupied with the cultural legacies of imperialism, both came from what was once known as the 'Third World', both taught in 'the West', both made theoretical use of post-structuralism. It became conventional to distinguish Said's debt to Foucault from Spivak's to Derrida and there is, indeed, a certain point to the convention: Spivak was both the translator into English of Derrida's *Of Grammatology* and a famously 'obscure' deconstructionist critic (Derrida, 1974; Spivak, 1999, 423–31; Eagleton, 1999); Said's understanding of 'Orientalism' was as a 'discourse' in the specifically Foucauldian sense of 'an enormously systematic discipline by which European culture was able to manage – and even produce – the Orient ... during the post-Enlightenment period' (Said, 1995, 3).

Said himself was almost entirely uninterested in SF, although he did note in passing that 'Verne's adventures ..., far from casting doubt on the imperial undertaking, serve to confirm and celebrate its success' (Said, 1993, 227). Nonetheless, his focus on British and French, and later American, scholarship during the post-Enlightenment period clearly runs parallel to our account of the origins of SF as a genre. Moreover, his interests, like ours, are in 'structures of feeling' (Said, 1993, 14). Neither in *Orientalism* nor in *Culture and Imperialism*, where the scope is widened to include the non-Western world in general, as distinct from the East in particular, is this simply a matter of ideas reflecting political or economic interests. Rather: 'Orientalism is – and does not simply represent – a considerable dimension of modern political–intellectual culture' (Said, 1995, 12). Said sees these discourses, which work to 'support, elaborate, and consolidate the practice of empire' (Said, 1993, 14), as functioning by way of a system of binary oppositions, in which the West, its possessions, attributes and ethnicities, are valorised positively against the inferior status of colonised peoples. The 'major component in European culture', he concluded, is 'the idea of European identity as a superior one in comparison with all the non-European peoples and cultures' (Said, 1995, 7). Western accounts of the Orient were thus primarily an effect of the West's own fantasies about the Eastern Other, rather than of any referential 'reality' within the 'Orient'. The obvious implication for SF is that its constructions of alien Others will tend to function in analogous fashion.

Spivak, by contrast, engages directly with what, in our account as in many others, is SF's founding text, Shelley's *Frankenstein*. Spivak's enthusiasm for deconstruction revolves around its capacity to sustain a vigorous theoretical 'anti-essentialism' in the face of European pretensions to 'know' the essences of both themselves and others. Witness the famously tortuous discussion of 'subaltern' speech, where she argues for the theoretical superiority of Derridean deconstruction over Foucauldian genealogy (and Deleuzian rhizomatics). 'Derrida', she writes, '... articulates the *European* Subject's tendency to constitute the Other as marginal to ethnocentrism and locates *that* as the problem of all logocentric ... endeavors' (Spivak, 1988, 292–93; cf. 1999, 279–81). This argument, first aired in a 1988 essay, led her to the conclusion that the 'subaltern cannot speak', a conclusion which is neither explicitly reaffirmed nor yet entirely withdrawn in the version included in *A Critique of Postcolonial Reason* in 1999 (Spivak, 1988, 308; 1999, 308–11). Spivak reads *Frankenstein* as a similarly deconstructive text, a critique, rather than an affirmation, of 'the axiomatics of imperialism in substance and rhetoric' (Spivak, 1999, 115). Frankenstein's refusal to create a second female monster, on the grounds that this would lead to 'a race of devils', speaks the 'language of racism – the dark side of imperialism understood as social mission' (Spivak, 1999, 134). The monster himself is transformed into a version of the 'native informant', subjected to a civilising education, but who nonetheless cannot finally be contained either by the text or by the master–slave relationship (Spivak, 1999, 135, 137–38, 139–40). 'Shelley gives to the monster the right to refuse the withholding of the master's returned gaze,' Spivak concludes, so that the demand to be heard by Frankenstein becomes a request 'for the colonial female subject' (Spivak, 1999, 140).

There is clear force to this reading and good extratextual reason, never actually cited by Spivak, to suppose that Shelley might have had direct acquaintance with, and been opposed to, the conditions of colonial slavery. In 1815 she spent some weeks at Clifton near Bristol, one of the centres of the Atlantic slave trade. As Miranda Seymour plausibly speculates,

> Mary could see black men being worked on Bristol Quay; she could hear the callously pragmatic views of those who had owned and now technically employed them. Surrounded by troubling evidence that abolition had brought little change of attitude ..., Mary was provided with a new element of the story she began to write the following summer. (Seymour, 2001, 139)

But the evidence Spivak and Seymour cite from the novel is less persuasive. When Frankenstein speaks of a 'race of devils', the term is used as a synonym for species, rather than as a racist category for distinguishing between humans. Nor is the monster's 'yellow skin, black hair and giant limbs', cited by Seymour, necessarily suggestive of any specifically racial identity: monsters do tend to be monstrous, and these particular monstrosities were as likely inspired by Northern English or Irish industrial workers as by African former slaves. At the level of textual analysis there is, then, comparatively little to suggest that this particular master–slave dialectic is necessarily colonial in character. Indeed, the few direct references to imperialism quoted by Spivak (Spivak, 1999, 136–38) are all oddly extraneous to the creator–creature relationship itself.

Let me draw attention, nonetheless, to two methodologically significant aspects of Spivak's analysis. First, she is clear both that *Frankenstein* betrays 'plenty of incidental imperialist sentiment' and that 'imperialism does not produce unquestioned ideological correlatives' in its narrative structuring (Spivak, 1999, 133). In short, the novel's relation to imperialism is contradictory. This is absolutely right and, moreover, likely to be true for the genre as a whole, albeit not for every individual text. As Rieder observes, drawing on an interesting parallel between SF and ethnology, 'The double-edged effect of the exotic – as a means of gratifying familiar appetites and as a challenge to one's sense of the proper or the natural – pervades early science fiction' (Rieder, 2008, 4). In short, the genre was at once ideological, in the pejorative sense, and yet also critical. It is, in fact, one of the strengths of Williams's notion of structure of feeling – and we have been arguing here that SF is underpinned by a distinctively modern structure of feeling – that these are necessarily compounded of different and even 'directly contradictory elements' (Williams, 1963, 38). So, when Said describes Verne's SF as simply supportive of imperialism, we should be wary of too ready an assent. Captain Nemo, the most famous and arguably the most interestingly complex character in Verne, is actually, as we know from *L'île mystérieuse* (*Mysterious Island*), the sequel to *Vingt mille lieues sous les mers*, the Indian Prince Dakkar, driven to piracy by the barbarism of British imperialism.

Second, Spivak is also clear that postcolonial readings by no means exhaust the textual possibilities of Shelley's novel, so that, at one point, she quite explicitly concedes that other readings are possible, 'for instance that the monster is the nascent working class' (Spivak, 1999, 137). The latter is a view I have myself canvassed elsewhere (Milner, 2005, 227–28). What interests me here, however, is the logic of the relationship between different such readings. For Spivak, as a good deconstructionist, plurality of readings is a necessary consequence of the nature of language: in Derrida's phrase, 'signified meaning ... always signifies again' (Derrida, 1978, 25). We might wish to qualify this position, however, for although any complex text is indeed likely to be open to a plurality of readings, this need not imply the kind of radical relativism one finds in Derridean versions of polysemy. There are both empirical and logical criteria against which different accounts might be measured and judged either stronger or weaker. This is particularly so, moreover, when engaged in what is primarily a literary–geographical rather than a literary–critical question, here that of, quite literally, locating SF. With these two cautionary methodological observations established – that both the genre itself and most of its individual texts will have a necessarily contradictory relationship to their contexts and that, whilst pluralities of reading are to be expected and welcomed, some readings are nonetheless likely to be better than others – let us proceed to consider two recent applications of postcolonial theory to SF, Istvan Csicsery-Ronay's much-cited essay on 'Science Fiction and Empire' and Rieder's *Colonialism and the Emergence of Science Fiction*.

Both of these place great stress on SF's colonial context. Csicsery-Ronay argues that the entire trajectory of the genre's history is best understood as a correlate of imperialism. 'The dominant sf nations', he writes, 'are precisely those that attempted to expand beyond their national borders in imperialist projects: Britain, France, Germany, Soviet Russia, Japan, and the US' (Csicsery-Ronay, 2003, 231). Rieder repeats this proposition in almost identical terms, except that Russia is rhetorically de-Sovietised and Japan omitted (Rieder, 2008, 3). As generalisations go, this sounds plausible enough, but only until one proceeds to ask about imperial powers that didn't produce SF, such as ancient Rome (*pace* Lucian), or China; or about important SF nations that clearly weren't imperialist, such as Čapek's Czechoslovakia or Lem's Poland. Csicsery-Ronay's response to the latter is to hazard the improbable suggestion that Čapek and Lem, neither of whom was either Austrian or Hungarian, be considered late products of the Austro-Hungarian Empire (Csicsery-Ronay, 2003, 243n). Even in Čapek's case this sounds implausible, given that he was a leading Czech liberal nationalist, close friend and admirer of Thomas Masaryk, the first President of the Czechoslovak Republic (Čapek, 1969), and one of the new republic's prominent intellectuals. But it is still less plausible for Lem, who was actually born in Lvov, now in Ukraine but then already in Poland, some three years after the collapse of the dual monarchy. True, he eventually moved to Krakow, previously capital of the Nazi General Governorate, but only in 1946, by which time the city was both Polish and Communist. The connections seem tenuous, to say the least. What interwar Czechoslokia and post-war Poland do share with the other SF nations, however, is a common status as industrialised or industrialising. Bohemia, as the Czech lands were then called, was the single most industrially developed province in the entire Habsburg Empire.

It is, no doubt, true that 'colonialism is a significant context for early science fiction' (Rieder, 2008, 2), just as, in Said's phrase, 'the novel ... and imperialism are unthinkable without each other (Said, 1993, 84). But both the novel in general and SF in particular are equally unthinkable without capitalist relations of production, or without patriarchal gender relations, or without systematic heterosexism. Which is why Marxist, feminist and queer readings are readily available, not only for *Frankenstein*, but for SF texts more generally. None of these can define what is distinctive about the genre, however, that is, how it differs from the realist novel, the romance or the detective novel. Such differences can be addressed adequately, it seems to me, only through the question raised in the previous chapter, that of the relation between science and technology and its place in the dialectic of Enlightenment and Romanticism. And the geographical reach of this dialectic is much better indicated by measures of industrialisation than of colonialism (or capitalism or patriarchy). The test case is Communist Russia, which was in no obvious sense an imperialist power during the 1920s, and became only very eccentrically so during the post-Second World War period, but remained obsessively preoccupied with industrialisation for most of its comparatively short history.

Both Csicsery-Ronay and Rieder tend to conflate European and American 'imperialisms'. For Rieder, as for Said, the continuity between Anglo-French and American hegemony is simply assumed. Rieder quotes Lenin's *Imperialism: The Highest Stage of Capitalism* with enthusiasm (Rieder, 2008, 26, 140), but fails to register that one of this text's strengths is to distinguish very sharply between the specific forms of late nineteenth- and early twentieth-century European imperialism and the colonial policies of earlier periods in the histories of capitalism and of pre-capitalist societies like ancient Rome (Lenin, 1969, 81–82). In these terms, the United States was only ever a very minor imperialist power and has, in any case, retreated into decolonisation. Contemporary American militarism functions on an unprecedentedly global scale, no doubt, but it does so, not to establish a specifically American colonial empire, but rather to sustain the conditions of possibility for an increasingly transnational world economic system. Where the older British and French colonial interests were secured, not least against each other, by the brute fact of colonial possession, the global interests of transnational corporations, and the global reach of transnational popular culture, SF included, are sustained by the 'free' flow of markets rather than by direct politico-juridical coercion.

Csicsery-Ronay registers this difference by way of reference to Michael Hardt and Antonio Negri's *Empire* (Hardt and Negri, 2000), which he plausibly reads as itself a quasi-science-fictional text. But he does so only to insist, a little misleadingly, that imperialism has been transformed into, rather than succeeded by, Empire. So he writes that SF has throughout been 'driven by a desire for the imaginary transformation of imperialism into Empire', where the latter is understood as the kind of 'postmodern empire' created by global market capitalism (Csicsery-Ronay, 2003, 232). This conflation of imperialism and Empire occludes important historical differences between the older European imperialisms and late capitalist globalisation; and between the imperialist subtexts often present in British, French and German SF, their comparative absence from Russian and

Japanese SF, and their very distinctive insertion into the ideologies of Empire in recent American SF, most obviously in cyberpunk. Moreover, it also homogenises each of these to an unwarranted extent: not all European SF is actually 'about' imperialism at any fundamental level; some that is, is nonetheless anti-imperialist in character; and not all postmodern SF is 'about' Empire; some that is, is nonetheless anti-capitalist in character. At one point Csicsery-Ronay grudgingly concedes the latter, but only so as to insist, against the weight of his own immediately previous admission, that 'the technoscientific Empire that makes sf possible has much in common with Jameson's negative totality' (Csicsery-Ronay, 2003, 241).

There is, doubtless, much to be said for Csicsery-Ronay's argument that SF 'extols and problematizes technology's effects' and that '[w]ith imperialism, politics became technological' (Csicscery-Ronay, 2003, 233). But one could just as easily substitute industrialisation for imperialism in the latter sentence; and there seems no good reason, other than postcolonial theoretical orthodoxy, not to do so. Again, there is much to be said for his observation that SF functions by 'managing the abstract techno-political leap ... from a nation among nations to a global culture' (Csicsery-Ronay, 2003, 235). Except that this is much more obviously true of American SF, from Asimov's *Foundation Trilogy* through to *Star Trek*, than of its European precursors. It simply isn't true, however, that the imaginary world-model of the entire genre is 'technoscientific Empire' (Csicsery-Ronay, 2003, 236). To the contrary, like the European empires themselves, each an empire among empires dominated by a nation among nations, nineteenth- and early–mid twentieth-century European SF tended to imagine its future worlds in distinctly national terms. This is obvious for the scientific romances of Verne and Wells, but almost equally so for Boulle's *La planète des singes* and Wyndham's *The Day of the Triffids*. Only with Houellebecq and Ballard is European literary SF annexed to Empire and, even then, only incompletely so. Csicsery-Ronay and Rieder have each raised important questions about SF's complicity with imperialism, but any adequate cultural geography of the genre must address both the significance of Czech and Polish SF and the important differences between the SF produced in relation, respectively, to European imperialism, the Soviet Russian experiment, and twenty-first-century globalised late capitalism. The obvious theoretical alternative is suggested by world-systems theory.

2. World-Systems Theory and Science Fiction: The Anglo-French Core

The more specific details of Wallerstein's method need not detain us here. Suffice it to say that his enduring concern has been with how capitalism functions as a world system, comprising a 'core', 'periphery' and 'semi-periphery'. 'Core–periphery', he explains, 'is a relational concept', referring, firstly, to the degree of profitability of production processes, secondly, the degree of monopolisation necessary to sustain such profitability and, thirdly, the degree of state patronage necessary to sustain such monopolies. 'Core-like processes', Wallerstein writes, 'tend to group themselves in a few states and to constitute the bulk of the production activity in these states. Peripheral processes tend to be scattered among a large number of states and to constitute the bulk of production activity in these states.' Some states, he adds, 'have a near-even mix of core-like and peripheral products. We may call them semiperipheral' (Wallerstein, 2004, 28). This, in outline, is the model Moretti applies to comparative literature, which we might be able to apply, in turn, to the global SF field.

World-systems theory first appeared in Moretti as a means to understand a relatively small number of exceptional texts: Goethe's *Faust*, Herman Melville's *Moby-Dick*, Wagner's *Der Ring des Nibelungen*, Joyce's *Ulysses*, Ezra Pound's *The Cantos*, Eliot's *The Waste Land*, Robert Musil's *Der Mann ohne Eigenschaften* and Gabriel García Márquez's *Cien años de soledad* (Moretti, 1996, 1–2). Unlike their canonical equivalents in French or English literature, he argues, these were '*world* texts, whose geographical frame of reference is no longer the nation-state'. They were also each products of the system's semiperiphery, sites of 'combined development', where 'historically non-homogeneous social and symbolic forms, often originating in quite disparate places, coexist in a confined space' (Moretti, 1996, 50). The argument resurfaces in more explicitly quantitative and sociological guise in *Atlas of the European Novel*, where it becomes a map of how the Franco-English cultural core pre-empted the development of other national literatures, whilst simultaneously opening up positive possibilities for innovation in the periphery. Citing Roberto Schwarz on Brazil (Schwarz, 1992, 29), Moretti writes of how 'peripheral' literatures can be 'sustained' by 'historical backwardness'. 'A new space encourages paradigm shifts', he observes,'because it poses new questions – and so asks for new answers ... The outcome of a new geographical space, these forms then produce *a new fictional space* ... A new space that gives rise to a new form – that gives rise to a new space. Literary geography' (Moretti, 1998, 195–97).

Moretti subsequently expanded on this analysis to advance an ambitious map of how comparative literature might be refigured as a discipline. He argued that the study of *Weltliteratur* can no longer be conceived simply as national literature writ large, 'literature, bigger', but must rather be reorganised around entirely different categories and conceptual problems. It 'is not an object,' he continues, 'it's a *problem*, and a problem that asks for a new critical method.' The model he proposes, adapted from Wallerstein, is that of a world literary system, simultaneously '*one*, and *unequal*: with a core, and a periphery ... bound together in a relationship of growing inequality.' If this is how the system functions, then the appropriate mode of analysis will become 'distant reading', he concludes, where distance '*is a condition of knowledge*', permitting the analyst 'to focus on units ... much smaller or much larger than the text: devices, themes, tropes – or genres and systems' (Moretti, 2000, 55–57). The result is a history of the modern novel understood as a 'system *of variations*', in which pressure from the Anglo-French core tends towards uniformity, whilst variable local realities in the periphery and semiperiphery tend towards difference. Tendency and counter-tendency produce a series of localised structural 'compromises', between foreign plot, local characters and local narrative voice, in which the 'one-and-unequal literary system' becomes embedded into the form itself (Moretti, 2000, 58–66).

Moretti's conjectures excited much controversy, both in the review in which it was published (Prendergast, 2001; Orsini, 2002; Kristal, 2002; Arac, 2002) and in scholarly comparatism more generally (Apter, 2003, 253–56; Spivak, 2003, 107–109n; Parla, 2004). In response, he conceded to Prendergast that other kinds of literature might well follow different patterns from the novel; and to Parla and Arac that even the English novel was itself originally a peripheral development in relation to an earlier Spanish core (Moretti, 2003, 75, 79). But he refused to retreat from the world-systems perspective itself, conceding very little indeed to Kristal's objection that the approach is necessarily 'occidentalist' or 'occidentocentric'. This was also Spivak's objection: 'this *is* nationalism,' she wrote, 'US nationalism masquerading as globalism' (Spivak, 2003, 108n). Moretti's response, directed at Kristal rather than Spivak, but equally applicable to both, is that 'Theories will never abolish inequality: they can only hope to explain it' (Moretti, 2003, 77). The combination of world-systems theory and distant reading clearly has some real purchase. It is unclear, however, why exactly it should become *the* method of comparative literary studies, as distinct from one amongst many. As Spivak asks: 'Why should the ... whole world as our object of investigation be the task of every comparativist ...?' (Spivak, 2003, 108n). The method nonetheless seems oddly appropriate to the particular questions we are attempting to answer in this chapter.

Moretti demonstrates that the novel became central to nineteenth-century European culture through the international predominance of its British and French variants, rather than as a set of discrete national entities. The nineteenth-century literary economy, he argues, comprised 'three Europes. With France and Britain always in the core; most other countries always in the periphery; and in between a variable group, that changes from case to case' (Moretti, 1998, 174). Using the volume of translations recorded in the various national bibliographies as key empirical indicators, he shows how French novelists were more successful in the Catholic South and British in the Protestant North, but that the whole continent read Scott, Bulwer-Lytton and Dickens, Dumas, Eugène Sue and Victor Hugo (Moretti, 1998, 178–79). Bulwer-Lytton's *The Coming Race* was, of course, a key text in nineteenth-century SF history; and Hugo was one of Verne's mentors. Moretti also shows how the long rivalry between these 'two narrative superpowers' was eventually won by France, 'making Paris ... the Hollywood of the nineteenth century'. By the mid-nineteenth century, translations of French novels into Italian outnumbered British by a ratio of eight to one, whilst even those into Danish were running only roughly even (Moretti, 1998, 184). The novel 'closes European literature to all external influences', he concludes, and then 'proceeds to deprive most of Europe of all creative autonomy: two cities, London and Paris, rule the entire continent for over a century, publishing half (if not more) of all European novels. (Moretti, 1998, 186)

What is true for the novel in general is also true for SF. Conceived in England and France, at the core of the nineteenth-century world literary system (Shelley, Bulwer-Lytton and, above all, Verne and Wells), it continued in both countries throughout the twentieth and into the twenty-first centuries (through Huxley, Orwell, Lewis, Wyndham, Hoyle, Clarke, Moorcock, Ballard, Banks, MacLeod and Miéville in Britain, Rosny, France, Renard, Spitz, Boulle, Merle, Walther, Brussolo, Arnaud, Dantec and Houellebecq in France). The United States has a fitful presence in the early tradition, essentially through Poe and Bellamy, but each of these is arguably more significant for their impact on the Anglo-French core, through Verne and Morris respectively, than on America itself. Verne and Wells are clearly crucial. In 1990, the last year in which the *UNESCO Statistical Yearbook* published figures for the most frequently translated authors, Verne was the fourth most translated author in the world, Wells the sixty-eighth (UNESCO, 1990, 7–110, 7–111). In 2011, UNESCO's online *Index Translationum* had Verne in second place, with 4606 new translations recorded between 1979 and 2011 (UNESCO, 2011). The University of Illinois holds translations of Wells's work in nineteen different European languages, including fifty-three titles in French, forty-seven in Spanish and thirty-two in German (Parrinder, 2005, 2). First published in England in 1895, *The Time Machine* was translated into French and Brazilian

Portuguese as early as 1899, into Hungarian in 1900, Russian in 1901, Italian in 1902, German in 1904 and Czech in 1905; *War of the Worlds*, published in England in 1898, was translated into Dutch, Hungarian and Norwegian in 1899, into French in 1900, German and Italian in 1901, Spanish in 1902 and Czech in 1903 (Parrinder and Barnaby, 2005, xxiii–xxv).

3. The European Semiperiphery

It is crucial to Moretti's application of Wallerstein's model that semiperipheral status is itself conducive to new cultural possibilities, in short, that a new space gives rise to a new form, a process with no direct equivalent in the original world-systems model of the global political economy. For Moretti, as not for Wallerstein, the distinction between periphery and semiperiphery amounts to that between simple cultural reception and imitation on the one hand, creative cultural innovation on the other. Which is why Moretti sees the literary system's semiperiphery as variable and changing from case to case. There is a danger here that the argument might collapse into near-tautology: if the only evidence of semiperipheral status is comparative cultural creativity, then one cannot logically use semiperipheral status to explain comparative cultural creativity. I intend to sidestep this question, however, by simply assuming that the distinction between periphery and semiperiphery can be established by other criteria, even though I am not in a position to do so here. The semiperipheral SF societies are, then, those which can be seen, retrospectively, as having substantially contributed to the global SF field and the evolving global SF selective tradition, the peripheral societies those which cannot.

The semiperipheral SF cultures are thus: the Weimar Republic (Gail, von Harbou and Lang, von Hanstein) and early Soviet Russia (Belyaev, Bogdanov, Bulgakov, Mayakovsky, Platonov, Alexei Tolstoy, Zamyatin); inter-war Czechoslovakia (Čapek, Troska); Communist Poland (Fialkowski, Lem, Wisniewski-Snerg) and late-Communist Russia (Altov, Bilenkin, Bulychev, Emtsev and Parnov, the Strugatsky brothers, Tarkovsky); inter-war North America (the genre's expansion into a whole range of new mass media, which we might well describe as 'the Gernsback moment'); and, finally, post-Second World War Japan (Abe, Hoshi, Komatsu, Murukami, Honda, Tezuka, Oshii). The periphery, by contrast, comprises those cultures that have received texts from and even to some extent imitated the Franco-British and American–Japanese cores, but did not independently contribute to the development of the global selective tradition. This includes both late nineteenth-century Japan and early twentieth-century Poland. Verne's *Le Tour du monde en 80 jours* was translated into Japanese as early as 1879, and six more of his *Voyages extraordinaires* in the early 1880s. These prompted a series of Japanese imitations, the best known of which is probably Oshikawa Shunrō's *Kaitei gunkan* (*Undersea Warship*), a reworking of *Vingt mille lieues sous les mers*. Wells's *The Time Machine* and *The War of the Worlds* were translated into Polish in 1899, prompting a series of Polish imitations, which led Andrzej Juszcyzk to the conclusion that the earliest 'Polish writers of science fiction ... worked more or less consciously under Wells's spell' (Juszczyk, 2005, 126). His examples include Jerzy Żulawski's lunar trilogy, *Na Srebrnym Globie* (*On the Silver Globe*) (1901), *Zwyciezca* (*The Victor*) (1908) and *Stara Ziemia* (*The Old Earth*) (1910), Antoni Słonimski's sole SF novel, *Torpeda Czasu* (*Time Torpedo*) (1924) and Bruno Winawer's *Doktor Przybram* (1924). Again, however, these do not acquire any lasting international significance, that is, they do not enter into the global SF selective tradition.

Setting aside the American and Japanese cases for the moment, we might begin by asking what kind of structural compromises occurred in the European semiperiphery. The most influential instance of Weimar SF was Lang's *Metropolis*, which had its first theatre release in January 1927, and is still one of the most expensive films ever made in Germany, costing DM 5,000,000 and very nearly bankrupting Universum Film Aktiengesellschaft. It was directed by Lang and scripted by von Harbou, both of whom had admired Wells's *The Sleeper Awakes* and clearly drew on it as a source. Apparently, Wells disliked their film, in part precisely for this reason (Schenkel, 2005, 96–99). Unlike Wells's Graham, Lang and von Harbou's hero and protagonist, Freder, is not literally woken from a 103-year long sleep, but his encounter with Maria nonetheless awakens him, for the first time, to the realities of exploitation and oppression in the city his father rules. Initially, neither protagonist has any real understanding of how their city works, even though Wells's London legally belongs to Graham and Lang and von Harbou's Metropolis to Freder's father, Joh Fredersen. But the clearest debt to Wells is in the architecture of the dystopian cityscape, which functions as a synecdoche for social catastrophe both in *The Sleeper Awakes* and in *Metropolis*.

That catastrophe is a massively exploitative class structure, vertically stratified between the darkest proletarian depths and the high city inhabited by the privileged classes. So, when Graham and Asano travel from the Business Quarter to the Underside, they penetrate 'downward, ever downward, towards the working places' (Wells, 2005c, 193–94). And, when Freder asks of his father 'wo sind die Menschen ... deren Hände Deine Stadt erbauten? [where are the people ... whose hands built your city?]', the camera cuts immediately to a shot of the workers descending by lift to the subterranean factories, as Fredersen retorts 'Wo sie hingehören ... in die Tiefe [Where they belong ... in the depths]' (Lang, 2002). Such vertical social stratification, which would become a standard trope in SF cinema, had no equivalent in Wells's or Lang and von Harbou's contemporary reality, where cities still tended to be stratified horizontally. The film's crowds and riots similarly echo those in Wells's novel, just as the profoundly masculinist relationship between Freder and Maria echoes that between Graham and Ostrog's niece, Helen Wotton. 'Do not forget the people', Helen urges Graham, 'who faced death, death that you might live' (Wells, 2005c, 140) and, when he finally wills the world to its people, 'Oh! Father of the World! ... I knew you would say these things' (Wells, 2005c, 215). The equivalent in *Metropolis* is in the closing scene, where Maria inspires Freder to unite capital and labour: 'Hirn und Hände wollen zusammenkommen [Head and hands want to join together]'; 'aber es fehlt ihnen das Herz dazu ... Mittler Du, zeige ihnen, den Weg zueinander ... MITTLER ZWISCHEN HIRN UND HÄNDEN MUSS DAS HERZ SEIN! [but they don't have the heart to do it ... Oh mediator, show them the way to each other ... THE MEDIATOR BETWEEN HEAD AND HANDS MUST BE THE HEART!]' (Lang, 2002).

The difference is obvious, however. Where Wells's novel ends in the midst of civil war, with both its outcome and Graham's own personal fate left deliberately unresolved, Lang and von Harbou's film concludes with the fully realised reconciliation of exploiter with exploited. In specifically German terms, this can be read as either Social Democratic or National Socialist and is very possibly both, if only because neither could have been achieved so cheaply in any imaginable historical reality. A Social Democratic solution would have required active structures of co-partnership, like those in the post-war Federal Republic; a National Socialist solution, the active suppression of working-class resistance, like that in the Third Reich. But *Metropolis* avoided the serious issues it raised, by substituting effect for idea, both the histrionic effects of the Freder–Maria relationship and the elaborate special effects of its cityscape. The latter is what finally excites our admiration in the film, then; not its ideas, which are rarely better than trite by comparison with *The Sleeper Awakes*, but rather the effects used to represent the city visually. It is in this respect that *Metropolis* most creatively reworks the legacies of the Anglo-French core, thereby providing the template for later cinematic SF cityscapes, from Cameron Menzies' *Things to Come* and Scott's *Blade Runner* to Proyas's *Dark City* and Besson's *The Fifth Element/Le Cinquième Élément*.

A similar cultural pattern can be observed in early Soviet Russia. By

1917, Verne and Wells were the most popular of all foreign authors published in Russian translation (Cockrell, 2005, 74). Alexei Tolstoy's *Aelita* (1924) is indebted to both, whilst Mikhail Bulgakov draws on more specifically Wellsian motifs in *Rokovye yaitsa* (*The Fatal Eggs*) (1925), *Sobach'e serdtse* (*The Heart of a Dog*) (1925) and *Master i Margarita* (*The Master and Margarita*) (1929–39) (Cockrell, 2005, 81–83). The key figure, however, is Zamyatin, who published Russian translations of *The Time Machine*, *The War in the Air* and *The Sleeper Awakes* in 1919–20 and wrote introductory commentaries to each of these and to the twelve-volume edition of Wells's collected works published in 1924–26 (Cockrell, 2005, 87). The original 1922 version of the latter is full of breathless admiration: 'almost all Wells's tales are constructed around brilliant, unexpected scientific paradoxes; all his myths are as logical as mathematical equations. And that is why we of today ... find this logical fantasy so compelling' (Zamiatin, 1997, 260).

Wells, Zamyatin insisted, is 'one of the greatest, most weighty and most interesting English writers' and 'the most contemporary of contemporary writers' (Zamiatin, 1997, 268, 274). The final version, reworked two years later, retained virtually all its initial enthusiasm (Zamiatin, 1970). Yet Zamyatin's *Mi* was nonetheless predicated on a powerful critique of exactly the kind of scientific positivism enjoined by Wells. As we noted in chapter 6, its Sole State is ruled by mathematics rather than by the Benefactor. The 'dystopian turn' commonly associated with Huxley and Orwell, and with mid twentieth-century Anglo-American SF more generally, is actually effected in Russia much earlier. Which is precisely why Orwell and Huxley were drawn to argue about the full extent of their respective borrowings from Zamyatin. This turn, which had far-reaching consequences for the shape of late twentieth-century SF, provides an unusually telling example of a structural compromise between the then dominant Anglo-French utopian positivism and local Russian characters and voice.

The pattern is repeated in inter-war Czechoslovakia. Verne had been translated into Czech as early as the 1870s, Wells not until *Ostrov doktora Moreaua* (*The Island of Doctor Moreau*) in 1901, but thereafter the latter was to prove the more decisive influence (Mánek, 2005, 166). Čapek visited Wells during his tours of England and Scotland and subsequently recalled the occasion with affection (Čapek, 1934; 1925, 180–81; Vocadlo, 1975, 105–15). Wells, in turn, repeatedly visited Czechoslovakia, often on Čapek's invitation, and they maintained regular contact until the latter's death in December 1938 (Mánek, 2005, 167). Nonetheless, Čapek's own work tended to poke fun at much that Wells most believed in, from science to socialism. In Čapek's last great novel, *Válka s mloky*, G. H. Bondy, the quintessentially capitalist captain of industry, celebrates the foundation of the Salamander-Syndicate with a promise that: 'A k jinému se ty potvory nehodí ... než aby se s nimi podnikala nějaká utopie. [And for nothing else are those damned beasts suited ... than that some Utopia should be achieved with them].' Lest the reader miss the reference, the appendix that immediately follows, 'O Pohlavním Životě Mloka [Of the Sexual Life of the Newts]', pointedly advises that: 'Viz v tom směru příslušnou literaturu [In this respect the reader is referred to the relevant literature] ... Paul Adam, H. G. Wells, Aldous Huxley' (Čapek, 1998, 112–13; 1937a, 152–53).

In *R.U.R.* itself, the comic prologue uses the character of Helena Gloryová, and her 'Liga humanity', which aims to liberate the robots from human oppression (Čapek, 1966, 28; 1961, 21–22), to parody precisely the kinds of progressive feminism Wells admired. The play's indictment of the robot revolutionary leader, Radius, also suggests a very different understanding of Lenin, and by extension of Stalin, to Wells's own: 'Nechci žádného pána ... Chci být pánem jiných ... Já chci být pánem lidí [I don't want any master. I want to be master over others ... I want to be master over people]' (Čapek, 1966, 49; 1961, 45). And the religiosity underpinning Čapek's critique of capitalist robotics and robotic communism stands diametrically opposed to Wells's atheistic scientism. So, when Harry Domin, R.U.R.'s production manager, tells Helena of old Rossum's pioneering work in robotics, he does so in terms that come close to Shelley's account of Victor Frankenstein:

> Víte, chtěl jaksi vědecky sesadit Boha ... Nešlo mu o nic víc než podat důkaz, že nebylo žádného Pánaboha zapotřebí. Proto si umanul udělat člověka navlas, jako jsme my.
> [He wanted to become a sort of scientific substitute for God, you know ... His sole purpose was nothing more or less than to supply proof that Providence was no longer necessary. So he took it into his head to make people exactly like us.] (Čapek, 1966, 16; 1961, 7)

The robot is, without doubt, one of the most significant innovations in the whole of inter-war SF, a new and immensely productive generic device that bequeathed a new word to the English and French languages. And it too seems to be the effect of a structural compromise between Anglo-French core plotlines and local Czech characters and voice.

Polish SF came to international prominence much later than Czech, and in the context of an imposed post-war Communism, as distinct from a threatened inter-war liberal democracy. Under Communism, however, both Wells and SF received an official seal of approval, and thereby became significant presences in the general culture. Key figures in Polish SF during this period included Fialkowski and Wisniewski-Snerg, but by far the best known was Lem, who famously judged *The War of the Worlds* 'najświetniejsze dzieło [the most brilliant work]' for its 'socjologiczna wyobraźnia [sociological imagination]' (Lem, 1974, 193, 195, cited in Juszczyk, 2005, 146). 'The importance of Wells's work on Lem is twofold', Juszczyk writes, 'firstly, there is a strong sense of Wells's leading role in the history of science fiction ... secondly, there are subtle but clear similarities between some of Lem's novels and stories and some of Wells's work' (Juszczyk, 2005, 145). Like Wells, Lem was scientifically trained; like Wells, he was a would-be polymath; and, like Wells, he was a child of the Enlightenment rather than Romanticism. Like Wells, Lem experimented with both utopia and SF; indeed, Suvin judges his *Obłok Magellana* one of 'the first utopia in world literature which successfully shows new characters creating and being created by a new society' (Suvin, 1979, 269).

Yet, there is an obvious and crucial difference, for where Wells retained a persistent optimism about the potentialities of scientific knowledge, an enduring focus in Lem, learnt from science itself, is that of the finite limits to what science can know. The paradigmatic case is *Solaris*, where all the efforts of the state-of-the-art Solaris Station, and of the science of solaristics more generally, including the characteristically positivist decision to bombard the planet with X-rays, fail to discover anything of significance about the conscious planetary intelligence they attempt to understand and contact. As the novel's central protagonist and narrator, Kris Kelvin, observes of the 'symetriada' the planet creates:

> Obserwujemy okruch procesu, drganie jednej struny w orkiestrze symfonicznej nadolbrzymów i mało tego, bo wiemy – ale tylko wiemy, nie pojmując – że równocześnie nad i pod nami, w strzelistych otchłaniach, poza granicami wzroku i wyobraźni zachodzą krocie i miliony równoczesnych przekształceń, powiązanych z sobą jak nuty matematycznym geometryczną, ale wobec tego my jesteśmy głuchymi jej słuchaczami.
>
> [We observe a fraction of the process, like hearing the vibration of a single string in an orchestra of supergiants. We know, but cannot grasp, that above and below, beyond the limits of perception or imagination, thousands and millions of simultaneous transformations are at work, interlinked like a musical score by a mathematical counterpoint. It has been described as a symphony in geometry, but we lack the ears to hear it.] (Lem, 2002, 138; 1971, 121).

Jameson rightly describes this argument, which is as much Lem's as Kelvin's, as an 'unknowability thesis' (Jameson, 2005, 107–18), a thesis that would have made no sense at all either to Wells or to Verne. At the close of *The War of the Worlds*, not only are the Martian invaders defeated, but they and their biology are also known and understood by the anonymous narrator and his science. The originality of Lem's text in this respect can surely be read as resulting in part from one of Moretti's structural compromises between the core and semiperiphery. If the idea of alien intelligence came from Wells, then that of its utter incomprehensibility can be plausibly explained as a loose correlate to the Polish experience of Russian-imposed Communism as so devoid of meaning as to reach the point of complete opacity.

For late-Communist Russia, the equivalent figures are the brothers and longstanding co-authors, Arkady and Boris Strugatsky. Here, again, we encounter the kind of structural compromise Moretti predicts. Slusser and Chatelain observe that, in all of the brothers' work, 'there is an abiding fascination with a particular aspect of Wells – alien invasion – and beneath this, at various levels of reference, a single work, *The War of the Worlds*' (Slusser and Chatelain, 2005, 292). The obvious example is *Vtoroe nashestvie marsian* (*The Second Invasion from Mars*) (1968), which is written in the form of a sequel to Wells's novel. But Slusser and Chatelain detect the trace of *War of the Worlds* in less obvious locations, notably *Piknik na obochine* (1972), where, they argue, 'the action … clearly focuses, as with Wells, on the inadequacy of human reactions to the alien event' (Slusser and Chatelain, 2005, 296). They mount a parallel case for *Za milliard let do kontsa sveta* (*A Billion Years to the End of the World*) (1978), translated into English as *Definitely Maybe*, where the Wellsian subtext derives from *The War of the Worlds*, but also, contrapuntally, from *The Invisible Man* (Slusser and Chatelain, 2005, 298–301). Unlike Wells, however, and very much like Lem, the Strugatsky brothers do not imagine the alien other as ultimately known or knowable. The analogy that gives *Piknik na obochine* its title bespeaks a version of the alien, not so much as hostile, but as simply indifferent to our very existence.

It is worth quoting the relevant encounter between their Nobel Laureate, Dr Valentin Pilan, and Richard M. Noonan, an electronic equipment supervisor, attempting to make sense of the apparently abandoned alien artefacts scattered throughout the Zone. It is as if they were the remnants of a picnic, Valentin suggests:

> Пикник. Представьте себе: лес, проселок, лужайка … Звери, птицы и насекомые, которые всю ночь с ужасом наблюдали происходящее, выползают из своих убежищ. И что же они видят? На траву понатекло автола, пролит бензин, разбросаны негодные свечи и масляные фильтры. Валяется ветошь, перегоревшие лампочки, кто-то обронил

> разводной ключ. От протекторов осталась грязь, налипшая на каком-то неведомом болоте... ну и, сами понимаете, следы костра, огрызки яблок, конфетные обертки, консервные банки, пустые бутылки, чей-то носовой платок, чей-то перочинный нож, старые, драные газеты, монетки, увядшие цветы с других полян
> A picnic. Picture a forest, a country road, a meadow ... The animals, birds, and insects that watched in horror through the long night creep out from their hiding places. And what do they see? Gas and oil spilled on the grass. Old spark plugs and old filters strewn around. Rags, burnt out bulbs, and a monkey wrench left behind. Oil slicks on the pond. And of course, the usual mess – apple cores, candy wrappers, charred remains of the campfire, cans, bottles, somebody's handkerchief, somebody's penknife, torn newspapers, coins, faded flowers picked in another meadow. (Strugatsky and Strugatsky, 2011; 1978, 102)

'Я понял, – сказал Нунан. – Пикник на обочине. [I see. A roadside picnic]', Noonan comments. 'Именно [Precisely]', Valentin replies: 'Пикник на обочине какой-то космической дороги [A roadside picnic, on some road in the cosmos]' (Strugatsky and Strugatsky, 2011; 1978, 102–3). This, too, can be read as evidence of a structural compromise between tropes and topoi deriving from the Wellsian core and very different semiperipheral motifs generated by a distinctly Russian understanding, born of Tsarism and Stalinism alike, of politico-social life as a condition of near-universal powerlessness.

4. From the Semiperiphery to the Core: North America and Japan

Darker undercurrents not withstanding – one thinks of Nemo and Moreau – Verne and Wells had generally written from within a self-confidently optimistic positivism, often bordering on the utopian. SF in Germany, Russia and *Mitteleuropa* generally abandoned this liberal futurology, opting either for an explicitly communist utopianism or, more interestingly, for dystopia, whether communist or capitalist, a theme later reimported into the Anglophone world by Orwell, that most un-English of English icons. Positivistic SF would be resumed in inter-war America, however, where, as we have seen, Gernsback coined the term scientifiction to describe the genre and traced its origins back retrospectively to Verne and Wells (and also Poe), although not, significantly, to the Eastern Europeans or to Shelley (Clute and Nicholls, 1993, 311). But this would be a positivism in a very different register, nonetheless, an escapist response to the Great

Depression rather than the easy celebration of scientific triumphalism. Hence, the quasi-Marxian character of Asimov's early Futurianism. This second epistemic shift is vital and was clearly a distinctly American achievement. The point needs to be stressed, however, that the United States was still, during the 1920s and 30s, very much nearer to the semiperiphery than to the core of the world literary system: for much of the twentieth century, British manufacturers retained a stranglehold on Anglophone publishing outside North America; even as late as 1996, the United Kingdom annual output of books amounted to 107,263 titles, the United States only to 68,175 (UNESCO, 1999, IV-82-89).

The core of the world literary system would, in fact, slowly shift from the London–Paris axis towards New York. But the 'Golden Age' of American SF is, nonetheless, the product of a significantly earlier moment, when the United States remained an essentially semiperipheral literary economy. At one point, Moretti asks why, in comparably 'peripheral' circumstances, the USA had failed to produce a paradigm shift akin to that of Latin American magic realism. His answer is that

> success and failure are highly *contingent* results ... the United States *could* indeed have produced a paradigm shift in the history of the novel in the mid nineteenth century ... On the other hand ... paradigm shifts are extremely rare events, and therefore what needs to be explained is not ... their absence ..., but rather their occurrence. (Moretti, 1998, 196n)

No doubt, this is so. But there is the additional alternative possibility, that North American 'backwardness' *did* in fact produce such a shift, not at the level of the 'modern epic', but in a marginal sub-form that would later generalise itself across the entire field of popular culture, from novel to film to television, so as to become the nearest we might ever have to a postmodern epic. This increasingly American form became, in turn, the core of the SF sub-system of the world literary system, and would therefore, in turn, itself collide with the substantive realities of later semiperipheral cultures, most especially in Japan.

The history of American SF is so familiar as to hardly warrant repetition. Suffice it to say that, during the inter-war period, the genre flourished both in Canada and the United States, and that the latter very rapidly became near-hegemonic, a situation which continued through the New Wave, feminism, Afrofuturism, cyberpunk and the new humanism of writers like Robinson. Moreover, North American hegemony extended from print to film and television. Despite this eventual dominance, we need to remember that the achievement was originally located on the semiperiphery of the world literary system. The structural compromise between the then dominant forms of Anglo-French scientific romance and more local North American registers is performed with wonderful precision in the Gernsback moment. Gernsback himself was, of course, a German-speaking immigrant, born Gernsbacher, who had only arrived in the United States in 1905. He was familiar with German-language SF and quite probably also with the first German-language SF magazine, *Der Orchideengarten*. His opening editorial for *Amazing Stories* promises its American readers the best that European SF could offer, that is, Verne and Wells – a promise it would keep – but also two American writers, Poe, who would not have been accorded an equivalent status in Britain, and Bellamy, who would not in either core literary economy (Gernsback, 1926, 3). The magazine itself, Gernsback's associated interests in broadcasting and his assiduous efforts to cultivate a fan base for scientifiction all suggest the mechanisms by which an essentially European literary genre would be reconstituted as North American and relocated in and around the audio-visual mass media. Gernsback didn't make this happen, any more than he made the Hugo Awards, but he is, nonetheless a wonderfully appropriate synecdoche for the entire process, a historical equivalent to the human similes in Miéville's *Embassytown*, but one who does not, thankfully, become a metaphor.

Contemporary American (and, to a lesser extent, British) SF was exported into Japan during the immediate post-Second World War period, in part as a result of the American military occupation. The genre's new Japanese semiperiphery responded to its new (Anglo-) American core much as the United States had responded to European SF, that is, by productively reworking inherited forms in ways that registered local Japanese peculiarities. The key Japanese SF writers – Kōbō Abe, Shinichi Hoshi, Sakyo Komatsu, Kenzaborō Ōe, Murakami – all achieve this kind of structural compromise. So, for example, the cruel evolutionism of Abe's 1959 *Daiyon kanpyōki* (*Inter Ice Age 4*), often claimed as the foundational text of post-war Japanese SF, can be read as recalling that of Clarke's *Childhood's End* (Tatsumi, 2011, 343). So Murakami's *Sekai noowari to hādo-boirudo wandārando* plays on Gibson's 'Johnny Mnemonic' even more obviously than his *ichi-kyu-hachi-yon* (*1Q84*) does on Orwell's *Nineteen Eighty-Four*. The decisive breakthrough, however, comes in the way Japanese writers, directors and animators appropriate the products of the American audio-visual media. Thematically, this is spectacularly evident in Honda's *Gojira* and the twenty-seven movies which followed between it and Ryuhei Kitamura's 2004 *Gojira: Fainaru Wōzu*, which rework the conventions of the American monster movie, through the prism of the distinctively Japanese experience of American nuclear attack, barely displaced into that of nuclear testing. Formally and technically, however, the crucial innovations are the synthesis of American comic-book SF with an older Japanese 'manga' tradition – the term dates from 1814 – to produce contemporary manga SF; and the synthesis of American animation with manga to produce anime.

Tezuka's 1949 reworking of Lang's *Metropolis* is perhaps the earliest example of SF manga, his *Tetsuwan Atomu* (*Mighty Atom*) certainly the best known, albeit as *Astro Boy*. Tezuka adapted *Tetsuwan Atomu* for television anime in 1963, in an interesting early example of the now widespread process by which manga, television anime and feature film anime are produced in combination. As Orbaugh explains, 'The most common path is for a narrative to start out as serialized manga and, after proving its popularity, to be remade into an animated television series, and later remade again into one or more feature films' (Orbaugh, 2009, 117). Many of the latter have met with international acclaim, notably Oshii's *Gōsuto In Za Sheru/Kōkaku Kidōtai* (*Ghost in the Shell*), Hideaki Anno's *Shin Seiki Evangerion* (*Neon Genesis Evangelion*) and Katsuhiro Otomo's *Akira*. Japanese SF has, then, moved from the genre's periphery to its semiperiphery and, in some respects, now threatens to rival American SF at the core. The sheer scale of the achievement is worth recording:

> manga and anime have become Japan's most significant artistic exports. Popular manga are translated into dozens of languages, available in bookshops throughout the developed world. Feature-length anime by well-known directors are commonly released worldwide ... In 2005, the global market for anime reached 233.9 billion yen (US$2.1 billion) ... from their first iterations ... manga and anime have been fundamentally linked with the development of sf as a genre in Japan. (Orbaugh, 2009, 112)

This seems to have little or no connection with Japan's imperialist past, certainly no more than Lem's fiction or Čapek's to the ill-fated Habsburg Empire, but much with its post-war role as a centre of technological and cultural innovation. Which is why I conclude that, although postcolonial theory can produce some limited insight into particular aspects of the genre's history, especially its early years in Britain and France, world-systems theory provides a more generally persuasive theoretical account of the cultural geography of SF. As we have seen, Moretti has been accused of occidentalism, a charge previously directed at Wallerstein himself (Dussel, 1998). A parallel accusation could perhaps be levelled at my own argument here. In self-defence, I can only comment that, writing from

Australia as I do, in what is very definitely a peripheral SF culture, I have no obvious vested interest in valorising the global system's cultural core. I could add that Australian SF has been unjustifiably neglected by the global SF selective tradition, a neglect I will attempt to redress, to some limited extent, in my closing chapter. But what such neglect means, in Moretti's terms, is precisely that Australia, like Latin America, still remains at the periphery of the global SF system. No doubt, Latin American SF scholars can make a good case for changing this state of affairs with respect to their own cultures, as I will shortly attempt for Australia. But that is their problem and this is mine. Either way, the world-systems approach seems to work.

9

The Uses of Science Fiction

We set out to answer four main questions: what, positively, was SF? what, negatively, wasn't it? when was it? and, finally, where was it? Our answer to the first question, developed in chapters 2 and 3 and elaborated in chapter 4, was that SF is a 'selective tradition', in Williams's terms, and that this selective tradition is produced and reproduced institutionally by the SF subfield of the general cultural field, defined in terms borrowed loosely from Bourdieu. Our answer to the second, developed in chapters 5 and 6, was that SF, utopia, dystopia and fantasy are analytically distinct but cognate genres, the relationship between which can be represented as a classical Venn diagram. The answer to the third, outlined in chapter 7, was that the genre is underpinned by a distinctly modern 'structure of feeling', in Williams's sense, which assumes that sciences normally can and normally will be applied as technologies, a structure of feeling which dates only from the early nineteenth century and is structured around what Adorno and Horkheimer called 'the dialectic of Enlightenment' and also a countervailing 'dialectic of Romanticism'. The answer to the last, given in chapter 8, was that the global SF field is organised as a core–periphery system, in Moretti's terms, where the core was originally Anglo-French but later moved to the United States, the semiperiphery variously German, Russian, Czech, Polish and Japanese, and the rest of the world, including Australia where I live and work, essentially peripheral. In this last chapter, I want to pull together some of these different threads, to address the specific question of the possible uses of SF, especially the future story, as negative or positive predictors of possible real-world future developments.

1. Future Stories and Futurologies

In the preceding chapters, I argued, *inter alia*, against what I've seen as overly prescriptive versions of SF criticism, whether the prescriptions be aesthetic, political or, as is most common, a combination thereof. SF can be liberal or conservative, socialist or fascist, or not very political at all and, nonetheless, still be SF; it can be canonical literature or pulp fiction or something nicely middlebrow in between and, nonetheless, still be SF. This might seem to suggest an implicit or actual hostility to the idea of the genre's having any practical political or ethical effectivity. This is not my intent, however. I certainly do not mean to suggest the kind of relativism that became *de rigeur* during high postmodernism, only that what Eagleton says of literature in general is also true of SF in particular: 'There is no such thing as a literary work or tradition which is valuable *in itself*... "Value" is a transitive term: it means whatever is valued by certain people in specific situations' (Eagleton, 1996, 11). This need not imply that we attempt to abstain from value judgements, an impossible task since valuing is something we all do all the time, whenever we debate with others the films we've seen or the books we've read. It means only that those values should not enter into the defining framework of academic study, as they clearly do for Suvin, Jameson and Freedman, for example in their policing of the boundaries between SF and fantasy, or between true and false nova.

We can and we do distinguish between what we see as better and worse texts, between those that are mindfucks and those that aren't, as my sons would have it, between more or less writerly and readerly texts, as Barthes had it, more or less open and closed texts, as Eco, between the more or less ideologically manipulative, the more or less patriarchal, and so on. And insofar as these distinctions are acceptable to wider valuing communities, then we can and we do engage in meaningful conversation about the value of texts. Valuing is fine; the category mistake is to attempt to predefine the content of an academic discipline or subdiscipline, such as SF studies, in terms of any particular set of aesthetic or political values. Weber theorised this problem through the distinction between value relevance and value freedom. 'The problems of the empirical disciplines', he wrote,

> are ... to be solved 'non-evaluatively'. They are not problems of evaluation. But the problems ... are selected by the value-relevance of the phenomena treated ... cultural (ie., evaluative) interests give purely empirical scientific work its direction. It is ... clear that these evaluative interests can be made more explicit and differentiated by the analysis of value-judgements. (Weber, 1949, 21–22)

This is the view I want to advance here, that SF studies as a field can be value-free, but that the particular arguments propounded within it will nonetheless be value-relevant.

Political or ethical concerns are, then, neither irrelevant nor unimportant. Indeed, much SF has been both deliberately intended by its authors and deliberately received by its readers as crucially value-relevant. Some, but not all, SF consists in future stories and some, but not all, is concerned either to advocate what its authors and readers see as desirable possible futures or to urge against what they see as undesirable possible futures. In short, the future story can be used as a kind of futurology. SF of this kind is intended to be politically or morally effective, that is, to be socially useful. '*We badly need a literature of considered ideas*', the Australian SF writer and critic, George Turner, argued in 1990: '*Science fiction could be a useful tool for serious consideration, on the level of the non-specialist reader, of a future rushing on us at unstoppable speed*' (Turner, 1990, 209). Three years earlier, in the 'Postscript' to what is by common consent his best SF novel, *The Sea and Summer*, Turner had written that: 'We *talk* of leaving a better world to our children, but in fact do little more than rub along with day-to-day problems and hope that the long-range catastrophes will never happen.' This particular novel, he explained, 'is about the possible cost of complacency' (Turner, 1987, 318). A very similar argument was recently mounted by Paolo Bacigalupi, the American SF writer, whose *The Windup Girl* was co-winner, with Miéville's *The City and the City*, of the 2010 Hugo Award for Best SF Novel. As Bacigalupi has made clear, his fiction is inspired by concerns as serious as Turner's: 'Mostly, I write these versions of the future because I'm worried about what seems to be happening, and I'm worried that we as a society aren't particularly interested in changing our ways' (Bacigalupi, 2009a). If some, but not all, SF writers understand their work thus, then the least SF criticism can do, by way of return, is to ask how well they succeed. This isn't by any means the only question one can pose to SF, merely one of many, but it matters nonetheless.

What especially interests me here is the genre's treatment of possibly catastrophic future developments, such as nuclear war and extreme climate change. In *The Seeds of Time* Jameson describes postmodern politics as exhibiting a cultural 'blockage' that prevents us from imagining the future except as 'an eternal present and, much further away, an inevitable catastrophe' (Jameson, 1994, 65–66, 70). Later, he would observe that 'it is easier to imagine the end of the world than to imagine the end of capitalism', adding that we also now 'witness the attempt to imagine capitalism by way of imagining the end of the world' (Jameson, 2003, 76). Žižek quotes Jameson's quip approvingly, before proceeding to contrast the international response to climate change with that to the 2008 financial crisis:

> save the planet from global warming … save the AIDS patients, save

> those dying for lack of funds for expensive treatments and operations, save the starving children ... all this can wait a little bit, but the call 'Save the banks!' is an unconditional imperative ... The panic was ... absolute, a trans-national, non-partisan unity ..., all grudges between world leaders momentarily forgotten in order to avoid *the* catastrophe. (Žižek, 2010, 334)

The contrast is well taken, but Jameson's initial diagnosis nonetheless runs the risk of mistaking true for false consciousness, to use slightly outdated terms. For what he reads as the socio-pathology of postmodern culture is far better understood as a Suvinian cognition effect, since, as a matter of actual fact, it has now become easier to destroy human civilisation than to overthrow capitalism.

This has been so, in principle, since the American nuclear attacks on Hiroshima and Nagasaki in August 1945 and, in practice, since the first accumulation of large American and Russian nuclear stockpiles during the 1950s. The Stockholm Institute for Peace Research calculates that, as at January 2011, eight states, America, Britain, China, France, India, Israel, Pakistan and Russia, possessed between them a total of about 20,530 nuclear warheads, 5,000 of which were ready for use and 2,000 on high operational alert, each typically far more powerful than the bombs that destroyed Hiroshima and Nagasaki, (SIPRI, 2011, 319-320). This is, by any reasonable calculation, more than sufficient to destroy human civilisation. Something similar can be said of climate change. The reason it has become so comparatively easy to imagine the large-scale inundation of major coastal cities is, quite simply, because the global climate is already warming at an appreciable rate. There is near-consensus amongst climate scientists that current levels of atmospheric greenhouse gas are sufficient to alter global weather patterns to disastrous and possibly catastrophic effect (Hegerl et al., 2007, 727) and also strong evidence that recent increases in heat waves and flooding are related to climate change (Schneider, et al., 2007, 796).

Paul Brians traced the first Anglophone fictional atomic war to 1895, but it is clear from his study that such stories were heavily concentrated in the Cold War period (Brians, 1987). Science-fictional representations of nuclear war and its possible aftermaths seem to have provided the Cold War generations with a primary adjustive mechanism through which to think the unthinkable. Well-known examples include Wyndham's *The Chrysalids* (1955), Hans Hellmut Kirst's *Keiner Kommt Davon* (*No One Will Escape*) (1957), Walter M. Miller's *A Canticle for Leibowitz* (1960) and Robert Merle's *Malevil* (1972). Climate change, by contrast, is a more recent motif.

Natural catastrophes, including flooding, are common enough in SF, perhaps especially so in Britain, where important examples included Wyndham's *The Kraken Wakes* (1953) and Ballard's *The Drowned World* (1962), but these were typically unrelated to real-world concerns over global warming. This might now be changing, however, as proto-ecological thematics become increasingly present in SF. Le Guin's *The Dispossessed* exhibited quite explicitly environmentalist politics as early as 1974 and Arthur Herzog's *Heat* explored the fictional possibilities of a runaway greenhouse effect in 1977. Robinson's *Pacific Edge* (1990) is an ecotopia, and his *Science in the Capital* trilogy (2004–7) pits the scientist-protagonist, Frank Vanderwal, and colleagues at the National Science Foundation against global warming, rising sea levels and the stalling of the Gulf Stream. Atwood's *Oryx and Crake* (2003) and *The Year of the Flood* (2009) trace the dynamics of American corporate capitalism through to anthropogenic ecological collapse. Karen Traviss's *Wess'har Wars* series (2004–8) is ecofeminist in both intent and effect. David Mitchell's 2004 *Cloud Atlas* and Winterson's *The Stone Gods* each combine narrative complexity and historical awareness with environmentalist thematics and SF tropes and topoi. And Bacigalupi's *The Windup Girl* is, of course, set in a twenty-third century Thailand overwhelmed by rising sea levels as a direct consequence of global warming.

We argued, in chapter 7, that SF has been predicated upon a dialectic of Enlightenment and Romanticism. For the great dialectical philosophers, such as Plato, Hegel and Marx, dialectic goes beyond mere binaristic antagonism only insofar as it eventually overcomes itself, in what the Germans call *Aufhebung*. To date, however, the dialectic of Enlightenment and Romanticism seems permanently stalled at the level of unresolved antagonism. Yet it isn't difficult to imagine what resolution would entail, at least in outline: a synthesis of Enlightenment science and the Romantic critique of science into some sort of Romantic science. Ironically, this option was actually available to early nineteenth-century Romanticism, which developed initially, as Rigby very persuasively argues, not as a generalised critique of science per se, but as a specific critique of particular Baconian and Newtonian versions of science (Rigby, 2004, 24). That critique was especially effective in the biological sciences, moreover, where mechanistic and atomistic models seemed especially inappropriate. It is no accident that Erasmus Darwin, the very 'Dr Darwin' cited in Shelley's 1818 Preface to *Frankenstein*, was both a poet, admired by Coleridge and Wordsworth, and a proto-evolutionist scientist, nor that his grandson, Charles, would credit Goethe as precursor to *On the Origin of Species* (Rigby, 2004, 29-30). If this type of Romantic science has any twenty-first century equivalent, then it is in the kinds of environmental science that alerted SF to the more dangerous possibilities of science-as-technology. To quote Bacigalupi again: 'Environmental science is telling us a lot about our future ... whether we're talking about global warming ... or a loss of genetic diversity in our food supplies, or the effects of low-dose chemicals on human development' (Bacigalupi, 2009a).

2. Antipodean Utopias

We noted in chapter 8 that Australian SF remains peripheral to the global SF system. Yet, there is a long history of what Adam Roberts described as 'works that located utopias and satirical dystopias on the opposite side of the globe' (Roberts, 2005, 56), that is, in Australia. His earliest example is Joseph Hall's 1605 *Mundus alter et idem sive Terra Australis ante hac semper incognita lustrata* (*A World Other and the Same, or the Land of Australia until now unknown*), the latest Nicolas Edme Restif de la Bretonne's 1781 *La Decouverte Australe par une homme-volant* (*The Discovery of Australia by a Flying Man*) (Roberts, 2005, 56–57, 85–86). Sargent's bibliography begins slightly later, with Peter Heglin's 1667 *An Appendix To the Former Work, Endeavouring a Discovery of the Unknown Parts of the World. Especially of Terra Australis Incognita, or the Southern Continent*, and proceeds to list something like 300 'Australian' print utopias and dystopias published during the period 1667–1999 (Sargent, 1999). But there are many others: neither Roberts nor Sargent mention Denis Veiras's *L'histoire des Sévarambes*, first published in part in English in 1675, in whole in French in 1679 (Veiras, 2006; 2001). The point to note is that European writers made extensive use of Australia as a site for utopian imaginings from well before the continent's actual conquest, exploration and colonisation, for the very obvious reason that it remained one of few real-world *terrae incognitae* still available for appropriation by such fantasy.

Most of these early antipodean utopian fictions took the form of an imaginary voyage narrated by travellers on their return home. So, Veiras's Captain Siden is en route to Batavia, when he is shipwrecked on the coast of Sevarambia, somewhere in what would now be Western Australia. He lives amongst the camel-riding Sevarambians for nearly fifteen years, studies their language, constitution and religion, takes three wives and fathers sixteen children before eventually being given permission to return to Europe (Veiras, 2001, 383). Such imaginings became less plausible when European explorers eventually brought back detailed accounts of Australia's climate, topography and people. As an immediate result, the utopias were progressively relocated further into the interior, but the realities of inland exploration soon proved equally disappointing. The subgenre of 'lost world' stories of ancient communities hidden in the desert nonetheless attained high popularity in the 1890s (Healy, 1978). Thereafter, however, in Australia as elsewhere, utopias were increasingly superseded by future-fictional uchronias. Robyn Walton cites Robert Ellis Dudgeon's *Colymbia*, published in 1873, as the first Australian science-fictional utopia (Walton, 2003, 7), although Joseph Fraser's *Melbourne and Mars* (Fraser, 1889), the diaries of a merchant able to travel between Melbourne and Mars more easily than we do today between Melbourne and London, is better known.

Moreover, once again in Australia as elsewhere, as the twentieth century proceeded, utopias were also increasingly displaced by dystopias. The best-known of these Australian SF dystopias are almost certainly Shute's nuclear 'doomsday' novel, *On the Beach*, and Turner's climate change dystopia, *The Sea and Summer*. *On the Beach* was, by Australian commercial standards, an astonishing success. First published in 1957, it had two printings in that year, a third in 1958 and a fourth in 1959. Subsequent reprintings followed regularly, the title remaining more or less continuously in print thereafter, the most recent to my knowledge being Random House's 2009 Vintage Classic. In 1978, the *UNESCO Statistical Yearbook* listed Shute as the most translated of all Australian writers and the 133rd most translated author in the world, with ninety-six translations during the period 1961–65, twenty-two in 1973 alone (UNESCO, 1978, 915). *On the Beach* was translated into Danish, Dutch and Japanese as early as 1957, Norwegian and German in 1958, Italian in 1959, French in 1968. According to the Nevil Shute Norway Foundation's[10] by no means exhaustive calculations, there are now translations in Bulgarian, Czech, Finnish, Greek, Greenlandic, Gujurati, Hungarian, Icelandic, Marathi, Polish, Portuguese, Romanian, Russian, Serbo-Croat, Slovak, Slovenian, Telugu, Urdu – and Klingon. First published in 1987, *The Sea and Summer* is an expanded version of a 1985 short story, 'The Fittest', which had also

10 'The Nevil Shute Norway Foundation web site is dedicated to the writing, wisdom and philosophy of Nevil Shute Norway. It is a tribute to his skill that more than fifty years after his death, Nevil Shute's works are still enjoyed by so many people around the world. The Nevil Shute Norway Foundation web site is for, by, and of Nevil Shute readers everywhere. It exists primarily for the exchange of news, opinions, and similar information among readers. Those interested in researching specific aspects of Nevil Shute's life and work will find the site an excellent place to start. It serves as a means of contact with other Shutists, as well as providing much specific Shute related information' (Nevil Shute Norway Foundation, 2011).

explored the fictional possibilities of the effects of global warming. Substantially less profitable than *On the Beach*, in 1988 *The Sea and Summer* nonetheless won both the Commonwealth Writers' Prize and the Arthur C. Clarke Award for best SF novel published in Britain (the previous year's had gone to Atwood for *The Handmaid's Tale*).

A Hollywood film version of *On the Beach*, produced by United Artists as a 'solid prestige job' (Walker, 1991, 815), appeared in 1959, directed by Stanley Kramer. It ran for over two hours and featured Gregory Peck as Dwight Towers, the commander of the American submarine *USS Scorpion*, and Ava Gardner and Fred Astaire, somewhat improbably, as the main Australian characters, Moira Davidson and John Osborne (Kramer, 1959). Filming began near Shute's own home at Langwarrin, thirty miles south of Melbourne, and continued in or near Melbourne during the spring of 1958. At a time when domestic Australian cinema had fallen into near-decrepitude, the film excited 'massive public curiosity' (Smith, 1976, 138). Kramer won a BAFTA for best director in 1960, Ernest Gold a Golden Globe for best score, and the film was nominated for two Oscars, although it won neither. In 2000 a telemovie version followed, which relocated the story from 1963 to 2007 and renamed the ship the *USS Charleston*. Directed by Russell Mulcahy, it featured Armand Assante as Towers, Rachel Ward as Davidson and Bryan Brown as Osborne, and was distributed by Channel 7 in Australia, Showtime and Hallmark in the United States, AXN in Japan. It won two Australian Film Institute awards in 2000 and was nominated for two Golden Globes the following year. More recently, BBC Radio 4 broadcast a radio version as its Classic Serial over a two-week period in November 2008. Dramatised by Mike Walker and directed by Toby Swift, Towers was played by William Hope, Davidson by Indira Varma and Osborne by James Gordon-Mitchell (Smith, 2008). By contrast, *The Sea and Summer* has been out of print for over a decade and has never been adapted for film, television or radio.

As we noted in chapters 5 and 6, Williams, Suvin, Jameson, Freedman and the early Moylan all exhibit clear antipathy to dystopia, essentially on the grounds that it tends, in Jameson's phrase, 'to denounce and ... warn against Utopian programs' (Jameson, 2005, 199). But, as we argued there, many dystopias, including those most disliked by Williams, Suvin and Jameson, do actually function as implicitly utopian warnings, rather than as anti-utopias in the strict sense of this term. This is true, I would argue, for both *On the Beach* and *The Sea and Summer*. Writing in the Australian newspaper, *The Age*, in 2008, Peter Christoff, the then Vice President of the Australian Conservation Foundation, observed that *On the Beach* had 'helped catalyse the 1960s anti-nuclear movement'. My own personal experience, for what it is worth, tends to bear out this judgement. As I recounted in chapter 1, Shute's novel was the first SF print text aimed at adults that I ever read and it propelled me into CND and thence, indirectly, into a whole series of further radical causes.

Comparing the threat of nuclear war in the 1950s with that of global warming in the early twenty-first century, Christoff warned that 'Like the characters in *On the Beach*, we are ... suffering from a radical failure of imagination.' What is interesting about this, quite apart from the cultural politics of global warming, is that he assumed Shute's novel would still retain a hold on the Australian public imagination over half a century after its publication. Indeed, when Christoff sought to alert *The Age*'s readers to the more alarming consequences of runaway climate change, he deliberately invoked the threat to the very beaches Shute had iconicised in the 1950s: 'So imagine at the end of this century ...,' he writes, 'summers without many of our beaches, if sea levels rise by even as little as 20 to 50 centimetres and storms scour away the rest' (Christoff, 2008, 13). When Christoff connected *On the Beach* to climate change, he did so precisely to urge the need for a parallel contemporary effort to imagine the unimaginable. 'These are distressing, some will argue apocalyptic, imaginings,' he admits. 'But without them, we cannot undertake the very substantial efforts required to minimise the chances of their being realised' (Christoff, 2008, 130). *The Sea and Summer*, it seems to me, had in fact attempted this two decades previously, but with less apparent success than *On the Beach*. The immediate question I want to pose here, then, is why the one novel was so much more politically and sociologically successful than the other.

3. *On the Beach* and *The Sea and Summer*

Both Shute and Turner lived in Melbourne and both had begun with literary ambitions very far removed from SF. By the time of the latter's death in 1997, however, he had become in effect the genre's Australian elder statesman. Both *On the Beach* and *The Sea and Summer* are set mainly in and around Melbourne, a vividly described, particular place, terrifyingly transformed into the utterly unfamiliar. The first is set during the second year after a full-scale nuclear war in the northern hemisphere, so that its subject matter becomes nothing less than the slow extinction of the last affluent remains of the human race. The second describes, in its core narrative, a world of mass unemployment and social polarisation, in which rising sea levels have resulted in the inundation of the city's bayside suburbs. When Shute first discussed the cover design for *On the Beach* with Heinemann, he had suggested 'a scene of the main four or five characters standing together quite cheerfully highlighted on a shadowy beach of a shadowy river – the Styx' (Smith, 1976, 129). Unusually, Heinemann did exactly as he asked. This juxtaposition of light and shade, cheerfulness and death, provides a nicely economical representation of the novel's central organising principle, what I will call its 'apocalyptic hedonism', a textual erotics deriving from the simultaneous juxtaposition of the terrors of imminent extinction and the delights of yet more immediate hedonistic affluence. There is no equivalent in *The Sea and Summer*, which is structured around the opposition between a core narrative dealing with the 'Greenhouse Culture' of the mid twenty-first century and a frame narrative set very much later in a slowly cooling world. Let us explore some of the crucial differences between the two texts.

On the Beach opens with a young Australian naval officer, Lieutenant-Commander Peter Holmes, still sore from a day spent partly on the beach and partly sailing, drowsily recalling the Christmas barbecue of two days earlier (Shute, 2009, 1). The 'short, bewildering war … of which no history … ever would be written' is introduced into this quintessentially Australian idyll at exactly the moment when Holmes and his wife, Mary, are planning to meet at their club and go on for a swim (Shute, 2009, 2–3). It closes with Towers and Davidson, he aboard the *USS Scorpion* heading south from the Heads, she ashore near Port Lonsdale, and an analogous, though now much darker, juxtaposition, that between the bottle of brandy and the Government-issue suicide tablets, between the 'big car' with 'plenty of petrol in the tank' and the nuclear submarine (Shute, 2009, 312, 310). Both opening and closing passages thus attain their primary narrative effectivity precisely through their apocalyptic hedonism. Similar motifs recur throughout the text: Osborne's new red Ferrari, for example, 'washed and polished with loving care' (Shute, 2009, 146), and his enthusiastic pursuit of what must be the very last Australian Grand Prix; his Uncle Douglas's sturdy determination to work through the Pastoral Club's wine cellar – 'we've got over three thousand bottles of vintage port left in the cellars … and only about six months left to go, if what you scientists say is right' (Shute, 2009, 97); and the fishing trip on the Jamieson River (Shute, 2009, 270–78) made possible by a Government decision to bring forward the trout season 'for this year only' (Shute, 2009, 229).

Asked her opinion of Melbourne during the filming of *On the Beach*, Ava Gardner is reputed to have judged it 'the perfect place to make a film about the end of the world'. Apocryphal or not, the remark has provoked much subsequent umbrage in Melbourne. And yet Gardner – or perhaps the Sydney journalist Neil Jillett, in whose article the quotation first appeared – was absolutely right. Both Melbourne in particular and Australia in general were indeed ideal locations for a film or book about the end of the world. Like the British settler colonies in North America, those in Australia had a longstanding and historically by no means unrealistic sense of themselves as unusually affluent and hedonistic societies. Unlike the North American colonies, however, those in Australia also suffered from an almost equally longstanding, and perhaps less realistic, sense of themselves as unusually exposed to the threat of invasion from the Asiatic north. Australian culture has thus been peculiarly conducive to the genesis of dystopian collective fantasies of racial extinction, for example the late nineteenth-century race-war dystopias, such as Kenneth Mackay's 1895 *The Yellow Wave* (Mackay, 2003). Fantasies of this kind acquired a much wider audience during the Cold War, however, as a result of the sudden coincidence of a runaway nuclear arms race with a general economy of affluence.

On the Beach became the single most influential nuclear war dystopia, despite exciting very little respect in academic literary criticism, in part precisely because of this apocalyptic hedonism. And it is interesting to note how the effect is achieved. As we have seen, the young Williams distinguished between 'Putropia', 'Doomsday' and 'Space Anthropology', admitting to an intense dislike of the first two, primarily because he saw them as evidence of a structure of feeling that pitted 'the isolated intellectual' against the 'masses', conceived as 'at best brutish, at worst brutal'. Whatever we make of the examples Williams himself gives, it is clear that this analysis will not work for Shute. For there is no sense of any of the latter's characters as isolated intellectuals: they are Navy men and Navy wives, Government scientists, farmers and farmers' daughters. And they are fully integrated into, rather than separated from, the surrounding population, who are themselves neither brutal nor brutish, but commendably ordinary and ordinarily commendable. When the *Scorpion* sails into Cairns, searching for possible survivors, the novel records that:

> Through the periscope they could see streets of shops shaded with palm trees, a hospital, and trim villas ...; there were cars parked in the streets and one or two flags flying ... The cranes were trimmed fore and aft along the wharves and properly secured ... Cairns looked exactly as it always had before. The sun shone in the streets, the flame trees brightened the far hills, the deep verandas shaded the shop windows ... A pleasant little place to live in the tropics, though nobody lived there ... (Shute, 2009, 78–79)

Here, surely, is the key to the novel's status, that it does exactly what Williams thought Doomsday novels couldn't, that is, it depicts a universal catastrophe, stoically and democratically endured, precisely as a cautionary tale. As Towers muses, 'Maybe we've been too silly to deserve a world like this' (Shute, 2009, 89). This, in turn, explains both its socio-political effect on the nuclear disarmament movement and its intertextual effect in film, television and radio.

In *The Sea and Summer*, by contrast, there is neither generalised affluence nor properly apocalyptic catastrophe. As the core narrative opens, the poor 'Swill' already live in high-rise tower blocks, the lower floors of which are progressively submerged, the wealthier 'Sweet' in suburbia on higher ground. In 2033 a third of Australia has been set aside for Asian population relocation, by 2041 the global population has reached ten billion and the cost of iceberg tows and desalinisation projects has brought the economy close to bankruptcy (Turner, 1987, 29–30). On his sixth birthday in 2041, Francis Conway and his nine-year-old brother, Teddy, are taken by their parents, Alison and Fred, to see the sea. What they find is a concrete wall 'stretching out of sight in both directions'. Francis's mother surprises him, however, by explaining that 'This is Elwood and there was a beach here once. I used to paddle here. Then the water came up and there were the storm years and the pollution, and the water became too filthy.' 'It must be terrible over there in Newport when the river floods,' she continues: 'A high tide covers the ground levels of the tenements' (Turner, 1987, 23–24). In 2044 Fred Conway is laid off and commits suicide, leaving Allie and the boys to move to Newport (Turner, 1987, 30–34), where they meet Billy Kovacs, the Tower Boss, who becomes Alison's lover, Francis's mentor and the reader's guide to the social geography of an Australian dystopia.

Where the narrative voice in Shute is that of the omniscient author, Turner's text is deliberately polyphonic. Its core narrative traces the development of the Greenhouse Culture through a set of memoirs and diary extracts written by five key protagonists, Alison Conway, Francis Conway, Teddy Conway, Nola Parkes and Captain Nikopoulos, during the years 2044–61. Where Shute's narrative proceeds in strict chronology, Turner's core narrative is counter-chronological, beginning and ending in 2061, but moving through the 2040s and 50s as it develops. Where *On the Beach* has a relatively simple structure of nine chapters, *The Sea and Summer* is organised into a main narrative comprising two parts set in the mid twenty-first century, and a frame narrative comprising three shorter parts set later, amongst 'the Autumn People' of the 'New City' in the Dandenongs (Turner, 1987, 3–16, 87–100, 315–16). The latter depicts a utopian future society, busily using submarine archaeology to explore the drowned remains of the 'Old City'. As with the critical dystopias we examined in chapter 6, a primary effect of this frame narrative is to blunt the force of dystopian inevitability driving the core narrative.

Both in philosophical aesthetics and in the kinds of literary criticism aligned with philosophy, the canonical artwork has conventionally been understood as paradigmatic, in the sense of realised ideal rather than that of mere instance. As David Roberts observes, the 'essential theoretical function' of normative aesthetics, from Kant and Hegel to Lukács and Adorno, is that of 'determining the paradigmatic work of art' (Roberts, 1990, 44). This was as true of Leavis on the cultural right, for whom Lawrence became the contemporary embodiment of the 'Great Tradition', as for Lukács on the cultural left, for whom Thomas Mann represented the highest achievement of contemporary 'critical realism' (Leavis, 1955; Lukács, 1963). And it remains true for Bloom, for whom Shakespeare's *Lear* is 'at the center of centers of canonical excellence ... primal aesthetic value, free of history and ideology' (Bloom, 1994, 65). Such criticism often appears to deduce its particular literary–critical judgements from more general propositions, but on examination those propositions tend to presuppose the judgements they produce. In short, their procedures are quasi-tautological. For the kind of sociology produced by Bourdieu and his colleagues, by contrast, even popular fiction can be considered paradigmatic insofar as it does empirically provide culturally effective models of thought and action.

In this sociological sense, Shute's *On The Beach* is *the* paradigmatic nuclear war dystopia, but Turner's dystopia is clearly not, or at least not yet, the paradigmatic climate-change dystopia Christoff hoped for. We might be able to explain this difference using the model of the SF field developed in chapter 3. In terms of the map of the field shown in Figure 3, where, then, should we locate Shute and Turner? My answer is represented in Figure 7. *On the Beach* was first published by William Heinemann, a major British commercial publisher with offices in London, Toronto and Melbourne, and by William Morrow, a major American commercial publisher, in New York. *The Sea and Summer* was published by Faber and Faber, the largest British 'independent' publisher, as it likes to describe itself, in London and Boston. Faber isn't quite Bourdieu's Minuit, but it might well be the closest English equivalent, for it too has Beckett in its back-list. *On the Beach* was massively profitable, but won no awards; *The Sea and Summer* substantially less profitable, but nonetheless critically acclaimed. Finally, we might note that, where Shute made a good living as a professional commercial writer, Turner had been in receipt of state patronage, through a writer's fellowship from the Australia Council's Literature Board.

I conclude, then, that Shute's novel would be in a roughly similar location to Verne's fiction, in the space indicated by scientific romance. Turner's would be roughly proximate, but nonetheless significantly removed

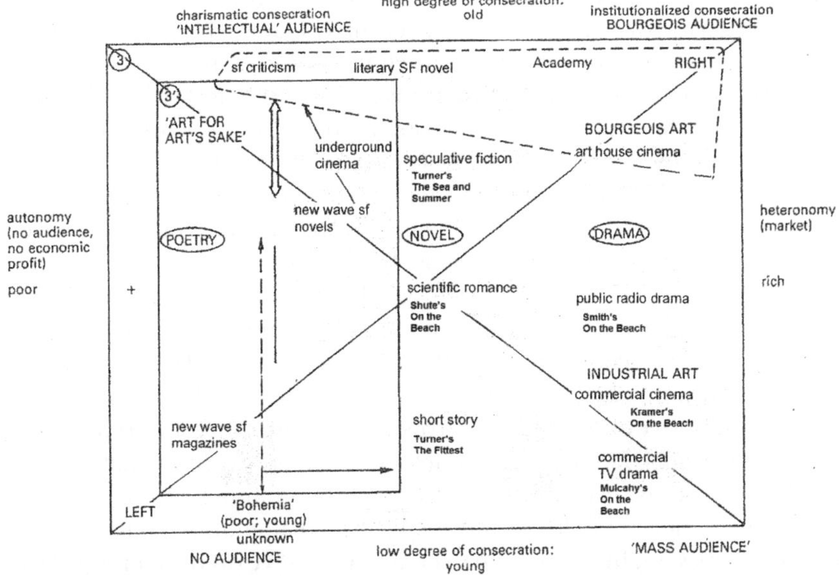

Figure 7: Nevil Shute, George Turner and the global science fiction field.

towards the area demarcated by the broken line in Bourdieu's diagram, which outlines the overlap between the restricted economy of symbolic profit, charismatic consecration by the intelligentsia and institutionalised bourgeois art. It would fall somewhere between the nineteenth-century French society novel and psychological novel, perhaps closest to the latter, in the space we marked as speculative fiction. Turner almost certainly intended *The Sea and Summer* as a literary SF novel, but it isn't clear as yet whether this ambition will ever be realised. I have also mapped into Figure 7 the approximate locations of the short story that inspired *The Sea and Summer* and of the film, television and radio adaptations of *On the Beach*. The three adaptations occupy locations equivalent to Bourdieu's nineteenth-century dramatic forms, that is, further towards the heteronomous end of the field than either of the novels. The spatial proximity of Shute's novel to the three adaptations suggests something of the mechanisms by which it became paradigmatic and Turner's did not. In the short term, at least, the more popular and less literary of the novels was much more likely to be adapted for radio, film and television.

As we noted in chapter 3, however, the transformation of symbolic into economic capital normally occurs only over the relatively long term. Such investments are always speculative, since for every Beckett there will always be a plethora of indefinite loss-makers. So the question remains as to whether *The Sea and Summer* will eventually emerge from Faber's back-list to become a possible paradigmatic climate-change dystopia. No doubt, it is too early to tell, but there are reasons to believe it might, if only because the politics of climate change shape contemporary political discourse much more powerfully than in the 1980s. The Kyoto Protocol came into force in 2005 and, for all its undoubted deficiencies, now provides an international framework for climate change mitigation strategy that would have been possible only in SF during the 1980s. In Australia itself, the Labor Party won the 2007 federal election, as surely as the conservative parties lost it, substantially over this very issue; and, if Labor ran quiet on the question at the following election, the Australian Greens did not and were rewarded, partly as a result, with a combined total of ten seats in the federal parliament, the most ever held by an Australian third force. Moreover, the 2010–11 summer floods which followed more or less immediately after the 2010 election served to deliver a visceral reminder of the reality of imminent ecological crisis to those still in denial about climate change. Cultural critics might not be able to do much to stave off the consequences of environmental catastrophe, but they can, perhaps, try to persuade someone, somewhere, to republish Turner's novel, maybe turn it into a film, even a television series. In the meantime, I will settle for the conclusion that there are suitably apposite tales of resonance and wonder, intelligence and warning, available in dystopian SF. We just haven't learnt to value them properly, not yet anyway.

4. Anticipations of Phil Chase

I began with an autobiographical account of my early encounters with SF and will end in very similar register, not with memories of Hampson's Dan Dare, but rather in anticipation of the environmentally activist President Phil Chase in Robinson's *Science in the Capital* trilogy. I have argued against the kind of prescriptive SF criticism that inscribes values into its subject matter, but nonetheless in favour of value-relevant scholarship. If it hasn't become obvious, I will now finally declare my own hand: philosophically, I am an ecosocialist, politically, a fully paid-up, card-carrying, but often regrettably inactive, member of the Australian Greens. I am an ecosocialist, in part, because I remain completely unpersuaded by liberal environmentalist arguments to the effect that 'free' markets are essentially beneficent institutions: the market isn't the solution, it's the problem. But also, in part, because I cannot subscribe to the socialist tradition's longstanding belief in the desirability of economic growth. Marx and Engels, for example, famously insisted that 'the development of productive forces … is an absolutely necessary practical premise' for the transition to post-capitalist society, 'because without it *want* is merely made general … and all the old filthy business would necessarily be reproduced' (Marx and Engels, 1970, 56). No matter how obviously defensible a proposition this must have seemed to nineteenth-century socialists, the continuous development of the productive forces had by the twenty-first century already *become* the old filthy business of capitalism.

No doubt, Marx was absolutely right to insist that the competitive accumulation of capital will necessarily generate an increase in what he termed the 'organic composition of capital', that is, the proportion of constant capital, or dead labour, in relation to the proportion of variable capital, or living labour (Marx, 1970, 612); that this will, in turn, produce a long-run tendency towards declining rates of profit; which, in their turn, will produce periodic crises of over-accumulation with all the human misery these generate (Marx, 1972, 211–13). The socio-political corollary of this economic tendency is the contradiction between capital and labour. But what Marx's model ignored was that this selfsame process of competitive accumulation also produces a corresponding increase in the proportion of dead nature in relation to living nature, railway sleepers in relation to trees. Contemporary environmental science and ecology suggest that the contradiction between capital and nature might actually be at least as important as that between capital and labour. O'Connor has defined this 'second contradiction' as capitalism's tendency to destroy the natural environment on which production depends, simply because there is 'no profit in maintenance or preservation … The profit is in expansion, accumulation, and marketing' (O'Connor, 1998, 317). But nature, unlike labour, is not a social actor and must therefore be represented politically by some human force or not at all. In party political terms, the Greens perform this function, which is why I chose to become a member.

This does not, however, mean that I espouse the kind of SF criticism that will somehow prescribe Green outcomes. It means only that, as an individual reader with particular interests and concerns, I have become increasingly underwhelmed by the kind of SF that cheerfully takes as its starting point the destruction, serious or comic, of the only planet we might ever have. The last-man trope was both original and inventive when first deployed in the figure of Shelley's Lionel Verney, still deftly comic in Adams's Arthur Dent and Grant and Naylor's Dave Lister, but had become tritely sentimental by the time Proyas's John Koestler farewelled Caleb, Abby and their rabbits (Shelley, 2008; Adams, 1985; Grant and Naylor, 1988–93; Proyas, 2009). I find myself in some sympathy, then, with Geoff

Ryman's *Mundane Manifesto*, even if the phrase 'mundane SF' comes as close to oxymoron as anything in the genre's selective tradition (Ryman, 2006; Ryman, 2009). What I want to see, in print, in film, on radio and on television, is SF that takes environmental problems as seriously as Cold War SF took the threat of nuclear war. It need not be dystopian, although it might well be so, if only because, as Bacigalupi said, the likely future outcomes seem increasingly unpleasant. But there will also be a place for the type of utopian imaginings implicit in Turner's frame narrative. Indeed, part of the strength of Robinson's *Science in the Capital* trilogy is that it succeeds, as Rigby rightly observes, in locating utopian possibilities 'in the thick of the disaster scenario itself, exploring better and worse ways of responding to crisis and catastrophe, with a view to envisaging how the horizon of a better future might be held open, rather than dictating how that future should be designed' (Rigby, 2011, 76). The collection of 'short stories from a damaged planet', edited by Mark Martin with an 'Introduction' by 350.org's Bill McKibben (Atwood et al., 2011) – a collection which includes a short prose-poem by Atwood, stories by Mitchell and Bacigalupi, and an extended extract from Robinson's *Sixty Days and Counting* – is as good a start as any, but obviously not itself the paradigmatic climate-change novel we might yet hope for.

To conclude by returning to my autobiographical subtext, I should explain that parts of this book were written in the unusual circumstance of a house flooded from end to end. The southern hemisphere summer of 2010–11 subjected large areas of Brazil, Southern Africa and Eastern Australia to extensive flooding. In Australia, the north-eastern state of Queensland reported the highest rainfall, most widespread flooding and severest cyclone season on record. During December and January, catastrophic floods cost thirty-five lives across the state and caused something like a billion Australian dollars' worth of damage. They were followed in January by extensive flooding along the border between the states of Victoria and New South Wales. On 2 February, Tropical Cyclone Yasi roared out of the Pacific and into Queensland, devastating towns and cities already struggling to cope with the floods. It was a category four storm, 900 miles across, which generated winds of up to 155 mph on landfall. It moved inland, slowing down to category two by the time it reached the desert city of Alice Springs, which it drenched in torrential rain. It threw out cyclonic waves of tropical moisture across eastern Australia, one of which reached Melbourne at about 8.30 on the evening of 4 February. What happened next was very small beer by comparison with Queensland, but nonetheless quite unprecedented in the thirty years I had lived there. We had nearly 130 mm of rain in 24 hours, most of it falling in less than 90 minutes. The nearby canal burst its banks, the water rose over my doorstep and under the French windows and then spread through the house, which, like most in Australia, is a single-storey bungalow. Throughout the suburb, and others nearby, homes were similarly affected. We've been clearing up ever since: in the first few days we threw out ruined carpets and furniture; in August we replaced the warped floorboards; in October the cracked bathroom and kitchen tiles. By the time I eventually sent the manuscript for this book off to the publisher, conditions seemed to have returned to what passed for normality in the early twenty-first century Greenhouse Culture. But I fear this may be only temporary. Because I live in Elwood, only a few minutes walk from the beach where Alison Conway used to play as a little girl.

Afterword

I decided on the book's closing sentence in February 2011, only a week or so after my house had flooded, and wrote the whole of the final chapter towards its concluding encounter with the young Alison Conway. But other quite unrelated events eventually convinced me that this little flood was ultimately a very small matter, not only in relation to the collective life of Australia, but also to my own personal biography. As narrative, the book ends where it ends. But as autobiography there is more to add. I began work on the book in West Yorkshire in late 2007, whilst tending to my teenage sweetheart and first love, Kathryn Turnier (née Wench), who was dying from pancreatic cancer. I completed the first draft in Victoria over the Australian summer of 2011–12, during the early part of which I had tended to my sister, Joyce Morton (née Milner), who was dying from an ovarian cancer that had metastasised into her liver. There was a truly fearful symmetry to the occasion of the book's composition, if only because Kathy and Joyce had known each other well. They had attended the same girls' grammar school, eaten at the same school dinner table, played in the same school hockey teams, and Kathy had also been Joyce's bridesmaid. And I remain haunted by vivid memories of their youthful beauty, energy and enthusiasm. I wouldn't want for a moment to claim that this parallelism is suggestive of environmental, rather than genetic, explanations for their illnesses. Probably not. But I would want to ask, as I have on a previous occasion: 'Why is that you can never find an earth-shattering scientific invention when you really need one?' (Milner, 2005, v). The answer surely lies in a deep structural contradiction between the emancipatory potential of scientific research, on the one hand, and the political economy of globalised late capitalism, on the other. As Clarke and Pohl's Mevrouw Vorhulst observes in *The Last Theorem*: 'Oh, there's plenty of money for research – as long as what is being researched is some kind of weapon' (Clarke and Pohl, 2008, 120). Many of our scientists know this to be the case, so too do most of our smarter SF writers. But it is strange how little attention the issue commands in contemporary SF, few honourable exceptions aside, Ian McEwan's *Solar* (2010), for example, which handles it to richly comic effect. McEwan does so, of course, in relation to climate change, which might mean that this 'Afterword' isn't so much a second conclusion as a restatement of the first. But it needed saying, anyway.

Works Cited

I. Texts

NOVELS, SHORT STORIES, POETRY

Kōbō Abe, *Daiyon kanpyōki* (Tokyo: Hayakawa Shobo, 1964 [1959]).

Douglas Adams, *The Hitch Hiker's Guide to the Galaxy* (London: Pan Books, 1979).

David Andrade, *The Melbourne Riots and How Harry Holdfast and His Friends Emancipated the Workers. A Realistic Novel* (Melbourne: Andrade & Co., 1892).

Isaac Asimov, 'The Evitable Conflict', *Astounding Science-Fiction*, June 1950: 48–68.

—, *I, Robot* (Greenwich: Fawcett, 1970 [1950]).

—, *The Foundation Trilogy* (New York: Doubleday & Company, 1982 [1951–53]).

Margaret Atwood, *The Handmaid's Tale* (London: Virago, 1987 [1986]).

—, *The Blind Assassin* (Toronto: McClelland and Stewart, 2000).

—, *Oryx and Crake* (London: Bloomsbury, 2003).

—, *The Year of the Flood* (London: Bloomsbury, 2009).

—, Paolo Bacigalupi, T. C. Boyle, Toby Litt, Lydia Millet, David Mitchell, Nathaniel Rich, Kim Stanley Robinson, Helen Simpson and Wu Ming 1, *I'm With the Bears: Short Stories from a Damaged Planet*, intro. Bill McKibben, ed. Mark Martin (London: Verso, 2011).

Paolo Bacigalupi, *The Windup Girl* (San Francisco, Night Shade Books, 2009b).

Francis Bacon, 'New Atlantis', in *The Major Works*, ed. Brian Vickers (Oxford: Oxford University Press, 2002 [1627]).

J. G. Ballard, *The Drowned World* (New York: Berkley Books, 1962).

—, *The Burning World* (New York: Berkley Books, 1964).

—, *Crash* (London: Jonathan Cape, 1973).

—, *The Atrocity Exhibition*, with author's annotations (San Francisco: RE/Search Publications, 1990 [1970]).

Iain M. Banks, *Consider Phlebas* (London: Macmillan, 1987).

—, *The State of the Art* (London: Orbit, 1993 [1991]).

—, *The Hydrogen Sonata* (London: Orbit, 2012).

Edward Bellamy, *Looking Backward, 2000–1887*, ed. Alex MacDonald (Peterborough: Broadview Press, 2003 [1888]).

Eando Binder, 'Adam Link Faces a Revolt', *Amazing Stories*, May 1941: 70–93.

James Blish, *Earthman, Come Home* (New York: Putnam, 1955).

—, *A Case of Conscience* (New York: Ballantine Books, 1958).

—, *They Shall Have Stars* (London: New English Library, 1968).

Pierre Boulle, *La planète des singes* (Paris: Poche, 1963).

Ray Bradbury, *The Martian Chronicles* (New York: Doubleday, 1950).
—, *Fahrenheit 451* (New York: Ballantine Books, 1953).
Dorothy Bryant, *The Kin of Ata Are Waiting for You* (New York: Random House, 1971).
Mikhail Bulgakov, *Rokovye yaitsa* (Moscow: Nedra, 1925).
—, *Master i Margarita* (Moscow: Moskva, 1966–67 [1929–39]).
—, *Sobach'e serdtse*, ed. Avril Pyman (London: Bristol Classical, 1994 [1925]).
Edward Bulwer-Lytton, *The Coming Race*, ed. David Seed (Middletown: Wesleyan University Press, 2007 [1871]).
Ernest Callenbach, *Ecotopia* (Berkeley: Banyon Books, 1975).
Tommaso Campanella, *La città del Sole* (Milan: Feltrinelli economica, 1979 [1602]).
Karel Čapek, *War with the Newts*, trans. M. and R. Weatherall (London: George Allen and Unwin, 1937a).
—, *Válka s mloky. Továrna na Absolutno* (Chomutov: Milenium, 1998 [1922]).
Charles Carter, *The Island of Justice* (Melbourne: Gordon & Gotch, 1901).
A. Bertram Chandler, 'New Wings', *Astounding Science-Fiction*, April 1948: 71–87.
Pierre Teilhard de Chardin, *L'Avenir de l'Homme* (Paris: Seuil, 1959).
Suzy McKee Charnas, *Motherlines* (New York: Berkley, 1979).
Charles Chilton, *Journey into Space* (London: Herbert Jenkins, 1954).
—, *The Red Planet* (London: Herbert Jenkins, 1956).
—, *The World in Peril* (London, Herbert Jenkins, 1960).
John Christopher, 'The New Wine', in Edmund Crispin (ed.) *Best SF: Science Fiction Stories* (London: Faber, 1955).
Arthur C. Clarke, *Childhood's End* (New York: Ballantine Books, 1953).
—, *Rendezvous with Rama* (London: Victor Gollancz, 1973).
— and Frederick Pohl, *The Last Theorem* (London: HarperCollins, 2008).
Murray Constantine, *Swastika Night* (London: Victor Gollancz, 1937).
Hercule-Savinien de Cyrano de Bergerac, *L'Autre Monde ou les États et Empires de la Lune*, ed. Margaret Sankey (Paris: Lettres modernes, 1995 [1657]).
Maurice G. Dantec 'Là où tombent les anges', *Le Monde*, 21 September 1995.
—, *Babylon Babies* (Paris: Gallimard, 2001).
Eleanor Dark, *Prelude to Christopher* (Sydney: P. R. Stephensen & Co., 1934).
Samuel R. Delany, *Triton* (New York: Bantam, 1976).
Philip K. Dick, *The Simulacra* (New York: Ace Books, 1964).
—, *Do Androids Dream of Electric Sheep?* (New York: Doubleday, 1968).
—, *Ubik* (New York: Doubleday, 1969).
—, *The Philip K. Dick Collection*, ed. Jonathan Lethem, three vols (New York: Library of America, 2009).
Greg Egan, *Permutation City* (London: Millennium, 1994).
T. S. Eliot, *The Waste Land*, ed. Tony Davies and Nigel Wood (Buckingham: Open University Press, 1994 [1922]).
Harlan Ellison (ed.), *Dangerous Visions* (Garden City: Doubleday, 1967).
— (ed.), *Again, Dangerous Visions* (Garden City: Doubleday, 1972).
Gustave Flaubert, *Salammbô*, intro. Pierre Moreau (Paris: Gallimard, 1974 [1862]).
E. M. Forster, 'The Machine Stops', in *The Eternal Moment and Other Stories* (London: Sidgwick and Jackson, 1928).

Anatole France, *Sur la pierre blanche* (Gloucester: Dodo Press, 2008 [1905]).
—, *L'île des pingouins* (Paris: Calmann-Lévy, 1960 [1908]).
Joseph Fraser, *Melbourne and Mars: My Mysterious Life on Two Planets. Extracts from the Diary of a Melbourne Merchant* (Melbourne: E. W. Cole, 1889).
Enrique Gaspar, *El Anacronópete* (Barcelona: Gomez Soler, 1887).
Sally Gearhardt, *The Wanderground: Stories of the Hill Women* (Watertown: Persephone Press, 1979).
Ralph Gibson, *Socialist Melbourne* (Melbourne: Communist Party, Victorian State Committee, 1938).
William Gibson, 'Johnny Mnemonic', in *Burning Chrome* (New York: Ace Books, 1987 [1981]).
—, *Zero History* (London: Penguin, 2011 [2010]).
Charlotte Perkins Gilman, *Herland* (New York: Pantheon Books, 1979 [1915]).
William Golding, *The Lord of the Flies* (London: Faber, 1954).
Otfrid von Hanstein, 'Utopia Island', trans. Francis Currier, *Wonder Stories*, May 1931: 1352–97, 1471; June 1931: 76–128.
Thea von Harbou, *Metropolis, roman* (Berlin: A. Scherl, 1926).
Peter Heglin, *An Appendix To the Former Work, Endeavouring a Discovery of the Unknown Parts of the World. Especially of Terra Australis Incognita, or the Southern Continent* (London: Philip Chetwinde, 1667).
Robert A. Heinlein, 'If This Goes On ——', *Astounding Science-Fiction*, March 1940: 117–51.
—, *Starship Troopers* (New York: Putnam, 1959).
—, *Orphans of the Sky* (New York: Putnam, 1964 [1941–51]).
—, 'Requiem', in *Requiem: New Collected Works by Robert A Heinlein and Tributes to the Grand Master*, ed. Yoji Kondo (New York; Tor Books, 1992 [1940]).
Arthur Herzog, *Heat* (New York: Signet, 1977).
Russell Hoban, *Riddley Walker* (London: Jonathan Cape, 1980).
Michel Houellebecq, *La poursuite du bonheur, poèmes* (Paris: La Différence, 1992).
—, *Le Sens du combat, poèmes* (Paris: Flammarion, 1994).
—, *Les Particules élémentaires* (Paris: J'ai lu, 2000a).
—, *Atomised*, trans. Frank Wynne (London: Heinemann, 2000b).
—, *La Possibilité d'une île* (Paris: Fayard, 2005).
—, *La carte et le territoire* (Paris: Flammarion, 2010).
—, *The Map and the Territory*, trans. Gavin Bowd (London: Heinemann, 2011).
William Dean Howells, *A Traveler from Altruria* (New York: Harper, 1894).
Aldous Huxley, *Crome Yellow* (London: Chatto and Windus, 1921).
—, *Point Counter Point: A Novel* (London: Chatto and Windus, 1928).
—, *Brave New World* (Harmondsworth: Penguin, 1955a [1932]).
—, *Island: A Novel* (London: Chatto and Windus, 1962).
Captain W. E. Johns, *Kings of Space* (London: Hodder and Stoughton, 1954).
—, *Return to Mars* (London: Hodder and Stoughton, 1955).
—, *The Edge of Beyond* (London: Hodder and Stoughton, 1958).
James Joyce, *Ulysses* (London: John Lane, Bodley Head, 1936 [1922]).
Hans Hellmut Kirst, *Keiner Kommt Davon; Bericht von den letzten Tagen Europas* (Vienna: K. Desch, 1957).

William Lane, *The Workingman's Paradise: An Australian Labour Novel*, by John Miller (pseud.) (Sydney: Edwards, Dunlop & Co., 1892).

Philip Latham, 'The Xi Effect', in Edmund Crispin (ed.) *Best SF: Science Fiction Stories* (London: Faber, 1955).

Ursula K. Le Guin, *The Left Hand of Darkness* (New York: Ace Books, 1969).

—, *The Dispossessed: An Ambiguous Utopia* (London: Harper Collins, 1996 [1974]).

Stanisław Lem, *Obłok Megallana* (Warsaw: Iskry, 1955).

—, *Śledztwo* (Warsaw: Wydawn, Ministerstwa Obrony Narodowej, 1959).

—, *Solaris*, trans. Joanna Kilmartin and Steve Cox, in *Solaris; The Chain of Chance; A Perfect Vacuum* (London: Faber, 1971).

—, *Solaris*, posłowie Jery Jarzebski (Krakow: Wydawnictwo Literackie, 2002 [1961]).

C. S. Lewis, *Out of the Silent Planet* (London: The Bodley Head, 1938).

—, *Perelandra* (London: The Bodley Head, 1943).

—, *That Hideous Strength* (London: The Bodley Head, 1945).

Jack London, *The Iron Heel* (New York: Macmillan, 1958 [1908]).

Lucian of Samosata, 'The True History', in *The Works of Lucian of Samosata: Volume II*, trans. H. W. Fowler and F. G. Fowler, Vol. II (Oxford: Oxford University Press, 1905).

—, *Alēthēs Historia*, in *Luciani Opera*, ed. M. D. Macleod, Vol. I (Oxford: Oxford University Press, 1972).

St Luke, The Gospel According to Luke, in the Bible, Authorised Version (Oxford: Oxford University Press, 1960).

Kenneth Mackay, *The Yellow Wave: A Romance of the Asian Invasion of Australia*, ed. Andrew Enstice and Janeen Webb (Middletown: Wesleyan University Press, 2003 [1895]).

Gabriel García Márquez, *Cien años de soledad* (Madrid: Catedra, 1997 [1967]).

Ian McEwan, *Solar* (London: Jonathan Cape, 2010).

Herman Melville, *Moby-Dick; or, The Whale* (New York: Harper Brothers, 1851).

Robert Merle, *Malevil* (Paris: Gallimard, 1972).

Judith Merril (ed.), *England Swings SF: Stories of Speculative Fiction* (New York: Ace Books, 1968).

Richard C. Michaelis, *Looking Further Forward, an Answer to 'Looking Backward' by Edward Bellamy* (Chicago: Rand, McNally, 1890).

China Miéville, *Perdido Street Station* (London: Pan, 2001 [2000]).

—, *The Scar* (London: Macmillan, 2002).

—, *Iron Council* (New York: Del Rey, 2004).

—, *The City and the City* (London: Macmillan, 2009).

—, *Embassytown* (London: Macmillan, 2011).

Walter M. Miller, *A Canticle for Leibowitz* (Philadelphia: Lippincott, 1960).

David Mitchell, *Cloud Atlas* (London: Hodder and Stoughton, 2004).

Vol Molesworth, *The Stratosphere Patrol: The Adventures of Captain Lon Wynter* (Sydney: Transport Publishing, 1943).

—, *Spaceward Ho! The Further Adventures of Captain Lon Wynter* (Sydney: Transport Publishing, 1943).

—, *The Three Rocketeers: Being the Further Adventures of Lon Wynter* (Sydney: Trans-

port Publishing, 1944).
Mary Ann Moore-Bentley, *A Woman of Mars* (Sydney: Edwards, Dunlop & Co., 1901).
Thomas More, *Utopia: Latin Text and English Translation*, ed. George M. Logan, Robert M. Adams and Clarence H. Miller (Cambridge: Cambridge University Press, 1995 [1516]).
William Morris, *News From Nowhere, or An Epoch of Rest*, ed. J. Redmond (London: Routledge and Kegan Paul, 1970 [1890]).
Haruki Murakami, *Sekai no owari to hādo-boirudo wandārando* (Tokyo: Kodansha International, 1985).
—, *ichi-kew-hachi-yon*, Book 1 (Tokyo: Shinchosa, 2009a).
—, *ichi-kew-hachi-yon*, Book 2 (Tokyo: Shinchosa, 2009b).
—, *ichi-kew-hachi-yon*, Book 3 (Tokyo: Shinchosa, 2010).
Robert Musil, *Der Mann ohne Eigenschaften* (Hamburg: Rowohlt, 1967 [1930–42]).
George Orwell, *Nineteen Eighty-Four: A Novel* (London: Secker and Warburg, 1949).
—, *The Road to Wigan Pier* (Harmondsworth: Penguin, 1962 [1937]).
—, *Nineteen Eighty-Four: The Facsimile of the Extant Manuscript*, ed. P. Davison (London: Secker and Warburg, 1984).
—, *Nineteen Eighty-Four* (Harmondsworth: Penguin, 1989 [1949]).
Marge Piercy, *Woman on the Edge of Time* (New York: Kopf, 1976)
—, *He, She and It: a novel* (New York: Knopf, 1991).
Plutarch, *Peri tou empainomenou prosōpou to kuklō tēs selēnēs*, with an English translation by Harold Cherniss, in *Plutarch's Moralia*, Vol. XII, Loeb Classical Library (London: Heinemann, 1957 [*c.*AD 71]).
Edgar Allan Poe, *The Narrative of Arthur Gordon Pym* (New York: Harper, 1838).
Frederick Pohl and Cyril Kornbluth, 'Gravy Planet', *Galaxy*, June 1952: 4–61; July 1952: 108–59; August 1952: 104–59.
—, *The Space Merchants* (London: Heinemann, 1955).
Ezra Pound, *The Cantos of Ezra Pound* (New York: New Directions, 1970 [1915–62]).
J. B. Priestley, *Saturn Over the Water* (London: Heinemann, 1961).
—, *The Shapes of Sleep: A Topical Tale* (London: The Book Club, 1963).
François Rabelais, *La vie de Gargantua et de Pantagruel*, in *Oeuvres complètes*, ed. Guy Demerson (Paris: Seuil, 1973 ([1532–64]).
Ernest Renan, *La Réforme intellectuelle et morale*, ed. P. E. Charvet (Cambridge: Cambridge University Press, 1950 [1871]).
J. W. Roberts, *Looking Within: The Misleading Tendencies of 'Looking Backward' Made Manifest* (New York: A.S. Barnes, 1893).
Kim Stanley Robinson, *Pacific Edge* (New York: Tor Books, 1990).
—, *Forty Signs of Rain* (London: HarperCollins, 2004).
—, *Fifty Degrees Below* (London: HarperCollins, 2005).
—, *Sixty Days and Counting* (London: HarperCollins, 2007).
—, *Galileo's Dream* (London: HarperCollins, 2009).
—, *2312* (London: Orbit, 2012).
J. K. Rowling, *Harry Potter and the Goblet of Fire* (London: Bloomsbury, 2000).
Joanna Russ, *The Female Man* (London: Women's Press, 1985 [1975]).
Geoff Ryman (ed.), *When It Changed: Science into Fiction, an Anthology* (Manchester:

Carcanet Press, 2009).
Robert Sabatier, *Le Sourire aux lèvres* (Paris: Albin Michel, 2000).
W. W. Satterlee, *Looking Backward and What I Saw* (Minneapolis: Harrison and Smith, 1890).
Mary Shelley, *Frankenstein, or The Modern Prometheus*, ed. M. K. Joseph (Oxford: Oxford University Press, 1980 [1818]).
—, *The Last Man*, ed. Morton D. Paley (Oxford: Oxford University Press, 2008 [1826]).
Oshikawa Shunrō, *Kaitei gunkan* (Tokyo: Holp Shuppan, 1974 [1900]).
Nevil Shute, *On the Beach* (London, Toronto and Melbourne: Heinemann, 1957).
—, *On the Beach* (London: Mandarin, 1990 [1957]).
—, *On the Beach* (London: Vintage Books, 2009 [1957]).
B. F. Skinner, *Walden Two* (New York: Macmillan, 1948).
Erwin K. Sloat, 'When Time Stood Still', *Amazing Stories*, July 1939: 76–93.
Antoni Słonimski, *Torpeda Czasu* (Warsaw: Czytelnik, 1967 [1924]).
Catherine Helen Spence, *A Week in the Future*, ed. Lesley Durrell Ljungdahl (Sydney: Hale & Iremonger, 1987 [1889]).
Norman Spinrad, *Bug Jack Barron* (New York: Walker & Co., 1969).
Olaf Stapledon, *Last and First Men* (London: Methuen, 1930).
Robert Louis Stevenson, *The Strange Case of Dr Jekyll and Mr Hyde* (London: Longmans, Green & Co., 1886).
Arkady and Boris Strugatsky, *Vtoroe nashestvie marsian: zapiski zdravomysli a shchego* (Leningrad: SP Smart, 1990 [1968]).
—, *Piknik na obochine*, in *Za milliard let do kontsa sveta; Piknik na obochine; Gadkie lebedie* (Saint Petersburg: Alians Pozisoft, 1993 [1972]).
—, *Za milliard let do kontsa sveta*, in *Piknik na obochine*, in *Za milliard let do kontsa sveta; Piknik na obochine; Gadkie lebedie* (Saint Petersburg: Alians Pozisoft, 1993 [1978]).
—, *Roadside Picnic*, trans. Antonina W. Bouis (London: Victor Gollancz, 1978).
—, *Piknik na obochine*, online version of the full Russian text at http://www.shnaresys.com/roadside/picnic/parallel.htm (last accessed November 2011).
J. R. R. Tolkien, *The Fellowship of the Ring* (London: George Allen and Unwin, 1954).
—, *The Two Towers* (London: George Allen and Unwin, 1954).
—, *The Return of the King* (London: George Allen and Unwin, 1955).
Alexei Tolstoy, *Aelita* (Moscow: Raduga, 1991 [1924).
Karen Traviss, *City of Pearl* (London: HarperCollins, 2004).
—, *Crossing the Line* (London: HarperCollins, 2004).
—, *The World Before* (London: HarperCollins, 2005).
—, *Matriarch* (London: HarperCollins, 2006).
—, *Ally* (London: HarperCollins, 2007).
—, *Judge* (London: HarperCollins, 2008).
George Turner, 'The Fittest', in David King and Russell Blackford (eds) *Urban Fantasies* (Melbourne: Ebony Books, 1985).
—, *The Sea and Summer* (London and Boston: Faber, 1987).
Noel Turner, 'Letter VIII', in *Candid Suggestions in Eight Letters to Soame Jenkins, Esq.* (London: W. Harrod, 1782).
A. E. van Vogt, 'Dormant', in Edmund Crispin (ed.) *Best SF: Science Fiction Stories*

(London: Faber, 1955).
—, *The War Against the Rull* (New York: Simon and Schuster, 1959).
Denis Veiras, *L'Histoire des Sévarambes*, ed. A. Rosenberg (Paris: Champion, 2001 [1679]).
—, *The History of the Sevarambians: A Utopian Novel*, ed. J. C. Laursen and C. Masroori (New York: State University of New York Press, 2006 [1675–79]).
Jules Verne, *Cinq semaines en ballon* (Paris: Hetzel, 1863).
—, *De la terre à la lune* (Paris: Hetzel, 1865).
—, *Le Docteur Ox* (Paris: Hetzel, 1874).
—, *L'île mystérieuse* (Paris: Hetzel, 1874).
—, *Le Sphinx des glaces*, two vols (Paris: Hetzel, 1897).
—, *Twenty Thousand Leagues Under the Sea*, trans. William Butcher (Oxford: Oxford University Press, 1998 [1872]).
—, *Vingt mille lieues sous les mers* (Paris: Poche, 1999 [1869–70]).
—, *Paris au XXe siècle* (Paris: Hachette, 1994).
Harl Vincent, 'Barton's Island', *Amazing Stories Quarterly*, 7 (2), 1934: 6–27.
Arthur Dudley Vinton, *Looking Further Back*ward (Albany: Albany Book Co., 1890).
Virgil, *The Georgics: A Poem of the Land*, trans. and ed. Kimberley Johnson (London: Penguin, 2009 [29 BC]).
Kurt Vonnegut, *Cat's Cradle* (New York: Holt, Rinehart and Winston, 1963).
H. G. Wells, *The Chronic Argonauts* (London: Royal Society, 1888).
—, *The Stolen Bacillus and Other Incidents* (London: Methuen, 1895).
—, *The Invisible Man* (London: C. Arthur Pearson, 1897).
—, *In the Days of the Comet* (London: The Century Co., 1906).
—, *The War in the Air* (London: George Bell, 1908).
—, *Men Like Gods* (London: Cassell, 1923).
—, *The Dream* (London: Jonathan Cape, 1924).
—, *The Scientific Romances of H. G. Wells* (London: Victor Gollancz, 1933b).
—, *Seven Science Fiction Novels* (New York: Dover Publications, 1950 [1934]).
—, *The Shape of Things to Come: The Ultimate Revolution*, ed. J. Hammond (London: Everyman, 1993 [1933]).
—, *The Island of Doctor Moreau: a critical text of the 1896 London first edition*, ed. L. E. Stover (Jefferson: McFarland, 1996 [1896]).
—, *The Time Machine: An Invention*, ed. L. E. Stover (Jefferson: McFarland, 1996 [1895]).
—, *The First Men in the Moon* (London: Victor Gollancz, 2001 [1901]).
—, *A Modern Utopia*, ed. Gregory Glaeys and Patrick Parrinder (London: Penguin, 2005a [1905]).
—, *The War of the Worlds*, ed. Patrick Parrinder (London: Penguin, 2005b [1898]).
—, *The Sleeper Awakes*, ed. Patrick Parrinder (London: Penguin, 2005c [1899]).
Morris West, *The Navigator* (London: Collins, 1976).
Bruno Winawer, *Doktor Przybram* (Warsaw: Czytelnik, 1961 [1924]).
Jeanette Winterson, *The Stone Gods* (London: Hamish Hamilton, 2007)
William Wordsworth, 'The Ruined Cottage', in *Poetical Works*, ed. E. de Selincourt and Helen Darbishire (Oxford: Oxford University Press, 1949 [1798]).
John Wyndham, *The Day of the Triffids* (London: Michael Joseph, 1951).

—, *The Kraken Wakes* (London: Michael Joseph, 1953).
—, *The Chrysalids* (London: Michael Joseph, 1955).
Henry Lewis Younge, *Utopia or Apollo's Golden Days* (Dublin: George Faulkner, 1747).
Evgenii Zamiatin, *We*, trans. G. Zilboorg, Introduction by P. Rudy (New York: E. P. Dutton, 1952 [1924]).
E. Zamiatine, *Nous autres*, trans. B. Cauvet-Duhamel (Paris: Gallimard, 1929).
Yevgeny Zamyatin, *Mi* (New York: Inter-Language Literary Associates, 1967 [1920–21]).
—, *We*, trans. Mirra Ginsburg (New York: Viking Press, 1972).
Jerzy Żulawski, *Na Srebrnym Globie* (Krakow: Wydaw, Literackie, 1975 [1901]).
—, *Zwyciezca* (Krakow: Wydaw, Literackie, 1979 [1908]).
—, *Stara Ziemia* (Krakow: Wydaw, Literackie, 1979 [1910]).

MAGAZINES, COMICS AND GRAPHIC NOVELS

Yu Aida, *Gansuringa Garu* (Tokyo: ASCII Media, 2002–).
Jean-Claude Forest, *Barbarella* (Paris: Eric Losfeld, 1964).
—, *Barbarella: Les Colères du Mange-Minutes* (Paris: Kesselring, 1974).
—, *Barbarella: La Semble-Lune* (Paris: Horay, 1977).
—, *Barbarella: Le Miroir aux Tempêtes* (Paris: Albin Michel, 1982).
Frank Miller, *Batman: The Dark Knight Returns* (New York: DC Comics, 1986).
Alan Moore and Dave Gibbons, *Watchmen* (New York: DC Comics, 1986–87).
Osamu Tezuka *Metropolis* (Tokyo: Ikuei Shuppan, 1949).
—, *Tetsuwan Atomu* (Tokyo: Kobunsha, 1951–68).
Katsuhiro Otomo, *Akira* (Tokyo: Kodansha, 1982–90).
Masamune Shirow, *Appurushīdo* (Tokyo: Kodansha, 1985–89).
—, *Gōsuto In Za Sheru/Kōkaku Kidōtai* (Tokyo: Kodansha, 1989–97).
Naoko Takeuchi, *Bishōjo Senshi Sērā Mūn* (Tokyo: Kodansha, 1992–97).
2000 AD (London: IPC Magazines/Fleetway/Rebellion, 1977–).
Action Comics, (New York: DC Comics, 1938–).
All Star Comics, (New York: All-America Publications/DC Comics, 1940–51).
Amazing Spider-Man, The (New York: Marvel Comics, 1963–).
Amazing Stories, (New York: Experimenter Publishing/Ziff-Davies, Universal Publishing, 1926–2005).
Analog Science Fact and Fiction (New York: Condé Nast/Dell Publications, 1960–).
Astonishing Stories (New York: Popular Publications, 1940–43).
Astounding Stories (New York: Clayton Magazines/Street and Smith, 1930–38).
Astounding Science-Fiction (New York: Street and Smith, 1938–60).
Bifrost (Saint Mammès: Éditions Le Bélial, 1996–).
Captain America Comics (New York: Timely Comics/Marvel Comics, 1941–50).
Cosmic Stories (Holyoke: Albing Publications, 1941)
Der Orchideengarten (Munich: Drerlanderverlag, 1919–21).
Detective Comics (New York: DC Comics, 1939–).
Eagle (London: Hulton Press, IPC Magazines, 1950–69, 1982–94).

Fantastic Four, The (New York: Marvel Comics, 1961–).
Fantasy (London: George Newnes, 1938–39).
Fantasy: The Magazine of Science Fiction (London: Temple Bar, 1946–47)
Fantax (Paris: Éditions Mouchot, 1946–49, 1950–51).
Fiction (Paris: Éditions Office de Publicité Technique et Artistique, 1953–90).
Future Fiction (New York: Columbia Publications, 1939–43)
Galaxie (Paris: Nuit et jour, 1953–59).
Galaxie (Paris: Éditions Office de Publicité Technique et Artistique, 1964–77).
Galaxis-Magazin (Munich: Arthur Moewig Verlag, 1958–59).
Galaxy Science Fiction (New York: World Editions/Robert Guinn/Universal Publications, 1950–80).
L'An 2000 (Paris: Éditions du Puits Pelu, 1953–54)
Lunatique (Paris: Éditions Eons, 2005–).
Marvel Comics (New York: Timely Comics/Marvel Comics, 1939–57).
Magazine of Fantasy and Science Fiction (New York: Mercury Publications/Spilogale, 1949–).
Métal Hurlant (Paris: Les Humanoids Associés, 1974–87, 2002–4).
Meteor (Roubaix: Artima/Aredit, 1953–77).
New Worlds (London: Pendulum Publications, 1946–47).
New Worlds (London: Nova Publications/Roberts & Vinter/David Warburton, 1949–70).
Perry Rhodan (Rastatt: Verlagsunion Pabel-Moewig, 1961–).
Science Fantasy (London: Nova Publications/Roberts & Vinter, 1950–66).
*Star*Line* (Covina: Science Fiction Poetry Association, 1978–).
Startling Stories (New York: Pines Publications, 1939–55).
Stella (Stockholm: Svenska Familj-Journalean Svea, 1886–88).
Stirring Science Stories (Holyoke: Albing Publications, 1941–42).
Super Science Stories (New York: Popular Publications, 1940–43)
Tales of Wonder (London: Walter Gillings, 1937–42).
Terra SF (Munich: Arthur Moewig Verlag, 1957–86).
Thrilling Wonder Stories (New York: Pines Publications, 1936–55).
Tit-Bits Science Fiction Comics (London: Associated Newspapers, 1953).
Utopia Magazin (Rastatt: Erich Pabel Verlag, 1955–59)
Utopia Zukunftsromane (Rastatt: Erich Pabel Verlag, 1953–68)
Wonder Stories (New York: Pines Publications, 1930–36).
X-Men, The (New York: Marvel Comics, 1963–).

THEATRE

Aristophanes, *Ornithes*, intro. Benjamin Bickley Rogers (London: Bell, 1906 [414 BC]).
Karel Čapek, *W.U.R. Werstands Universal Robots*, trans. Otto Pick, (Prague: Lipsko, Orbis, 1922).
—, *R.U.R. (Rossum's Universal Robots). A Fantastic Melodrama*, trans. Paul Selver (New York: Doubleday, 1923).

—, *Bílá nemoc* (Prague: Fr. Borovny, 1937b).
—, *Power and Glory. A Drama in Three Acts*, trans. Paul Selver and Ralph Neale (London: Allen and Unwin, 1938).
—, *Věc Makropulo: komedie o třech dějstvích s přeměnous* (Prague: Fr. Borovy, 1941 [1922]).
—, *R.U.R. (Rossum's Universal Robots). A Play in Three Acts and an Epilogue*, trans. Paul Selver, in *The Brothers Čapek, R.U.R. and The Insect Play* (Oxford: Oxford University Press, 1961).
—, *R.U.R. Rossum's Universal Robots. Kolektivní Drama o Vstupní Komedii a Trench Dejstvích* (Prague: Ceskoslovensky Spisovatel, 1966 [1921]).
Johann Wolfgang von Goethe, *Faust. Der Tragödie* (Stuttgart: E. Klett, 1981 [1808, 1832]).
Vladimir Mayakovsky, 'The Bedbug', in *The Complete Plays of Vladimir Mayakovsky*, trans. Guy Daniels (New York: Washington Square Press, 1968).
—, *Klop*, ed. Robert Russell (Durham: University of Durham, 1985 [1929]).
Jean Touissant Merle and Antoine Nicolas Béraud, *Le Monstre et le magicien* (Paris: Chez Bezou, 1826).
Richard Brinsley Peake, 'Presumption, or the Fate of Frankenstein', in Jeffrey N. Cox (ed.) *Seven Gothic Dramas 1789–1825* (Athens: Ohio University Press, 1992 [1823]).
Jules Verne and Adolphe d'Ennery, *Voyage à travers l'impossible* (Paris: J.-J. Pauvert, 1981 [1882]).
Richard Wagner, *Der Ring des Nibelungen* (Leipzig: J. J. Weber, 1863).

FILM

J. J. Abrams (dir.), *Star Trek* (Paramount Pictures: 127 mins, 2009).
Hideaki Anno (dir.), *Shin seiki Evangerion Gekijō ban: Shito Shinsei* (Production IG, Gainax: 115 mins, 1997).
— (dir.), *Shin seiki Evangerion Gekijō ban: Air/Magokoro o, Kimi ni* (Production IG, Gainax: 87 mins, 1997).
Roy Ward Baker (dir.), *Quatermass and the Pit* (Hammer: 97 mins, 1967).
Ford Beebe and Saul A. Goodkind (dir.), *Buck Rogers* (Universal: 237 mins, twelve episodes, 1939).
Luc Besson (dir.), *Le Dernier Combat* (Les Films du Loup: 92 mins, 1983).
— (dir.), *The Fifth Element/Le Cinquième Élément* (Gaumont/Pathe: 126 mins, 1997).
James Cameron (dir.), *The Terminator* (Orion Pictures: 108 mins, 1984).
— (dir.), *Terminator 2: Judgement Day* (Tristar: 139 mins, 1991).
— (dir.), *Avatar* (20th Century Fox: 162 mins, 2009).
David Cronenberg (dir.), *Scanners* (Avco-Embassy Pictures, 103 mins, 1981).
— (dir.), *The Dead Zone* (Paramount: 103 mins, 1983).
— (dir.), *Videodrome* (Universal: 89 mins, 1983).
— (dir.), *The Fly* (20th Century Fox: 95 mins, 1986).
— (dir.), *Crash* (Alliance Communications: 96 mins, 1996).
— (dir.), *eXistenZ* (Alliance Atlantis and Serendipity Point Films: 93 mins, 1999).

Guillermo del Toro (dir.), *El espinazo del Diablo* (Warner Sogefilms A.I.E.: 107 mins, 2001).
— (dir.), *El laberinto del fauno* (Warner/Telecinco Cinema: 112 mins, 2006).
Sergei Eisenstein (dir.), *Ivan Grozniy*, Part 1 (Mosfilm: 99 mins, 1944).
Gordon Flemyng (dir.), *Dr Who and the Daleks* (AARU Productions: 82 mins, 1965).
Henrik Galeen (dir.), *Alraune* (Ama-Film GmbH/Universum Film Aktiengesellschaft: 108 mins, 1928).
Terry Gilliam (dir.), *12 Monkeys* (Universal: 127 mins, 1997).
Jean-Luc Godard (dir.), *Alphaville: Une Étrange Aventure de Lemmy Caution* (Pathé Contemporary/Chaumiane-Film: 99 mins, 1965).
Didier Grousset (dir.), *Kamikaze* (Gaumont: 90 mins, 1986).
Ishirō Honda (dir.), *Gojira* (Toho: 96 mins, 1954).
Peter Jackson (dir.), *The Lord of the Rings: The Fellowship of the Ring* (New Line Cinema/Time Warner: 178 mins, 2001).
— (dir.), *The Lord of the Rings: The Two Towers* (New Line Cinema/Time Warner: 173 mins, 2002).
— (dir.), *The Lord of the Rings: The Return of the King* (New Line Cinema/Time Warner: 201 mins, 2003).
Ryuhei Kitamura (dir.), *Gojira: Fainaru Wōzu* (Toho: 125 mins, 2004).
Stanley Kubrick (dir.), *Dr Strangelove* (Columbia: 94 mins, 1964).
— (dir.), *2001: A Space Odyssey* (Metro Goldwyn Mayer: 143 mins, 1968).
— (dir.), *A Clockwork Orange* (Warner Brothers: 137 mins, 1971).
Stanley Kramer (dir.), *On the Beach* (United Artists: 134 mins, 1959).
Fritz Lang (dir.), *Metropolis* (Universum Film Aktiengesellschaft: 180 mins, 1926).
— (dir.), *Metropolis* (Transit Film/Friedrich Wilhelm Murnau Stiftung: 124 mins, 2002).
Ang Lee (dir.), *Wo hu cang long* (EDKO Film: 120 mins, 2000).
George Lucas (dir.), *Star Wars* (20th Century Fox: 121 mins, 1977).
Chris Marker (dir.), *La Jetée* (Argos Films: 28 mins, 1964).
Georges Méliès (dir.), *La Voyage dans la lune* (Gaston Méliès: 14 mins, 1902).
Lothar Mendes (dir.), *The Man Who Could Work Miracles* (London Films: 82 mins, 1936).
William Cameron Menzies (dir.), *Things to Come* (London Films: 89 mins, 1936).
Andrew Niccol (dir.), *Gattaca* (Columbia: 106 mins, 1997).
— (dir.), *S1m0ne* (New Line Cinema: 117 mins, 2002).
— (dir.), *In Time* (20th Century Fox: 115 mins, 2011).
Mamoru Oshii (dir.), *Gōsuto In Za Sheru/Kōkaku Kidōtai* (Shochiku: 82 mins, 1995).
Katsuhiro Otomo (dir.), *Akira* (Toho: 125 mins, 1988).
Alex Proyas (dir.), *Dark City* (New Line Cinema: 96 mins, 1998).
— (dir.), *Knowing* (Escape Artists/Summit Entertainment: 121 mins, 2009).
Leni Riefenstahl (dir.), *Triumph des Willens* (Universum Film Aktiengesellschaft: 114 mins, 1935).
Franklin J. Schaffner (dir.), *Planet of the Apes* (20th Century Fox: 107 mins, 1968).
Ridley Scott (dir.), *Alien* (20th Century Fox: 119 mins, 1979).
— (dir.), *Blade Runner* (Blade Runner Partnership/ Warner Brothers: 114 mins, 1982).

— (dir.), *Prometheus* (Scott Free/ 20th Century Fox: 124 mins, 2012).
Steven Soderbergh (dir.), *Solaris* (20th Century Fox: 95 mins, 2003).
Stephen Spielberg (dir.), *Close Encounters of the Third Kind* (Columbia: 137 mins, 1977).
Frederick Stephani (dir.), *Flash Gordon* (Universal: 245 mins, six episodes, 1936).
Andrei Tarkovsky (dir.), *Solyaris* (Mosfilm: 169 mins, 1971).
— (dir.), *Ctankep* (Mosfilm: 163 mins, 1979).
François Truffaut (dir.), *Fahrenheit 451* (Universal: 112 mins, 1966).
Roger Vadim (dir.), *Barbarella* (Paramount: 98 mins, 1967).
Michael Vaughn (dir.), *Stardust* (Paramount: 122 mins, 2007).
Paul Verhoeven (dir.), *Robocop* (Orion Pictures: 103 mins, 1987).
— (dir.), *Total Recall* (Tristar: 113 mins, 1990).
— (dir.), *Starship Troopers* (Tristar: 129 mins, 1997).
Larry and Andy Wachowski (dir.), *The Matrix* (Warner Brothers: 1999).
James Whale (dir.), *Frankenstein* (Universal Studios: 71 mins, 1931).
Fred M. Wilcox (dir.), *Forbidden Planet* (Metro-Goldwyn-Meyer: 98 mins, 1956).
Robert Wise (dir.), *Star Trek: The Motion Picture* (Paramount: 132 mins, 1979).

RADIO PLAYS, RADIO SCRIPTS, PODCASTS AND OTHER HÖRSPIELE

Douglas Adams, *The Hitch-Hiker's Guide to the Galaxy: The Original Radio Scripts*, ed. Geoffrey Perkins (New York: Harmony Books, 1985 [1978–80]).
Robert Barr (dir.), *The Time Machine* (London: BBC Radio, 1949).
Alain Barroux (dir.), *Le Mystérieux Dr Cornelius* (Paris: France-Culture, 1978).
Samuel Beckett, 'All That Fall', 'Embers', 'Rough for Radio I', 'Rough for Radio II', 'Words and Music' and 'Cascando', in *The Complete Dramatic Works* (London: Faber, 1990).
Bertolt Brecht, *Die heilige Johanna der Schlachthöfe* (Berlin: G. Kiepenheur, 1932).
Damian Broderick, *Transmitters* (Sydney: ABC Radio National, 1984).
—, *Striped Holes* (Sydney: ABC Radio National, 1990).
—, *Time Zones* (Sydney: ABC Radio National, 1992)
—, *Schrödinger's Dog* (Sydney: ABC Radio National, 1995).
Marguerite Cassan (dir.), *Le Prisonnier de la planète Mars* (Paris: France-Culture, 1978).
—, *Renard, Maurice*, dir. E. Frémy (Paris: France-Culture, 1981).
Pierre-Arnaud de Chassy-Poulay (dir.) *Malheurs aux barbus* (Paris: RTF, 1951–52).
— (dir.), *Signé Furax* (Paris: Europe 1, 1956–60)
Charles Chilton, *Journey into Space: The Return from Mars* (London: BBC Audio Download, 2007 [1981]).
—, *Journey into Space* (London: BBC Audiobooks, 2008 [1953–54]).
—, *Journey into Space: Frozen in Time* (London: BBC Audiobooks, 2009 [2008]).
—, *Journey into Space: The Red Planet* (London: BBC Audiobooks, 2011 [1954–55])
—, *Journey into Space: The World in Peril* (London: BBC Audiobooks, 2011 [1955–56]).
—, *Journey into Space: Operation Luna* (London: BBC Audiobooks 2011 [1958]).

—, *Journey into Space: The Host* (London: BBC Audiobooks, 2011 [2009]).
Frédéric Christian (dir.), *Le Théâtre de l'Étrange* (Paris: France-Inter, 1963–74).
Alonzo Deen Cole (dir.), *Frankenstein* (Newark: Radio WOR-Newark, 1931).
Brian Daley, *The National Public Radio Dramatization: Star Wars* (New York: Del Rey, 1994).
—, *The National Public Radio Dramatization: The Empire Strikes Back* (New York: Del Rey, 1995).
—, *The National Public Radio Dramatization: The Return of the Jedi* (New York: Del Rey, 1996).
Friedrich Dürrenmatt, *Herkules und der Stall des Augias* (Zurich: Im Verlag der Arche, 1960 [1954]).
—, 'Das Unternehmen der Wega', in L. McGlashan and I. R. Campbell (eds) *Drei Hörspiele* (London: Harrap, 1966 [1954]).
Steve Eley and Jeremiah Tolbert, *Escape Pod*, 2005–.
Louis MacNeice, *The Dark Tower and Other Radio Scripts* (London: Faber, 1947 [first broadcast 1946]).
Nadia Molinari (dir.), *The State of the Art*, adapted by Paul Cornell (London, BBC Radio 4, 2009).
Lucas Moreno and Marc Tiefenhauer, *Utopod*, 2007–.
Toby Smith (dir.), *On the Beach*, adapted by Mike Walker (London, BBC Radio 4, 120 mins, 2008).
Tony C. Smith and Ciaran O'Carrol, *StarShipSofa*, 2006–.
Henri Soubeyran (dir.), *La Science-Fiction* (Paris: France-Culture, 1980–81).
Tom Stoppard, *Stoppard: The Plays for Radio 1964–1991* (London: Faber, 1994).
Dylan Thomas, *Under Milk Wood: A Play for Voices* (London: Dent, 1954).
Pierre Versins, *Passeport pour l'inconnu*, dir. Roland Sassi (Geneva: Société suisse de radiodiffusion, 1957).
Orson Welles (dir.), *The War of the Worlds*, adapted by Howard Koch (New York: CBS, 1938).
Adventures of Dan Dare – Pilot of the Future, The (Radio Luxembourg, 1951-1956).
Bed Bug, The (ABC Radio, 1981).
Blake & Mortimer (ORTF/France II, 1960–63).
Buck Rogers (CBS, 1932–46).
Brave New World (CBC Radio, 1956).
Canadia: 2056 (CBC Radio, 2007–).
Das Sternentor (Maritim, 2002–9).
Day of the Triffids, The (BBC Radio, 1957).
Demolished Man, The (ABC Radio, 1985).
Der Weganer-Sechsteiler (Europa, 1976–78).
Die Arrow-Trilogie (Europa, 1980).
Die Triffids (Westdeutscher Rundfunk, 1969).
Dimension X (NBC, 1950–51).
Drowned World, The (BBC Radio, 2009).
Earthsearch (BBC Radio, 1981).
Flash Gordon (MBS, 1935–36).
Foundation Trilogy, The (BBC Radio, 1973).

Frozen in Time (BBC Radio, 2008).
Hitchhiker's Guide to the Galaxy, The (BBC Radio, 1978–80 and 2004–5).
Host, The (BBC Radio, 2009).
Host Planet Earth (BBC Radio, 1965).
Johnny Chase, Secret Agent of Space (CBC Radio, 1978–81).
L'Apocalypse est pour demain (France Inter, 1977).
Les Tréteaux de la nuit (France-Inter, 1979–80)
Les Tyrans sont parmi nous (RTF, 1953).
Lights Out (NBC, 1934–47).
Limbo City (ABC Radio, 1979).
Lost Planet, The (BBC Radio, 1953).
Lost World, The (BBC Radio, 1938).
Lost World, The (BBC Radio, 1944).
Lost World, The (Radio New Zealand, 1980–81).
Macropoulos Secret, The (ABC Radio, 1988).
Mind Of Tracey Dark, The (Springbok Radio, 1974–78).
Moon Flower, The (ABC Radio, 1953).
Nebulous (BBC Radio, 2005–2008).
Nightfall (CBC Radio, 1980–83).
No Place To Hide (Springbok Radio, 1958–70)
Out of the Silence (Radio 3DB, 1934).
Per Anhalter ins All (Bayerischer Rundfunk, Südwestfunk and Westdeutscher Rundfunk, 1981–82).
Per Anhalter ins All 2 (Bayerischer Rundfunk, Südwestfunk and Westdeutscher Rundfunk, 1990–91).
Planet B (BBC Radio, 2009).
Planet Named Sheol, A (ABC Radio, 1986).
Probe (Springbok Radio, 1969).
Quiet Please! (MBS/ABC, 1947–49)
Radio Tales (NPR, 1996–2002).
Rendezvous with Rama (BBC Radio, 2009).
R.U.R. (BBC Radio, 1941).
Space Cadet (ABC, 1952).
Space Force (BBC Radio, 1984–85).
Space Patrol (ABC, 1950–55).
Strangers from Space (Springbok Radio, 1961–63).
Superman (MBS, 1940–52).
Time Machine, The (CBC Radio, 1948).
Time Machine, The (BBC Radio, 2009).
Trois hommes à la recherche d'une comète (France-Culture, 1980).
Vanishing Point, The (CBC Radio, 1984–91).
War of the Worlds, The (BBC Radio, 1950).
Witch's Tale, The (WOR/MBS, 1931–38).
X Minus One (NBC, 1955–58).

TELEVISION

Douglas Adams, *The Hitch Hiker's Guide to the Galaxy*, dir. Alan J. W. Bell (BBC Television: 6 × 32 mins, 1981).
Robert Barr (dir.), *The Time Machine* (BBC Television: 60 mins, 1949).
Jan Bussell (dir.), *R.U.R.* (BBC Television: 35 mins, 1938).
— (dir.), *R.U.R.* (BBC Television: 90 mins, 1948).
Rudolph Cartier (dir.), *Nineteen Eighty-Four*, adapted by Nigel Kneale (BBC Television: 120 mins, 1954).
Maurice Frydland (dir.), *Le Mystérieux Docteur Cornelius* (A2, Col.: 6 × 60 mins, 1984).
Bruno Gantillon (dir.), *Le Travail du furet* (FR 2: 100 mins, 1994).
Rob Grant and Doug Naylor, *Red Dwarf*, Series 1–6 (BBC Television: 36 × 30 mins, 1988–93).
Fred Hoyle and John Elliott, *A for Andromeda*, dir. Michael Hayes (BBC Television, 7 × 45 mins, 1961).
—, *The Andromeda Breakthrough*, dir. John Elliott and John Knight (BBC Television, 6 × 45 mins, 1962).
Lazare Iglésis (dir.), *L'Alpomega* (ORTF 1, Col.: 6 × 60 mins, 1973).
Peter Kassovitz (dir.), *La Guerre des insectes* (A2, Col.: 4 × 60 mins, 1981).
Nigel Kneale, *The Quatermass Experiment*, dir. Rudolph Cartier (BBC Television: 6 × 30 mins, 1953).
—, *Quatermass II*, dir. Rudolph Cartier (BBC Television: 6 × 30 mins, 1955).
—, *Quatermass and the Pit*, dir. Rudolph Cartier (BBC Television: 6 × 35 mins, 1958–59).
Nick Marck (dir.), 'Conversations with Dead People', *Buffy the Vampire Slayer* (Mutant Enemy Inc./20th Century Fox Television: 44 mins, 2002).
Nino Monti (dir.), *Bing* (FR3: 3 × 60 mins, 1991).
Russell Mulcahy (dir.), *On the Beach* (Showtime/Seven Network: 195 mins, 2000).
Daniel Moosmann (dir.), *Noir sont les galaxies* (A2, 4 × 60 mins, 1981).
Noël-Noël, *Le Voyageur des siècles*, dir. Jean Dréville (ORTF1, Col.: 4 × 60 mins, 1971).
Alain Page, *Le Mutant*, dir. Bernard Toublanc-Michel (TF1, Col.: 6 × 60 mins, 1978).
Dennis Potter, *Cold Lazarus*, dir. Renny Rye (BBC Television/Channel 4: 60 mins, 1996).
Pierre Sisser (dir.), *Astrolab 22* (TF1: 13 × 26 mins, 1985).
J. Michael Straczynski et al., *Babylon 5* (PTEN/TNT: 110 × 43 mins, 1993–98).
Bob Thénault (dir.), *Frankenstein* (ORTF 3: 95 mins, 1974).
Jacques Trébouta (dir.), *Le Grand secret* (A2, Col.: 6 × 60 mins, 1989).
Jules Verne, *L'île mystérieuse*, dir. Pierre Badel (RTF: 2 × 60 mins, 1963).
—, *Le Tour du monde en 80 jours*, dir. Pierre Nivollet (A2, Col.: 2 × 90 mins, 1975).
Michel Wyn (dir.), *Les Visiteurs* (TF1, Col.: 6 × 60 mins, 1980).
Adventures of Superman, The (ABC, 1952–58).
Aux Frontières du possible (ORTF2, 1971–74).
Battlestar Galactica (SciFi Channel, 2004–9).
Bishōjo Senshi Sērā Mūn (Toei Animation/ TV Asahi, 1992–97).
Blake's Seven (BBC Television, 1978–81).
Buck Rogers (ABC, 1950–51).

Captain Scarlet and the Mysterons (ATV, 1967–68).
Captain Video and his Video Rangers (DuMont Television Network, 1949–55).
Chōjiku Yōsai Makurosu (Mainichi Broadcasting, 1982–83).
De Bien étranges affaires (FR3, Col., 1982).
Doctor Who (BBC Television, 1963–89, 1996; BBC Cymru 2005–).
Doragon Bōru (Fuji TV, 1986–2011).
Farscape (Jim Henson Company/National Nine Network/Hallmark, 1999–2003).
Farscape: The Peacekeeper Wars (Hallmark Entertainment/Jim Henson Company, 2004).
Fireball XL5 (ATV, 1962–63).
Joe 90 (ATV, 1968–69).
Les Atomistes (ORTF 1, 1968).
Les Classiques de l'Étrange (ORTF 1, A2, Col., 1974–76).
LEXX (Sci-Fi Channel/Alliance Atlantic, 1997–2002).
Mājinga Zetto (Toei Animation/Fuji Television, 1972–74).
Megazōn Tsū Sun (AIC, Tatsunoko and Artmic, 1985–89).
Out of the Unknown (BBC Television, 1965–71).
Out of This World (ABC Television, 1962).
Outer Limits, The (ABC, 1963–65).
Raumpatrouille Orion (Bavaria Atelier GmbH/ARD, 1966).
Shin Seiki Evangerion (Gainax, Tatsunoko, 1995–96).
Smallville (The WB Television Network/The CW Television Network, 2001–11).
Space Command (CBC Television, 1953–54).
Stargate SG-1 (MGM/Showtime, 1997–2007).
Star Trek (Paramount, 1966–69).
Star Trek: Deep Space Nine (Paramount, 1993–99).
Star Trek: Enterprise (Paramount, 2001–5).
Star Trek: The Next Generation (Paramount, 1987–94).
Star Trek: Voyager (Paramount, 1995–2001).
Stingray (ATV, 1964–65).
Supercar (ATV, 1961–62).
Tetsujin 28-go (Fuji TV, 1963–66).
Tetsuwan Atomu (Mushi Productions, 1963–66).
Thunderbirds (ATV, 1965–66).
Torchwood (BBC Cymru, 2006–8).
Torchwood: Children of Earth (BBC Cymru, 2009).
Torchwood: Miracle Day (BBC Cymru, BBC Worldwide and Starz Entertainment, 2011).
Twilight Zone, The (CBS, 1959–64).
Vega 4 (ABC Television/Channel 7 [Australia], 1968).
X-Files, The (Fox Broadcasting, 1993–2002).

II. Criticism, History, Theory, Biography, Autobiography

Miguel Abensour, *Les Formes de l'utopie socialistes-communiste* (Paris: thèse pour le Doctorat d'État en science politique, 1973).

Theodor W. Adorno and Max Horkheimer, *Dialectic of Enlightenment*, trans. John Cumming (London: Verso, 1979).

Brian Aldiss, *Billion Year Spree: The History of Science Fiction* (London: Weidenfeld & Nicolson, 1973).

—, *Trillion Year Spree: The History of Science Fiction*, with David Wingrove (London: Victor Gollancz, 1986).

Louis Althusser, 'Ideology and Ideological State Apparatuses (Notes towards an Investigation)', in *Lenin and Philosophy and Other Essays*, trans. Ben Brewster (London: New Left Books, 1971).

— and Étienne Balibar, *Reading Capital*, trans. Ben Brewster (London: New Left Books, 1970).

Kingsley Amis, *New Maps of Hell: A Survey of Science Fiction* (London: Victor Gollancz, 1961).

Perry Anderson, *Passages from Antiquity to Feudalism* (London: New Left Books, 1974).

Marc Angenot and Darko Suvin, 'A Response to Professor Fekete's "Five Theses"', *Science Fiction Studies*, 15.3 (1988): 324–33.

Emily Apter, 'Global *Translatio*: The "Invention" of Comparative Literature, Istanbul, 1933', *Critical Inquiry*, 29 (2003): 253–81.

Jonathan Arac, 'Anglo-globalism?', *New Left Review*, (II) 16 (2002): 35–45.

Mike Ashley, *The Time Machines: The Story of the Science-Fiction Pulp Magazines from the Beginning to 1950* (Liverpool: Liverpool University Press, 2000).

—, *Out of This World: Science Fiction but Not as You Know It* (London: The British Library, 2011).

Isaac Asimov, *In Memory Yet Green: The Autobiography of Isaac Asimov 1920–1954* (New York: Doubleday, 1979).

—, *I, Asimov: A Memoir* (New York: Doubleday, 1994).

Brian Attebery, 'Science Fantasy and Myth', in George E. Slusser and Eric S. Rabkin (eds) *Intersections: Fantasy and Science Fiction* (Carbondale: Southern Illinois University Press, 1987).

Margaret Atwood, 'George Orwell: Some Personal Connections', in *Curious Pursuits: Occasional Writing 1970–2005* (London: Virago, 2005 [2003]).

—, 'Introduction', in *In Other Worlds: Science Fiction and the Human Imagination* (London: Virago, 2011a).

—, 'Dire Cartographies: The Roads to Ustopia', in *In Other Worlds: Science Fiction and the Human Imagination* (London: Virago, 2011b).

Aussiecon4, *The 68th World Science Fiction Convention* (Melbourne: Victorian Science Fiction Conventions Inc., 2010).

Raffaella Baccolini, 'Gender and Genre in the Feminist Critical Dystopias of Katherine Burdekin, Margaret Atwood, and Octavia Butler', in Marleen S. Barr (ed.) *Future Females, the Next Generation: New Voices and Velocities in Feminist Science Fiction* (Boston: Rowman and Littlefield, 2000).

— and Tom Moylan, 'Introduction: Dystopias and Histories', in Rafaella Baccolini and Tom Moylan (eds) *Dark Horizons: Science Fiction and the Dystopian Imagination* (London and New York: Routledge, 2003).

Paolo Bacigalupi, 'Interview', *SF Signal* 14 September (2009a). http://www.

sfsignal.com/archives/2009/09/interview-paolo-bacigalupi/.

Alain Badiou, *Infinite Thought: Truth and the Return to Philosophy*, trans. and ed. Oliver Feltham and Justin Clemens (London: Continuum, 2003).

—, 'Truth: Forcing and the Unnameable', in *Theoretical Writings*, ed. and trans. Ray Brassier and Alberto Toscano (London: Continuum, 2004).

M. M. Bakhtin, *The Dialogical Imagination: Four Essays*, ed. Michael Holquist, trans. Caryl Emerson and Michael Holquist (Austin: University of Texas Press, 1981).

Iain M. Banks, 'A Quick Chat with Iain M. Banks', *The Richmond Review* (1996). http://www.richmondreview.co.uk/features/banksint.html (accessed on 24 November 2011).

Michèle Barrett and Duncan Barrett, *Star Trek: The Human Frontier* (Cambridge: Polity Press, 2001).

Roland Barthes, 'The Structuralist Activity', in R. T. de George and F. M. de George (eds) *The Structuralists: From Marx to Lévi-Strauss* (New York: Anchor, 1972).

—, *S/Z*, trans. Richard Miller (New York: Hill and Wang, 1974).

—, *The Pleasure of the Text*, trans. Richard Miller (New York: Hill and Wang, 1975).

Jean Baudrillard, *Simulacres et simulation* (Paris: Éditions Galilée, 1981).

—, 'Two Essays', trans. Arthur B. Evans, *Science Fiction Studies*, 18.3 (1991): 309–19.

—, *Simulacra and Simulation*, trans. Sheila Faria Glaser (Ann Arbor: University of Michigan Press, 1994).

Matthew Beaumont, *Utopia Ltd.: Ideologies of Social Dreaming in England 1870–1900* (Leiden and Boston: Brill, 2005).

Sybille Bedford, *Aldous Huxley: A Biography, Vol. One: 1894–1939* (London: Chatto and Windus in association with William Collins, 1973).

Andrea L. Bell and Yolinda Molina-Cavilán (eds), *Cosmos Latinos: An Anthology of Science Fiction from Latin America and Spain* (Middletown: Wesleyan University Press, 2003).

Walter Benjamin, 'The Work of Art in the Age of Mechanical Reproduction', in *Illuminations*, trans. Harry Zohn (Glasgow: Collins, 1973).

Jeremy Bentham, 'Plan of Parliamentary Reform, in the Form of a Catechism', in *The Works of Jeremy Bentham*, Vol. 3, ed. John Bowring (Edinburgh: William Tait, 1843).

Daniel Bernardi, '*Star Trek* in the 1960s: Liberal-Humanism and the Production of Race', *Science Fiction Studies*, 24.2 (1997): 209–25.

Steven Best and Douglas Kellner, *The Postmodern Adventure: Science, Technology, and Cultural Studies at the Third Millennium* (New York: Guilford Press, 2001).

Russell Blackford, Van Ilkin and Sean McMullen, *Strange Constellations: A History of Australian Science Fiction* (Westport: Greenwood Press, 1999).

Karin Blair, 'Sex and *Star Trek*', *Science Fiction Studies*, 10.2 (1983): 292–97.

Everett F. Bleiler, with the assistance of Richard J. Bleiler, *Science-Fiction: The Gernsback Years: A Complete Coverage of the Genre Magazines* Amazing, Astounding, Wonder, *and Others from 1926 through 1936* (Kent: Kent State University Press, 1998).

Ernst Bloch, 'Nonsynchronism and the Obligation to its Dialectics', trans. Mark Ritter, *New German Critique*, 11 (1977): 22–38.

—, *The Principle of Hope*, trans. Neville Plaice, Stephen Plaice and Paul Knight (Oxford: Basil Blackwell, 1986 [1954–59]).

Clive Bloom, *Bestsellers: Popular Fiction since 1900* (London: Palgrave Macmillan, 2002).

Harold Bloom, *The Western Canon: The Books and School of the Ages* (New York: Harcourt Brace & Co., 1994).

Roland Boer, 'Political Myth: Fable, Politics and the Bible', *International Journal of the Humanities*, (2) 2 (2006): 1621–25.

Mark Bould, 'Rough Guide to a Lonely Planet, from Nemo to Neo', in Mark Bould and China Miéville (eds) *Red Planets: Marxism and Science Fiction* (London: Pluto Press, 2009).

—, Andrew M. Butler, Adam Roberts and Sherryl Vint (eds), *The Routledge Companion to Science Fiction* (London and New York: Routledge, 2009).

— and China Miéville (eds), *Red Planets: Marxism and Science Fiction* (London: Pluto Press, 2009).

— and Sherryl Vint, *The Routledge Concise History of Science Fiction* (London and New York, 2011).

Pierre Bourdieu, *Outline of a Theory of Practice*, trans. Richard Nice (Cambridge: Cambridge University Press, 1977).

—, 'The Field of Cultural Production, or: The Economic World Reversed', trans. Richard Nice, in *The Field of Cultural Production: Essays on Art and Literature*, ed. Randal Johnson (Cambridge: Polity Press, 1993).

Malcolm Bradbury and James McFarlane (eds), *Modernism 1890–1930* (Harmondsworth: Penguin, 1976a).

—, 'The Name and Nature of Modernism', in Malcolm Bradbury and James McFarlane (eds) *Modernism 1890-1930* (Harmondsworth: Penguin, 1976b).

Bertolt Brecht, 'A Short Organum for the Theatre', trans. John Willett, in *Brecht on Theatre*, 2nd edn (London: Eyre Methuen, 1974 [1949]).

Paul Brians, *Nuclear Holocausts: Atomic War in Fiction, 1895–1984* (Kent: Kent State University Press, 1987).

Damien Broderick, *Reading by Starlight: Postmodern Science Fiction* (London: Routledge, 1995).

V. M. Budakov, '*Dystopia*: An Early Eighteenth-Century Use', *Notes & Queries*, 57.1 (2010): 86–88.

Scott Bukatman, *Terminal Identity: The Virtual Subject in Postmodern Science Fiction* (Durham: Duke University Press, 1993).

Peter Bürger, *Theory of the Avant-Garde*, trans. Michael Shaw (Minneapolis: University of Minnesota Press, 1984).

George W. Bush, 'President Bush Announces New Vision for Space Exploration Program: Remarks by the President on US Space Policy', The White House, Office of the Press Secretary, 14 January (Washington, DC: 2004).

J. W. Campbell, 'Science-Fiction', *Astounding Science-Fiction*, 20, March 1938: 37.

Hadley Cantril, *The Invasion from Mars: A Study in the Psychology of Panic*, intro. Albert H. Cantril (Piscataway, NJ: Transaction Publishers, 2005).

Karel Čapek, *Letters from England*, trans. Paul Selver (London: G. Bles, 1925).

—, *Anglické Listy: pro vetsi nazornost provázené obrázky autorovymi* (Prague: Fr.

Borovny, 1934 [1924]).

—, *Ctení o T.G. Masrykovi* (Melantrich: V Praze, 1969).

Pascale Casanova, *The World Republic of Letters*, trans. M. B. Debevois (Cambridge, Mass.: Harvard University Press, 2005).

Michel de Certeau, *The Practice of Everyday Life*, trans. Steven Rendall (Berkeley: University of California Press, 1984).

Peter Christoff, 'The End of the World as We Know It', *The Age*, 15 January (2008).

Arthur C. Clarke, 'Hazards of Prophecy: The Failure of Imagination', in *Profiles of the Future: An Inquiry into the Limits of the Possible*, rev. edn (London: Victor Gollancz, 1974).

John Clute, David Langford and Peter Nicholls (eds), *The Encyclopedia of Science Fiction*, 3rd edn (London: Victor Gollancz/SF Gateway, 2011). http://sf-encyclopedia.com/.

John Clute and Peter Nicholls (eds), *The Encyclopedia of Science Fiction* (London: Orbit, 1993).

Roger Cockrell, 'Future Perfect: H. G. Wells and Bolshevik Russia, 1917–32', in Patrick Parrinder and John S. Partington (eds) *The Reception of H.G. Wells in Europe* (London: Continuum, 2005).

Paul Collins (ed.), *The MUP Encyclopaedia of Australian Science Fiction & Fantasy* (Melbourne: Melbourne University Press, 1998).

John R. Cook and Peter Wright, '"Futures Past": An Introduction to and Brief Survey of British Science Fiction Television', in John R. Cook and Peter Wright (eds), *British Science Fiction Television: A Hitchhiker's Guide* (London: I. B. Tauris, 2006).

Christine Cornea, *Science Fiction Cinema: Between Fantasy and Reality* (Edinburgh: Edinburgh University Press, 2007).

Anne Cranny-Francis, 'Sexuality and Sex-Role Stereotyping in *Star Trek*', *Science Fiction Studies*, 12.3 (1985): 274–84.

Bernard Crick, *George Orwell: A Life* (London: Secker and Warburg, 1980).

Tim Crook, *Radio Drama: Theory and Practice* (London and New York: Routledge, 1999).

Istvan Csicsery-Ronay, 'Science Fiction and Empire', *Science Fiction Studies*, 30.2 (2003): 231–45.

Jack Dann (ed.), *Dreaming Again* (Sydney: Voyager, 2008).

— and Janeen Webb (eds), *Dreaming Down-Under* (Sydney: Voyager, 1998).

Eric Lief Davin, *Partners in Wonder: Women and the Birth of Science Fiction* (Lanham: Rowman & Littlefield, 2006).

Hugo de Burgh, 'Investigating Corporate Corruption: An example from the BBC's *File on Four*', in Hugo de Burgh (ed.) *Investigative Journalism: Context and Practice* (London and New York: Routledge, 2000).

Samuel R. Delany, 'The Semiology of Silence: The *Science Fiction Studies* Interview', in *Silent Interviews: On Language, Race, Sex, Science Fiction, and Some Comics: A Collection of Written Interviews* (Hanover: Wesleyan University Press, 1994 [1987]).

Lester Del Rey, *The World of Science Fiction: 1926–1976: The History of a Subculture* (New York and London: Garland Publishing, 1980).

Jacques Derrida, *Of Grammatology*, trans. Gayatri Chakravorty Spivak (Baltimore:

Johns Hopkins University Press, 1974).
Enrique Dussel, 'Beyond Eurocentrism: The World System and the Limits of Modernity', in Fredric Jameson and Masao Miyoshi (eds) *The Cultures of Globalization* (Durham: Duke University Press, 1998).
Terry Eagleton, *Literary Theory: An Introduction* (Oxford: Blackwell, 1983).
—, *The Function of Criticism: From 'The Spectator' to Post-Structuralism* (London: Verso, 1984).
—, *Against the Grain: Essays 1975–85* (London; Verso, 1986).
—, *Literary Theory: An Introduction*, 2nd edn (Oxford: Blackwell, 1996).
—, 'In the Gaudy Supermarket', *London Review of Books*, 21.10 (1999): 3–6.
—, *After Theory* (New York: Basic Books, 2003).
Umberto Eco, *The Role of the Reader: Explorations in the Semiotics of Texts* (London: Hutchinson, 1981).
Harlan Ellison, '1967: Introduction Thirty-Two Soothsayers', in Harlan Ellison (ed.) *Dangerous Visions: 35th Anniversary Edition* (New York: Edgeworks Abbey/ibooks, 2002 [1967]).
Friedrich Engels, 'Herrn Eugen Dührings Umwälzung der Wissenschaft (Anti-Dühring)', in Karl Marx und Friedrich Engels, *Werke*, Band 20 (Berlin: Dietz Verlag, 1962).
—, 'Anti-Dühring: Herr Eugen Dühring's Revolution in Science', trans. E. Burns, in Karl Marx and Frederick Engels, *Collected Works*, Vol. 25 (London: Lawrence and Wishart, 1987).
Ferenc Fehér, 'The Pyrhhic Victory of Art in its War of Liberation: Remarks on the Postmodernist Intermezzo', in Andrew Milner, Philip Thomson and Chris Worth (eds) *Postmodern Conditions* (Oxford: Berg, 1990).
John Fekete, 'Doing the Time Warp Again: Science Fiction as Adversarial Culture', *Science Fiction Studies*, 28.1 (2001): 77–96.
Peter Fitting, 'Fredric Jameson and Anti-Anti-Utopianism', *Arena Journal*, (II) 25/26 (2006): 37–51.
Steven Earl Forry, *Hideous Progenies: Dramatizations of Frankenstein from Mary Shelley to the Present* (Philadelphia: University of Pennsylvania Press, 1990).
Carl Freedman, *George Orwell: A Study in Ideology and Literary Form* (New York: Garland, 1988).
—, 'Another Response to John Fekete', *Science Fiction Studies*, 16.1 (1989): 116–17.
—, *Critical Theory and Science Fiction* (Hanover: Wesleyan University Press, 2000).
—, 'Looking for Jake and Other Stories', *Foundation: The International Review of Science Fiction*, 97, Summer 2006: 108–13.
Philip French, 'Future Imperfect: The Hitchhiker Movie is clever but adds little to the Radio Original', *Observer*, 1 May (2005).
John Frow, *Genre* (London and New York: Routledge, 2006).
Ken Gelder, *Popular Fiction: The Logics and Practices of a Literary Field* (London and New York: Routledge, 2004).
Hugo Gernsback, 'A New Sort of Magazine', *Amazing Stories: The Magazine of Scientifiction*, April 1926: 3.
Jonathan Glancey, 'Sufferin' Satellites! We've Built the Future', *The Guardian G2*, 28 April (2008): 23–25.

Joan Gordon, 'Reveling in Genre: An Interview with China Miéville', *Science Fiction Studies*, 30.3 (2003a): 355–73.

—, 'Hybridity, Heterotopia, and Mateship in China Miéville's *Perdido Street Station*', *Science Fiction Studies*, 30.3 (2003b): 456–76.

Stephen Greenblatt, *Learning to Curse: Essays in Early Modern Culture* (London: Routledge, 1990).

Colin Greenland, *The Entropy Exhibition: Michael Moorcock and the British 'New Wave' in SF* (London: Routledge and Kegan Paul, 1983).

Jürgen Habermas, 'Modernity – an Incomplete Project', trans. Seyla Ben-Habib, in Hal Foster (ed.) *Postmodern Culture* (London: Pluto Press, 1985).

Richard J. Hand, *Terror on the Air! Horror Radio in America 1931–1952* (Jefferson: McFarland, 2006).

Michael Hardt and Antonio Negri, *Empire* (Cambridge, Mass.: Harvard University Press, 2000).

J. J. Healy, 'The Lemurian Nineties', *Australian Literary Studies*, 8.3 (1978): 307–16.

Gabriele C. Hegerl, Francis W. Zwiers, Pascale Braconnot, Nathan P. Gillett, Yong Luo, Jose A. Marengo Orsini, Neville Nicholls, Joyce E. Penner and Peter A. Stott, 'Understanding and Attributing Climate Change', in Susan Solomon, Dahe Qin, Martin Manning, Zhenlin Chen, Melinda Marquis, Kristen Averyt, Melinda M. B. Tignor and Henry LeRoy Miller, Jr (eds) *Climate Change 2007: The Physical Science Basis. Contribution of Working Group I to the Fourth Assessment Report of the Intergovernmental Panel on Climate Change* (Cambridge: Cambridge University Press, 2007).

Agnes Heller, 'The Contemporary Historical Novel', *Thesis Eleven*, 106 (2011): 88–97.

Veronica Hollinger, 'Contemporary Trends in Science Fiction Criticism, 1980–1999', *Science Fiction Studies*, 26.2 (1999): 232–62.

Nalo Hopkinson and Uppinder Mehan (eds), *So Long Been Dreaming: Postcolonial Science Fiction and Fantasy* (Vancouver: Arsenal Pulp Press, 2004).

Michel Houellebecq, *Contre le monde, contre la vie, essai sur Lovecraft* (Paris: Éditions du Rocher, 1991).

Peter Humm, Paul Stigant and Peter Widdowson (eds), *Popular Fiction: Essays in Literature and History* (London: Methuen, 1986).

John Huntington, *Rationalizing Genius: Ideological Strategies in the Classic American Science Fiction Short Story* (New Brunswick: Rutgers University Press, 1989).

Aldous Huxley, *Do What You Will: Essays* (London: Chatto and Windus, 1929).

—, *The Letters of D. H. Lawrence* (New York: Viking Press, 1932).

—, 'Foreword' to *Brave New World* (Harmondsworth, Penguin, 1955b [1946]).

—, *Letters of Aldous Huxley*, ed. Grover Smith (London: Chatto and Windus, 1969).

Andreas Huyssen, *After the Great Divide: Modernism, Mass Culture and Postmodernism* (London: Macmillan, 1988).

Luce Irigaray, 'Communications linguistique et spéculaire (Modèles génétiques et modèles pathologiques)', *Cahiers pour l'Analyse*, 3 (1966): 39–55.

Roman Jakobson, 'Closing Statement: Linguistics and Poetics', in Thomas A. Sebeok (ed.) *Style in Language* (Cambridge, Mass.: MIT Press, 1960).

Edward James, *Science Fiction in the Twentieth Century* (Oxford: Oxford University

Press, 1994).
— and Farah Mendlesohn (eds), *The Cambridge Companion to Science Fiction* (Cambridge: Cambridge University Press, 2003).
Fredric Jameson, *The Political Unconscious: Narrative as a Socially Symbolic Act* (London: Methuen, 1981).
—, *Late Marxism: Adorno, or, the Persistence of the Dialectic* (London: Verso, 1990).
—, *Postmodernism, or, the Cultural Logic of Late Capitalism* (London: Verso, 1991).
—, *The Seeds of Time* (New York: Columbia University Press, 1994).
—, 'Future City', *New Left Review*, (II) 21 (2003): 65–79.
—, 'The Politics of Utopia', *New Left Review*, (II) 25 (2004): 35–54.
—, *Archaeologies of the Future: The Desire Called Utopia and Other Science Fictions* (London: Verso, 2005).
—, 'Then You Are Them', *London Review of Books*, 31.17 (2009): 7–8.
Hans Robert Jauss, *Toward an Aesthetic of Reception*, trans. Timothy Bahti (Brighton: Harvester, 1982).
Henry Jenkins, '"Strangers No More, We Sing": Filking and the Social Construction of the Science Fiction Fan Community', in Lisa A. Lewis (ed.) *The Adoring Audience: Fan Culture and Popular Media* (London: Routledge, 1992a).
—, *Textual Poachers: Television Fans and Participant Culture* (New York: Routledge, 1992b).
Jan Johnson-Smith, *American Science Fiction Television: Star Trek, Stargate and Beyond* (London: I. B. Tauris, 2005).
Linda Jordan, *German Science Fiction in the Science-Fiction Magazines of Hugo Gernsback (1926–1935)*, MA Thesis (Montreal: McGill University, 1986).
Jean Jules-Verne, *Jules Verne: A Biography*, trans. Roger Greaves (London: Macdonald and Jane's, 1976).
Andrzej Juszczyk, 'H. G. Wells's Polish Reception', in Patrick Parrinder and John S. Partington (eds) *The Reception of H. G. Wells in Europe* (London: Continuum, 2005).
Paul Kincaid, 'On the Origins of Genre', *Extrapolation*, 44.4 (2003): 409–19.
Damon Knight, *The Futurians* (New York: John Day, 1977).
Patricia Köster, 'Dystopia: An Eighteenth Century Appearance', *Notes & Queries* 228 (ns 30.1) (February 1983): 65–66.
Efrain Kristal, '"Considering Coldly" ... A Response to Franco Moretti', *New Left Review*, (II) 15 (2002): 61–74.
Annette Kuhn, 'Introduction: Cultural Theory and Science Fiction Cinema', in Annette Kuhn (ed.) *Alien Zone: Cultural Theory and Contemporary Science Fiction Cinema* (London: Verso, 1999).
Jacques Lacan, 'The Mirror Stage as Formative of the Function of the I', in *Écrits: A Selection*, trans. Alan Sheridan (London: Tavistock, 1977).
Brooks Landon, *The Aesthetics of Ambivalence: Rethinking Science Fiction Film in the Age of Electronic (Re)Production* (Westport: Greenwood Press, 2002).
F. R. Leavis, *D. H. Lawrence, Novelist* (London: Chatto and Windus, 1955).
—, *Mass Civilization and Minority Culture* (Cambridge: Minority Press, 1930).
Ursula K. Le Guin, 'Head Cases', *The Guardian Review*, 22 September (2007): 17.
—, 'The Year of the Flood by Margaret Atwood', *The Guardian Review*, 29 August

(2009): 5.

Stanisław Lem, 'Posłowie', in H. G. Wells, *Wojna swiatów*, trans. Henryk Józefowicz (Cracow: Wydawnictwo Literackie, 1974).

V. I. Lenin, *Imperialism: The Highest Stage of Capitalism* (New York: International Publishers, 1969).

Jean-Marc Lofficier and Randy Lofficer, *French Science Fiction, Fantasy, Horror and Pulp Fiction: A Guide to Cinema, Television, Radio, Animation, Comic Books and Literature* (Jefferson: McFarland, 2000).

Roger Luckhurst, *Science Fiction* (Cambridge: Polity Press, 2005).

Georg Lukács, *The Historical Novel*, trans. Hannah and Stanley Mitchell (Harmondsworth: Penguin, 1969 [1963]).

—, *The Meaning of Contemporary Realism*, trans. J. and N. Mander (London: Merlin Press, 1963).

Georg Lukács, Hans Heinz Holz, Leo Kofler and Wolfgang Abendroth, *Conversations with Lukács*, ed. Theo Pinkus, trans. David Fernbach (London: Merlin Press, 1974).

Jean-François Lyotard, *The Postmodern Condition: A Report on Knowledge*, trans. Geoffrey Bennington and Brian Massumi (Minneapolis: University of Minnesota Press, 1984).

Bohuslav Mánek, 'A Welcome Guest: The Czech Reception of H. G. Wells', in Patrick Parrinder and John S. Partington (eds) *The Reception of H. G. Wells in Europe* (London: Continuum, 2005).

Jean-Michel Margot, 'Jules Verne, Playwright', *Science Fiction Studies*, 32.1 (2005): 150–62.

Karl Marx, *Capital: A Critique of Political Economy*, Vol. I, trans. S. Moore and Edward Aveling (London: Lawrence and Wishart, 1970).

—, *Capital: A Critique of Political Economy*, Vol. III, ed. Frederick Engels (London: Lawrence and Wishart, 1972).

— and Frederick Engels, *The Communist Manifesto*, trans. S. Moore (Harmondsworth: Penguin, 1967).

—, *The German Ideology*, Part One, trans. W. Lough, C. Dutt and C. P. Magill, ed. C. J. Arthur (London: Lawrence and Wishart, 1970).

Scott Matthewman, 'Rendezvous with Drama: More about BBC Radio's Sci-Fi Season', *The Stage*, 2 October (2008). http://blogs.thestage.co.uk/tvtoday/2008/10.

Patricia Melzer, *Alien Constructions: Science Fiction and Feminist Thought* (Austin: University of Texas Press, 2006).

Judith Merril, 'What Do You Mean: Science? Fiction?', in Thomas D. Clareson (ed.) *SF: The Other Side of Realism* (Bowling Green: Bowling Green University Popular Press, 1971).

China Miéville, 'Editorial Introduction', in China Miéville and Mark Bould (eds) 'Symposium: Marxism and Fantasy', *Historical Materialism: Research in Critical Marxist Theory*, 10.4 (2002): 39–49.

—, 'Weird Fiction', in Mark Bould, Andrew M. Butler, Adam Roberts and Sherryl Vint (eds) *The Routledge Companion to Science Fiction* (London and New York: Routledge, 2009a).

—, 'Cognition as Ideology: A Dialectic of SF Theory', in Mark Bould and China Miéville (eds) *Red Planets: Marxism and Science Fiction* (London: Pluto Press, 2009b).

— and Mark Bould (eds), 'Symposium: Marxism and Fantasy', *Historical Materialism: Research in Critical Marxist Theory*, 10.4 (2002).

Andrew Milner, *John Milton and the English Revolution: A Study in the Sociology of Literature* (London: Macmillan, 1981).

—, 'The Protestant Epic and the Spirit of Capitalism', in William Zunder (ed.) *Paradise Lost: Contemporary Critical Essays* (London: Macmillan, 1999).

—, *Re-Imagining Cultural Studies: The Promise of Cultural Materialism* (London: Sage 2002).

—, *Literature, Culture and Society* (London and New York: Routledge, 2005).

— and Jeff Browitt, *Contemporary Cultural Theory: An Introduction* (London and New York: Routledge, 2002).

— and Robert Savage, 'Pulped Dreams: Utopia and American "Golden Age" Science Fiction', *Science Fiction Studies*, 35.1 (2008): 31–47.

John Stuart Mill, *Hansard's Parliamentary Debates*, 3rd series, vol. 190, no. 1517, 12 March (London: Cornelius Buck, Paternoster Row, 1868).

Michael Moorcock, 'A New Literature for the Space Age', *New Worlds*, 48, 142 (1964): 2–3.

—, 'Ballard: The Voice', *New Worlds*, 50, 167 (1966): 2–3, 151.

Franco Moretti, *Signs Taken For Wonders: Essays in the Sociology of Literary Forms*, 2nd edn, trans. Susan Fischer, David Forgacs and David Miller (London: Verso, 1988).

—, *Modern Epic: The World System from Goethe to García Márquez*, trans. Quintin Hoare (London: Verso, 1996).

—, *Atlas of the European Novel 1800–1900* (London: Verso, 1998).

—, 'Conjectures on World Literature', *New Left Review*, (II) 1 (2000): 54–68.

—, 'More Conjectures', *New Left Review*, (II) 20 (2003): 73–81.

Sam Moskowitz, *Explorers of the Infinite: Shapers of Science Fiction* (Westport: Hyperion Press, 1974a).

—, *The Immortal Storm: A History of Science Fiction Fandom* (Westport: Hyperion Press, 1974b).

Tom Moylan, *Demand the Impossible: Science Fiction and the Utopian Imagination* (New York: Methuen, 1986).

—, *Scraps of the Untainted Sky: Science Fiction, Utopia, Dystopia* (Boulder, Colorado: Westview Press, 2000).

— and Rafaella Baccolini (eds), *Utopia Method Vision: The Use Value of Social Dreaming* (Frankfurt am Main, Oxford and Bern: Peter Lang, 2007).

Arno Münster (ed.), *Tagträume vom Aufrechten Gang: Sechs Interviews mit Ernst Bloch* (Frankfurt: Suhrkamp, 1977).

Patrick D. Murphy, *Ecocritical Explorations in Literary and Cultural Studies: Fences, Boundaries and Fields* (Lanham: Lexington Books, 2009).

Nevil Shute Norway Foundation. http://www.nevilshute.org/index.php (last accessed December 2011).

Peter Nicholls (ed.), *The Encyclopedia of Science Fiction: An Illustrated A to Z* (London:

Granada, 1979).

Barack Obama, 'President Barack Obama on Space Exploration in the 21st Century: Remarks by the President on Space Exploration in the 21st Century', The White House, Office of the Press Secretary, 15 April (Washington, DC: 2010).

James O'Connor, *Natural Causes: Essays in Ecological Marxism* (New York: Guildford Press, 1998).

Sharalyn Orbaugh, 'Manga and Anime', in Mark Bould, Andrew M. Butler, Adam Roberts and Sherryl Vint (eds), *The Routledge Companion to Science Fiction* (London and New York: Routledge, 2009).

Francesca Orsini, 'Maps of Indian Writing: India in the Mirror of World Fiction', *New Left Review*, (II) 13 (2002): 75–88.

George Orwell, 'Looking Back on the Spanish War', in *Homage to Catalonia and Looking Back on the Spanish War* (Harmondsworth: Penguin, 1966 [1943]).

—, 'Wells, Hitler and the World State', in *Collected Essays, Journalism and Letters, Vol. 2: My Country Right or Left*, ed. Sonia Orwell and Ian Angus (Harmondsworth: Penguin, 1970a [1941]).

—, 'Review', *Tropic of Cancer* by Henry Miller', *New English Weekly*, 14 November 1935, in *Collected Essays, Journalism and Letters of George Orwell, Vol. 1: An Age Like This*, ed. Sonia Orwell and Ian Angus (Harmondsworth: Penguin, 1970b [1935]).

—, 'As I Please', *Tribune*, 6 December 1946, in *Collected Essays, Journalism and Letters of George Orwell, Vol. 4: In Front of Your Nose*, ed. Sonia Orwell and Ian Angus (Harmondsworth: Penguin, 1970c [1946]).

—, 'Letter to Gleb Struve', 17 February 1944, in *Collected Essays, Journalism and Letters, Vol. 3: As I Please*, ed. Sonia Orwell and Ian Angus (Harmondsworth, Penguin, 1970d [1944]).

—, 'Review of *We* by E. I. Zamyatin', in *Collected Essays, Journalism and Letters of George Orwell, Vol. 4: In Front of Your Nose*, ed. Sonia Orwell and Ian Angus (Harmondsworth: Penguin, 1970e [1946]).

—, 'James Burnham and the Managerial Revolution', in *Collected Essays, Journalism and Lettersof George Orwell, Vol. 4: In Front of Your Nose*, ed. Sonia Orwell and Ian Angus (Harmondsworth: Penguin, 1970f [1946]).

—, 'Letter to Gleb Struve', 21 April 1948, in *Collected Essays, Journalism and Lettersof George Orwell, Vol. 4: In Front of Your Nose*, ed. Sonia Orwell and Ian Angus (Harmondsworth: Penguin, 1970g [1948]).

—, 'Letter to F. J. Warburg', 30 March 1949, in *Collected Essays, Journalism and Letters of George Orwell, Vol. 4: In Front of Your Nose*, ed. Sonia Orwell and Ian Angus (Harmondsworth: Penguin, 1970h [1949]).

—, 'Why I Write', in *Collected Essays, Journalism and Letters of George Orwell, Vol. 1: An Age Like This*, ed. Sonia Orwell and Ian Angus (Harmondsworth: Penguin, 1970i [1946]).

—, 'Letter to Francis A. Henderson (extract)', in *Collected Essays, Journalism and Letters of George Orwell, Vol. 4: In Front of Your Nose*, ed. Sonia Orwell and Ian Angus (Harmondsworth: Penguin, 1970j [1949]).

—, 'Inside the Whale', in *Collected Essays, Journalism and Letters of George Orwell, Vol. 1: An Age Like This*, ed. Sonia Orwell and Ian Angus (Harmondsworth: Penguin,

1970k [1940]).
—, 'Notes on the Way', *Time and Tide*, 6 April 1940, in *Collected Essays, Journalism and Lettersof George Orwell, Vol. 2: My Country Right or Left*, ed. Sonia Orwell and Ian Angus (Harmondsworth: Penguin, 1970l [1940]).
—, 'Prophecies of Fascism', *Tribune*, 12 July 1940, in *Collected Essays, Journalism and Letters of George Orwell, Vol. 2: My Country Right or Left*, ed. Sonia Orwell and Ian Angus (Harmondsworth: Penguin, 1970m [1940]).
Jale Parla, 'The Object of Comparison', *Comparative Literature Studies*, 41.1 (2004): 116–25.
Patrick Parrinder, 'Introduction: Learning from Other Worlds', in Patrick Parrinder (ed.) *Learning from Other Worlds: Estrangement, Cognition and the Politics of Science Fiction and Utopia* (Liverpool: Liverpool University Press, 2000).
—, 'Introduction: An Outline of Wells's Reception in Europe', in Patrick Parrinder and John S. Partington (eds) *The Reception of H. G. Wells in Europe* (London: Continuum, 2005).
— and Paul Barnaby, 'Timeline: European Reception of H. G. Wells', in Patrick Parrinder and John S. Partington (eds) *The Reception of H. G. Wells in Europe* (London: Continuum, 2005).
Christopher Pawling (ed.), *Popular Fiction and Social Change* (London: Macmillan, 1984).
Constance Penley, *NASA/TREK: Popular Science and Sex in America* (London: Verso, 1997).
Robert M. Philmus (ed.), *H. G. Wells: The Island of Doctor Moreau: A Variorum Text* (Athens: University of Georgia Press, 1993).
Renato Poggioli, *The Theory of the Avant-Garde*, trans. Gerald Fitzgerald (Cambridge, Mass.: Harvard University Press, 1968).
Frederick Pohl, *The Way the Future Was: A Memoir* (New York: Ballantine Books, 1978).
Christopher Prendergast, 'Negotiating World Literature', *New Left Review*, (II) 8 (2001): 100-121.
Thomas Pynchon, 'Foreword', in George Orwell, *Nineteen Eighty-Four: The Centennial Edition* (New York: Plume, 2003).
Jimmie L. Reeves, Mark C. Rodgers and Michael Epstein, 'Rewriting Popularity: The Cult Files', in David Lavery, Angela Hague and Maria Cartwright (eds) *Deny All Knowledge: Reading the X-Files* (London: Faber, 1996).
John Rieder, *Colonialism and the Emergence of Science Fiction* (Middletown: Wesleyan University Press, 2008).
Kate Rigby, *Topographies of the Sacred: The Poetics of Place in European Romanticism* (Charlottesville: University of Virginia Press, 2004).
—, 'Imagining Catastrophe: Utopia and Dystopia in a Warming World', *Arena Journal*, (II) 35/36 (2011): 57–77.
Adam Roberts, *Science Fiction* (London: Routledge, 2000).
—, *The History of Science Fiction* (Basingstoke: Palgrave Macmillan, 2005).
—, 'A Brief Note on Moretti and Science Fiction', in Jonathan Goodwin and John Holbo (eds) *Reading Graphs, Maps, Trees: Responses to Franco Moretti* (Anderson, SC: Parlor Press, 2011).

David Roberts, '*Marat/Sade*, or the Birth of Postmodernism from the Spirit of the Avant-Garde', in Andrew Milner, Philip Thomson and Chris Worth (eds) *Postmodern Conditions* (Oxford and New York: Berg, 1990).
—, *The Total Work of Art in European Modernism* (Ithaca: Cornell University Press, 2011).
— and Peter Murphy, *Dialectic of Romanticism: A Critique of Modernism* (London: Continuum, 2004).
Robin Roberts, *Sexual Generations: 'Star Trek: The Next Generation' and Gender* (Urbana: University of Illinois Press, 1999).
Kim Stanley Robinson, 'Notes for an Essay on Cecilia Holland', *Foundation: The Review of Science Fiction*, 40, Summer 1987: 54–61.
—, 'Remarks on Utopia in the Age of Climate Change', *Arena Journal*, (II) 35/36 (2011): 8–21.
Lacey Rose, 'Hollywood's Most Expensive Movies', *Forbes*, 12 September (2005).
Andrew Ross, *Strange Weather: Culture, Science and Technology in the Age of Limits* (London: Verso, 1991).
Joanna Russ, 'The Image of Women in Science Fiction', in *The Country You Have Never Seen: Essays and Reviews* (Liverpool: Liverpool University Press, 2007).
Geoff Ryman, 'The Mundane Manifesto', *New York Review of Science Fiction* 226 (2006 [2002]): 4–5.
Edward W. Said, *Culture and Imperialism* (London: Chatto and Windus, 1993).
—, *Orientalism*, rev. edn (New York: Pantheon Books, 1995 [1978]).
Lyman Tower Sargent, 'Themes in Utopian Fiction in English before Wells', *Science Fiction Studies*, 10 (1976): 275–82.
—, *British and American Utopian Literature, 1516–1985: An Annotated, Chronological Bibliography* (New York: Garland, 1988).
—, 'The Three Faces of Utopianism Revisited', *Utopian Studies*, 5.1 (1994): 1–37.
—, 'Australian Utopian Literature: An Annotated, Chronological Bibliography 1667–1999', *Utopian Studies*, 10.2 (1999): 138–73.
—, 'In Defense of Utopia', *Diogenes*, 53.1 (2006): 11–17.
Martin Schäfer, *Science Fiction als Ideologiekritik? Utopische Spuren in der amerikanischen Science-Fiction Literatur 1940–1955* (Stuttgart: Metzler, 1977).
Elmar Schenkel, 'White Elephants and Black Machines: H. G. Wells and German Culture, 1920–45', in Patrick Parrinder and John S. Partington (eds) *The Reception of H. G. Wells in Europe* (London: Continuum, 2005).
Stephen H. Schneider, Serguei Semenov, Anand Patwardhan, Ian Burton, Chris H. Magadza, Michael Oppenheimer, A. Barrie Pittock, Atiq Rahman, Joel B. Smith, Avelino Suarez and Farhana Yamin, 'Assessing Key Vulnerabilities and the Risk from Climate Change', in Martin Parry, Osvaldo Canziani, Jean Palutikof, Paul van der Linden and Clair Hanson (eds) *Climate Change 2007: Impacts, Adaptation and Vulnerability. Contribution of Working Group 11 to the Fourth Assessment Report of the Intergovernmental Panel on Climate Change* (Cambridge: Cambridge University Press, 2007).
Robert E. Scholes, *Structural Fabulation: An Essay on Fiction of the Future* (Notre Dame: University of Notre Dame Press, 1975).
Paul Schrader, 'Canon Fodder: As the Sun Finally Sets on the Century of Cinema,

by What Criteria Do We Determine Its Masterworks?', *Film Comment* September/October, 2006: 33–49.

Roberto Schwarz, 'Misplaced Ideas', in *Misplaced Ideas: Essays on Brazilian Culture,* ed. John Gledson (London: Verso, 1992).

Martin Schwonke, *Vom Staatsroman zur Science Fiction: Eine Untersuchung über Geschichte und Funktion der naturwissenschaftlich-technischen Utopie* (Stuttgart: Ferdinand Enke, 1957).

David Seed, *Science Fiction: A Very Short Introduction* (Oxford: Oxford University Press, 2011).

Miranda Seymour, *Mary Shelley* (London: Picador, 2001).

Debra Shaw, *Women, Science and Fiction: the Frankenstein Inheritance* (London: Palgrave, 2000).

Lewis Shiner, 'Inside the Movement: Past, Present, and Future', in George Slusser and Tom Shippey (eds) *Fiction 2000: Cyberpunk and the Future of Narrative* (Athens: University of Georgia Press, 1992).

Viktor Shklovsky, 'Art as Technique', trans. Lee T. Lemon and Marion J. Reis, in Lee T. Lemon and Marion J. Reis (eds) *Russian Formalist Criticism: Four Essays* (Lincoln: University of Nebraska Press, 1965).

SIPRI (Stockholm Institute for Peace Research), *SIPRI Yearbook 2011: Armaments, Disarmaments and International Security* (Oxford: Oxford University Press, 2011).

George Slusser, 'Science Fiction in France: An Introduction', *Science Fiction Studies,* 16.3 (1989): 251–53.

— and Danièle Chatelain, 'A Tale of Two Science Fictions: H. G. Wells in France and the Soviet Union', in Patrick Parrinder and John S. Partington (eds) *The Reception of H. G. Wells in Europe* (London: Continuum, 2005).

Julian Smith, *Nevil Shute* (Boston: Twayne Publishers, 1976).

Vivian Sobchack, *Screening Space: The American Science Fiction Film* (New York: Ungar, 1987).

Susan Sontag, 'The Imagination of Disaster', in *Against Interpretation and Other Essays* (New York: Farrar, Straus & Giroux, 1966).

Gayatri Chakravorty Spivak, 'Can the Subaltern Speak?', in Cary Nelson and Lawrence Grossberg (eds) *Marxism and the Interpretation of Culture* (London: Macmillan, 1988).

—, *A Critique of Postcolonial Reason: Toward A History of the Vanishing Present* (Cambridge, Mass.: Harvard University Press, 1999).

—, *Death of a Discipline* (New York: Columbia University Press, 2003).

Bruce Sterling, 'Preface', in Bruce Sterling (ed.) *Mirrorshades: The Cyberpunk Anthology* (New York: Arbor House, 1986).

—, 'Cyberpunk in the Nineties', *Interzone: Science Fiction and Fantasy,* 38 (1990): 39–41.

John Sutherland, *Reading the Decades: Fifty Years of the Nation's Bestselling Books* (London: BBC Publications, 2002).

Darko Suvin, 'On the Poetics of the Science Fiction Genre', *College English,* 34.3 (1972): 372–82.

—, *Metamorphoses of Science Fiction: On the Poetics and History of a Literary Genre* (New Haven: Yale University Press, 1979).

—, *Positions and Presuppositions in Science Fiction* (Kent: Kent State University Press, 1988).

—, 'Utopianism from Orientation to Agency: What Are We Intellectuals under Post-Fordism to Do?', in *Defined by a Hollow: Essays on Utopia, Science Fiction and Political Epistemology* (Frankfurt am Main, Oxford and Bern: Peter Lang, 2010a [1997–98]).

—, 'A Tractate on Dystopia 2001', in *Defined by a Hollow: Essays on Utopia, Science Fiction and Political Epistemology* (Frankfurt am Main, Oxford and Bern: Peter Lang, 2010b [2001]).

Takayuki Tatsumi, 'A Cacophone Modernist', *Science Fiction Studies*, 38.2 (2011): 341–43.

A. J. P. Taylor, *The Oxford History of England, Vol. 15: English History 1914–45* (Oxford: Oxford University Press, 1965).

John Tulloch and Henry Jenkins, *Science Fiction Audiences: Watching Dr Who and Star Trek* (London: Routledge, 1995).

George Turner, 'Envoi', in *A Pursuit of Miracles: Eight Stories* (Adelaide: Aphelion Publications, 1990).

UNESCO, *UNESCO Statistical Yearbook* (Paris: UNESCO, 1978).

—, *UNESCO Statistical Yearbook* (Paris: UNESCO, 1990).

—, *UNESCO Statistical Yearbook* (Paris: UNESCO, 1999).

—, *Index Translationum* (Paris: UNESCO, 2011). http://www.unesco.org/xtrans/bsstatexp.aspx?crit1L=5&nTyp=min&topN=50 (accessed 19 November 2011).

Nicoletta Vallorani, '"The Invisible Wells" in European Cinema and Television', in Patrick Parrinder and John S. Partington (eds) *The Reception of H. G. Wells in Europe* (London: Continuum, 2005).

Jeff VanderMeer, 'The New Weird: It's Alive?' in Jeff and Ann VanderMeer (eds) *The New Weird* (San Francisco: Tachyon Publications, 2008).

A. E. van Vogt, *Reflections of A. E. van Vogt: The Autobiography of a Science Fiction Giant* (Lakemont: Fictioneer Books, 1975).

Jules Verne, 'Edgar Poe et ses ouevres', in *Textes oubliés*, ed. F. Lacassin (Paris: Union Générale, 1979).

—, 'Jules Verne Interviewed, 9 October 1903', in Patrick Parrinder (ed.) *H. G. Wells: The Critical Heritage* (London: Routledge, 1997).

Otakar Vocadlo, *Anglické listy Karla Capka* (Prague: Academia, 1975).

John Walker (ed.), *Halliwell's Film Guide*, 8th edn (London: Harper Collins, 1991).

Immanuel Wallerstein, *World-Systems Analysis: An Introduction* (Durham: Duke University Press, 2004).

Robyn Walton, 'Utopian and Dystopian Impulses in Australia', *Overland*, 173 (2003): 5–20.

Ben Ware, 'Williams and Wittgenstein: Language, Politics and Structure of Feeling', *Key Words: A Journal of Cultural Materialism*, 9 (2011): 41–57.

Donald Watt, 'The Manuscript Revisions of *Brave New World*', in Jerome Mecker (ed.) *Critical Essays on Aldous Huxley* (New York: G. K. Hall & Co., 1996).

Max Weber, *The Protestant Ethic and the Spirit of Capitalism*, trans. Talcott Parsons (London: Unwin, 1930).

—, *The Methodology of the Social Sciences*, trans. and ed. Edward A. Shils and Henry

A. Finch (New York: Free Press, 1949).
Phillip E. Wegner, *Imaginary Communities: Utopia, the Nation, and the Spatial Histories of Modernity* (Berkeley: University of California, Press, 2002).
—, 'Jameson's Modernisms; or, the Desire Called Utopia', *Diacritics*, 37.4 (2007a): 2-20.
—, 'Here or Nowhere: Utopia, Modernity, and Totality', in Tom Moylan and Rafaela Baccolini (eds) *Utopia Method Vision: The Use Value of Social Dreaming* (Frankfurt am Main, Oxford and Bern: Peter Lang, 2007b).
—, 'Ken MacLeod's Permanent Revolution: Utopian Possible Worlds, History and the *Augenblick* in the *Fall Revolution* Quartet', in Mark Bould and China Miéville (eds) *Red Planets: Marxism and Science Fiction* (London: Pluto Press, 2009).
—, 'Preface: Emerging from the Flood in Which We Are Sinking: or, Reading with Darko Suvin (Again)', in Darko Suvin, *Defined by a Hollow: Essays on Utopia, Science Fiction and Political Epistemology* (Frankfurt am Main, Oxford and Bern: Peter Lang, 2010).
René Wellek and Austin Warren, *Theory of Literature* (Harmondsworth: Penguin, 1976).
H. G. Wells, 'Preface' to *The Scientific Romances of H.G. Wells* (London: Victor Gollancz, 1933a).
Wikipedia, 'Definitions of Science Fiction', http://en.wikipedia.org/wiki/Definitions_of_science_fiction (last accessed December 2011).
Raymond Williams, *Culture and Society 1780–1950* (Harmondsworth: Penguin, 1963).
—, *The Long Revolution* (Harmondsworth: Penguin, 1965).
—, *Drama from Ibsen to Brecht* (Harmondsworth: Penguin, 1973).
—, *Television; Technology and Cultural Form* (Glasgow: Fontana, 1974).
—, *Marxism and Literature* (Oxford: Oxford University Press, 1977).
—, *Politics and Letters: Interviews with New Left Review* (London: New Left Books, 1979).
—, 'Notes on Marxism in Britain since 1945', in *Problems in Materialism and Culture: Selected Essays* (London: New Left Books, 1980a).
—, 'Base and Superstructure in Marxist Cultural Theory', in *Problems in Materialism and Culture: Selected Essays* (London: New Left Books, 1980b).
—, 'Utopia and Science Fiction', in *Problems in Materialism and Culture* (London: New Left Books, 1980c). (First published in *Science Fiction Studies*, 5.3 [1978].)
—, *Culture* (Glasgow: Collins, 1981).
—, 'The Tenses of Imagination', in *Writing in Society* (London: Verso, 1984).
—, 'A Defence of Realism', in *What I Came To Say*, ed. Neil Belton, Francis Mulhern and Jenny Taylor (London: Hutchinson Radius, 1989).
—, 'Nineteen Eighty Four in 1984', in *Orwell*, 3rd edn (London: Fontana, 1991 [1984]).
—, 'Film and the Dramatic Tradition', in John Higgins (ed.) *The Raymond Williams Reader* (Oxford: Blackwell, 2001 [1954]).
—, 'Science Fiction', in Andrew Milner (ed.) *Tenses of Imagination: Raymond Williams on Science Fiction, Utopia and Dystopia* (Oxford and Bern: Peter Lang, 2010). (First published in *The Highway*, 48 [1956].).

Scott Wilson, *Cultural Materialism: Theory and Practice* (Oxford: Blackwell, 1995).

Judith Wilt, 'Introduction', in Judith Wilt (ed.) *Making Humans: Mary Shelley, Frankenstein, H. G. Wells, The Island of Doctor Moreau* (New York: Houghton Mifflin, 2003).

Rick Worland, 'Captain Kirk, Cold Warrior', *Journal of Popular Film and Television*, 16.3 (1988): 109–17.

Evgenii Zamiatin, 'H. G. Wells (1922)', in *A Soviet Heretic*, ed. and trans. M. Ginsburg (Chicago: University of Chicago Press, 1970 [1924]).

—, 'Wells's Revolutionary Fairy-Tales', trans. Lesley Milne, in Patrick Parrinder (ed.) *H. G. Wells: The Critical Heritage* (London: Routledge, 1997 [1922]).

Slavoj Žižek, *Enjoy Your Symptom! Jacques Lacan In Hollywood and Out*, rev. edn (London: Routledge, 2001).

—, *Living in the End Times* (London: Verso, 2010).

Index

Abe, Kōbō 166, 175
Abensour, Miguel 98
Abrams, J. J. 110
academic SF criticism 59
Adams, Douglas 76, 85, 121, 193
    The Hitchhiker's Guide to the Galaxy 51, 76, 85, 87
Adolph, José B. 100
Adorno, Theodor 49, 75, 78–79, 87, 143
Aeschylus 90, 91, 137
Afrofuturist SF 63, 174
Aldiss, Brian 31, 34, 39, 54, 55, 59, 85, 140, 153
Althusser, Louis 20
Altov, Genrikh 166
Amazing Stories [magazine] 13, 14, 31, 54, 84, 107, 108, 152, 175
American Golden Age SF 27
American New Wave 59, 62, 94, 101, 174
Amis, Kingsley 34
Amis, Martin 9
Anderson, Perry 142
Andrade, David 97
Andrevon, Jean-Pierre 52
Anemolius 89
anime 51, 176
Anno, Hideaki 176
anti-anti-utopianism 93–94
anti-critical dystopia 119
anti-nuclear movement 185–86, 189
anti-utopia 116, 118
anti-utopianism 93, 110, 116, 117
Aristophanes 90, 91, 137, 139
Arnaud, G.-J.165
Arthur C. Clarke Awards 63, 102, 185
Ashley, Mike 136–37
Asimov, Isaac 5, 6, 24, 57, 61, 162
    Foundation Trilogy 109
    Futurianism 60, 174
    I, Robot 109
    positronic robot 109
    psychohistory 109
    technological utopianism 107
Astounding Science-Fiction [magazine] 55, 60, 107, 152
Atwood, Margaret 57, 99, 118, 119, 155, 185, 194
    commercial success 63
    on critical dystopia 100–101
    on definition of SF 22–23
    on ending of *Nineteen Eighty-Four* 122–23, 135
    The Handmaid's Tale 118, 119, 120, 123, 185,
    Oryx and Crake 22, 155
    The Year of the Flood 22, 57, 155
Austen, Jane 9–10
Australia
    dystopian SF 184–92
    radio SF 73, 84, 86
    and SF geography 177
    as site of utopian imaginings 183–84
    television SF productions 52
    utopian SF 183–86
Australian Greens 192, 193
avant-garde movements
    and modernism 28–29, 60
    and SF intellectual formations 60–66

Baccolini, Rafaella 2, 118, 119, 120
Bacigalupi, Paolo 180, 182, 183, 194
Bacon, Francis 25, 90, 98, 137, 139, 143, 152
Badiou, Alain 135
Bakunin, Michael 91
Ballard, J. G. 6, 67, 85, 136, 165, 182
    and British New Wave 59, 62
    The Burning World 136
    place in SF history 96, 154, 162, 165
    The Atrocity Exhibition 62

Crash 96
The Drowned World 85, 182
Banks, Iain M. 77, 81, 83, 94, 95, 99, 105, 165
Consider Phlebas 83, 99
The Hydrogen Sonata 83
The State of the Art 77, 81–83
Barr, Robert 84
Barthes, Roland 37, 75, 179
Baudrillard, Jean 2, 13, 96–97, 154
Bazin, André 66
Beaumont, Matthew 99
Beckett, Samuel 11, 70
Behrens, Alfred 86
Bellamy, Edward 31, 95, 136, 137
controversy with Morris 98–99
Looking Backward 94, 97, 99, 112, 118, 136
place in SF history 108, 112–13, 165
Belyaev, Alexander Romanovich 166
Benedict, Ruth 147
Benjamin, Walter 47, 94
Béraud, Antoine Nicolas 44
Besson, Luc 48, 168
Bester, Alfred 86
Bilenkin, Dimitri Aleksandrovich 166
Binder, Eando 108
Blake, William 137
Blanche, Francis 74
Blay, John 86
Bleiler, E. F. 108
Blish, James 57, 145
Bloch, Ernst 3, 91–92, 109
Bloom, Clive 9
Bloom, Harold 12–14, 66, 67, 190
Boer, Roland 135
Bogdanov, Alexander 27, 166
Bould, Mark 1, 2, 103
Boulle, Pierre 162, 165
Bourdieu, Pierre 3, 9, 10, 11, 40, 41–45, 47, 54, 156, 178, 190–91,
boundaries of a field 54
field of cultural production 9, 10, 11, 41
field of power 41
habitus 42
model of the literary field 41, 156
Bradbury, Ray 6, 14, 28, 29, 59, 84, 85, 120, 145
Brave New World (Huxley)
accusations of plagiarism 124, 125
contrasted with *Mi/Nous autres* 130–32
as critical dystopia 118
ending of 130, 133
as literature 6, 13, 66
Orwell's objection to 125
purpose of 33, 125, 127
radio adaptations 86
setting 130
Brecht, Bertolt 24, 69, 101
de la Bretonne, Nicolas Edme Resif 183
Brians, Paul 181
Britain
broadcasting of radio and television 50
New Wave movement 62
radio SF 5, 73, 84–86
and SF geography 165
SF magazines 55–56
television SF 6–7, 51
British Library, *Out of This World* exhibition 136–37, 155
British New Wave 59, 62
Broderick, Damien 86
Bruehl, Hein 87
Bruno, Giordano 139
Brussolo, Serge 165
Bryant, Dorothy 100
Bulgakov, Mikhail 166, 169
Bulwer-Lytton, Edward 98, 165
Bulychev, Kirill 166
Burdekin, Katharine 118
Bürger, Peter 28, 29, 60
Burgess, Anthony 6, 35
Burroughs, William 35, 62
Butler, Octavia 63
Byron, George Gordon, 6th Baron 29

Callenbach, Ernest 100
Cameron, James 29, 48, 49
Campanella, Tommaso 90, 91, 137, 139
Campbell, Barry 86
Campbell, J. W. 55, 60, 61, 107, 152
Astounding Science-Fiction magazine 55, 60, 107, 152
Canada
radio SF 86
television SF productions 52
Čapek, Josef 126
Čapek, Karel 13, 14, 51, 84, 86, 94, 137
Bilá Nemoc (The White Plague) 47, 126
ending of *R.U.R.* 133
literary reputation 29, 47, 66, 117, 126

political stance 160
relationship with Wells 169
use of comedy 169–70
Válka s mloky (*War with the Newts*) 13, 35, 66, 169
Věc Makropulo (*The Macropoulos Secret*) 47, 86
see also R.U.R. (Rossum's Universal Robots)
capitalism
and labour 193
and nature 193
Carr, John Dickson 84
Carter, Charles 97
Carter, Chris 51, 54
Cartier, Rudolph 51
de Certeau, Michel 65
Chandler, A. Bertram 110
Chardin, Teilhard de 97, 99
Charnas, Suzy McKee 100
de Chassy-Poulay, Pierre-Arnaud 74
Chattwell, Helen 85
Chaviano, Daína 100
children
and radio SF 84
and television SF 51, 52
Chilton, Charles 5, 85
Christoff, Peter 185, 186
Christopher, John 85, 145
cinema 7
earliest SF blockbuster 48
earliest SF film 47–48
in Japan 175–76
SF landmarks 48–49
special effects 49
underground cinema 65–66
Clarke, Arthur C. 85, 86, 103, 165, 196
climate change 181, 185, 186, 190, 194, 197
Clute, John 2–3, 30, 66, 67, 91
cognition, role in SF 24
Cole, Alonzo Deen 73, 84
comedy SF 85, 86
comic books 55–56, 58
commercial radio, SF broadcasters 84, 88
commercial television, special effects in SF productions 50
comparative cultural studies 156
comparative literature, and world systems theory 163–65
Constantine, Murray 118
Cooper, Wyliss 84
Cornell, Paul 81
Correa, Hugo 100
Counter-Reformation 142
Cox, Erle 73
critical dystopia 116, 118–20, 135
critical technocracy 109
critical theory, and SF 1–2
critical utopia 99–101, 110
Cronenberg, David 65
Crook, Tim 73, 79
Csicsery-Ronay, Istvan 160, 161–62
cultural materialism 144
as method 70–73
cultural reception, process of 75
cyberpunk 27, 29, 59, 62, 63, 154, 162, 174
Cyrano de Bergerac, Hercule-Savinien de 137, 139
Czechoslovakia
industrialisation in inter-war years 160
and SF geography 166, 169–70

Dac, Pierre 74
Daley, Brian 86
Dan Dare (comic strip character) 4, 14–18, 20–21
Dantec, Maurice G. 59, 165
Dark, Eleanor 97
Darwin, Charles 182
Darwin, Erasmus 182
Davies, Russel T. 54
De Angelo, Carlo 73
Delany, Samuel R. 63, 99, 100
Derrida, Jacques 156–57, 159
Dick, Philip K. 6, 59, 67, 76, 79, 83, 94, 96, 151, 154
Do Androids Dream of Electric Sheep? 76
Philip K. Dick Collection 67
Ubik 76
Dickens, Charles 165
Diogenes, Antonius 137, 139
Disch, Thomas M. 62
Doctor Who [television series] 3, 6, 7, 13, 16, 51, 53, 54, 64, 110
doomsday dystopia 5, 145, 188
drama *see* cinema; radio drama productions; radio SF productions; television; theatre
Dudgeon, Robert Ellis 184
Dumas, Alexandre 149, 152, 165
Dürrenmatt, Friedrich 69, 70, 77, 79–81, 83, 87

Herkules und der Stall des Augias (*Hercules in the Augean Stables*) 69
Das Unternehmen der Wega (*The Mission of the Vega*) 79–81
dystopia 3, 14
in American pulp fiction SF 110
anti-critical dystopia 119
anti-utopia 116
antipathy to 115–20
in Australian SF 184–86
classic dystopias 119–20
critical dystopia 116, 118–20, 135
doomsday dystopia 5, 145, 188
in European SF 173
fallible dystopia 119
in literary SF 110, 145
Nineteen Eighty-Four 116–18, 119, 120–23
origins of term 89–90
political purpose of 127
and presentation of otherness 97
and the problem of endings 127–33, 129–30, 132–35
race-war dystopias 188
relation to utopia 98–99
in Russian SF 169
simple dystopia 119
turn in 1950s 110, 169
utopianism within 120, 185

Eagle [comic] 4, 17
Eagleton, Terry 2, 24, 25, 145, 179
Eastern Science Fiction Convention 61
Eco, Umberto 10, 75, 179
ecosocialism 192
ecotopia 182
Egan, Greg 155
Eisenhower, Dwight D. 113
Eisenstein, Sergei 29
Eliot, T. S. 26, 37, 39, 80, 81, 124, 145, 146, 163
Ellison, Harlan 56, 59, 62
Emtsev, Mikhail Tikhonovich 166
Engels, Friedrich 93, 121, 132, 192–93
English Revolution 144–45
Enlightenment 143, 145, 154, 161, 182
d'Ennery, Adolphe 43
environmental concerns 182, 193–94
Ermshwiller, Carol 63
estrangement, role in SF 24
ethnography, autobiography as 3, 7, 14
Euhemerus 137
eutopia 90

fallible dystopia 119
fan formations 64
fandom 65
fans 8–9
fantasy
cognition effects 106
definition of 22
exclusion from SF 101
influence of genre 89
and magic 24, 89, 102, 103, 106
and science fiction 3, 101–107
SF-fantasy hybrids 105, 106
utopian fantasy hybrids 104
utopian SF-fantasy hybrids 105
fanzine podcasts 74–75
fanzines 61, 65
Farmer, Philip José 62
Fascism 117–18
Faulkner, William 9
Fekete, John 79, 94
feminist SF 63, 174
Fénelon, François 90
Fiałkowski, Konrad 166
filking 65
film studies 13
Fiore, Joachim de 91
Flaubert, Gustave 149, 150
floods 194–95
forcing 135
Forster, E.M. 6, 27, 58, 124
Foucault, Michel 156
France
history of SF 165
literary field in second half of nineteenth century 42–44
location of early SF within literary field 43–44
radio SF 84, 87
SF magazines 56
France, Anatole 13, 66, 97, 165
Francis, H. G. 74
Franciscowski, Hans Gerhard 74
Frankenstein [novel] (Shelley) 29, 182
cinematic adaptations 48
ideas in 32, 34, 144
as literature 13
location in English literary field 44
novelty of 34, 140
place in history of SF 25, 31, 32, 34, 140, 153, 157

radio drama adaptations 73, 84, 86
relation to imperialism 158–59
Spivak's reading of 157–59
stage adaptations 44
telemovie adaptations 52
Frankfurt School 26
Fraser, Joseph 184
Free, Colin 86
Freedman, Carl 2, 24–25, 102
definition of SF 7
on distinctive linguistic register of SF 76–77
on dystopias 115
on pulp fiction 57
on SF genre 46
on utopia and SF 91, 94
French literary field 42–44
Fromm, Erich 147
Frow, John 12
future stories 178–83
Futurianism 60–61, 64, 109, 174
Futurians 60, 61
Futurism 60
futurologies 178–83

Gail, Otto Willi 166
Galeen, Henry 48
Gardner, Ava 187
Garfield, James A. 113
Gearhardt, Sally 100
Gelder, Ken 9–12, 13, 26, 30, 43
genre
and reproduction of form 36–37
structure of 35–36
as 'type' 12–13, 153
genre SF 107
fiction 9, 10, 12
novels 56–57, 58
Germany
radio SF 74, 87
television SF production 52
Weimar Republic SF 166, 167, 173
Gernsback, Hugo 61, 152, 153
Amazing Stories [magazine] 13, 31, 54, 107, 152, 175
background 55, 175
coining of term scientifiction 34, 173
place in history of SF 13, 31, 54, 55, 57, 107, 166, 175
Gernsback moment 166, 175
Gibbon, Dave 55, 58
Gibson, Ralph 97
Gibson, William 59, 140, 175
Gilliam, Terry 48
Gilman, Charlotte Perkins 97
global warming 181, 182, 185, 186
Godard, Jean-Luc 65, 66
Godfrey, David H. 85
Godwin, William 40
Goethe, Johann Wolfgang von 163, 182
Golding, William 6, 14, 35
Gothic, the 105
Grant, Rob 193
Grant, Ulysses S. 113
graphic novels 58
Great Fire of London 143
Greenblatt, Stephen 19
Grousset, François Paschal 43

Habermas, Jürgen 27, 28, 29
habitus 42
Haldeman, Joe 59
Hall, Joseph 183
Hanstein, Otfrid von 108, 166
Harbou, Thea von 48, 166, 167
Harrison, Benjamin 113
Hardt, Michael 161
Hayes, Rutherford B. 113
Hecateaus 137
Heglin, Peter 183
Heinlein, Robert A. 57, 84, 113, 116
'if this goes on' principle 116
Orphans of the Sky 57
'Requiem' 84
Starship Troopers 113
Heller, Agnes 150
Herzog, Arthur 182
Hillis Miller, J. 10
Historical Materialism [journal] 102
historical novel, affinities with SF 149–51, 152–53
history of SF 25, 44
in America 165, 166, 173–75
in Britain 165
and context of colonialism 160
in Czechoslovakia 160, 166, 169–70
development of genre 139
and dialectic between Enlightenment and Romanticism 143, 145, 154, 161
emergence of genre 12, 27, 28, 143, 149, 151, 153–54, 156
form and history 149–54
founding text 157

in France 165
genealogies 139, 140
in Germany 166, 167, 173
Gernsback moment 166, 175
and imperialism 160–62
and industrialisation 161, 162
in Japan 166, 167, 175–76
long histories 137–44
nineteenth-century SF novels 149
periodisation 27, 96–97
in Poland 160, 166, 167, 170–72
and relationship between science and technology 139–40, 142, 153, 154, 161
in Russia 123, 166, 168–69, 172–73
SF and the structure of feeling 144–49
Hoban, Russell 13
Hollinger, Veronica 1
Honda, Ishirō 48, 166, 175
Horkheimer, Max 49, 78–79, 87, 143
Hornig, Charles D. 108
Hoshi, Shinichi 166, 175
Houellebecq, Michel 63, 66, 67, 96, 99, 152–53, 162, 165
Les Particules élémentaires (*Elementary Particles*) 66, 152
La carte et le territoire (*The Map and the Territory*) 66–67, 153
Howells, William Dean 97
Hoyle, Fred 6, 165
Hugo Awards 13, 59, 60, 64, 74, 76, 102–103, 110, 145, 151, 175, 180
Hugo, Victor 165
Huntington, John 109
Huxley, Aldous 27, 30, 86, 94, 97, 98, 99, 117, 136, 145, 165
accusations of plagiarism against 124, 125
family background 124
literary reputation 6, 13, 66
pacifism 125
place in SF history 165
on purpose of dystopias 127
purpose of his dystopian writing 33
see also Brave New World
Hyman, Bruce 85

Iambulus 137
(ideal) state novel 92
ideology, and utopia 18–21
imperialism
conflation with Empire 161–62
in *Frankenstein* 158–59
and history of SF 160–62
in Verne 158, 159
Industrial Revolution 143, 144
industrialisation, and history of SF 160–61, 162
institutionalised bougeouis art 59

Jackson, Andrew 113
Jackson, Peter 102
Jakobson, Roman 75
Jameson, Fredric 3, 102, 145
Archaeologies of the Future 24, 26, 27, 91, 92, 93, 117, 151
on affinities between historical novels and SF 149–50, 150–51, 152
analysis of *Nineteen Eighty-Four* 116–17, 118, 119, 120, 121–22
on avante-garde movements 60
definition of SF 7, 26, 57–58, 103
on dystopia 116, 119, 120
exclusion of fantasy from SF 101
hermeneutics 18–19
on history of SF 25, 27, 30
on imagining the future 180–81
method and style 24–25
on modernism 28
on Philip K. Dick 59
The Political Unconscious 18, 24
Postmodernism, or, The Cultural Logic of Late Capitalism 28
on role of cognition in SF 25
on utopia as a subgenre of SF 46, 90–96, 151
Japan
anime 51, 176
manga 56, 176
and SF geography 166, 167, 175–76
television SF productions 51–52
Jauss, Hans Robert 75
Jenkins, Henry 8, 65
Jillet, Neil 187
Johnson-Smith, Jan 110
Joyce, James 124, 163
Juszcyzk, Andrzej 167

Kirst, Hans Hellmut 181
Kneale, Nigel 51
Knight, Damon 56
Komatsu, Sakyo 166, 175
Kornbluth, C.M. 6, 61

Kramer, Stanley 7, 185
Kristal, Efrain 164
Kubrick, Stanley 7, 13, 48

Lacan, Jacques 49
Lane, William 97
Lang, Fritz 13, 29, 48, 166, 167
 Metropolis 13, 48, 49, 167–68, 176
Langford, David 2–3
Lasser, David 108
last-man trope 193
Latham, Philip 145
Laurie, André 43
Lawrence, D. H. 10, 11, 124, 190
Le Guin, Ursula K. 86, 94, 95, 98
 on definition of SF 22
 The Dispossessed 63, 86, 99, 100, 139, 182
 environmental concerns 182
 The Left Hand of Darkness 13, 63
 literary reputation 13, 63
 speculative poetry 59
Leavis, F. R. 37, 39, 120, 144, 148, 190
Lee, Ang 102
Lee, Robert E. 113
Lem, Stanisław 13, 24, 66, 160, 171
 Obłok Magellana (*The Magellanic Cloud*) 171
 Śledztwo (*The Investigation*) 13
 Solaris 13, 66, 171–72
 solaristics 24, 171
Lenin, V. I. 61, 161, 170
Lessing, Doris 12, 107
Lewis, C. S. 5, 63, 106, 165
literary field, the
 Bourdieu's model of 41
 in England 44
 in France during second half of nineteenth century 42–44
 see also SF field
literary SF 58, 59, 66–67, 107, 145
literary sociology 156
literary theory 2
 postcolonial 156–62
literature
 and modernism 11–12
 nature of 58
 and popular fiction 9–14, 22, 26, 43, 58
 and SF 22, 26, 58, 66–67
Lofficier, Marc 44, 66
Lofficier, Randy 44, 66
Lourson, Laurent 87
Lovecraft, H. P. 59, 63
Lowndes, Robert 60
Lucas, George 48, 86,
Lucian of Samosata 137, 139, 144, 153
 Alēthēs Historia 140–42
Lukács, Georg 93, 149–50, 190
Lyotard, Jean-François 27

McEwan, Ian 196–97
McFarlane, James 28, 29
Mackay, Kenneth 188
McKeown, Bill 86
McKibben, Bill 194
MacLeod, Ken 165
Macvicar, Angus 85
magazines
 in America 13, 14, 54–55, 56, 57, 58, 107–110
 in Britain 55–56
 earliest 54
 in Europe 54
 in France 56
 podcasting 74
Maggs, Dirk 85
magic, and fantasy 24, 89, 102, 103, 106
manga 56, 176
Mann, Thomas 190
Marker, Chris 48
Márquez, Gabriel García 163
Martin, Mark 194
Marx, Karl 71, 93, 132, 182, 192–93
Mayakovsky, Vladimir 64, 86, 166
media and cultural studies, failure to consider radio 68–70
Méliès, Georges 47–48
Melville, Herman 163
Menzies, William Cameron 7, 48, 124, 168
Merle, Jean Touissant 44
Merle, Robert 165, 181
Merril, Judith 34, 59, 60, 62
Mi/Nous autres [novel] (Zamyatin) 117
 comic moments 131
 contrasted with *Brave New World* 130–32
 contrasted with *Nineteen Eighty-Four* 128–31
 as critical dystopia 118, 119, 120
 ending of 133
 as literature 66
 publication and translation 123–24
 review by Orwell 33–34, 124, 125

Michaelis, Richard C. 118
Michel, Johnny 60, 61, 109
Miéville, China 59, 63, 102, 103–104, 105, 106, 165, 180
The City and the City 102, 180
Embassytown 175
Iron Council 63, 102
Perdido Street Station 63, 102
military utopianism 112–13
Mill, John Stuart 90
Miller, Walter M. 181
Milton, John 143, 144
Mitchell, David 182
modernism
and the avant-garde 28–29
and culture of modernity 27
dialectic between Enlightenment and Romanticism 154
as high art 28
and literature 11–12, 29–30
and realism 30
usages of term 27
Molesworth, Voltaire 'Vol' 84
Molinari, Nadia 81, 83
Moorcock, Michael 59, 62, 165
Moore, Alan 55, 58
Moore-Bentley, Mary Ann 97
More, Thomas 25, 89, 90, 98, 105, 137, 138, 139, 144, 152, 153
Moretti, Franco 58, 137, 156, 163–65, 166, 172, 174, 176, 177, 178
Morris, William 95, 98, 99, 105, 118, 137, 145, 165
News from Nowhere 97, 99, 105, 118, 134
Morton, Joyce 196
Mosley, Walter 63
Moskowitz, Sam 31, 60, 61
Moylan, Tom 2, 99–101, 116, 118–20
Mulcahy, Russell 185
Murakami, Haruki 155, 166, 175, 187
Murphy, Peter 154
Musil, Robert 163

Nation, Terry 6, 7
natural catastrophes, SF representations of 182
nature, and capitalism 193
Naylor, Doug 193
Negri, Antonio 161
Nevil Shute Norway Foundation 184
New Left Review [journal] 70, 71
New Wave movements 27, 29, 57, 59, 63. 96
French 'nouvelle vague' 66
American New Wave 59, 62–63. 94. 97, 101, 174
British New Wave 40, 59, 62
New Weird 62, 63
New Worlds [magazine] 56, 62, 63
New Zealand, in radio SF 86
Newman, Sydney 6
Niccol, Andrew 49
Nicholls, Peter 3, 30, 66, 67, 91
Nineteen Eighty-Four [novel] (Orwell) 116, 117, 118, 119, 120–23, 175
Appendix on Newspeak 122–23, 134–35
contrasted with *Mi/Nous autres* 128–31
as critical dystopia 135
as dominant paradigm for post-war dystopia 14
ending of 134–35
Williams's analysis of 120–21, 122, 134–35
Niven, Larry 103
novum 23, 39, 47, 48, 49, 89, 91, 92, 148
Nowra, Louis 86
nuclear catastrophe, possibility of 181
nuclear war, SF representations of 181–82, 185–89, 190

Oakley, Barry 86
O'Bannon, Rockne 54
occidentalism 164, 176
Ōe, Kenzaboro 175
Orbaugh, Sharalyn 176
orientalism 157
Orwell, George 94, 98, 99, 136, 145, 165
anti-Fascism 117–18, 121
anti-Stalinism 116, 117
background 124
on Čapek's *R.U.R.* 126–27
intellectual context 123
literary reputation 6, 13, 14, 66
objection to *Brave New World* 125
place in SF history 165
political purpose of writings 116–18, 121–22
success as a writer 123
on totalitarianism 116–18, 121, 122
on Wellsian utopianism 33, 124–25
on Zamyatin's *Mi* 33–34, 123–24, 125
see also Nineteen Eighty-Four

Oshii, Mamoru 48, 59, 166, 176
Otomo, Katsuhiro 176
Out of This World exhibition 136–37, 155
Owen, Robert 91

Parnov, Eremei Iudovich 166
Parrinder, Patrick 39
Peake, Richard Brinsley 44
Penley, Constance 65
Perkins, Geoffrey 85
Pibouleau, Robert 87
Piercy, Marge 63, 93, 94, 95, 99, 100, 105, 118
He, She and It 118
Woman on the Edge of Time 93, 100, 105
Plato 137
Platonov, Andrey Platonovich 166
Playfair, Nigel 51, 84
Plutarch 139
Poe, Edgar Allan 13, 31–32, 34, 153, 165
poetry, and SF 59–60
Poggiolo, Renato 28, 29
Pohl, Frederick 6, 60, 61, 196
Poland
industrialisation in post-war period 160
and SF geography 166, 167, 170–72
Pollack, Frank L. 87
popular fiction
as genre fiction 12
and Literature 9–14, 26, 43
and science fiction 9
positivistic SF 173
post-structuralism 156
postcolonial literary studies 156
postcolonial literary theory
origins 156
and SF 157–62, 176
posthuman SF 154
Potter, Dennis 54
Pound, Ezra 163
Proudhon, Pierre-Joseph 91
Proyas, Alex 48, 168, 193
public broadcasting
in Britain 50
ideas and effects in SF productions 50
production of SF for radio 50
in United States 50
publishers 56
pulp fiction
American magazines 13, 14, 54–55, 56, 57, 58, 107–110
critical technocracy 109
dystopian turn 110
forms 108
social messianism 108
technological perfectibilism 108
utopianism in 107–110
Pynchon, Thomas 122, 123

Rabelais, François 25, 90, 137, 139
race-war dystopias 188
radio dramatic productions
adaptations 69
'Golden Age of Radio' 50
and media and cultural studies 68–70, 72–73
original works 69–70
see also radio SF productions
radio institutions 83–88
commercial radio SF broadcasters 84, 88
public radio SF broadcasters 83–88
radio SF productions
adaptations of existing works 84–85
affinity with SF literature 76, 88
aimed at children 84, 85
in America 73, 84, 86–87
in Australia 73, 84, 86
in Britain 5, 73, 84–86
in Canada 86
commercial broadcasts 84, 88
demise of 68, 88
differences from television drama 75
earliest productions 73
experimental potential 53, 53–54
forms 53, 76–83
in France 84, 87
in Germany 74, 87
lack of studies on 68, 72
in New Zealand 86
public broadcasts 84–88
in South Africa 84
special effects 50, 53, 87, 88
in Switzerland 87
radio technology, and science fiction 73–76
realism, and modernism 30
Reformation 142–43, 144
Renan, Ernest 97
Renard, Maurice 165
resonance and wonder, tales of 18–21

restricted economy 59–60
Rhysling Award 59
Rieder, John 159, 160, 161
Riefenstahl, Leni 29
Rigby, Kate 143, 182, 194
Roberts, Adam 137–39, 140, 142, 143
Roberts, David 29, 154, 190
Roberts, J. W. 118
Robinson, Kim Stanley 35, 94, 95, 145, 151–52, 174, 182, 192, 194
  Galileo's Dream 145
  Pacific Edge 152
  Science in the Capital trilogy 182, 192, 194
  2312 145
robots, origins of 7–8, 14, 170
rock music, inspired by SF 7
Roddenberry, Gene 110, 112, 113, 139
romance 9
Romantic science 182
Romanticism 143, 145, 154, 161, 182
Roosevelt, Theodore 113
Rosny, J.H. 165
Ross, Andrew 61, 109, 110
Rowling, J. K. 102, 106
R.U.R. (Rossum's Universal Robots) [play] (Čapek) 47, 131
  comic prologue 170
  as critical dystopia 118
  ending of 126, 132–33
  English stage adaptation 132
  as literature 13, 14, 66
  place in history of SF 47, 51, 170
  as political theatre 47
  radio dramatisations 84
Rushdie, Salman 10, 11
Russ, Joanna 34, 63, 99
Russia
  early Soviet era SF 166, 168–69
  late Communist era SF 172–73
  and SF geography 123, 166
Russian Formalism 23–24
Ryman, Geoff 194

Sabatier, Robert 99
Said, Edward 156, 157
St Augustine 91
Saint-Simon, Henri de 90, 137
Sargent, Lyman Tower 3, 90, 116, 183
Sartre, Jean-Paul 92
Sassi, Roland 87
Satterlee, W. W. 118
Saunders, G. K 86
Savage, Robert 61
Schäfer, Martin 107, 109
Scholes, Robert 144
Schrader, Paul 13
Schwartz, Benjamin 87
Schwartz, Roberto 163
Schwartz, Walter Andreas 87
science
  dangerous possibilities of science-as-technology 183
  Enlightenment view of 143
  finite limits of scientific knowledge 171
  relationship to technology 139–40, 142, 153, 154, 161
  Romantic science 182
  subject matter 152
Science Fiction League 64
Science Fiction Poetry Association 59
science fiction (SF)
  academic definitions 23–26
  application of category 7, 22
  content over form 22
  continuity across media 13
  definition of 22–23
  function of 25
  linguistic style 76–77
  as literary genre 7, 12
  and literature 22, 26, 58, 66–67
  nature of 178–79
  non-academic definitions 30–35
  as popular fiction 22, 26
  relationship to high culture or modernism 27
  role of cognition 24, 106
  scientific pretentions of 103
  understanding of science 139
  uses of 178–83
  see also history of SF; SF *headings* e.g. SF field
Science Fiction Studies [journal] 1, 102, 103
scientific romance 44, 54, 124
scientifiction 173
Scott, Ridley 29, 48, 168
Scott, Walter 150, 152
Seed, David 106–107
selective tradition 37–40
Selver, Paul 84, 127, 132, 133
Seymour, Miranda 158
SF community 13, 64
SF field 3
  boundary with canonical 'literary' field 67

central lines of development 45–46
drama 43–44, 47–54
in early twentieth century 44–45
global SF literary field 44–45, 156
heteronomous end 54
ideas and effects 45–47, 87–88
location of Shute and Turner 191
poetry 59–60
prose 54–59
restricted economy and institutionalised bourgeois art 59–67

SF, geography of
Anglo-French core 162–66
European semiperiphery 166–73
Japan 175–76
North America 173–75

SF selective tradition 3
distinguishing features 98, 105
functioning of 139
geographical provenance of 155
global 167
production and reproduction of 67, 178
utopian imaginings within 107

SF studies
beginnings of 1
and critical theory 1–2
value-freedom 179
value-relevance of phenomena treated 179–80

Shakespeare, William 153, 190
Shelley, Mary 73, 193
background 40, 158
The Last Man 32, 34, 126, 198
literary reputation 13, 44
place in history of SF 31, 136, 137, 140, 153, 155, 157
see also Frankenstein

Shelley, Percy Bysshe 29
Shiner, Lewis 63
Shklovsky, Viktor 75
short stories 58
Shubik, Irene 6
Shunrō, Oshikawa 167
Shuster, Joe 55
Shute, Nevil 5, 184, 186, 188, 189, 190
On the Beach 184, 185–86, 187–89, 190, 191

Siegal, Jerry 55
Skinner, B. F. 97, 99
slash fiction 65
slavery 158
Sloat, Erwin K. 108
Słonimski, Antoni 167
Slusser, George 56, 172
Smith, Cordwainer 86
Smith, E. E. 'Doc' 46, 107
social messianism 108
socialism 93
Socialist Workers Party 102
Sontag, Susan 49, 76
South Africa, radio SF 84
Space Anthropology 145
special effects
appeal of 53
in commercial television productions 50
cost of 49, 53
in film and television SF 87–88
in late nineteenth century French theatre 43–44
in public broadcasting television productions 50
in radio drama productions 50, 53, 87, 88

speculative fiction 22, 34, 59, 102
speculative poetry 59
Spence, Catherine Helen 97
Spielberg, Stephen 48
Spinrad, Norman 59, 62
Spitz, Jacques 165
Spivak, Gayatri Chakravorty 156, 157–59, 164
Staatsroman 92
Stapledon, Olaf 27, 30
Star Trek conventions 8
Star Trek [film and television franchise] 7, 51, 53, 54, 64, 65
and 1960s American liberalism 111
and American culture 111–12, 113–14
early episodes 7
films 48, 110, 112
market for 54
military utopia 112, 113
place in popular culture 110, 136
'Save Star Trek' campaign 64
and slash fiction 65
special effects 7
and symbiotic relationship with NASA 111–12
television series 51, 53, 64, 110, 112
utopianism in 95, 107, 110–14
visual aspects 46
see also Trekkers

Star Wars conventions 8

Star Wars [films] 48, 96
Sterling, Bruce 59, 63, 153
Stevenson, Robert Louis 3, 86
Stoppard, Tom 70
Straczynski, J. Michael 51, 54
structure of feeling 157, 159
  and SF 144–49
Strugatsky, Arkady 66, 166, 172
  Piknik na obochine (*Roadside Picnic*) 66, 172–73
  Vtoroe nashestvie marsian (*The Second Invasion from Mars*) 172
  Za milliard let do kontsa sveta (*A Billion Years to the End of the World*) 172
Strugatsky, Boris 66, 166, 172
  Piknik na obochine (*Roadside Picnic*) 66, 172–73
  Vtoroe nashestvie marsian (*The Second Invasion from Mars*) 172
  Za milliard let do kontsa sveta (*A Billion Years to the End of the World*) 172
Sutherland, John 9
Suvin, Darko 1–2, 3, 25, 26, 27, 60, 102
  on affinities between historical novels and SF 149
  on cognitive rationality and SF 138
  definition of SF 7, 103, 137
  on dystopias 115, 119, 120
  exclusion of fantasy from SF 101
  on Lucian 141
  on pulp fiction 57
  Metamorphoses of Science Fiction 1, 23, 24, 35, 46, 92, 137
  on structure of a genre 35–36
  on tradition 37
  on use and effect of knowledge in SF 46
  on utopia as a subgenre of SF 90–96, 138
Swift, Jonathan 137, 139
Switzerland, radio SF 87

Tarkovsky, Andrei 66, 166
Taylor, A. J. P. 68, 69, 76
Taylor, Zachary 113
technological perfectibilism 108
technological utopianism 107
technology, relationship to science 139–40, 142, 153, 154, 183
television
  adaptations from earlier radio programmes 76
  aimed at children 51, 52
  in America 51
  Australian productions 52
  in Britain 6, 6–7, 51
  Canadian productions 52
  experimental potential 53–54
  first broadcast 14
  forms 53
  French productions 52–53
  German productions 52
  Japanese productions 51–52
  'literary' adaptations 5
  national differences 51
  special effects 50, 53
  television institutions
  commercial broadcasters 50
  public broadcasters 50
  SF productions by commercial broadcasters 51–52
  SF productions by public broadcasters 5, 51, 52
television studies 13
textual poaching 65
Tezuka, Osamu 52, 166, 176
theatre
  as 'bourgeois art' 44
  French SF plays in late nineteenth century 43–44
Theopompus 137
Thomé, Martine 87
Tolkien, J. R. R. 102, 105, 106
Tolstoy, Alexei 27, 166, 169
del Toro, Guillermo 102, 106
totalitarianism 117, 121–22, 125–26, 128, 129
tradition, selective tradition 37–40
Traviss, Karen 182
Trekkers 8, 9, 64
Troska, J. M. 166
Truffaut, François 65, 66
Tulloch, John 65
Turner, George 180, 184, 186, 189, 190
  The Sea and Summer 184, 185, 186–87, 188, 190, 191, 192
Turner, Noel 90
Turnier, Kathryn 196

underground cinema 65–66
United States
  American New Wave 62–63
  commercial broadcasting 50
  contemporary militarism 161

'Golden Age' of SF 55, 174
liberalism in 1960s 111
NASA/TREK 111–12
place of *Star Trek* in popular culture 110
public broadcasting 50
radio SF 73, 84, 86–87
and SF geography166, 173–75
SF pulp fiction magazines 13, 14, 54–55, 56, 57, 58, 107–110
status of military 113–14
television SF 51
University of Liverpool, Science Fiction Collection 3
utopia
in American pulp fiction magazines 107–110
anti-anti-utopianism 93–94
anti-utopia 116, 118
Australia as site of 183–84
in Australian SF 184–86
as cognate literary form with SF 2, 90, 96
critical utopia 99–101, 110
definition 90
difference from SF 96
and ideology 18–21
military utopia 112–13
origins of term 89
in popular SF 107–14
relation to dystopia 98–99
in response or reaction against industrial society 97
in *Star Trek* film and television franchise 107, 110–14
as subgenre of SF 90–96, 107, 138
technological utopianism 107
in Wells's novels 33
Wellsian utopianism 124–25
within dystopia 120
see also dystopia
utopian fantasy hybrids 104
utopian SF-fantasy hybrids 105
utopian socialism 93
utopian studies 90

Vadim, Roger 48
VanderMeer, Ann 63
VanderMeer, Jeff 63
Vaughn, Michael 102
Veiras, Denis 183
Venn, John 104, 105
Verhoeven, Paul 48
Verne, Jules 23, 28, 105, 137
adaptations of works 52, 86
Cinq Semaines en ballon (*Five Weeks in a Balloon*) 149
De la terre à la lune (*From the Earth to the Moon*) 47, 105
Le Docteur Ox 54
L'île mystérieuse (*Mysterious Island*) 52, 159
imperialist sympathies 158, 159
influence of Poe on 31–32
literary reputation 6, 13
literary works 95
Paris au XXe siècle (*Paris in the Twentieth Century*) 95, 149
place in SF history 140, 149, 153, 155, 165
Le Sphinx des glaces (*The Sphinx of the Ice Fields*) 32
Le Tour du monde en 80 jours (*Around the World in 80 Days*) 43, 52, 167
translations of 167, 169
Vingt mille lieues sous les mers (*Twenty Thousand Leagues under the Seas*) 87, 140, 159, 167
Voyage à travers l'impossible (*Journey Through the Impossible*) 46–47
voyages extraordinaires novels 34, 43, 44, 46, 138, 139, 149, 167
on Wells 32
Versins, Pierre 87
Vincent, Harl 108
Vint, Sherryl 1, 2
Vinton, Arthur Dudley 118
Virgil 137
visual aspects of SF 46–47
Vogt, A. E. van 57, 145
Vonnegut, Kurt 13

Wagner, Richard 29, 163
Wakowski, Andy 49
Wakowski, Larry 49
Waldron, Winnie 86
Wallerstein, Immanuel 156, 162–63, 164, 166, 176
Walther, Daniel 165
Walton, Robyn 184
Washington, George 113
Weber, Max 143, 179
Wegner, Phillip E. 2, 26, 27, 28, 29, 30, 91, 94

weird fiction 59, 62, 63–64, 106
Welles, Orson 73, 77–79, 83
Wells, H. G. 23, 30, 61, 84, 85, 86, 87, 91, 97, 98, 136
adaptations of 51, 77–79, 84, 85, 86, 87
'The Chronic Argonauts' 155
comparison with Shelley 32
dislike of Lang's *Metropolis* 167
The Dream 124
film scripts 48
The First Men in the Moon 47, 87
influence on Lem 171
In the Days of the Comet 95
The Invisible Man 87, 172
The Island of Doctor Moreau 32, 86, 169
literary reputation 13, 31
The Man Who Could Work Miracles 44
Men Like Gods 95, 97, 124
A Modern Utopia 29, 95, 97, 100, 124
'The New Accelerator' 86
Orwell's antipathy to 33, 124, 125
place in SF history 27, 28, 33, 137, 138, 140, 144, 153, 155, 165
relationship with Čapek 169
The Science Fiction Novels 13
The Shape of Things to Come 33, 99, 124
The Sleeper Awakes 167, 168
'The Star' 87
The Stolen Bacillus and Other Incidents 54
Things to Come 44, 48, 124
The Time Machine 5, 25, 30, 51, 84, 85, 86, 136, 140, 165, 167
translations of 165–66, 167, 169
utopianism 95, 99, 100, 138
on Verne 32–33
The War of the Worlds 23, 34, 73, 77–79, 87, 167, 171, 172
works in *Amazing Stories* 108
Wells, Peggy 86
West, Morris 97
Whale, James 48
White, John Manchip 85
Wilcox, Fred M. 153
Williams, Raymond 3, 12, 14, 36
cultural materialism 70–73, 144
Culture and Society 144, 146
on dystopias 110, 115, 145, 188
on emergent cultures 149
on film 69
on levels of cultural form 12, 153
on 'the long revolution' 144
The Long Revolution 146–47, 148–49
Marxism and Literature 147–48
move away from criticism 94
on *Nineteen Eighty-Four* 120–21, 122, 134–35
on radio 69, 70
on selective tradition 37–40
on structure of feeling 144, 145–49, 159
Television: Technology and Cultural Form 69, 70, 72
on theatre 69
on types of contemporary literary SF 145
on utopia and dystopia 98–99
on utopia and SF 97–98
Winawer, Bruno 167
Winterson, Jeanette 13, 22, 182
Wiśniewski-Snerg, Adam 166
Wolfe, Gene 59
Wolff, Tobias 9
Wollheim, Donald 60, 61
Wordsworth, William 143
World Science Fiction Conventions 46, 61, 64, 74, 102, 155
World Science Fiction Society 102
world systems theory 156
and comparative literature 163–65
key concerns 162–63
and SF 165–76, 177
Wyndam, John 5, 57, 85, 87, 145, 162, 165, 181, 182

Younge, Henry Lewis 89

Zamyatin, Yevgeny 94, 98, 117, 119, 137
dystopian writing 128–30, 145
influence of Wells on 33–34, 125, 169
literary reputation 66, 123–24
place in SF history 27, 29, 137
translations of Wells 169
see also Mi/Nous autres
Žižek, Slavoj 180–81
Zoline, Pamela 62
Żulawski, Jerzy 167

Printed and bound by CPI Group (UK) Ltd, Croydon, CR0 4YY

09/06/2025

14685941-0002